MW00985144

Merze Tate

Merze Tate

THE GLOBAL ODYSSEY OF A BLACK WOMAN SCHOLAR

Barbara D. Savage

Yale UNIVERSITY PRESS

New Haven & London

Published with assistance from the foundation established in memory of Amasa Stone Mather of the Class of 1907, Yale College, and from the income of the Frederick John Kingsbury Memorial Fund.

Yale University Press books may be purchased in quantity for educational, business, or promotional use. For information, please e-mail sales.press@yale.edu (U.S. office) or sales@yaleup.co.uk (U.K. office).

Set in Adobe Garamond type by IDS Infotech, Ltd.
Printed in the United States of America.

ISBN 978-0-300-27027-3 (hardcover : alk. paper)
Library of Congress Control Number: 2023935185
A catalogue record for this book is available from the British Library.

This paper meets the requirements of ANSI/NISO Z39.48.1992 (Permanence of Paper).

10 9 8 7 6 5 4 3 2 1

In loving memory of

Mildred Savage Fields (1927–2013)

Walter M. Fields, Jr. (1918–1996)

In appreciation of

Joellen El-Bashir

Moorland-Spingarn Research Center

Howard University

Contents

Preface

To answer the question of how I came to be interested in Merze Tate is to acknowledge a role for both serendipity and intentionality. It is also to admit that sometimes our research subjects simply insist on finding us. After finishing a book in 2008 on race, religion, and politics, I began to research African American missionaries in the resources I always turn to first: Carter G. Woodson's *Journal of Negro History* and Howard University's *Journal of Negro Education.* I do that because they both hold so much often overlooked and excellent earlier scholarship.

The first article that popped up was not on Black missionaries, but instead it was by Tate, writing in the 1960s about her research into white missionaries from New England who went to the Sandwich Islands in the Pacific in the 1820s. In her account, their arrival represented the first step in the eventual annexation of Hawaii by the United States, which culminated in statehood in 1959. For much of the twentieth century, Black and female scholars were routinely denied the opportunity to publish in most academic journals in their fields. That is how Tate's writings ended up in the two journals on Black history even though her work was in diplomatic history and international relations.

I was familiar with Tate's name from her writings about World War II (the subject of my first book), but it was news to me that she was the prolific scholar she soon revealed herself to be. Tate's scholarly reach and range—more easily discoverable as research databases improved—immediately intrigued me, as did her extensive solo world travels. Her inspiring struggle in the 1920s and 1930s to become a scholar at a time when women and Black people were largely excluded from academic professions drew me in deeper. Her lifetime of pathbreaking publications also led me into intriguing fields of study far from my own training in African American history. The more I learned, the clearer it became that her extraordinary life story and prodigious body of work still had much to teach all of us.

That is how I became Tate's reluctant biographer. The resonances from her successes and struggles are universal, but they remain especially familiar to many of us who also have chosen to become scholars, albeit with the privileges that were denied her. Ultimately, the credit for my decision to study her life and engage her work goes to an unfunded collaborative project that in 2015 yielded a book, *Toward an Intellectual History of Black Women.* That collection included my first published work on Tate, the only scholar in the volume. Although I still resisted, it probably was already too late to turn back from what was revealing itself as a captivating life story full of travel adventures, relentless intellectual ambition, and prolific productivity.[1]

I had begun writing this book when I was invited in 2018 to participate in a Leverhulme Trust Research Project on Women and the History of International Thought, which had been inspired in part by our book on Black women. That resulted in two books: a collection of essays, *Women's International Thought: A New History,* and an annotated anthology of works by historical women, *Women's International Thought: Towards a New Canon.* Tate's life and her ideas receive attention in both, and this book also bears the influence of that collaboration.[2]

As is often the case with our most difficult and fulfilling endeavors, I had no idea how much work this project would be and how long it would take, even before the complications and delays caused by the 2020 pandemic. Tate's archival trail and her many travels have taken me by trains, planes, and cars from Philadelphia to Michigan, New York, Cambridge, and overseas to India, Thailand, Hawaii, and a year at Oxford. But as with all of my scholarly work, many days over many years were spent working in one of my favorite spaces, Howard University's Founder's Library and its rich collections in the Moorland-Spingarn Research Center.

After climbing the steps of the red brick building with its white columns, I opened the wooden doors and turned right, time after time pausing at a display case in the hallway with photographs tracing the history of the campus. That is where I first learned the architectural phrase "desire lines," a concept describing pathways made by foot veering from those laid out in concrete sidewalks. This book follows the desire lines of Merze Tate's life as she went her own way and made a place for herself in a world where the designated routes for a Black girl born in 1905 could not contain her ambitions, her brilliance, and her courage.

Getting to "why" Tate was driven to live the life she lived and do the work she did is also at the heart of this biographical project. She chose to advance her lifelong anti-racist and anti-colonial commitments expressly through her writing and her teaching over five decades. Her underlying intellectual desire and travel lust were the dual reinforcing drives in her life. For her, those powerful drives also enabled her sense of independence and personal freedom. If we are to respect those forces in Tate's life, as I do, then our ideas about women's pleasure and desire need to make room for a much broader reconceptualization of both.

One of the people who had begun to do just that theoretical work was a friend and contributor to *Toward an Intellectual History of Black Women,* Cheryl Wall, a Rutgers-based Black literary scholar who passed away suddenly in early 2020. At the time of her death, Wall was busily engaged in philosophical concerns captured in a posthumous essay in 2021. She spoke directly to what I have been searching for in explaining Tate's lifelong commitment to research and writing. Wall named that simply as "the pleasures of intellectual work." Claiming pleasure of any kind is often downplayed by women and, in her argument, by Black women in particular. That is why Wall argued explicitly for Black women to be able to "own the joy that their engagement with ideas produces."[3]

Wall's article encourages an embrace of intellectual work as a source of "profound pleasure" even under difficult circumstances, or perhaps especially so then. She quoted Zora Neale Hurston, who said: "Work is the nearest thing to happiness that I can find."[4] Wall urged us to develop and embrace a language of joy for intellectual desire and fulfillment. I certainly found that in great abundance in Tate's life, and in my own commitment to bring her story and her work to broader recognition, even though I lacked the language to explain it.

In 1905, the year of Tate's birth, the Black woman writer Fannie Barrier Williams described the plight of the "colored girl" of that era, who, though subject to the "tyranny of race prejudice"—"but yet, as meanly as she is thought of, hindered as she is in all directions, she is always doing something of merit and credit that is not expected of her. She is irrepressible. She is insulted, but she holds up her head; she is scorned, but she proudly demands respect." That description captures the boldness of Tate's spirit and life as well as anything.[5]

The "why" of her years of obsessive intellectual labor—and mine in this biography—is the joy and personal fulfillment it yields, beyond the satisfaction that comes from the way the work reflects political commitments and expands what we know about the fields in which we labor. Tate freely embraced, in Wall's words, "the transcendent experience that those of us fortunate enough to do intellectual work count as its ultimate pleasure." And for that, we should all be grateful, both to Tate and to Cheryl Wall for naming it for us.

Merze Tate

Introduction

On a spring evening in 1921, more than four hundred people crammed into a high school auditorium in Battle Creek, Michigan, to witness an annual student oratorical contest where one girl and one boy would be crowned winners. Merze Tate, a sixteen-year-old Black girl, stood in front of the predominately white audience and proclaimed into their silence that "for two hundred and forty-four years my ancestors were held in bonds of slavery, deprived of every opportunity for mental development, civil expression and hindered in their pursuits of human endeavor," and then saw continued hatred and denial after emancipation. But in a time of global war, whites had "called upon two million black men from Africa, from the West Indies, and from America, to fight that the world might enjoy the benefits of civilization. They fought as men, they fought nobly, they fought gloriously." Despite that, she argued, they were still denied liberty and the privileges of democracy.[1]

Tate did not falter as she made one bold plea after another. Saying, "Oh, America," she demanded that the "14,000,000 of my people" be extended a fair chance at jobs and freedoms open to recent immigrants. Taking seriously the "oratorical" nature of the contest, she reached back to anti-slavery rhetoric that deftly deployed the image of the heroic Black soldier:

> It was of a Negro soldier that Wendell Phillips, immortal statesman and orator, said: "But fifty years hence, when Truth gets a hearing, the

> Muse of History will put Phocion of the Greek, and Brutus for the Roman, Hampden for England, Fayette for France, choose Washington as the bright, consummate flower of our earlier civilization, and John Brown the ripe fruit of our noonday, then, dipping her pen in the sunlight, will write in the clear blue, above them all, the name of the soldier, the statesman, the martyr, Toussaint l'Ouverture."

With that, she rested her case for an end to racial inequality while teaching her audience about the continuing consequences of slavery, the sacrifices of Black soldiers from the United States, the Caribbean, and Africa, and the continued denial of "common justice" to Black people here and around the globe. By invoking Toussaint, she held high the name of the Black liberator warrior of Haiti, but she also honored the Black men in her own family who had served in the Civil War and the Spanish-American War, and her older brother who had been in the Navy in World War I.[2]

"Miss Merze Tate, a colored girl, was the winner for the girls' division of the contest, her subject being 'The Negro in the World War,' " the *Battle Creek Enquirer* reported the next day. That event marked the start of a public career that Merze Tate forged in a world that routinely disrespected Black women and men as intellectual, political, and moral inferiors.

Her courage and prodigious intellectual gifts would carry her far away from her native Michigan, first to a graduate degree in the 1930s from Columbia Teachers College. But that was just the beginning. Thanks to a fellowship from her Alpha Kappa Alpha sorority, she studied international relations at the University of Oxford, becoming in 1935 the first Black American to earn a graduate degree there. After teaching at southern Black colleges, she went on in 1941 to be the first Black woman to earn a Ph.D. in government from Harvard. From there, and against all odds, she assumed a professorship that lasted thirty-five years at the prestigious Howard University, a rare achievement for women of her generation and at any institution, whether Black or white.

Tate aspired to be an educator who was also a producer of new knowledge and not just a consumer of it. A gifted writer and extraordinary scholar, she published five groundbreaking books (including one from Harvard and one from Yale) and dozens of articles on the role of race in European and U.S. imperialism in Asia, the Pacific, Africa, and elsewhere. Her innovative work rivaled those of her male colleagues in the United States and abroad and in fields where few women worked then or now.

As a child, Tate became fascinated by maps, geography, and travel accounts. As a teenager, news of a war of global proportions mingled with accounts from Black men in her own family who returned from service abroad to continued racial discrimination in their home country. But their tales of travel also kindled her imagination and her determination to see the world and its wonders for herself. As an adult, she circled the globe twice, traveling alone. She set foot on every continent but two—Antarctica and South America. As one of the earliest Fulbright scholars, she spent a year in India in 1950 which allowed her to explore there, in Asia, and the Indo-Pacific. In her seventies, she finally made it to Africa—twice.

During her travels, she found herself in the presence of Adolf Hitler, Pope Pius XII, Jawaharlal Nehru, Indira Gandhi, and Desmond Tutu, to name a few. Her travel informed her work and vice versa. There are few substitutes for seeing first-hand the places one is studying. She mixed her missions, spending time researching in archives, touring in leisure, and enjoying the company of new friends and colleagues along the way.

The touchstones of her returns from travel were friends and families eager to hear of her adventures. She never married and had no children, and led a vibrant social life in Washington, across the United States, and around the world. Her leisure was fed by her broad intellectual and cultural interests, by her prowess at the bridge table, by her skills as a chef and party-giver, and by her gift for sustaining friendships across time and space. Tate moved in all these spaces with a hurried athletic grace of intentionality and purpose, dressed in the latest styles and finest fabrics popular in the social and professional worlds she inhabited, most often captured on the pages of Black newspapers.

This book tells the story of how a young Black girl, born in 1905 on an isolated farm in the center of Michigan, became a scholar and traveled the world with her cameras in hand. Her path-blazing achievements rested on her brilliance and her hard work but required a lifetime of struggle in what she called a "sex and race discriminating world."

The challenges Tate faced in making a place for herself as a Black woman scholar remain all too familiar today. She always credited her success to older women, Black and white, both in the United States and abroad, and to sacrifices made for her by her older sister. She was right about that. At key junctures, a diverse group of women deployed their limited financial and institutional resources to help a younger Black woman achieve her wildly ambitious dreams. Her life story is an inspiring example of Black familial and community solidarity and, more rare, of gender commitments across racial lines in the age of Jim Crow, segregation, and international racism.

She did not shy from advancing her own interests at a time when that was frowned upon for women even more than it is today. Nor did she cloak her anger when she faced manmade obstacles, especially those imposed by the men who dominated the academic profession and the institutions where she studied and worked.

Yet she was a single Black woman who was able to live a long, healthy life of independence and professional fulfillment, and, most importantly, personal freedom. The credit for that goes to her crystal clear sense of self, her fearlessness, and her intellect. She never wavered from her passionate commitments to educating, to producing knowledge, and to seeing as much of the world as possible.

Tate's belief in the emancipatory potential of education was expressed not only through her writing and teaching, but through her philanthropy. A mask of frugality hid many decades of her quiet but very shrewd stock market investments. With her proceeds, she donated over $2 million in the late 1970s to the educational institutions that trained her, the equivalent today of $9 million. Her generous gifts continue to do their work to this day, paying full scholarships for college students and providing research support for some preparing to become scholars. She laid up her treasures where they mattered most to her.

Tate also bequeathed us something few Black women have the power to generate: a historical archive. Large archival boxes at Howard now hold a vast array of written material from every stage of her long life, spanning decades of personal and professional correspondence, drafts of her published and unpublished works, and copies of her many talks and speeches. In a practice popular at the time, she created dozens of scrapbooks of her travels, including photographs, maps, and ephemera, but also of special occasions in her life. She also kept what was most meaningful to her emotionally, materials that would remind her of the love and care she shared with friends at home and around the world.[3]

Additional archival evidence of her life stretches from Oxford to India and back to Michigan, and is laid out as well on the pages of Black newspapers and academic journals. At the end of her career, she served as both an interviewer and an interviewee in the Black Women Oral History Project at Radcliffe's Schlesinger Library, leaving an unedited and unpublished transcript of her interview exceeding five hundred pages.

Facing that volume and variety of paper is daunting and the opportunity to sift through it all is not without its challenges, especially when studying someone committed to fashioning the narrative of her own life. But with fact-checking, and an acquired understanding of her personality, character, temperament, and intellectual tendencies, the scattered records of her life remain unusual and valuable historical sources.

With them, this book takes up its first task: to rescue Tate's life and her legacy from an obscurity imposed by the virulent racial and gendered politics of the academic world, both in her lifetime and ours. For sure, who Tate was and how she was able to live a fulfilling life and do all she did is fascinating, but that forms only a part of my work.

Only by excavating and critiquing her scholarship can we understand the life of her mind, which also is the aim of intellectual biography. Tate had an unusual capacity for both panoramic conceptual imagination and sustained archival research, accompanied by relentless ambition that refused to be stifled. It is only by studying her five decades of writing that we can learn why she and her ideas were so ahead of her time and yet remain so relevant to the world in which readers in the twenty-first century find themselves.

Her prolific publications and accolades bear witness to her intellectual prowess and persistence. At a time when women and most Black men were routinely excluded from academic publishing, Tate published five books as well as thirty-four journal articles and forty-five review essays.

An interdisciplinary scholar long before that approach was in vogue, the fields in which she wrote, diplomatic history and international relations, recognized the quality and significance of her work at the time, but never to the extent it or she deserved. Despite all of that, her life's work has all but disappeared from the narrative of American and African American intellectual, political, and cultural life, or for that matter, Black women's history.[4]

Tate's earliest writings take us into debates among African Americans in the 1930s about how best to educate Black college students for the political challenges facing them. She paid special attention to the preparation of Black women students and how to balance the demands of personal life with professional ambitions, whether a woman married or remained single or whether she became a mother or not. Tate was also an early advocate of science, technology, engineering, and mathematics fields for Black students, hoping that the sciences might be less susceptible to bias from race and gender.

Her lifetime of scholarship, spanning many eras and regions, is not rooted primarily in ideology or class, but is tethered theoretically to what should be called an "anti-racist geopolitics." She applied her critique to the history of the arms race and the annexation of Hawaii by the United States as well as to then-contemporary developments in India and Asia, the entire Pacific region, and in Africa. Her focus was on the methods of imperialism with racism operating as both a "how" and a "why." She concerned herself with the technologies of racialized imperialism, to include tools of violence like arms and weaponry, of course. But in her work on Hawaii, she extended her definitions to include missionaries and the business settler class.

She also marked U.S. imperialism as beginning early in the nineteenth century, and in Hawaii and not, as usually argued, with the Spanish-American War in 1898. Race, the history of slavery, the Civil War, and its aftermath stand at the center of her analysis, especially on questions about labor. Tate detailed the role of race and the work of settler colonialists not only in Hawaii but in Oceania more broadly, including in Papua New Guinea, Fiji, Australia, and New Zealand. She argued that the United States and Great Britain reached an early rapprochement in that region, one of the first signals of an emerging Anglo-American alliance still much in evidence in the trilateral security pact of Australia, the United Kingdom, and the United States announced in 2021.

Tate also rejected the notion of "non-self-governing territories," conceptualized after World War II to be applied to colonized lands in Africa in particular. She argued that it mattered little whether an international legal relationship with a more powerful nation was called a "strategic area," "trust territory," "Crown colony," or "mandate"; to her, all such forms diminished the sovereignty and independence of the weaker partner. Tate's view was distinct from those, like Ralph Bunche, W. E. B. Du Bois, and Rayford Logan, who had accepted the compromise implicit in the earlier "mandates" of the League of Nations and the later embrace of "trust territories" by the United Nations. For her, the explicit power imbalance persisted regardless of the label applied, and to expect a different political outcome from what remained a subservient position for former colonies was naive.

Her final work was an investigation into the expansion of railroads, deep-sea ports, mineral extraction, and international corporate capitalism in post-independence Africa of the 1970s. For her, the building and controlling of that infrastructure by external international capital had the potential to be as efficacious as weaponry in dominating and controlling the political and economic future of the continent. That work remained unpublished, but her attention to the power of global capital's movement was no less prescient as she worried about modern forms of re-imperialization, especially as realized through what would later be called "enclave economies."

Tate's self-proclaimed identity was as a historian, and I honor that. However, she was not invested in disciplinary squabbles and claims, and her professional treatment would not have been changed by her choice of discipline in an academic world rife with racial and gender restrictions. Her unusual training and capacious intellect positioned her to be among the first to embrace the value of interdisciplinarity, borrowing methods from diplomatic, economic, and political history as well as international relations.

That was complemented by her careful study of geography and geopolitics, which led her toward a concept of comparative imperialism within regions and across continents, whether in the Pacific or in Africa. Her reading, her research, her teaching, and her travels left her more realistic as well about the hoped-for potential at the historic Asian-African Conference held at Bandung, Indonesia, in 1955. She was boldly skeptical of the view that an Afro-Asian alliance might be easily realized among nations with such varying economic strengths and cultural and political differences, despite a history of shared imperialism.

No political label or discipline or school can serve as shorthand for the range and theoretical sophistication of Tate's works and ideas. Her life and her work also force the realization that the political categories we apply to most historical subjects, including in African American studies, are too narrow and too few. Our list of canonical political thinkers, irrespective of their race, is too exclusionary to capture the full range and richness of political thought on race and imperialism and much more. This is especially true when we ignore the work of historical Black women thinkers like Tate.

Tate's life and work also raise the question: What has been the intellectual loss of nearly a century of racial segregation and gender exclusion in history and international relations, the humanities and social sciences, and the natural sciences as well? That is part of a broader problem in academia, where Black and women scholars and thinkers are less likely to be studied, taught, or cited, and are more often subject to blunt categorization or appropriation.

There is plentiful evidence of African American thought on the nexus between race, empire, capitalism, and colonization both inside and outside academic settings. That merely highlights that, at the same time, most other scholars, with rare exception, continued to deny or ignore the racialized political reality in the topics they studied and the worlds where they lived. The more compelling line of inquiry is: How did Tate and others manage to reject the prevailing notions in their fields and produce stellar scholarship that defied convention while their academic colleagues continued to follow received wisdom, rarely challenge it, and earn great academic success, including for the "discovery" of ideas long ago explored by overlooked Black scholars like Tate?

Tate's life, travels, and work require us to revise and extend broader themes in twentieth-century American and African American history, women's history, the history of education, diplomatic history, and international thought. For most of the twentieth century, most Black academics were "segregated scholars" who spent their careers at historically Black colleges and universities ("HBCU"), yet their lives and works have not received the close study they deserve, with rare exceptions. Tate would be one of the few women in that group and one whose credentials and publications rivaled or outpaced her male peers, Black and white.[5]

Invisible to the majority white world, Black educators formed a close-knit network that included those working in high schools, colleges, and universities. Tate freely shared her knowledge more widely as a "public intellectual" through lectures and speeches in a Black civic sphere of Black audiences in political and social clubs, churches, sororities and fraternities, on campuses, and through the Black press. Tate's active life in that network spans the 1930s through the 1980s, providing a window on the struggles of the generation raised during Jim Crow but who lived through the civil rights era and the transition to "desegregation."

Black domestic travel has been studied as plagued by racism and Black international travel presented as an escape from U.S. racism. Both are true, but neither captures the full range of travel practices of Black Americans who went abroad with great intentionality, but for a wide variety of reasons. Tate rarely traveled anywhere in the world without running into or staying with other Black Americans. Some were there for professional reasons or for leisure and pleasure, some were students and scholars like Tate. Others were artists, athletes, religious leaders, missionaries, journalists, members of the military, or attached to other U.S. government agencies.

Tate was part of that large cohort of Black American world travelers. Her extensive and detailed unpublished travel accounts bring that reality to life. Through her, we can see how international travel helped form Black people's ideas about American and African American exceptionalism and privilege, and about other "darker peoples" of the world in India, Asia, and Africa.

Tate's location in Washington and at Howard University invites a reconsideration of that southern city's place in twentieth-century Black intellectual and political life. The District was home to an unusually large well-educated

Black community. As the nation's capital, the city held all three branches of the federal government, as well as its libraries, museums, archives, and foreign embassies. Only there would Tate have been able to realize her scholarly ambitions, making full use of those resources, especially at the Library of Congress and the National Archives. Tate's life reminds us of the city's singularity and significance, including what it means to study colonialism in a peculiar political space that lacks voting congressional representation and true home rule.

Two of the major tropes in Black women's history, archival absence and silence, are contested here by "archival abundance" and studied self-invention. The first pleases a biographer but the other can confound.

Here, an archive scattered around the world speaks, filtered through my reliance on the methodological tools of narrative history, bringing along habits of studied skepticism and interpretive authority. This is the particular creative work that can only come from deep immersion in archival remnants from many sources, then brought together in the faithful telling of a life's journey.

To cherry pick and interpret archival records, texts, or photographs in support of a predetermined argument, trope, or ideology can be an ethical disservice to the objects of our research. This can be especially troubling in studying Black people who have so long suffered from just those kinds of practices by earlier generations of scholars. Indeed, those were the very issues that birthed the need for the field of Black history at the turn to the twentieth century.

Even so, there certainly are times when Tate was self-consciously silent and, on rare but telling occasions, misleading. As for what she might have redacted or withheld, one can only guess, but the areas of her life about which she saved little and spoke and wrote even less are the most private—her religious faith and her physically intimate relationships.

After over a decade of work, I still respect the fact that parts of Tate's life remain simply unknowable. When we reach that limit, the urge to invent risks mythmaking, errors, and unfounded conclusions. Archives must be interrogated, critiqued, and judged carefully for sure, but they do still matter for what only they can and do reveal. This book is testament to that belief and practice.

Toward the very end of this project, after years of "hearing" Tate's voice in the pages of her correspondence, her transcribed oral interviews, and her published and unpublished writings, I was able for the first time to hear her voice when audiotapes of those interviews were released. On paper, she is as bold and confident as her ideas and the life she lived. But when I listened to her voice, recorded in her seventies, I hear a lilting, soft-spoken, erudite woman whose speech reminds me of the Black women who taught me in the segregated schools of Virginia in the 1960s and the retired Black schoolteachers who now share pews with me at church.

I realized more clearly in that moment that Tate must have known that if her voice and her ideas were going to be heard and heeded, then writing was the way she was going to have to do that. In her academic and professional work, she was writing to make herself heard in spaces where Black women's voices were absent or unwelcome or overpowered.

And so she wrote constantly. First, as a scholar, but also dabbling in journalism, travel writing, creating little poems and ditties, and in the age before email, writing copious letters, both personal and professional. Her decision to save so much of what she wrote makes my work possible, as well as her prolific body of published scholarly work, which equals and exceeds that of most of her generational peers.

To understand how Merze Tate was able to do all she did and build a life of personal and intellectual freedom for herself, we must return to where her story and this book begin and end: Michigan.

CHAPTER I

"Her Own Story"

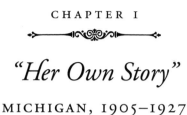

MICHIGAN, 1905–1927

Cold, snowy weather in early February is rarely newsworthy in central Michigan. But in 1905, the *Isabella Enterprise* in Mount Pleasant was forced to take note. One "blizzard bearing day" after the other had battered the region with temperatures plummeting as low as 17 degrees below zero. Howling winds whipped up tall snow drifts that froze and refused to budge. The expected 6:50 p.m. train got stuck and could not arrive until the middle of the next day. Intrepid rural federal delivery mail carriers were "great sufferers," as they were unable to navigate the "drifted roads."[1]

On February 6, Myrtle Tate went into labor as this fierce storm raged. Seeking the help of the local doctor was impossible in the snow. So a neighbor, her German American friend Verne Fish, helped deliver the baby girl. When the weather cleared, the doctor made it out on his horse and sleigh to place drops in the baby's eyes and to cut her tied tongue.[2] Then he carried news of the birth back to the county clerk. Having seen neither the baby nor the mother, the official recorded the child's race as "white," usually a safe assumption there. But in this case, the clerk was mistaken. Both of the parents called themselves "colored" and the Census designated them as "Black." The child did not learn of the error until more than a quarter century later, when she applied for a passport.[3]

The middle of Michigan was an unlikely place for a Black child to be born in 1905. Less than one percent of the state's 2.5 million residents were Black, and in rural areas they were fewer than half a percent. This child was born there because her grandparents had migrated to the area from Ohio after the Homestead Act of 1862 made tracts of land available in exchange for clearing and farming it. They had been among several Black families from Hocking County, Ohio, who traveled six weeks in caravans of ox-drawn covered wagons for nearly four hundred miles to reach the pine-forested land of Mecosta, Isabella, and Midland counties in Michigan.[4]

Myrtle and her husband Charles were born into two of those families, he to the Tates in 1864 while they were still in Ohio and she to the Letts in Michigan in 1875. They both came from that minority of Black people who were free well before the Civil War, and in this case for more than a generation. The couple had married in 1901, after their first marriages ended in divorce. Myrtle Tate had filed on the grounds of non-support to end her marriage to Edward Cross, a member of another Black settler family. With three young children to raise, she had quickly remarried. So although this new baby was the Tate couple's first-born, she had three older half-siblings: two brothers, Herschel and Theo, ages ten and six, and a sister, Thelma, age eight; another brother, Keith, would join the family two years later.[5]

When it came time to name their daughter, Myrtle Tate decided her first name would be "Vernie," to honor her good neighbor who had delivered the child. But for her middle name, she chose "Merze," which was unusual, especially for a girl. That name, which the child came to be known by, served as a first and lasting mark of difference for the rest of her long life.

When Merze Tate was asked as an adult about the origins of her name, she deflected. This was her habit when she did not want to discuss something she found painful or, in this case, simply odd or perhaps unflattering to her mother. She would say only that she was named after a character in a novel that her mother had read, but that the book had been destroyed in a fire, a telling detail designed to end the inquiry.[6]

Like most names, Merze Tate's tells us more about the parent than the child. It seems likely that the novel her mother had read was *Merze: The Story of an Actress,* published in 1888 by Marah Ellis Ryan, a prolific writer known for her popular sentimental novels of white heroines of the American West. However, this particular novel was set not in the West, but in Kentucky, Ohio, and Virginia in the period immediately after the Civil War.[7]

Like most sentimental novels, its plot follows the heroine's search for happiness as an orphan in Kentucky who yearns above all else for education, books, and learning—ambitions that are ridiculed and denied because she is female. The heroine emerges as a voracious reader who marries but still wants to be a classical actress, well-educated, and able to support herself financially. In contrast to most romantic novels, the happy ending here is that the heroine does not have to give up her marriage for her lucrative acting career and is able to have both.

The convoluted narrative rests on many themes that would have appealed to Myrtle Tate. Like the heroine, she too had been orphaned when her mother died shortly after giving birth to her, although she was raised by her father's sister alongside her cousins. She had completed sixth grade and loved reading and learning, marking her among the literate at a time when that status was not presumed, especially among Black people. She later became known in her community for her gifts in elocution, dramatic readings, and recitations. Her first marriage was to a man who did not or could not support her or their children, similar to the protagonist's financially irresponsible father in the book. So the novel's theme of a woman attaining financial independence would have had a particular appeal.

The novel's heroine embodied a rural woman's search for greater freedom than most women knew and to be realized through books, education, and a career. By choosing to name her daughter after this character, Myrtle Tate may have projected her own yearnings on her baby girl. She seemed to hope for her a life that would bring more independence and adventure than her own, including more opportunities for education and professional work, and the chance to travel beyond Michigan to see a wider world.

Myrtle Tate's identification with the heroine makes sense, but what she most likely could not identify with are the servile Black characters that drive the dialogue when the heroine is living on a plantation in Virginia while training to be an actress. The contrast between the heroine's quest for freedom, independence, and opportunity and the portrayal of the Black characters' insistence on remaining tethered to the South is a central paradox of the novel. Raised in the rural Midwest in isolation from a large Black community, perhaps Myrtle Tate felt little kinship with the southern Black former slaves who, unlike her family, could not leave, or she made peace with their presence or simply chose to ignore them while she decided to name her daughter after the book's white heroine.

A motherless child's sense of loss and limitation rarely abates, even though Myrtle Tate remained closely connected with her father and surrounded by loving kin. Reading the book may have rekindled dreams of a life for herself different from the one she was living. When she had reached the age when she would make decisions about her future as an adult, her choices would not have been many. Like most Black women at the end of the nineteenth century, her vocational and financial options were few whether she lived in the Midwest, the North, or the South.

But in this case, geography and circumstance would have imposed even greater restrictions on her, absent an ability or willingness to move away from the only home she knew. Women who wanted to move or migrate in this period had far fewer options than men, without beckoning relatives elsewhere; they also had limited kinds of work available, and often they had to stay put because of family caretaker responsibilities. If she wanted marriage or children, which would have been expected in that era, even the number of Black male partners near where she lived in rural Michigan would have been extremely limited.

Myrtle Tate's fate was to spend all of her life in southwest Michigan near the place of her birth. Yet she named her daughter after the independent, adventuresome, professionally successful, financially independent heroine "Merze." Perhaps she hoped that her daughter, born in 1905, might have a different future and a better chance of reaching a dream of freedom and learning than she had when she was born in 1875.

In the novel, the protagonist was asked by her adopted daughter about her peculiar name. The daughter asks, "Merze? Is that from Mercy?" to which her mother replied, "I do not know what it is from, dear." The daughter persists: "I think it must be from Mercy," and the mother accedes. From that exchange comes the pronunciation that would follow Myrtle Tate's Merze, as "Merce," with the "z" softened to a "c" sound.

When Merze Tate spoke toward the end of her life of her upbringing in rural Michigan, her deep admiration for her family's history as homesteaders was clear. She repeated what she could not have known but would only have been told—a true story of tough, hardworking people who cut pine trees to build log cabins, frame homes, churches, and schools. They cleared the land they claimed in hopes of making tillable soil in a place with a short growing season that limited the options for good farming.

The people who raised her were proud of their toil and independence, even though it was a life of grueling hard labor and limited financial yield. Her mother, Tate later reported, was so prideful that in old age she refused to accept Social Security because she considered it charity. By any objective measure, the family would have been considered poor, but Tate explained that "we were never poverty-stricken" and "never went to bed hungry." As far as

Merze Tate, standing, with her mother, Myrtle, and brother Keith (Zhang Collection, Western Michigan University Archives)

their clothing, they were "a little bit better than the average person" because her mother sewed beautifully for her family and for others, a skill she taught her younger daughter.[8]

Their life of hardscrabble independence also included the hardships of geographic isolation in an era before cars and trucks, made even worse by long, harsh winters. It was not the case that the Black families who traveled together from Ohio had formed one new community, as had happened in southwestern parts of the state. "I don't want you to think that these counties were settled completely by colored. They were only a small group along with whites," Tate explained. Instead, they were scattered depending on where land or work was available, since not all of them ended up owning land.[9]

Maintaining ties with other Black families required planning, travel, and good weather, as Tate described: "Maybe on Sunday we'd go in the horse and buggy four or five miles to a colored family to have dinner or they would come to ours. Or if we went to church out of our area, I'd have those associations with the Crosses or the Letts. But my everyday associations would be with the neighbors." When her family members attended church in their own area, they would be the only Black people there.[10]

Even the most cursory survey of a manuscript census of Tate's home county reveals pages and pages of "W's," only rarely interrupted by the isolated small family groupings of "B's," signifying the racial imbalance. In reporting her childhood memories, she painted a picture of near idyllic relations with white neighbors, but she actually only ever names one: the Fish family, which lived on the next farm. Tate remembers being told that the two mothers nursed each other's babies and watched over each other's children. Even this recollection of mutuality of need was a reversal of the usual trope of Black women nursing white southern children.

Although she never acknowledged it in her accounts of the family, public records and Tate's personal correspondence reveal that when she was only seven, her mother and father separated. By a Bill of Separation, her father deeded one farm to Tate's mother for her support and that of his children, and retained a nearby farm for himself. Her mother was alone again, but this time with five children rather than three.[11]

For the rest of her life, Merze Tate let ambiguity cloud those facts. She did the same to conceal that her mother's first marriage had ended not by her husband's death but in divorce. Tate's adult withholding of specifics that were well known to her and everyone who knew her family is a relic of an age when divorce and separation were uncommon and sometimes seen as scandalous. It may also reflect her own sense of shared shame, or both. But without a doubt, it also comports with familiar self-narrating tendencies to expunge, abridge, elide, and redact anything that reflected badly on what she later called "her own story."

Indeed, one emotional upheaval after the other marked the early years of her life. The year after her parents' legal separation, a local newspaper reported that the family had suffered a fire that destroyed their home and most of their possessions. Myrtle Tate's father, with whom she had remained close, died during this period. Soon she was seriously ill herself, requiring her older

Merze Tate, bottom, with her brother Keith in the center, brothers Theo and Herschel, and sister, Thelma (Zhang Collection, Western Michigan University Archives)

daughter, Thelma, who had earned a teaching certificate from Central Michigan Teacher's College, to return home from Grand Rapids to care for her.

During this time, the younger children attended school in Grand Rapids for a year, long enough for Merze to win first place in an essay-writing contest. A year later, her best playmate, a girl her age from a neighboring family, died of pneumonia when they were both twelve. Of that, Tate would only say in later recollections that she learned then that she was no longer afraid of a dead body, having touched her friend's in its coffin. Her descriptions of the joy and loss of that friendship stand out because she makes no mention of childhood times spent with anyone else, including with her family.[12]

These unsettling and traumatic events all came in quick succession. Perhaps both to deny their impact on her and to cast her family legacy heroically, Tate created an alternative public narrative and took control of her own life story. The memories that animated Tate's later accounts of her young life are centered not on her family but on school, where her exploits as a brilliant student brought her acclaim and affirmation early and often. Tate's start of school overlapped almost exactly with her parents' separation and presented her with opportunities to excel and make her family proud, and, as they saw it, their race, too.

Tate's formal education began at the Rolland Township, School No. 5, a one-room frame building close to her home that she and her younger brother attended together. The "curriculum was not limited to the three R's, but included geography, history, horticulture, orthography, and physiology." It was during these early school years that the idea of traveling to see the world captivated her young mind: "My geography books were illustrated with fascinating pictures of the Acropolis, the Pyramids, the Cape of Good Hope, Victoria Falls, Mandalay, Siam, Singapore, Hong Kong, Zanzibar, Australia, New Zealand, the Fiji Islands, Niagara Falls, the Grand Canyon, 'Old Faithful' in Yellowstone park, the huge Redwood tree in California through which a carriage could pass, and the Christ of the Andes. How I dreamed of seeing some of these far way places with strange-sounding names."[13]

Based on her vivid descriptions, it seems likely that Tate's teacher introduced her students to the thrilling travel narratives in the *Zig Zag Journeys* series. The books featured a group of boys going on trips with their teacher, accompanied by dialogue detailing the political and natural history of the places they visited. The exquisite etchings of places, scenes, buildings, maps, and people must have been even more enchanting before easily available travel photography images. The travelers in the books were all male and white, but this seemed in no way a deterrent to Tate's desire as a young Black girl to one day see all the fascinating places sketched in the books.[14]

Many years later, Tate remembered having to walk eight miles a day to get to and from her high school in Blanchard. As her brother's education ended in eighth grade, she usually walked alone. She recalled making the trip after blizzards when the snow was up to her hips and in spring thaws when the water rose above her ankles, proudly never missing a day. To pass the time, she memorized and recited aloud Gray's "Elegy Written in a Country Churchyard" or

Tate, second from left in the back row, with her tenth-grade class in Blanchard, 1921 (Zhang Collection, Western Michigan University Archives)

parts of Chaucer's "Canterbury Tales" in old English or portions of Ernest Henley's "Invictus" or his "England, My England" or parts of the Declaration of Independence or Lincoln's "Gettysburg Address."[15]

Like her sister before her, who had graduated as valedictorian at Blanchard, Tate was an excellent student and at the top of her class. Her hopes of graduating ended abruptly in tenth grade when fire destroyed the school, imperiling Tate's college plans. If the younger sister was to go to college, she needed first to study at another accredited high school.[16]

To do that, Tate left home at fifteen and moved a hundred miles away to attend Battle Creek High School. In 1921, before modern highways and easy access to cars, that was a long way from home. This decision speaks loudly of the value that she, her mother, and her family placed on educating the girls in their family. While her brothers would have greater mobility and a wider range of laboring and farming possibilities, the vocational options for the daughters would be quite limited without a formal education. Domestic work, which elsewhere depended on Black women, was a luxury for the very few white midwestern families wealthy enough to afford servants. Her older brother Herschel had moved to Battle Creek to work, and that may have played a role in her going there, although he was not at that point in a position to offer her a place to live.

That's why, even though she was in high school, the city directory for 1922 lists Tate as a "maid." She could only afford to finish high school if she worked and lived with white families for room and board and some cash. One year she cooked and cleaned for an elderly woman and her companion; when the three of them were alone, she cooked and they ate together, but when the woman had company, Tate served the food to her and her guests.[17]

The move to Battle Creek would prove fortuitous for Tate despite the difficulty of leaving home and working while going to school. The city of 36,000 was larger and less isolated than Blanchard or Mount Pleasant. Although its Black population was small—about a thousand people—the city long had a reputation as a haven for ex-slaves, including the renowned abolitionist Sojourner Truth, who died and was buried there in 1883. The city's public schools were open to the small number of Black students. The high school had its first Black graduate in 1877, and about a dozen others by the time Tate arrived. Still, with such a historically small Black population, she was one of the few Black students in the school, where all of the teachers were white.[18]

Compared with schools near Tate's home, her new high school was much bigger, in a new modern building, with better educated teachers and a more advanced curriculum, including subjects she enjoyed such as ancient and medieval history. As is often the case, good teachers can make all the difference in a student's life. For Tate, it was her history teacher, a young "Miss Glass," who inspired her in ways that guided her ambitions for many years to come. Evelyn Glass had graduated from Battle Creek High before becoming a Phi Beta Kappa at the University of Michigan in 1920, returning to teach high school history by emphasizing geography and maps depicting adventures of travel and exploration.

Her teacher also fed Tate's growing appetite for travel when she told her students about her own recent summer adventures in Europe. Glass was only eight years older than Tate, but in June 1921 she had sailed from New York to Liverpool, returning from Glasgow to Montreal at the end of August; she toured England, Scotland, and several European countries. On another trip, Glass attended a summer school session for high school teachers in Oxford. Tate first heard about Oxford from her, saying that "she told the class so much about it," the beauty of the town and the university, and the historical grandeur and aura of excellence. Her high school history teacher who loved to travel inspired Tate to want to be the same.[19]

Battle Creek High offered other opportunities, including the student oratorical contest with which we began. When Tate won as a junior, that achievement came after the many upheavals in her family, after her high school had burned down, after her recent relocation from Blanchard, and while she was working her way through school. Her speech advocating for fair treatment for Black citizens rested on the wartime record of service of Black men. She likely came to that topic from reading Black newspapers and magazine coverage of the heroism and unfair treatment of Black soldiers during and after the war, including during the racial violence that took place in numerous cities during the Red Summer of 1919. She also likely had conversations with her older brother Herschel, who had served in the Navy during the war and later became very engaged in Black civic, literary, and political clubs in Battle Creek.[20]

Her teachers may have played a role too, but in Tate's recollections she emerges already as the solo star of her own story. She explained that she wrote and then memorized her speech by reciting it aloud while she did housework or walked to school. "And some people who heard about it and heard I was so good," she recalled, "one person who was supposed to have been the one to win it, dropped out." Tate had reason to be proud of herself. She was living on her own, working to support herself, and still earning straight A's in all of her classes.[21] That she was exceeding her white peers was a credit to her individual determination, but her family and others also would have seen her success as a victory against notions of African American intellectual inferiority even more prevalent then than now.

Tate had begun what would be the defining feature of her life: intellectual ambition and a relentless pursuit of education and knowledge. Over forty years later, Battle Creek native Helen Smith Kaiser mailed Tate a long letter, asking "remember me?" and reminding her that when she was a child "you used to live with us," likely as live-in help. After updating Tate on her parents and her siblings, Kaiser wrote, "I remember so well how hard you worked to go to school and [am] so happy that you have had such a beautiful life. You really deserve the best." Her reputation as a hardworking, high achieving student was set early and it was long seen as inspiring in the memories of people who knew her then.[22]

Notice of her academic success earned her an offer from a local white businessman to help send her for a year to Western State Normal School in Kalamazoo. Tate's hometown newspaper in Blanchard, under the banner headline "Former High School Student Making Good," recounted how she had walked to school as a child, received highest honors, paid her own way through Battle Creek High School, gotten the best grades, and was now on her way to Western. How this information and its particular framing made its way into print is not clear, but the content presented certainly met her and her family's approval.[23]

Descended from free Blacks who migrated from Ohio into the Northwest Territory, Tate seemed to have been spared from a childhood of abject poverty and the daily humiliations and the worst dangers associated with racial segregation, discrimination, and violence. Living in small numbers and scattered in rural pine forests and farmlands may have kept everyday public interactions at a minimum, but Tate also had a lifelong tendency to minimize challenges or difficulty in her recollections.

Unlike many of her generation, Tate also had access to an unusually advanced elementary and high school education. Her parents and other family members were literate and able to assist her as an eager young student. In an era when most young Black women were forced to leave school and work or assume caretaking duties, her family did not require that of her and helped support her quest for education.

A clipping of the article about winning the Hinman contest remained among Tate's possessions until her death, and its substance would often be repeated as the core of the narrative of her own life as a student of exceptional intellect and determination. But it also reveals, both in its presentation and its preservation, that she would never be reticent to self-promote and to celebrate her hard work and personal achievements, a quality often frowned upon in young women. This also serves as early evidence of her ample ego strength.

Tate did not report being daunted by the prospect of moving alone again to go to college in Kalamazoo. To her, it was a short move, less than thirty miles west of Battle Creek, the place where she already had learned to be on her own. Once she had left her mother at age fifteen, she would find herself at home in many places, but Blanchard and Isabella County would never again be among them.

When Tate entered Western State Normal School at seventeen, she was attending a college that was only two years older than she was. Established initially to offer a teacher training certificate program, by 1920 the school also awarded bachelor degrees. The college continued to grow and evolve throughout the following decades, and eventually it was renamed Western Michigan University in 1957.[24] Tate entered college with the ambition for not just a teacher's certificate, but for a bachelor's degree with the hope of becoming a high school history teacher.

Tate in her college graduation photo, 1927
(Zhang Collection, Western Michigan University Archives)

Kalamazoo, situated 150 miles west of Detroit and 150 miles north of Chicago, was a city of about 70,000 people, with a small Black community of 800. The city was also home to Kalamazoo College, but it was Western that drew students like Tate into its teacher training program. She would be one of only a handful of Black students there.[25]

Just as her high school teacher had encouraged and influenced Tate, at Western she encountered faculty members who also exposed her to a wider world and, perhaps even more important, to women who modeled academic careers. Tate was most inspired by Nancy Scott, her modern European history professor with a doctorate from the University of Pennsylvania in 1909 who specialized in Czechoslovakian and Slavic affairs and international law. Scott also spent an academic year studying in Prague, traveling throughout Europe, and staying for a month in Geneva observing the League of Nations. She lectured frequently on international affairs to local civic and women's groups and later advised on international programs for the American Association of University Women. Tate considered her a mentor, and they stayed in touch until Scott's death in Kalamazoo four decades later, in 1967.[26]

Tate could see in Scott what the life of a woman professor trained in history and international affairs might offer, including opportunities to travel and study abroad. It was not until 1921 that three Black women became the first to earn Ph.D. degrees. So Tate's tutelage by a woman with Scott's training was a rarity and a benefit from being at a white institution. Her professor was engaged as well in debates about women who chose education, economic independence, and careers over marriage and domestic home life. In defending that choice, which had been her own, Scott cautioned against stereotyping women like her as "old maids" and discriminating against them as masculine and non-maternal. Instead, she wrote in 1926, "the mother-spirit in women" was separate from "physical motherhood" and found expression in work as teachers, nurses, and social workers. Although itself an essentialist sentiment, it did robustly vindicate women who chose those professions, particularly at a time when marriage often disqualified them for employment.[27]

Tate took full advantage of the course offerings at Western State even as she had to work to support herself. She soon was on her way to earning another straight-A record, but she became so sick that she was forced to miss a year out of school after earning her teaching certificate in 1925: "I was ill. It wasn't mental. It was just overwork." Tate never was more specific about her illness, saying only that it had been misdiagnosed. A letter of recommendation years later disclosed that the doctor thought she had tuberculosis, a disease whose stigma, often racialized, was discordant with her narrative of her life. She recovered well enough to use the teaching certificate she had already earned to work at an elementary school in Cass County, which had a small Black community. Her ambition had not waned—for even when she was there and when she was ill, she took correspondence courses with the college so that she could continue to work on a bachelor's degree.[28]

Once she had returned to college, her financial needs persisted, and word of her plight reached back to Battle Creek, including to members of its small

Tate in Michigan, around 1925 (Zhang Collection, Western Michigan University Archives).

Black community. On stationery carrying the familiar Black women's club motto "We Lift as We Climb," Mae Guy of the Dardanel Art Club wrote Tate in 1925: "We would like to hear from you as we are planning on helping you a little financially and feel that you are very deserving." The Battle Creek Board of Education also awarded her some funds to help her in college.[29]

But Tate most credited money from her sister Thelma with enabling her to finish college without working herself into complete exhaustion again. Her sister had taught elementary school, but later moved to Detroit where she shared a home with her brother Theo. After passing the civil service exam, she

Tate in Michigan, 1925
(Moorland-Spingarn, Howard University)

had taken a secure and relatively well-paying position with the post office, an unusually early opportunity for a Black woman to achieve.

Her sister Thelma's life as a young woman by then had included a brief marriage that ended in a divorce on the grounds of extreme cruelty; she later remarried, this time more happily to a fellow post office worker, James Hayes. It is unclear why she left teaching, but opportunities for Black teachers were very limited and salaries for all teachers were low. Detroit was the rare school system that would hire married women as schoolteachers, but at a time when only 4 percent of students were Black and the majority in only two schools, the prospects for Black teachers remained extremely limited even in the face of growing teacher shortages.[30]

With the financial security provided by her sister, Tate pleaded with the college for permission to complete the bachelor's degree as quickly as possible by taking extra heavy course loads. The dean refused to consent, fearing that Tate would have another breakdown, but in an early sign that she would never take "no" for an answer, she took her request to the school's president. When he saw that she had maintained straight A's the previous term while taking six courses, he was so impressed that he wrote a note: "Permit her to take what she wishes." His word carried the day, despite the objection of another administrator who viewed Tate's record and argued that something must be wrong with the curriculum if she could finish it in three years.[31]

After she was released to take as heavy a load of courses as she wanted, Tate graduated in 1927, with straight A's, and posted the highest academic record ever at the school; she was one of 100 bachelor degree recipients among 559 graduates. Although she did not realize it at the time, she also became the first Black student to earn a degree there, as others had left with a teaching certificate only. Her reputation as a brilliant, hardworking student would become central to her self-identity, and her stellar record brought Tate both local and broader notice. A special correspondent to the *Christian Science Monitor* posted an article detailing how she had worked her way through college, finishing with highest honors while completing her course in three years. The article's title, "Negress Wins School Honors," marked Tate's race and gender as part of what made the achievement newsworthy.[32]

A schoolteacher outside Philadelphia read that article and wrote to congratulate Tate, identifying himself as a principal of "a white faculty of a large public school for colored children." He asked if she could write "in a few hundred words the story of your life efforts, with your guiding principles, that I may use it as a stimulus for the worthy older girls here who would like to follow in your footsteps?" Whether she wished for it or not, Tate had been elevated at age twenty-two into a role model, for Black girls in particular.[33] The exceptionalist narrative of her early academic success also brought with it obligations as an ambassador and racial representative.

When college officials went to place their star graduate of 1927 in a job, they were surprised to discover that despite her record there was not a single position available in the state of Michigan for a Black high school teacher. The school's newness and its inexperience with Black graduates, especially one with a bachelor's degree, may explain the ignorance of the racially restrictive policies and practices that effectively limited Black teachers to jobs teaching Black students. In 1926 only 40 of Detroit's 5,800 teachers were Black, and they all worked on the elementary school level. Although Black students could attend predominately white schools, ironically, the Black population in most cities in Michigan had not yet reached numbers sufficient to create all-Black schools, particularly at the high school level.[34]

At the time, neighborhoods and schools were overlapping sites of white resistance. Tate graduated two years after the infamous case of Ossian Sweet in Detroit poignantly captured the state's racial environment. Sweet, a Black physician, bought a house in an all-white neighborhood, where he and his family were forced to defend themselves against a white mob, resulting in one death. Sweet and members of his family were put on trial in a case that attracted national attention and resulted in a hung jury, then a mistrial, and finally an acquittal, but not without first visiting great trauma, financial ruin, and tragedy on the Sweet family.[35]

But Tate would not have needed to look toward Detroit for evidence that Michigan was no racial utopia. In the 1920s, the Ku Klux Klan built a very well organized presence in the Midwest, and Michigan ended up with more Klansmen than any southern state, including in the rural counties in the central part of the state where her family lived. Crosses burned in Mecosta County, just north of Grand Rapids and neighboring on the area where Tate's family lived. The anti-Black, anti-Catholic, anti-Jewish, anti-immigrant views found fertile ground despite the very small and isolated numbers of people who were not white or not Protestant.[36]

In this racialized environment, securing a good education for Black children became a flashpoint for political organizing in Michigan, especially in the state's urban Black communities such as Detroit and Grand Rapids. Demands for more opportunities for Black schoolteachers were part of the resulting protests, which became more urgent with the increased migration of Black citizens during and after World War I.

Even if white officials at Western were oblivious to the racial politics in their home state, it is hard to imagine that Tate was unaware of the limited opportunities for Black teachers, including her own sister. Even her later account acknowledges as much: "But they couldn't place me because at that time, there was no public school, or private school probably, in the state of Michigan, hiring colored people at the senior high school level. In Detroit there were elementary teachers. I had any number of friends who were teaching in the elementary grades. But no one in the high school." She should have been aware of the policy and practice when she started to look for a job but perhaps assumed that her fate would differ because, like her Miss Glass, she had a bachelor's degree.[37]

But disappointed she was, as this particular distinction of being "the first" did not come her way. The Detroit school system, which had the state's largest number of Black students, did not hire its first (and only) Black high school teacher until 1934, a man who got the job only after a concerted campaign by Black citizens there. And in Battle Creek, where Tate had gone to high school, the public schools did not hire their first Black teacher until 1946.[38]

What is remarkable about Tate's moment of racial awakening is that she had lived twenty-two years before it happened. Most accounts of Black lives feature an incident when a Black child comes face to face with racism and with their parents' or their community's powerlessness to change it. Tate claims never to have known segregation or discrimination or the sting of racism growing up, only to face it trying to get her first job as a college-educated Black woman. Even this adds to her sense of racial exceptionalism, having grown up in places where the number of Blacks was not yet large enough to be rigidly segregated, but where racial discrimination obviously was never entirely absent.

Tate was resilient even if disappointed and remained stubbornly committed to teaching history at the high school level. She had a choice: if she wanted to teach high school, she would not be able to do it in her native state. To their credit, the administrators at Western were determined to help her realize her ambition and to avoid the embarrassment of not being able to place their top student. Knowing that she was still without funds, they loaned her the money necessary to travel and interview for jobs in other states. Tate would always be grateful for this act of generosity, and never forgot how her alma mater had invested in her.

Her job search was limited to cities, in her words, "where there were colored high schools," which were the only places hiring Black high school teachers. Neighboring states with larger numbers of Black people were already confronting shifting racial demographic changes that brought larger proportions of Black youths into urban school systems. Midwestern school systems that had been "integrated" earlier in the twentieth century were, with increasing numbers of Black migrant children, becoming as segregated as the residential neighborhoods in which Blacks were restricted by racial covenants and redlining.

This is how Tate came to interview in St. Louis, Cincinnati, and Indianapolis. In St. Louis, she felt unprepared for a surprise examination in history conducted by the white superintendent and the all-white school board. At first, she "was trembling almost with fear," but once she heard the questions, she felt that some "divine guidance must have come because every question they put to me, it seemed that the answer was on the tip of my tongue." It did not take long for her ironclad confidence to reassert itself and for her to realize that "I probably knew more than the school board members."[39]

These visits also were the beginning of her introduction to a small but growing national network of college-educated Black people, especially schoolteachers. Indeed, some of the people she met during these interviews later developed into lifelong friends. Among them were Susie Williams and her sister Frances Williams, daughters of the principal of the prestigious Sumner High School in St. Louis.

Tate succeeded in getting job offers in all three cities. In the end, she chose to teach in Indianapolis, she said, because it offered to pay her a hundred dollars more because of her experience teaching white high school students through Western's on-campus student teaching program. Racially-based pay disparities played in her favor in that instance. But she also chose Indianapolis because it was nearer to her family in Michigan, especially her sister in Detroit, the family member to whom she felt closest.[40]

But she also already had set her sights on loftier goals in places farther away. She had applied for and received a teaching fellowship at Howard University. It was the choice not taken probably for financial reasons, but the school known as the mecca of Black higher education had already attracted her ambition.[41]

Tate would always praise her Michigan heritage because she also saw it as a key distinction in her identity as a Black person. "I was born in Michigan, not in Mississippi," she would say many decades later. "That probably has made all the difference in my life." She wondered aloud what would have happened to her "if she had seen the light of day in Bolivar County, or any other county in Mississippi, the daughter of a landless and far-from-free sharecropper, instead of in Michigan, the granddaughter of forever free homesteaders, free to till their soil, free to produce a surplus to sell for money with which to purchase tools, implements, horses, more land, and to build a frame house."[42]

Her litany of "free" ended with her recognition that "this was Chippewa Indian territory, preempted by Germans, Irish, Scotch-Irish, Scots, English, and Scandinavians, with the Indians relegated to a reservation near Mt. Pleasant." Even as she acknowledged that the "free" land that her grandparents had settled under the Homestead Act of 1862 was land formerly occupied by Native peoples, she also seemed to deflect the responsibility for that on those white settlers who came first, and not on her ancestors who arrived later.[43]

Tate's upbringing on her family's land in Michigan was a midwestern expression of rural Black life outside the more familiar southern settings of the early twentieth century. Descended from free Blacks who migrated from Ohio into the Northwest Territory, she also was spared a childhood of abject poverty and one steeped in the daily humiliations and dangers of racial segregation and discrimination.

Her parents and other family members were literate and able to assist her as a young student. She also had access to an unusually advanced elementary and high school education, which was a substantial advantage at a time when fewer than 20 percent of Americans could claim the same. In an era when most Black women were forced to leave school and work at a young age or to assume caretaking duties, her resilient mother and her family were able to help her earn a college degree in Michigan in 1927 and emerge as a self-confident, independent young Black woman full of unrelenting ambition and determination.

Tate had left Blanchard to go to high school in Battle Creek and on to Kalamazoo for college. Racial discrimination required her to leave Michigan to do the work for which she had sacrificed so much to train. Her years in Indianapolis became transformative ones in her long journey to become not only a high school teacher, but a world traveler, a scholar, and a cosmopolitan woman.

CHAPTER 2

"Distinguished Colored Men and Women"

INDIANAPOLIS—ENGLAND—EUROPE—WASHINGTON, 1927–1932

When Tate started her teaching job in Indianapolis in 1927, she moved into a Black community that was in a bustling capital city crossed by several major railroad lines. Although the city and its Black population grew during World War I, many more southern migrants passed through the city, often to get to Chicago or Detroit, or if they stayed in-state, to steel-industry jobs in Gary. But some settled in Indianapolis. By the end of the 1920s, the Black population had grown to 44,000, or 12 percent of the city's population.[1]

Blacks in the city built a vibrant commercial, cultural, and political community to serve their needs. In 1910, Madame C. J. Walker moved her manufacturing headquarters from St. Louis to Indianapolis; her enterprises and her philanthropy helped bolster a growing local Black economy. The city's Indiana Avenue was home to eight blocks of Black businesses as well as venues for Black entertainers, dances, bands, and other leisure activities. Political and civic groups, women's clubs, and churches provided the energy and spaces for community organizing. Political engagement among Black women was especially strong; in 1913, they founded one of the earliest local chapters of the NAACP in the country and led it with an all-female board and officers. With funds from Walker, they also established a Black YWCA in 1914, to complement the Black YMCA that had been organized in 1910 after the white Y rejected all Black applicants.[2]

Whites in power noticed and fought against the growing presence of Black people there and in other Indiana cities. The state legislature passed policies of racial restriction in 1900 that limited service in the state militia to white men, prohibited interracial marriage, and permitted but did not require segregated schools. Indiana was also home to a powerful Ku Klux Klan that dominated the state's Republican Party in the 1920s. Its merger with the party meant that most Black Republicans in Indiana began to vote Democratic long before the Roosevelt years.[3]

Support for the Klan in Indianapolis led to the creation of a White Supremacy League, also known as the White People's Protective League. True to either of its names, the group and its supporters worked to separate everything in the city by race and succeeded in passing a racialized residential zoning law. They nominated candidates for mayor and took over the school board. Over the objection of Black parents, the board then segregated all elementary schools. In order to prevent Black students from attending existing white high schools, the city announced a plan in 1922 to build a new all-Black high school.[4]

The Black community in the city fought back because most were offended by the imposition of a segregated school system in the Jim Crow style that they also feared would be inadequately funded. They worked with the NAACP and sued to block the school's construction, but without success. Still dissatisfied, Black community leaders forced the city to commit to hiring only Black teachers for the school; otherwise, those opportunities would continue to be denied them, perhaps even in an all-Black school. Teachers had to be recruited from across the country because there were so few Black teachers trained for the high school level in Indiana.

Black community members did succeed in naming the school Crispus Attucks High, rather than Thomas Jefferson High as the board had proposed. If there was to be a Black high school, they reasoned, it would bear the name of a Black revolutionary hero and not that of a slaveholding president. The fight against the segregated school was lost, but the symbolic victory in its naming at least honored that struggle.

When Tate joined the new faculty at Crispus Attucks, she described it as a "collection of distinguished colored men and women from various parts of the country." Most of them were experienced teachers, some with advanced degrees, who had moved in order to teach Black high school students at a time when educational opportunities were very limited. Even when it opened in 1927, it was already overcrowded, confirming community fears of underfunding. In time, the school would become a revered community institution as it trained Black students from all over the city and from all socioeconomic backgrounds. The school also hosted musical offerings, lectures, performances, and sporting events, making it an influential social and cultural setting as well.

Hired to teach history, Tate was mentored by more seasoned colleagues, Black women who modeled their deep commitment to provide an excellent education for their students. Her first supervisor was Iva Marshall, a Hunter College graduate who had come from the revered Dunbar High School in Washington to chair the history and social science division at Attucks. Marshall met and married another Attucks teacher, Tilford Davis, who had come from Kansas City. Both would become lifelong friends with Tate.

The teachers who were drawn to work at Attucks impressed Tate with their training and their sense of racial duty and introduced her to a new social world of educated Black people who also knew how to have fun in their leisure. For the first time, Tate lived in a large, urban Black community with rich cultural, social, and political networks. She was welcomed into the swirl of women's clubs, teas, and luncheons in Black Indianapolis. After long being one of a few Black students and never having had a Black teacher, Tate seemed to quickly acclimate herself to this new environment, and with enthusiasm.

Playing bridge, a game that came to popularity at that time, was a key to that social world. Tate knew nothing of the game, having never seen a card or a deck of cards in her mother's home. When she was invited to join a bridge club, she set about learning the game from a fellow Attucks teacher, an expert card player and a man she later called a "boyfriend." She lived in an efficiency apartment where he would join her to play Honeymoon Bridge, a version that can be played by two people rather than four: "I learned the denominations and the values of ace and king and queen and jack. And he would bet me a kiss that he would win. And I would bet him a kiss that I would win. So it didn't make any difference who won or who lost. So that's how I learned to play bridge. A most auspicious arrangement which we played for some time."[5]

Tate's mind and temperament were particularly well suited for the game. She was a quick study, had a gift for mathematics, and soon developed keen instincts for a game that rewarded her near photographic memory, her competitive urge, and her comfort with risk taking and strategic thinking. At her first bridge party, she played well enough to win first prize. "From that time on, I thought I knew bridge," she recalled. The game would remain one of the great joys of her life, opening the way to the busy social world of Black bridge clubs and to tournament-level play where she would become a master player. Later, the game also served as a second language of sorts, as she often played it in her international travels with people who did not speak English.[6]

Tate's social life flourished, and her name appeared frequently in the society pages of the local Black newspaper, the *Indianapolis Recorder,* which featured accounts of her being at parties and women's clubs. She and her colleague Iva Marshall hosted bridge parties for "The Nines," a women's social club. Tate also belonged to "The Pierettes," which the paper called "a charming and an illustrious group of young folk" who held dances and bridge parties. She held a bridal shower at her home when Marshall married Tilford Davis at St. Rita's Catholic Church, a Black parish in the city. She hosted gatherings for "The Club of Eight," including one that was called "one of the prettiest parties of the season," featuring musical performances, bridge, and a four-course luncheon with a travel motif of "ice cream in the shape of planes and trams." She sponsored after-theater parties at the Coffee Pot, a restaurant located in the Walker Theater complex, which had opened in 1927. Her busy social life also included traveling with a group of friends in 1931 to the Kentucky Derby, where they were feted at a large dinner.[7]

After all of her hard work, illness, and isolation in college, Tate's immersion in Black cultural life in Indianapolis brought her into social circles and professional networks that would sustain and nourish her emotionally and intellectually for the rest of her life. She later was recruited to join two Black sororities, Sigma Gamma Rho, which had been established at Butler University in Indianapolis in 1922, and Alpha Kappa Alpha, founded at Howard in 1908, making it the first Black sorority. Tate chose the AKA's because they were the oldest and because of the Howard connection. She was made a member in April 1931, joining her good friend and now "Soror" Iva Marshall Davis. Her AKA sorority sisters overlapped with members of the various clubs and groups to which Tate belonged, but sorority membership also brought her into a larger national network of college-educated Black women.[8]

Tate participated in public educational events too, providing lectures on "Negro history" at the YWCA for the local Business and Professional Club; her six-part series featured talks on Blacks in history, music, literature, poetry, education, and art. On another occasion, she spoke to young women at the Y on the topic "The Art of Being a Girl." She attended meetings of the Fortnightly Library Club, which included discussions of recent books such as Robert Moten's *What the Negro Thinks* and Nella Larsen's novel *Passing.*[9]

Seeing first-hand the difference that a college degree was making in her life, Tate also recruited and recommended women graduates from Attucks to her alma mater Western State and helped support them financially. The

Tate in Indianapolis, early 1930s (Moorland-Spingarn, Howard University)

school's president wrote to her that "your own record here was so satisfactory that your recommendation of any of your girls will be sufficient." When he offered to provide a scholarship for tuition, Tate replied, "I shall supplement this with $50 for the student's books," revealing her early commitment to providing educational opportunity for others.[10]

Tate obviously was enjoying her time in Indianapolis, and she liked teaching high school history, but her mind remained restless and her intellectual ambitions continued to grow. She took extension courses from Indiana University professors who traveled to Indianapolis to teach evening classes, expanding her language skills beyond English and Spanish by taking more French classes and, for the first time, German. In another sign of her broadening academic interests, she also studied European history with Frank Lee Benns, a prominent scholar in the field whose book *European History Since 1870,* published in 1930, became a classic.[11]

Like many Black schoolteachers, including some at Attucks, Tate spent summers in New York City taking classes at Teachers College at Columbia University in order to earn a master's degree, at a time when segregation limited access to graduate education in the states where they worked. In typical fashion, she managed to complete the program there in record time, thanks to her frenetic pace and intellectual intensity:

> I would leave the last possible day from Indianapolis after I had taught up until one o'clock, catch the Spirit of St. Louis, which was the crack train between St. Louis and New York, to get to New York the next day to register at the intersession courses at Columbia. At that time they had an intersession, the summer session, and another intersession that you could take advantage of if you were ambitious in the summer school work. So I would get the Pullman so I would have a night's rest and I would have my dinner en route and be at Columbia University the next morning for registration and to start classes.[12]

Her first two summers of study had her taking three or four courses a term on the history of education or on teaching. By the end of her time there, her focus had shifted to graduate courses on English constitutional history, the British empire in the nineteenth and twentieth centuries, and seventeenth- and eighteenth-century Europe. Even her final education course was on the history of European education. Though she wrote little of her leisure time during her summers in New York, it is hard to imagine that the Black social and literary world did not attract her time and attention, as she on occasion boarded at the Emma Ransom YWCA house in Harlem.[13]

After finishing her degree, Tate had promised herself the reward of a first trip overseas in the summer of 1931. It was only when applying for her passport that she discovered that she was listed as "white" on her birth certificate, a matter of some confusion. When the nationally circulated *Chicago Defender* and the *Pittsburgh Courier* ran a photograph in their articles about her travel plans, the public persona that Tate had begun cultivating as a high school student now had taken fuller form.

> One of those touring Europe this summer is Miss Merze Tate, a teacher of history in the Crispus Attucks high school, Indianapolis. Miss Tate will study French history at the Sorbonne and make a special survey of the International colonial exposition now in Paris. While a student at Battle Creek high school, Miss Tate won first place in the Hynman [*sic*] oratorical contest, the only Race person to win such an honor. She took her bachelor of arts degree from Western State Teachers college in Kalamazoo with a straight A record, the highest ever made there. She received her master of arts degree from Columbia University in 1930. Miss Tate is a member of the Alpha Kappa Alpha sorority.

Elsewhere, other newspapers reported that Tate was one of three Black women teachers going to study at the Sorbonne that summer. But it was Tate's habit to self-report on her own singularity whether as a student, teacher, or traveler. Her welcome into Black Indianapolis and its vibrant public intellectual life had helped transform the brilliant, ambitious, striving Michigan farm girl into a young woman of the educated Black elite who would now begin to realize her girlhood dream of traveling the world.[14]

Tate's solo journey abroad began with a train trip from Indianapolis to Detroit and then to Montreal. After staying in the YWCA there and touring the city, Tate boarded the S.S. *Montrose,* a Canadian ocean liner that would sail eight days for Cherbourg. The travel diary she began when she boarded ship reveals her habit of meticulous recordkeeping about what she did, who she met, what she observed, and how she spent her money, but little about what she felt.

On June 18, 1931, she wrote, in fledgling French: "The (mail) steamer Montrose, a Canadian Pacific Line boat, left Montreal at eleven in the morning. I am the only Negro woman. The travelers are very pleasant." Her nationality would be apparent anytime she spoke, but her caramel-colored skin would mark her race. Tate had an ease for conversation with strangers that served her well then and during a lifetime of travel to come. By the third day, she was drinking afternoon tea and playing bridge at night with her fellow passengers.[15]

The prospect of idyllic days at sea was broken by news that a passenger in third class had committed suicide and that his body was to be buried at sea. On Sunday, she attended an Anglican service, and began to suffer from some

Tate en route to Europe, 1931
(Zhang Collection, Western Michigan University Archives)

seasickness, but by the next day she wrote only, "Just another day at sea." She enjoyed the rest of the journey with her new friends, attended lectures and recitals, and continued to play bridge after tea and dinner.

Once the *Montrose* landed at Cherbourg, Tate took a train to Paris where she went directly to the Sorbonne to arrange lodging for her stay there. She soon traveled with a group of new French friends to a bathing resort in Boulogne, finding that "I was the only colored girl there. I certainly had many stares." Back in the city, she mastered the Metro and traveled several times with her camera to the Colonial Exposition, which was France's attempt to present in one place the diverse cultures of the lands under its imperial control. Tate was amazed by seeing so many visitors from all over the world, but once again she also noted, "I am quite a curiosity myself."[16]

While lingering intentionally at the American Express offices on July 1, Tate met a large group of other "colored Americans," including Sadie Warren, the owner of the *Amsterdam News,* Augusta Savage, the sculptor, and several other young women. She was happy to join that group of writers, teachers, and artists who were as eager as she was to explore the city, including its salons and nightlife.

It was through this group of Black women that Tate likely first learned of Grace Walker, a Black American woman who specialized in dramatic monologues featuring Black poetry accompanied by music. She had studied at Cambridge that year and at the Royal Academy of Dramatic Art in London before heading to Paris. Three days after encountering the group, Tate arranged a meeting with her and learned that she was heading to the Geneva School of International Relations for a summer session to study and to lecture. Walker made a powerful impression on her and inspired her to decide abruptly to spend precious weeks of her first trip to Europe in summer school in Geneva.[17]

Four days later, Tate boarded a train to Switzerland and shared a compartment with H. H. van Gessel of Holland, a wealthy gentleman who had worked in Geneva for many years, and the two struck up a conversation. The travel culture of the 1930s permitted much more ease of interaction with strangers and brought less suspicion and more help for a solo traveler. With his assistance, she secured a room on Parc des Bastions, an easy walk to the school, the Musée d'Art, and the Cathedrale St. Pierre, where she attended services on Sundays. While Tate was in Geneva, van Gessel, his wife, and seven children entertained her many times at their lakeside estate with its dramatic mountain views, taking tea under the trees by the water or inviting her along on their family excursions to France. Tate enjoyed her time with the family because of their warmth and generosity to her, and she marveled that his wife spoke English, his children spoke French, his mother spoke Dutch, and the servants spoke German, Javanese, and French.

As soon as she arrived in Geneva, Tate presented herself at the School of International Relations and requested to be admitted to the program. Being both bold and supremely confident in her own abilities, Tate had traveled there hurriedly and without any pre-arrangements. Her daring was rewarded when Lucie and Alfred Zimmern, the school's founders, granted her permission to enter the summer program, for which she paid thirty dollars in tuition. Alfred Zimmern had been named that year as the first Montague Burton Professor of International Relations at Oxford, and he was eventually seen as one of the founders of the then new field; he had been a deputy director at the League of Nations and later helped with the founding of UNESCO.

But it was the school's co-director, Lucie, a classically trained soprano and pianist, who had invited Grace Walker as part of her political vision of international education that placed recitals and cultural exchanges alongside more traditional lectures. Tate also found herself in familiar company, as most of the summer students were female teachers from the United States. Indeed, the city of Geneva was host to the many ambitious young women who had moved there to help run the day-to-day work of the League of Nations, something perhaps best captured in a popular well-researched trilogy by the Australian writer Frank Moorhouse. Tate was drawn easily into the world she found in the city, including the intense schedule of daytime lectures, evening cultural events, and outings.[18]

Alfred Zimmern opened the session with four lectures, one on the ideals of the school and three on international relations. Scholars and officials associated with the League of Nations lectured on economics, the mandate system, political philosophy, the opium crisis, and current tensions in Spain, India, and the Soviet Union. Among the succession of prominent international scholars were Fernand Maurette, a French economist and geographer at the League's International Labour Organization, who delivered three lectures on the problems of international migration, and Bertil Ohlin, a League-affiliated Swedish economist who spoke on the world depression and later shared a Nobel Prize in economics in 1977 for his theory of international trade. Tate also heard a lecture on "The Spirit of Man" by Sir Sarvepalli Radhakrishnan, an Indian scholar of philosophy and comparative religion who was named a professor at Oxford in 1936 and who, after his retirement, became vice president and then president of India in the late 1950s and 1960s.[19]

Grace Walker's two appearances at the conference struck an emotional nerve. In the first, Walker lectured on "The American Negro in Art and Literature," framing her presentation of poems by the writers Countee Cullen, Claude Mackay, Langston Hughes, and Jean Toomer. Walker's recent training at the Royal Academy in London may have added dramatic power to her elocution skills: she received a standing ovation.[20]

In a later evening session, Walker joined with the Black American classical concert pianist Lorenza Jordan Cole in an evening recital. Cole, only five years older than Tate, was trained at Juilliard and had come to London in 1930 to study with Tobias Mathey, then the world's greatest living piano teacher. Percival Parham, well known for his arrangements of spirituals and the poetry of Langston Hughes, joined them on stage. Walker talked about the meanings of spirituals before Cole played them; Cole then played some of her usual repertoire, selections by Black classical composers Nathaniel Dett and Samuel Coleridge-Taylor. "The large audience was taken away," Tate wrote, "and refused to go home even after the program had ended."[21]

Paulette Nardal, an Afro-Martiniquais journalist and part of the Négritude movement, described Walker as one "among the young coloured American women who come every year to acquire the fine intellectual or artistic touch which only the old continent and especially France can give." But when Nardal saw her appear elsewhere, the power of the performances of African American literature and music overwhelmed her and left her in awe of Walker's "quiet implicity," her "stirring contralto," and her "composure" in presenting "modern Afro-american poetry" that reflected "racial solidarity which comes from common suffering."[22]

The final lecture that Tate attended before preparing to leave Geneva was "The Negro Problem in the U.S.A." presented by Everett Stonequist, a recently graduated student of the sociologist Robert Park. Tate judged his lecture "an unusually fine and just interpretation of the problem." That may not sound like much of an analysis, but it was rare for Tate to do more than note names and identification. On the same day, for example, she noted simply that she also visited the League of Nations where she "was received by Mr. Phelps Stokes," traveling on behalf of the fund benefitting education for African Americans and Africans.[23]

Dramatic performances of Black literature and poetry or classical renditions of Negro spirituals were a common form in Black cultural settings, such as schools and churches, including in Indianapolis. But one is left to wonder how it must have felt to experience the power of the familiar in that setting and in an audience where Tate was likely the only Black person present other than the performers themselves. Her diary notes are written in a tone of pride and awe, but she says nothing directly beyond that. She did, however, write out the details of Cole's formal training and collected her contact information in the states, planning to stay in touch once they were both back.

Tate formed her earliest ideas about the field of international relations during that summer in Geneva. They included Lucie and Alfred Zimmern's recognition of the unjust treatment of Black people in the United States as important to their shared conception of international studies. Being in Geneva had a profound effect on the professional and personal decisions Tate would make after she returned home.

A panoramic photograph of the Geneva School session of 1931 captures a large group of students assembled outside on a sunny day. Near the back on the top row is the face of a lone Black woman in a sea of white faces. The woman in the picture was not Tate, but Lorenza Jordan Cole. Tate missed the photo because she left Geneva early, two weeks before the school was to end, but after she had witnessed Walker and Cole. She spent her final day in Geneva with the van Gessels and a large group of visitors from Holland for a final outing by car through the Savoy mountains into nearby Annecy, France. The evening closed back in Geneva with a large group dinner in Bellerive where she gathered suggestions on hotels and contacts for the journey ahead of her.[24]

The next day, August 8, she was on her way, full speed ahead as she seemed to try to make up for the time "lost" to the summer session. By evening, the Mitropa train line brought her into Germany where she stayed three days before taking another train to Amsterdam.[25]

As often happens for first-time American visitors to Europe, Tate seemed overwhelmed by the scale and age of what she saw on her travels. She had a keen visual sensibility and took many photographs, but her diary from that point on read like a running account of all that she was seeing and doing and what she was hearing from tour guides, as if she were suffering from sensory overload. This was especially true during her time at the Rijksmuseum, where she saw the power of the works of Rembrandt, Vermeer, and others. Her on-foot explorations continued at a rapid pace as she continued on to Brussels and Waterloo, which she describes in vivid, panoramic terms.

Tate took a train on August 17 from Brussels to Ostende to board a steamer for a very rough crossing of the channel to get to London for two days. After a hasty tour of all the major historical sights, she made time for gift shopping before setting off to Oxford, Leamington, and Shottery to visit Shakespeare's home and the cottage where his wife, Anne Hathaway, grew up. Birmingham and Liverpool were her last train stops, and again, her detailed descriptions of museums, art, and historical sites filled her diary and reflected her fascination with military history and technology.[26]

By the end of the day, she was on the Atlantic aboard the *Duchess of Richmond.* Unlike her original crossing, she made only one entry about her return trip: "Regular voyage at sea. The ocean was as perfect as could be. We were entertained with motion picture, concert & whist tournament." Now a seasoned traveler, she made no mention of the individual days as they passed at sea. She also did not note whether she was the only Black woman aboard, a status to which she had become even more accustomed.

Tate had kept a meticulous cash accounting of every cent she spent on the trip, a sign of her frugality. Her nine weeks away had cost her $919.29, with the largest purchases being her two Atlantic crossings: $105 each way. One of her largest recurring expenses was for film and processing, as she took her camera everywhere she went. She later placed and labeled the photographs from that trip in a scrapbook, a creative habit she also used for mementos, souvenirs, and articles, not just from her travels, but from her busy social and professional life at home. This became a permanent practice that preserved reminders of her joyous and exciting times while also documenting a life she came to view as historically significant after first receiving public notice for excelling as a high school student in Michigan.

She spent significant amounts on transportation on land and the costs of studying in Geneva. A generous tipper in her travels, she also spent liberally on gifts for friends and family, but she seemed to lodge and eat at very modest cost. She liked hats, however, and bought several in Paris. Her final expenditures were for tickets from Montreal back to Detroit and then from Detroit to Indianapolis, where she arrived just in time to prepare to return to her job.[27] And with that she moved from a summer spent mostly being "the only Negro woman" back to the all-Black intellectual and social world in which she lived and worked.

Tate's re-immersion in the social world of Black Indianapolis must have been both familiar and jarring after a summer of European travel and life outside the racial restrictions of her home country. She soon settled back into the job and daily life she had left behind during her summer in Europe and England. She began to look for a house in Indianapolis. But her exposure to the architecture, art, and natural beauty of the countries and cities still fired her imagination and left her excited to share the details of her travels and her studies with friends, students, and the larger community. She presented a two-part evening public lecture in November in the auditorium at Attucks. Using her creativity as a teacher, the program featured pipe organ and violin music to precede her first talk, then an intermission, followed by music by the school's band, her second lecture, and more music. She illustrated her talk with maps and shared her photographs.[28]

Her imaginative multimedia approach not only enlivened the event to draw a larger audience, but the student musical performances also permitted her to charge money for it as part of fund raising for a project Tate had begun working on in the spring before she sailed to Europe: a Travel Club for students, with the very specific goal of taking a trip to Washington, D.C., the following spring of 1932.

Tate's goal also was to make sure that lack of money would not be a barrier for any student who wanted to go. Defraying the costs of the trip in the middle of the depression would require nonstop fund raising by the students, who sold candy daily and floral arrangements for Mother's Day and Memorial Day. Sponsoring the trip became a community project as she and her students worked hard to solicit money from local Black businesses, Black men's and women's clubs, sororities, stores, and individual donors.[29]

Tate's summer abroad was too intense not to have changed her. When the head of the Indianapolis AKA chapter, Hattie Edwards, mentioned to her that their sorority had recently funded a fellowship for international study, Tate did not hesitate to apply. Begun as part of a broader effort to support educational opportunities for its members, the sorority created a fund to help with tuition fees for advanced international study for members who already had master's degrees. In 1928, the group announced that the plan was "now a reality" and that the fellowship "has created in the heart of the thinking members of the public a new appreciation of what we, as a sorority, are doing." The first international award had gone to Ethel Grubbs, a mathematics and physics teacher in Washington, D.C., who had used it to study mathematics at the University of Berlin in 1928–1929. The second fellowship enabled Hazel E. Browne, a college teacher from Louisville, to study English philology in Germany.[30]

Never one to shy away from last-minute opportunity, Tate hurriedly submitted her application in time for the selection committee's meeting at the AKA's annual meeting, or "boule," in December in Cincinnati. She attended what was to be her first large AKA gathering along with three other delegates from Indianapolis. On the application form, she wrote that she planned to study the history of England and modern Europe at either Oxford or the University of London, but she underlined "Oxford" to signal that it was her first choice.[31]

More than two hundred members of the sorority attended the conference, which was held between Christmas and New Year's. The committee that selected the fellowship recipient relied on a point system; Tate outscored the other two applicants, but barely. Because it was a close call, there was considerable resentment over the fact that she had so recently become a member, but there was nothing in the rules that spoke to that.

That she was so new and attending her first annual meeting also meant that few of her sorors knew who she was or anything about her other than what they read on the application. This may also have mattered more because Tate had joined as a graduate member and therefore had not participated in a college chapter on a Black campus.

The committee sent her name forward to the body as a whole but added that, in the future, the length of time an applicant had been a member should be considered an eligibility factor. In the end, Beatrice Scott, the organization's head, brought the group to unanimity in support of Tate. But the bitterness over such a new member receiving the fellowship lingered, and it soon had consequences for Tate.[32]

Despite the unexpectedly good news of the $1,000 fellowship, Tate had given little thought to how one actually gets admitted to graduate study at Oxford. More pressing, however, was her teaching and her work planning and helping her students raise funds for the promised spring Travel Club trip to Washington. Enthusiasm for the trip had continued to build as had the number of students who wanted to go. The Black community's investment in the students' campaign had yielded $2,500, enough to make sure every deserving student could go. This was an extraordinary achievement during a time of economic hardship and yet another measure of deep communal commitment to the education of these young Black students.

On March 27, Easter Sunday afternoon, forty-three students boarded a special car on the Big Four Route train from Indianapolis bound for Washington. Many of the students received some assistance and five of them had their entire trip paid in full. Sleeping overnight on the train, they pulled into Union Station in the capital the next morning.

They checked into the Black-owned Whitelaw Hotel, a building in Renaissance Revival style that had been designed by a Black architect in 1919. The hotel often hosted traveling Black entertainers and other prominent Black visitors to segregated Washington. Its location in the vibrant U Street corridor and Shaw neighborhood near Howard University was very convenient; the girls would stay in the hotel and the few boys on the trip would lodge on the Howard campus.

Blacks who traveled in the United States during this period always had to navigate the restrictions of rampant racial segregation, taking care about where they could stay. Most of the students' meals seemed to have been taken on the train or at the Whitelaw Hotel, or on Howard's campus. Tate's characteristic meticulous attention to detail was deployed here to protect her young charges from the humiliation and sometimes danger that met Black travelers as they sought lodging or food.[33]

But what they saw was shaped by her commitment to teaching history and giving her Black students a sense of possibility even in the age of Jim Crow. The itinerary for the trip had all the hallmarks of the frenetic travel pace Tate favored. They visited the White House, the Lincoln Memorial, the Washington Monument, the Bureau of Engraving and Printing, and the Library of Congress; they also took a night tour of monuments to appreciate their beauty when illuminated. Of special interest to Tate was a visit to two Smithsonian buildings and an opportunity to see the *Spirit of St. Louis,* Charles Lindbergh's

Cherry Blossom Tour, Crispus Attucks High School, in 1932; Tate is fourth from left in the front row (Zhang Collection, Western Michigan University Archives)

plane. Their local congressman, Louis Ludlow, had arranged for the students to visit both the House and Senate galleries and to tour the Capitol building.

Tate organized buses to take the students outside the city so they could tour Mount Vernon and the Naval Academy at Annapolis, where they witnessed cadets in training. At the tomb of the Unknown Soldier at Arlington Cemetery, the ROTC boys laid a wreath that had been made by Attucks students. She also made sure the bus drove them through Embassy Row, or what she called the "legation section" of the city, as well as Rock Creek Park and Georgetown.

She did not neglect significant African American sites. They visited the home of Frederick Douglass, Miner Teachers College, and Howard University. There, they were received by T. J. Anderson, a professor who had previously taught at Attucks, and by the first Black president of the university, Mordecai Johnson, who addressed the students before they met other Black faculty, toured the medical school, and took in a swimming exhibition. A travel club from Dunbar High School entertained the group, and one night the students went to the theater. Their train departed at eleven o'clock on Wednesday night, and the students again slept and ate en route, finally making their triumphant return to Indianapolis the following evening at six, all thanks in part to a dedicated nationwide network of Black educators.

As ordinary as the trip might seem now, in 1932 it rightly was portrayed by Tate and Black newspapers as a racial breakthrough. Tate's published account of the trip carried the headline "Should Colored Children Travel?" The trip disproved those who believed that "colored youth" were incapable of traveling in a group without incident, she said, reporting that the students drew attention to themselves only because they were so well-behaved:

> White and colored alike marveled at the splendid conduct of the group. The dining car waiters appeared to be bubbling over with joy. They stated it was the greatest pleasure they had had to serve two dining cars of well behaved educated colored youth. Compared with white groups of students, one waiter declared that our children were 'perfect.' The railroad representatives spoke of the attractiveness and neatness of our coach when it arrived in Washington after forty-three had occupied it nineteen hours.[34]

Later, the students' parents thanked Tate when their mothers, coordinated by Frances B. Coston, gave her a surprise party and a gift of a traveling bag in appreciation for organizing the "Cherry Blossom Tour" and caring for their children.[35]

Far more was at stake than the opportunity to expose Attucks students to their nation's capital. By making themselves visible as tourists and students, they announced that America was their country too. But they also had been taught that they represented their race at a time when white surveillance enforced legally sanctioned segregation and discrimination. The students bore the burden of demonstrating that they were both capable and deserving to claim a place in public civic culture. The pride that the Black porters expressed was no doubt shared by the community in Indianapolis that had raised the money to give them this opportunity. Photographs of the travel club show that the students were overwhelmingly female, so the trip was also intended to instill in young Black women a lesson in the value of communal travel, even though Tate herself was unafraid to travel alone. But the gender disparities also reflected a common pattern of boys being drawn into physical labor and other work at early ages.[36]

By including Black institutions, Tate showed her students that there were nurturing and nourishing places for ambitious, hardworking young people beyond Indianapolis. She made sure to give her students a vision of their own futures at a time when public spaces and most economic and educational opportunities were still closed to them. Seeing both federal and Black Washington also provided the students with an understanding of both worlds, troubled though their coexistence was. More than that, Tate shared her philosophy about the value of travel to relieve provincialism, inspire, and transform.

CHAPTER 3

"Sail to the Future"

OXFORD–EUROPE, 1932–1935

Only after the Cherry Blossom Tour was over did Tate follow through on what she had learned about women in the United States applying for graduate study at Oxford. She would need to be recommended by the American Association of University Women, which at the time refused to admit Black women as members. Tate had missed their March 1 deadline but, undaunted, she applied on April 12 and marshalled an arsenal of recommendation letters that far exceeded the number required. Aside from her AKA chapter president, she relied primarily on contacts from her college years at Western.

The person who seemed to capture Tate's drive and determination best was not one of her teachers but Marion Terpenning, the wife in a college professor's family who had hired Tate to live and work in their home:

> I think she is the most ambitious person I have ever known. Brutus would have withdrawn his accusation of ambition against Caesar if he had seen Merze first. She has a good mind and an aggressive personality, and evidently made up her mind in childhood to scale the heights in spite of all the obvious obstacles in the path of a colored child. It is partly because I have such great sympathy with her because of the handicaps under which she has labored toward her present achievements—earning all her own way through high school and college, fighting, successfully, an attack of tuberculosis, getting an all-A record here in college in spite

> of her hours of housework—that I should be so glad to see her get the distinction and pleasure of the year at Oxford.

In her enthusiasm to cite all that Tate had overcome, Terpenning also revealed that her year away from college may have been because of tuberculosis.[1]

Tate's brilliance and performance as a student were beyond dispute among those who had taught her; one professor called hers the "most active undergraduate mind that it has been my privilege to teach." But they were also quite direct in trying to convince the organization that she would be a safe choice despite her race and that indeed she was exactly the kind of Black young woman they could recommend to Oxford. She was called "a distinct credit to her race or any race for that matter" by one teacher, and another wrote of her "refinement and culture." Another argued that in college "Miss Tate's dignity and good taste in her relationship with the other students overcame any problem of racial difference."[2]

Nancy Scott, Tate's European history professor and mentor, attested to her "keenly penetrating mind, tireless energy and much ambition," but also felt the need to point out: "She is not very dark skinned, has regular features, and beautiful hair. She is tall and slender, dignified in bearing. She dresses neatly and well. Her voice is good, her enunciation clear. Among English people she would be looked upon, I imagine, very much as are the high class Hindu students." Scott knew enough about Oxford to slot Tate into a familiar category among colonial subjects who were students.

The head of the Michigan AAUW portrayed herself as an expert on the particular kind of Black person Tate was and reassured her English counterparts that Tate still knew her racial place despite all her achievements and abilities: "I was brought up in Missouri so I have always known colored people. . . . From all reports that I can get about her she is one of these rare educated colored women who knows how to adjust herself inconspicuously and tactfully in whatever situation she may be placed."[3]

It took until June 1 for the AAUW to recommend and forward Tate's application to Oxford for the coming fall term. One reason for the delay was the mention of tuberculosis, triggering concern that Tate's health might not be strong enough for two years of intense work at Oxford. When asked, Tate explained that physical exhaustion from working too hard had caused her year-long breakdown; she was suspected of having tuberculosis but the doctor was never able to confirm it, and that since then she had been in good health. Tate's reluctance about her illness may also reflected her fear of the racialized stigma that attached in particular to TB in that period. With that assurance, Esther Brunauer of the AAUW forwarded to Oxford Tate's application to study for a Bachelor of Letters degree (B. Litt.) in Modern History and International Relations. Tate was one of only two American women to be recommended that year, at a time when there were few women students at Oxford.[4]

When Grace Hadow, the principal of Society of Oxford Home Students, received the materials from the AAUW, neither Tate's race nor health provoked concern. Her handwritten notes on the file identify Tate as "a negress: evidently a remarkable & interesting young woman"; she reported that "several of the Committee thought that her preparation in modern history was not quite thoro enough, but felt that she was the sort of person who would make up her deficiencies if given the opportunity." Despite her excellent record at Western, it was "evidently rather an elementary sort of place," and not on the approved list of institutions eligible for admission for "senior status"—that is, for a second degree or a graduate-level degree program.

Hadow and others at the society wanted to accept her. Their idea was to admit her to their only one-year program, a diploma in economics, and allow her to read in international relations; if she "proved unexpectantly good" they "*might* be able to recommend her for the B. Litt degree." But even for that, since it was the summer vacation, Tate would have to wait until the next year to apply for admission.[5]

Hadow explained all this to Tate in a letter on June 25, taking care to reassure her that her application showed "sufficient ability," but explaining that the only one-year program was for a non-degree diploma. Degree programs, she explained, required sufficient funding for two years in residence; admission required an entrance exam, which was offered only in December and February. The earliest they could answer about the one-year non-degree diploma program would be in the fall, so she advised Tate to wait and reapply the next year in 1933.[6]

Tate seemed to accept this suggestion and to begin preparing herself to wait a year, which would have suited her better, too. She traveled in late August to Los Angeles to see the Summer Olympics and to attend a summer AKA boule meeting there. Earlier, she had boldly asked and been denied a request that the sorority double the amount of the fellowship from $1,000 to $2,000 to enable her to be at Oxford for more than one year. She now wanted to make a personal appeal to the national AKA leadership to defer her award for one year.

She may have made things worse for herself by overbidding a weak hand. The leaders who had approved her award over objections were no longer in power, and the new principals were not sympathetic to her pleas. Under the rules of the fellowship as they interpreted them, not only would she have to use the money in 1932 but she could only use it for the primary institution she had named on her application—Oxford.[7]

In a panic, on August 18 Tate cabled Hadow from California: "Fellowship must be used this year or forfeited will accept any place regular or nonregular student." By cable exchanges, the Society of Oxford Home Students agreed to admit her, but again only for its one year diploma in economics, which Tate accepted on August 28. Whatever appreciation Tate might have felt about being accepted into the diploma program despite the lateness of her application would soon dissipate.[8]

Tate immediately launched a writing campaign reiterating that she still wanted to study in "the field of pure history—Modern European, English History and Constitutional and International Relations. True I have pursued Economics and Political Science courses but only for a better background for my history." She made her ambitions clear: "I hope some day to become a professor in one of our large colored universities. A certificate in history or social training would mean so much to me in applying for such a position." Tate had deflected the question of whether she had the money for a second year of study, and she also ignored Oxford's insistence that Western must first be added to its list of approved institutions, something which seemed unlikely.[9]

In her later recollections, Tate admitted that the idea of saying she was going to Oxford was "unwise" and a product of her own naivete. She remembered that "there was all this talk about, 'Merze Tate thinks she's going to Oxford. When did she get that idea in her head? Now she has to go through the AAUW. They don't even let a Negro come join the organization. How does she think she's going to get a recommendation from them?' " She heard from colleagues at Attucks that people around town, Black and white, were asking, " 'who is that woman at your high school who thinks she's going to Oxford?' And there had been bets up that I would get in and I wouldn't get in. Well, I did."[10]

Tate's decision in late August to go to Oxford for the start of the term in October left her with one month to prepare to leave. Apparently, she did not intend to return to Indianapolis, as she sold a house that she had only recently bought. She hurriedly resigned her position at Attucks after five years of teaching there, leaving the school to find a last-minute replacement.

The "Cherry Blossom Tour" of Washington that she had organized for her students became her parting gift to the Black community that had helped transform her into a woman now on her way to study at one of the world's greatest educational institutions. Friendships and professional networks she formed in the city would follow her the rest of her life, especially her close relationships with Iva Marshall Davis and her circles of AKA sorors, schoolteachers, and bridge players. Of the man who had taught her honeymoon bridge, she later said without any sign of regret that "he was merely a boyfriend. We didn't marry. Maybe if I'd stayed around longer, we would have. . . . And I'll not call his name. He's been married three times."

Tate was willing to sacrifice her job, her personal relationships, and her proximity to family for what she saw as a once-in-a-lifetime opportunity for her and also for the Black American women she saw herself as representing. Her newfound financial independence and her willingness and ability to forgo familial obligations enabled her to pull up stakes. She was going to Oxford for what she knew would be at least two years, in spite of not having secured any funding for the second year. Her intellectual ambition overrode all else even though she was admitted to a non-degree diploma program in a subject she did not want to study. She believed that once she was there, she would make her way into the program she wanted to pursue.

"I am sailing from New York September 30 on the S. S. Bremen," she wrote R. F. Butler at the Society for Home Students as she planned her leave from Indianapolis. Once news of her admission spread in AKA circles and Black newspapers, earlier skepticism and resentments turned into congratulations and good wishes.

On her way to New York, Tate stopped in Philadelphia at the invitation of her sorors in the local AKA chapter who entertained her and showered her with gifts for her trip. They saw her as an exemplar of cosmopolitan modern Black womanhood, defined by the ability to travel and study abroad—their aim in funding the fellowship. Her AKA sorors had made it possible for her to afford to go to Oxford, and that friendship with them would sustain her over a lifetime.

The next day she was at sea.[11]

On her third Atlantic crossing in two years, Tate spent five days at sea traveling aboard the S.S. *Bremen* from New York City to Southampton. Fall brought rough seas and cold, dreary weather to accompany her uncertainty about her last-minute decision to go to Oxford. Her thoughts turned philosophical as she reflected on what she had left behind and the uncertainties ahead. A poem she titled "Thoughts on the S. S. Bremen" sketched out her feelings about her new adventure:

The sea is rough and dark and misty
The foam is thick the wind ever whistling
But the big ship Bremen pushes on
Leaving New York in the distant beyond.
Breaking the billows that around her do foam
Pushing straight on to her port at home
So must I like the *Bremen* be
Break the waves that would o'erwhelm me.
Leave the past in the distant beyond
Sail to the future through the port's unknown
Never wavering a mile from my course
Sail each day as the Bremen sails.
Til that blessed time when the port's won
And the captain says, "Your trip was well done."

With the dark imagery of the stormy sea, Tate's fears of the unknown are barely beneath the surface, even as she identifies herself as being as intrepid as the most renowned high-speed turbine ocean liner of the day. The sense of loss from her sudden uprooting seemed to engulf her even as she toughens herself with religious imagery for comfort at journey's end. Yet it was too late to turn back.

In a second poem, "Thoughts on Entering Oxford," Tate left no doubts about the source of her determination and the responsibility that came with this new opportunity:

When I consider what before me lies
A chance to make a name a chance to die
A chance to gather from these ancient walls
Covered with ivy, hiding famous halls
What this mother of learning is ready to bestow
On one who has the courage and strength to go
Through endless hours of toil and grief and joy
I think of constant strife without these walls
And wonder if our lives are worth the while
We spend on earth nurturing petty whiles
Then I recall who best bear his yoke may serve him best
This relieves my mind and then I rest
And make my one big wish a prayer to be
A credit to my race and to my sorority.

Tate's great ambition to go to Oxford was not matched by her knowledge of that university. Organized uniquely as a constellation of separate residentially based colleges, its structure did not resemble institutions in the United States or even in England, for that matter, except for Cambridge. Each college was an independent academic and social world unto itself, with guarded access only for its members. The university had recently codified in 1927 its intention to remain predominately for men by imposing a quota on the number of women students in residence to 840, held to less than a quarter of the number of men. Women students could attend lectures and take examinations, but they were excluded from much of the rest of the university, including a prohibition on taking meals in any of the all-male colleges.[12]

There were four residential colleges for women when Tate arrived, but she had been admitted to the Home Society, where students did not share a common residence, boarding instead in private homes or in residential facilities hosted by Catholic or Anglican nuns. The society's students included many from outside England, including those like Tate from the United States. It took two more decades, until 1952, before the society became Oxford's fifth college for women and was renamed St. Anne's College.

All three of the women who admitted Tate were affiliated with social work, settlement house, and other institutions aimed at bettering the lives and education of women, including in the Oxford community outside the university. Grace Hadow, the society's principal, had studied English literature at Oxford's Somerville College. After a stint at Bryn Mawr in the United States, she had returned to become a tutor and then a lecturer at Lady Margaret Hall in 1909. She was strongly committed to adult education for women, especially rural women, because she saw that as key to their participation in civic culture. In 1929, she assumed the head of society, where she worked closely with the Butler sisters, Violet and Ruth, who were members of a prominent Oxford academic and literary family. Ruth was Hadow's vice principal and Violet, a tutor at St. Hugh's, had studied modern history, economics, and political science.[13]

This small, dedicated group warmly welcomed Tate into the marginalized and close-knit world of women at Oxford. They had admitted her despite their reservations about the strength of her academic training, a general skepticism applied to foreign institutions. Hadow helped arrange housing for her and introduced her to other women in the Home Society and at Oxford. Violet Butler recommended lectures in history and offered her tutorial sessions needed for an economics diploma. After their first meeting, Butler wrote Hadow that Tate still had her mind set on graduate work in history, and until that was resolved, it seemed useless to try to get her to do work that she did not want to do.

Indeed, as soon as she arrived, Tate began a campaign for permission to do more advanced work in history. Her admission into the "senior status" needed for graduate work depended on Oxford recognizing her degree from Western State, which the university formally refused to do despite her legalistic arguments based on her reading of their own rules. Tate saw the decision as a reflection of a British disregard for teachers' colleges, including her summer master's degree from Columbia's Teachers College. She wrote them that she was "extremely disappointed" by the decision, but agreed to begin work on the diploma in economics and political science, her only option at that point. She also did not understand or would not accept how different were American and Oxford modes of graduate training: the latter provided little classroom training but relied instead on tutorials and independent work that also assumed an advanced prior knowledge of the subject.[14]

Despite her worries and disappointments, Tate was exhilarated about being at Oxford, which she called a "dream of a place." She settled into the world of women at Oxford, thanks to the professional generosity of the women at the Home Society who included her in teas, dinners, and excursions. "Well, when I arrived, and went to the college to which I was assigned, in my mailbox," she recalled, "a box already labeled in my name, I had a stack of letters, notes, and so on from different people inviting me. 'I'm so and so. Will you come to my house such and such a date for tea?' I also had letters from clubs asking me to join." She also became completely enamored with the university's ancient academic traditions and nomenclature.[15]

Rarely shy about new activities, Tate said "yes" when some other women students asked her to join a punting club. With access to a boat of their own, the women used it as a place to take lunch or tea, or simply for the fun of moving on the water. Frequent tea parties with the other women led to even more invitations for tea or lunch. She especially enjoyed the many rich cultural offerings, including debating events, musical performances, and theater by the Oxford Dramatic Society.

Oxford was also a city of students on bicycles, so she learned to ride. With the help of a friend, she overcame her fear of falling, bought a used bike, painted it, got a bell and a basket, and joined her fellow students. Her only complaint about Oxford was its lack of reliable central heating. She was accustomed to Michigan's frigid snowy winters, but the cold inside the school's buildings was hard on her. "It isn't a bitterly cold climate," she recalled, but she quickly learned that "you go outside in England to get warm," meaning that the British fondness for long daily walking was a necessity in fall, winter, and spring.[16]

Despite her embrace of the place, Oxford was undoubtedly the most white, male setting she had ever been in. Her status as the only Black American certainly marked her as different, although she made no mention of any hostilities or incidents directed at her. She also remembered that in her first year, Oxford admitted its first Chinese women and two women from Turkey. The only other Black woman she knew was an undergraduate from Lagos; "I guess they went liberal that year," she would later say. What she was witnessing was Oxford's limited extension of its institutional largess to the colonized or racialized student subject, whether from India, Africa, or the United States, here being slowly extended to women.[17]

The Nigerian student later known as Kofoworola Aina Ademola was a member of a highly educated family and later spoke and wrote of her time at Oxford, including of her "American friend," Merze Tate. Ademola's memories included evidence of their shared "youthful exuberance" among women friends, including punting and falling into the river. The academic atmosphere suited Ademola, as if she had been "tossed in a sea of intellect with highly earnest students who keep themselves occupied in trying to emerge from the surging whirl. She gradually discovered that they were on dry land and that she was among a sympathetic crowd."[18]

Tate had settled into that social world there nicely, even if the sympathy and niceness cloaked deeper patronizing attitudes. But by the end of the fall term, the question of her student status remained unresolved, even as Butler clearly saw that Tate found the work on economics uninteresting and merely plodded through her assigned work. In a congenial but direct manner, Violet Butler wrote to Tate that she had received a letter from Zimmern, in which he was "quite encouraging" but still recommended against her trying to get into the B. Litt. program as a research student. He too suggested, as had Hadow and Butler, that she do a probationary period with extra reading before applying. That Zimmern had agreed with Hadow and Butler disheartened Tate, as did his refusal to take her under his supervision, which had been her expectation, however unrealistic.[19]

It would have been risky for Tate to accept that route, because if she failed at the end of the probationary terms to gain Zimmern's strong support for her application to the B. Litt. program, she would have been expected to leave the next summer, with nothing to show for her year at Oxford. As her tutor,

Butler understood Tate's frustration even as she agreed that she was not yet prepared for the research degree work: "Perhaps it is fair to give my opinion on the work that you have done for me. I feel that it is quite good,—very sensible and workmanlike; but with the best will, I can't find in your work on this (uncongenial) subject, evidence of your capacity for original work, though I have nothing to say in the opposite direction." With that, Butler left open the possibility that if Tate were able to do the work that actually interested her, she would be able to overcome deficiencies.[20]

As a student Tate had always excelled, often by speeding ahead of her peers. She now faced the new and difficult experience of having Oxford advise her to do remedial work while also disregarding her hard-earned degrees at white institutions in the United States, the achievements of which she was most proud. But in more practical terms, she also knew that the $1,000 from the AKA would barely support her through one year at Oxford, and she would need some way of securing funds to stay longer.

Oxford's refusal to bend rules for her or to accept her own estimation of her abilities angered Tate, but it did not destroy her confidence in her intellectual abilities or her capacity for sustained hard work. It also did not diminish her willingness to advocate on her own behalf or her stubborn sense of entitlement to follow her own desires. In her end-of-term meeting with Hadow in 1932, she affirmed what she had decided to do—to jettison the work toward a diploma in hopes of being admitted to the research degree program. Doing that would also allow Tate to begin working on what truly interested her, what Butler referred to as her "League of Nations questions."[21]

The women affiliated with the Home Society had continued to support Tate emotionally through this period of academic uncertainty. They seemed genuinely committed to her success despite their concerns about her preparedness, and they admired her smarts, her easy sociability, her determination, and her capacity for hard work. At Hadow's suggestion, Tate's host family prepared a Thanksgiving meal for her, which surprised and touched her. "We did our humble best to celebrate the occasion with a rather special supper, including cranberry jelly!" her hostess wrote. "How childishly interested Americans are in food!"[22]

Hadow was concerned about where Tate would spend the Christmas holiday, since she could not travel home. "I ought to have thought of this earlier," she wrote, "but Miss Tate has seemed so eminently capable of taking care of herself that I forgot to ask if her vacation plans were settled." A Home Society supporter asked, "Is there not a 'Lady Somebody' in London who helps foreign students to find homes in the Vacation?" Indeed, Tate spent part of the Christmas break as the guest of a Sir Robert and Lady Craig in Edinburgh, where she also attended a Student Christian Movement Conference, an early ecumenical group with links to what became the World Council of Churches. Once back in London, she spent the rest of her holiday in the reading room of the British Museum as she moved forward with her planned academic work, not in economic and political theory, but in history and international relations.[23]

In the spring of 1933, Tate continued to be tutored by Butler, and to read, attend lectures, and begin work on disarmament, a topic suggested by Zimmern in the wake of the World Conference on Disarmament held in Geneva in 1932. She spent the long Easter vacation reading and researching in the Bibliothèque Nationale, Paris. At the end of the term in June, she was not required to leave, which was good news for her, but her formal admission to the B. Litt. required that her thesis topic be approved by the Social Studies faculty—again, however, not until after the fall term began in October. Her status at Oxford was still unsettled, although she had reason to be optimistic that she would achieve her goal of being admitted to the degree program.[24]

By summer, having been away from the United States for nine months, Tate may have had a longing for family, old friends, and familiar faces, especially since it was clear that she would need to remain away from the United States for at least two more years to get a degree. Oxford required that someone local be authorized to act on her behalf in case of accident or disability, and when Hadow, at Tate's request, agreed in June 1933 to take on that role as her "responsible person" in case of illness, Tate unexpectedly attached very specific instructions—neither requested nor required—to be followed in case of her death. "In case of death please make the following disposition of my body: Have the heart cremated and the ashes sent to my mother, Mrs. Myrtle Tate, Blanchard Michigan, U. S. A. The remainder of my body I wish to be given or sold to a medical college for study. My many illnesses should make my body extremely valuable."[25]

In what feels like an emotional low point, Tate also still saw herself, even in death, as embodying a specialness, an exceptionalism. That belief in her own uniqueness and worthiness—here taken to an extreme in a time of crisis—would remain one of her most persistent personal characteristics and one from which she drew strength and courage and a sense of entitlement. But she also was very prideful, stubborn, and dedicated to advancing and protecting a public persona of academic brilliance and racial exceptionalism, something that her affiliation with Oxford had elevated but also now deeply imperiled. Her fiercely protected self-image permitted no hint of failure.

When the term ended, she spent part of June touring England. In July, she revisited old friends in Switzerland, acquaintances from her time there two summers earlier.[26]

The question of money began to loom larger even though she had been able to draw on funds of her own back in the States, including some cash freed by selling her house. Ever resourceful, she advertised in *Le Figaro* in Paris, a newspaper she believed to be favored by French gentility, to offer her services as an English tutor. She was hired by the Comte and Comtesse Jean de Geoffre de Chabrignac to tutor their daughter in August and September at their summer home near Montelimar in the south of France. Tate enjoyed this arrangement because she tutored in the mornings, giving her the afternoons for leisure and outings, and for playing bridge in French with her hosts and their guests.[27]

Once back at Oxford for the start of the term, she resumed her studies, and toward the end of the term, much to her relief, she was admitted to the B. Litt. program and the faculty approved "The Movement for Disarmament, 1853–1914" as her thesis topic. Zimmern was traveling in the United States that autumn and winter, so Tate worked under the supervision of James L. Brierly, the Chichele Professor of International Law and Diplomacy.[28]

Just when she finally won what she had been advocating for since before her arrival at Oxford, Tate now faced the same problem that confronted other U.S. students that fall. Bank closures and failures in 1933 froze the transfer of funds from the States to those living abroad, or in many cases, erased bank holdings of those who were relying on them, like Tate. The administration at Oxford, including at the Home Society, intervened to secure additional sources of funds for those students.

Pridefully independent and opposed to financial obligation, Tate resisted the help being offered: "I do not like the thought of having a heavy indebtedness hanging over me when everything is so unsettled at home. I believe that the best thing for me to do is to return home and earn some money, straighten out my property there and return here in a year or so." But she had a change of heart, although she agreed to only limited assistance, and only in loans needed to cover her fees for the upcoming two terms, with the expectation that she would be able to gather other funds somehow from her own resources.[29]

When those funds were not forthcoming, she was forced to rely even more on Hadow and others at Oxford who were searching for funds for her and other students. At Tate's suggestion, Hadow sought help from sources in the States, too, including the AAUW, but their funds had been depleted by similar requests. Tate was able to stay at Oxford thanks to Hadow's persistence in cobbling together small loans and grants and to her sister Thelma who once again loaned her money to stay in school. With her financial crisis abated, Tate continued to work intensely on her thesis, including over the long Easter vacation which she once again spent partly at the Bibliothèque Nationale in Paris.[30]

Tate was working steadily toward the May deadline to submit her B. Litt. thesis when another crisis struck: she had a bicycle accident, which caused a debilitating fracture of her foot, landing her in a succession of convalescent, nursing, and rehabilitation homes outside Oxford, thwarting her access to needed books and materials. Rather than ask to have her schedule for submission and defense delayed, Tate decided to submit the thesis on time and then defend it in an oral exam. Her two examiners were Ernest Llewellyn Woodward and Agnes Headlam-Morley, who were both historians at Oxford. After her oral defense, her examiners decided neither to pass or to fail her, but to postpone a final decision until after the summer vacation, presumably to allow for Zimmern's re-engagement.

This came as a shock to Tate, who had been so confident of passing her viva that she had either written or provided the content for an article in the nationally circulated Black newspaper the *Pittsburgh Courier*'s edition for June 20, 1934, that announced in bold type "Merz [*sic*] Tate Is Awarded B. Litt. At Oxford." The article portrayed her as having made her defense from "an invalid's chair," while noting that she was still confined to a nursing home but remained hopeful that she would see more of Europe before returning.[31]

The lack of an outright approval of her work left Tate despondent at a time when she was moving from one convalescent home to another for treatment of her foot. On June 15, she wrote to Hadow from St. Leonards-on-Sea in Hastings in East Sussex: "The great pity is that in the final analysis—and in simple language—I have failed." This shook Tate at her psychological core. Indeed, her strong sense of self rested in part on the fact that since childhood she had been praised for her intellect and treated like a genius—until Oxford flexed its institutional power.

Not only did she feel a deep personal failure, but she also believed that she had faltered in carrying her burden of racial and gender representation. She continued:

> I beg this of you because I do not want you to use me as a standard for judging others of my race. I know that this is too much to ask for most

> members of your race judge the colored race by one or two whom they have known instead of each person individually. But I consider you so far superior to most people that I dare to hope you may be a little wiser in this respect. If ever another young coloured woman should apply to come up to Oxford I hope that you will judge her on her own merits and not think of me and all the trouble I caused. There are hundreds of coloured women in America who would come up to Oxford and be successful for they would have money enough to live free from financial worries and brains sufficient to pass any examination. It is most unfortunate that I as a pioneer had to face so many difficulties and then not succeed. It is the first great failure of my life but I am anxious that others should not suffer because of my failure.

For Tate to mention race in this way reveals her sense of shame and extreme emotional state. But it also shows her willingness to use racial appeals to try to get the outcome she wanted, something she would resort to again in the future as a discursive weapon, usually disingenuously for the purpose of making her case. But her boldness and personal pride were still fully in place: "I have never asked for special favours at Oxford and have never expected any," she concluded, "but now considering that I may be four thousand miles away in October, I do think that the Social Services Board could come to some decision about my thesis."[32]

Tate soon began to argue with tenacious ingenuity that the lack of decision, even after Zimmern had been consulted, was somehow still in her favor: "it must be that I have not *absolutely* failed, for it would be very simple to make a statement to that effect." That was opening enough for Tate to continue to insist that an answer come sooner rather than later. The examiners were impressed with the amount of work and reading that Tate had done, but felt it had not yielded a thesis that critically engaged other scholarship or permitted her to make new arguments or findings. What she had written was too broad and the historical background she presented was insufficient. Tate contorted that explanation to mean that she had done too much or written too much for a B. Litt. thesis and that perhaps what she had done should qualify as a D. Phil. thesis instead, a request that was denied.[33]

The uncertainty about the status of her work could not be resolved until after Oxford resumed for the fall term, so in the interim she did what seemed to bring her the most solace: she traveled. Although her foot was still painful and she could not walk unassisted, she proceeded to visit much of Germany, to stay with her old friends in Switzerland, and to tutor as she had done the previous summer. She had decided to spend time in Germany on her way to France because she and an unnamed Black American woman who was studying at the Sorbonne wanted to see the three hundredth anniversary of the Passion Play staged at Oberammergau. They agreed to meet in Heidelberg before heading to Munich, where they would then travel on third-class student train tickets to see it.[34]

The new Nazi regime made its presence known to Tate when she tried to enter the country from Belgium on a two-year visa she had obtained when she was in the States. Under their new policy, only one-year visas would be honored, so Nazi officials denied her entry and forced her to return to Belgium to get a new visa. Equipped with German language skills but traveling on a cane and very little cash, Tate was left stranded waiting for a return train, but when offered food while she waited, she refused. Despite the day's delay, she eventually reunited with her friend in Heidelberg and they made their way to Munich and on to Oberammergau.[35]

The Passion Play in Oberammergau captured Tate's imagination. Her interest also reflected once again her own shifting religious sensibilities and her embrace of Catholic historic sites and visual iconography. By 1930, the "Nazification" of the play had only worsened its anti-semitic depictions, but it had continued to draw the famous, not least Hitler himself. Yet Tate was especially drawn to visual spectacle, and the play certainly provided that. The power of the lifelike dramatizations by ordinary people who "lived" in character remained a highlight of her time in Europe, and later became the subject of an illustrated lecture she delivered after her return to the United States.[36]

When Tate arrived at the Château des Roches in July to begin her tutoring job, she found a letter from Hadow advising her to come up for examination again the next summer, rather than trying to force a decision in the fall term when she was likely to fail. Tate thanked Hadow for her concern and help and expressed her appreciation for Zimmern's friendship, but she replied with pride and defiance. "You need not worry about my pressing the Board for the B. Litt. Degree in October or anytime. I do not now, and I hope I shall never, ask for anything from any institution which it is not perfectly willing to grant me."[37]

Tate returned to London in October. Once the term commenced, Hadow was able to clarify why the committee had not either accepted or rejected her thesis "straight out." She explained: "What is unusual in your case is that they have, I think, been anxious to give you every consideration and instead of a direct rejection have given themselves time to re-consider your work. It would, perhaps, really have been kinder to be harsher, and so to have saved you suspense. I do not, of course, know what the final verdict will be, but I think it is very probable that they will suggest your trying again."[38]

Hadow's letter seems an accurate and kind depiction of what happened, but it conceals the busy efforts behind the scenes to give Tate a second chance. Zimmern detailed to C. V. Butler, Tate's tutor, the terms under which she would have the best chance to succeed. She would need to narrow her topic to a much shorter chronological period; and she should focus the scope of her work. He also insisted that she immediately do additional tutorial work in European history with the prominent historian Mary Coate of Lady Margaret Hall. Only if that went well would he consider supporting her readmission.[39]

Tate had little choice but to accept these conditions. So she began to work with Coate. In her view, Tate "has no idea of really scholarly detail or critical methods" but impressed Coate with her capacity for sustained intellectual work. At the end of the probationary program, she recommended to Zimmern that he support Tate's readmission to the B. Litt. program. Reassured, Zimmern backed Tate's readmission but with a new and much narrower thesis topic.[40]

Coate conferred with Agnes Headlam-Morley of St. Hugh's College before suggesting that she be named Tate's thesis supervisor—advice Zimmern followed. Headlam-Morley was an Oxford-trained modern European historian, and the daughter of a prominent diplomatic historian, Sir James Wycliffe Headlam. Only three years older than Tate, she had only recently been appointed a tutor at St. Hugh's and taught in the school of philosophy, politics, and economics. Much later, in 1948, she would become the first woman to hold an endowed chair at Oxford. Under Headlam-Morley's guidance, Tate set about reading and researching her topic, Tate and Hadow having secured additional loan monies to see her through the upcoming two terms.[41]

But even as she continued to do her work, Tate's shame and furor over not having received the B. Litt. degree the first time around had not abated. Her willingness to fight for herself sometimes obscured her recognition that she had allies who were earnestly trying to help her. She issued a harsh warning to the ever patient and polite Hadow in terms that baffled and angered her as she reported to her vice principal, Butler: "It really is pathetic to see how determined she is that everyone's hand is really against her." Hadow reassured Tate that if she were to get the degree, that "speaks for itself, if not there is no need to say she tried & failed."[42]

Tate lost herself in her research and writing. On April 16, her mother, Myrtle Tate, in a single-page letter written in lead pencil, filled with misspellings, and addressed only to "Oxford University," explained that it had been three months since anyone in the family had heard from her daughter. She pleaded for news of any trace of her daughter or any "information about her be it good or bad, please let me know the facts." Tate's mother had reached out in desperation, but still, as a mark of her own pride and propriety she also included postage for the reply. The poignant letter captures the stress, shame, and secrecy under which Tate was laboring, but it also reveals a lack of consideration for her own family who worried about her well-being. Hadow answered the letter, giving Tate's mother a current mailing address for her daughter.[43]

She was living partly in London and partly in Oxford as she continued to work under supervision from Headlam-Morley, who, like Hadow, tried to balance support with growing impatience. Reporting to Violet Butler on April 26, Headlam-Morley wrote: "She is, as you say, rather difficult to deal with as every normal difficulty she encounters is transformed into a grievance. She does sometime (quite unintentionally I think) cause a good deal of unnecessary trouble but is very quick to reprimand me if I keep a chapter a little longer than she thinks necessary!"[44]

In many respects, the process she describes seems typical of the tensions and frustrations of advising graduate student work; to her credit, even when she grew frustrated, she remained sympathetic to Tate. "Whether or not she will get the degree I cannot prophesy but I have not hinted my doubts to her as she already suffers from lack of confidence," she confided to Butler. "I *hope* she will get the degree but cannot feel certain about it."[45]

At noon, the day the thesis was due, Headlam-Morley had called Hadow to report that she had received a scrap of paper from Tate saying the thesis would not be finished. An hour later, Tate did turn in the thesis, but the next day, realizing that Hadow had received an extension for her, she made a plea to have it returned so she could recheck that the pages were in the proper order, a final measure of her anxiety.[46] Her oral examiners made for a very formidable team: J. L. Brierly, the international law expert, and C. A. W. Manning, who would later emerge as a staunch defender of apartheid in his native South Africa. This time, Tate's revised thesis and her defense of it met the approval of both.[47]

Hadow was among the first to congratulate Tate, writing, "am so glad to hear of your success & to know that all your hard work is rewarded." Word of the outcome of the defense soon reached Headlam-Morley. "I gather Miss Tate had quite a happy time with Prof. Brierly and Prof. Manning. It was entirely her own show," she wrote, adding that she was "delighted at Miss Tate's success which I really do think she deserved after all her hard work." Zimmern shared that sentiment. "I hear that Miss Tate has achieved her ambition," he wrote Butler. "I must send her a line to congratulate her on this relief after so much inhalation. I think the verdict was right on both occasions," referring to the past failure and the present success.[48]

Whatever relief or joy Tate might have felt from earning her coveted B. Litt. seemed to have been subsumed immediately by her written demands that her supporters at the Home Society erase all evidence of what she saw as her prior failure. She demanded that Hadow and Butler follow her instructions on what was to be said, insisting that doing this would "relieve me from making long explanations in America." She outlined exactly what she wanted them to write, telling them that "these are the facts that I should be pleased to have definitely stated." One of her claims was that she had been required to write an "entirely different thesis" the second time around. When Butler wrote her statement, she explained that it was not unusual for students to fail the first time through. That was handed on to Tate but since it did not follow her script, it is unlikely that she ever used it.[49]

Tate's insistence on this particular narrative was not merely self-protection from the deep shame she felt personally over what she saw as a humiliating failure, although it certainly was that too. Nor was her panicky approach to Hadow merely irrational paranoia that Oxford was going to broadcast news of her delay to degree. It was the fact that she had prematurely publicly announced to friends and others that she had earned the degree a year earlier.

With degree received, Tate made another urgent request to Hadow about what to say and what not to say, demanding that she write the AKA's a letter "which will make my sorors feel that the recipient of the $1000 fellowship did not waste their money or their time." This Hadow dutifully did. Tate had already secured letters of recommendation from Brierly, Zimmern, and Headlam-Morley and sent them to her placement file at Teacher's College at Columbia. With all that done, she had accomplished her mission and secured silence around her delay to degree.[50]

Even after three long and sometimes difficult years away, Tate was not eager to return immediately to the United States. Instead she decided to study German at the University of Berlin, to spend two or three weeks again in France tutoring, and to see friends in Geneva and attend the opening of the League

Tate in her Oxford regalia (Moorland-Spingarn, Howard University)

of Nations. She would be following in the footsteps of her friend Ethel Grubbs, who had used her AKA fellowship to study in Germany, as well as other Black scholars like Du Bois. Surprisingly, it was not unusual for students at Oxford to do this even in this period; Dean Rusk did the same in 1935 and so did Eric Williams in 1938.[51]

But by 1935 Berlin was frightening. Hitler and the Nazi regime's attacks on Jews had grown even more vociferous since her time there just the summer before. As she traveled, she stayed in German homes recommended by friends in England, to save money but also to immerse herself in the language, which she already understood more than people thought.[52] Years later she recalled that when she stayed in a Jewish home: "And they weren't going out. They wouldn't go, they just stayed off the street. Maybe once a week would walk way across town to a Jewish market to buy their food rather than two blocks to a newer one, trying to help the Jewish people you see. But the activity would be just someone came in and played bridge in the evening. So I played bridge in German." Her staying with Jewish families provided them with a little money, at a time when the streets were full of troops, talking loudly and threateningly about the Jews, and terrifying her hosts.[53]

In Berlin, she enrolled on August 1 in the German Institute for Foreigners, where students from all over the world studied the language. Her instructor taught the students Nazi philosophy and took the class on required excursions:

a working men's camp, founded to begin military-style training; the Ship Habensberg on the Hohenzollern Canal, with a mechanical device for lifting ships through the locks. The most harrowing outing was to the Sports Palace for an evening rally, where they were given excellent seats near the front:

> And this whole Sports Palace had large cavernous signs . . . with slogans against the Jews. I didn't know it was going to be an anti-Jewish thing. 'Women' translated in English, 'Women and children, the Jew is your undoing.' And 'Down with world Jewry.' And all this around the walls of this enormous Sports Palace, it was a public meeting against the Jews. And then this Spartchoir, these men with tremendous voices, with all the rancor and vigor that they could put in their voice, speaking against the Jew. They went on and on. Streicher was the Jew baiter. And he spoke and you know, frothed at the mouth. All that just, hatred. And then Hitler came in and of course the people went mad. Oh you know, just mad when he came in. And it was just a meeting to work the people up against the Jews. . . . But that was the most unpleasant situation that I experienced. It wasn't directed against me but I felt the agony in my heart.

At her next class, "our professor lectured us on not being correct in not standing and saluting" when the crowd sang "Deutschland Uber Alles."[54]

Tate wrote a letter to a friend at Oxford condemning what she had witnessed, but it was censored and delayed two or three months; when it arrived, "they had deleted all these things I'd said about Streicher and Hitler." She believed that the authorities had actually looked for her, since she had described her itinerary in the letter, but that they never found her because she stayed in private homes and not in hotels, "and they probably thought I was a white American or a white Englishman." At the end of her class on August 21, Tate received a certificate verifying her three-week course of study.[55]

With that accomplished she left for Geneva, where she received a letter forwarded from London offering her a job as dean of women and history teacher at Barber-Scotia College in Concord, North Carolina. Leland Cozart, the school's dean, had gotten Tate's information from the placement office at Columbia. She quickly accepted the position by cable, wiring only "Cozart, Barber-Scotia, Concord, North Carolina, Accept, Tate" because she was so low on money she had to make every single word count.[56]

"The position is not what I had hoped to secure," she wrote Hadow, "but after the financial losses and worries of the past three years I am thankful for anything." The salary was "miserable," she explained. But her greater ambitions remained intact, since she saw the position as only temporary and she was already "looking forward to something better for next year in Washington, D. C."[57]

Just as she had done on her journey to Oxford, Tate spent some of her time as she made her way home aboard the S.S. *Europa* crafting another poem:

> The sea is calm and the sky is blue,
> They meet together as one—not two.
> The good ship *Europa,* though huge in port
> Appears only a toy on the ocean floor.
> So like our lives when they stand alone,
> But how insignificant with those of the world.
> All we may learn, all we may know,
> Is naught compared with what's to be known.
> All we can do in this world so wise,
> Is to do our best at every time.
> When all is finished and all are called,
> Whether we're great or whether we're small
> Will not matter to the one above;
> All He asks for is our love.

Her devotion to the sonnet form was not overwhelmed even by her exhaustion, and she once again used it to capture her gratitude and relief, but also a sense of spiritual awe and faith about her future.

Tate came home to enter the next phase of the life she was building for herself. She brought her Oxford degree and memories of her life and travels in England and Europe back with her. In many ways, she really was just getting started.

CHAPTER 4

"A Narrow Life, But a Rich One"

NORTH CAROLINA–CAMBRIDGE–BALTIMORE, 1935–1942

With a heightened sense of resolve and achievement, Tate set sail for New York on September 4, 1935, heading toward a country still suffering its own economic crisis and one where the tenets of Nazism were not unfamiliar. Traveling by train the day after her arrival, she made time during a stop in Washington to meet with Charles Wesley, chairman of the history department at Howard University, probably to remind him of her interest in working there. With that done, after three years of riding the rails in England and Europe, she boarded a Jim Crow train south. The train crossed by bridge into Virginia, stretching above the Potomac through Alexandria, then the Rappahannock through Fredericksburg, and later the James through Richmond. It then crossed the state line for the long, slow ride into the deep rural center of North Carolina to reach Barber-Scotia College, a small Black women's Presbyterian junior college in the mill town of Concord.[1]

The school that had brought Tate to North Carolina could hardly have been more different from Oxford in its history, mission, and size. Founded in 1867 by Presbyterians, it attracted Mary McLeod Bethune, who studied there in 1893. It evolved by merger in 1932 to become Barber-Scotia College, with a mission to educate Black women schoolteachers and social workers. It was on its way to accreditation as a junior college in 1936, later to graduate its first class as a four-year institution in 1945. In 1954, it became co-ed, welcoming all regardless of race, and today continues to educate and train its predominately Black student body.[2]

Its history and mission, including its religious origins, were typical for most historically Black educational institutions established during the Reconstruction period to educate Black southerners for the work of lifting a race of people newly freed from enslavement. These private religiously affiliated institutions assumed this responsibility because southern state legislatures refused or were slow to fund Black schools at any level, and especially for higher education.

Although Tate had not attended a predominately Black college, most of the schoolteachers she had served with in Indianapolis and many of her AKA sorors had, so this was not an unfamiliar world to her. But the location, the small scale, and the provincialism stood in stark contrast to Oxford, London, and Paris, where she had spent much of her time researching and writing. One big advantage of being in North Carolina, however, was that it had twelve Black colleges, creating a large, energetic social network of Black educators.

Tate had no real appetite for her position as dean of women. Her predecessor had a reputation for being very strict with the women students, unsurprising for the time and for a religiously funded institution. From the very beginning of her tenure, Tate, only thirty years old, was a very different kind of dean. She had never had to chafe under strict rules on her own comings and goings, and she clearly had no interest in imposing such requirements on the students at Barber-Scotia. Word of her liberal approach spread quickly on the small campus, and the women students requested her as chaperone for a bus trip for a football game at nearby Johnson C. Smith College in Charlotte, where many of the students had boyfriends. The men met the women at the bus and took them off to the game; Tate let them socialize for a long time after the game before heading back to Barber-Scotia. Rather than going and watching over them, which may have been the practice before her, Tate simply elected to go off to a dormitory and read, circling back well after the game had ended.

With that, her reputation was cemented, and the students always requested her on future excursions. In looking back decades later at her approach, she called herself a "modern woman," and a new type of dean of women who would not be "tight on the girls." That attitude and her lingering English accent distinguished her, but her views on how best to educate young Black women were consistent with ideas then being advocated by other Black women educators and deans, including Lucy Diggs Slowe, the dean of women at Howard and one of the original founders of two Black women's organizations, the AKA sorority and the National Association of College Women.[3]

Tate's own lively social life included faculty and staff members who worked at the cluster of nearby Black colleges or who convened from farther away for academic conferences. The founding conference of the Association of Social Science Teachers from Black colleges was held at Johnson C. Smith College in 1935. It drew distinguished scholars from around the country, including W. E. B. Du Bois, and, from Howard, Ralph Bunche, Charles Wesley, Harold Lewis, among others. All of the women faculty members at Barber-Scotia, regardless of their field of interest, attended the gathering, and at the end of the day invited the men back to their campus. Or at least they invited all the men except Du Bois, who, according to Tate, the women all considered too old for socializing, as he was then nearing seventy.[4]

Tate reminisced that life in Concord in the time of rigid racial segregation was not unbearable, "because I was young enough to adjust. I was happy. I was delighted to be there, to even have a position. And I don't remember being miserable at any time. It was a narrow life, but a rich one." She also brought a bit of Oxford's traditions to the campus, instituting a May Day celebration modeled after the one at Magdalen College, famous for its sunrise choristers from the top of its towers. At Barber-Scotia, she went out into the countryside to cut piles of dogwood blooms to dress up the trees on campus overnight. The next morning she had girls singing at daybreak from various parts of the campus, including from the belfry, followed by breakfast outside. This may not have had the power of the Oxford gathering but it certainly would have been more pleasant in May temperatures in North Carolina than those at a darkened drizzling dawn on the chilly Cherwell and Thames near Christ Church Meadows.

Being back in the United States allowed Tate to reconnect with the social and professional network that mattered to her most, the women of Alpha Kappa Alpha. When they gathered in December 1935, at Virginia Union University in Richmond for their annual conference and boule, Tate prepared a very long report on her three years away; it later took up nearly three full pages when it was published in their member publication, the *Ivy Leaf*. Her account also reached a broader reading public through extended summaries of her presentation printed in Black newspapers.[5]

Tate recounted in great detail her life and times at Oxford, and her many travels in England and Europe. Her gift for vivid descriptive writing and the power of her visual memory made up somewhat for the length of the piece, but her particular habit of mind made it difficult for her to impose editorial perspective on her own work. She told of an extraordinary three years in the life of a young Black woman who felt she had the right to speak with authority and at length, just as she had as a sixteen-year-old high school student.

Her extended essay's simple title, "Three Years in England," carried the subliminal purpose of the piece. Yes, she expressed her sincerely felt gratitude to her sorors, gracefully, and yes, she regaled her readers with tales of her travels to Germany, Geneva, Paris, Bavaria, Chartres, and Oberammergau. But most prominent was her need to explain why it took her three years to get her Oxford degree.

The complexity of her personal pride and competitive nature, her sense of the burden of racial representation, and the lingering post-traumatic stress of what she considered her shameful "failure" to pass her viva the first time is laid bare in a long, convoluted explanation she concocted to obscure it. The truth in this case was actually more powerful than the story she embellished. That she was able to master the research and writing needed to complete the B. Litt., with little supervision, under the financial stresses and after the accident, demonstrated even more clearly her brilliance, resolve, resilience, and toughness. And the fact that so many women at the Home Society and Zimmern were invested in her success also speaks to their admiration of her and those qualities. But any hint of failure or vulnerability seemed at odds both with her self-image and the public persona she wanted to present and protect.

In this essay, Tate again explained her feelings of obligation that extended well beyond her own personal achievement, just as she had written to Hadow while waiting for word on her examination results:

> Throughout the three years I spent in England I was ever conscious of being a pioneer representing AKA in particular and Negro womanhood in general. The latter fact was impressed upon me by the circumstance that I was the first Colored American woman to matriculate at Oxford and, as far as I know, *the first colored American to receive a higher* degree at that University. . . . In both curricula and extra-curricula activities, in both the lecture and drawing room, I was continually mindful of my representing a race which is ever striving against almost unsurmountable difficulties, to reach seemingly unattainable heights in history.

Her need to devise this cover-up speaks once again to the thing she feared most—academic failure. Her sense of self rested on her intellectual abilities, compounded by her competitive need to achieve new racial milestones and to represent black womanhood in particular.

That she had succeeded against all odds also fed her dream of eventually becoming a scholar. Being the "first colored American" with a graduate degree from Oxford placed her achievement above that of Alain Locke, the first and, at the time, the only black Rhodes scholar, who did not achieve that distinction. That statement, which was in fact true, would be central to her reputation then and for the rest of her life.

If Tate approached the return to her sorority with some trepidation, her invitation to speak in Indianapolis in the spring of 1936 offered her a more purely joyful homecoming in a community that had welcomed her as a newly minted college graduate in 1927. The occasion was the annual Monster Meeting of the Senate Avenue YMCA. Since its inception in 1905, this nationally recognized forum had hosted Black college presidents, scholars, and political figures, all of them men. Even attendance at the forum also was largely closed to women, but Tate broke the gender barrier by being the first Black woman invited to give the keynote address. She would remain the only woman keynote speaker until her return in 1952.[6]

People who were present described Tate's talk, "International Relations," as "the best address ever heard from any woman, regardless of race." After her talk, she adjourned for another hour to meet with a group of young people, giving them a "close up" about student life at Oxford. She also spoke at a breakfast meeting of the Fortnightly Literary Club, where she had been a member, entertaining members with tales of travels in Paris, Berlin, and many other spots in Europe. Despite her abrupt departure for Oxford in the fall of 1932, her old friends showed their pride in her and seemed happy to celebrate her achievements four years later.[7]

True to her own prediction, Tate remained at Barber-Scotia for only one year. She was prescient about the timing of her departure, but not about her destination. In 1936, when no position in Washington came her way, she was enthusiastic to accept a new job at Bennett College in nearby Greensboro.

Bennett College had been established in 1876 with Methodist support, serving first as a co-educational day school to help meet the need for Black teachers and ministers. But in 1926, it was converted to a Black woman's college, making it one of two, along with Spelman College in Atlanta, dedicated to that mission. With a campus of thirty-eight acres and recent additions of a new dormitory, library, classroom buildings, laboratories, a refectory, and a chapel, Bennett was a beautiful and well-appointed campus. At the time of its shift to women only, it was providing training at the high school level and two

Tate at Bennett College, 1936
(Moorland-Spingarn, Howard University)

years of college, which had enabled many of its graduates to meet the requirements to become teachers.

When David Jones, a Black native of Greensboro and a graduate of Wesleyan College, returned home in 1927 to assume the presidency of the college, it had only ten students. By 1932, with assistance from his gifted and hardworking colleague Dr. Willa Player, it had been transformed into an accredited four-year college and eliminated its high school program. Bennett's president was married to the former Susie Williams of St. Louis, whom Tate had met when she interviewed for a job at the high school where Susie's father was the principal. Susie Jones served in various administrative positions at Bennett and also was instrumental in helping to sustain and grow the college over the twenty-nine years of their tenure there. The two women were able to renew and deepen what became a lifelong friendship.

Tate arrived in 1936 to a beautiful college campus around a green landscape and magnolia trees. But the college remained quite small, with three hundred students. However, Greensboro was much larger than Concord and home to North Carolina A & T, a prominent land-grant Black co-educational school right across the street.[8]

As one of eight new faculty members, Tate was hired to teach history. She was relieved not to have duties as dean of women, as she never enjoyed the disciplinary aspect of that job, which also distracted from her own reading and teaching. She had been guest speaker at the college's first homecoming convocation earlier that year and she already knew most of the faculty. Here she would first work with Flemmie Kittrell, who had just become the first Black woman to receive a Ph.D. in nutrition and home economics from Cornell. The world of those affiliated with Black academic institutions was small and tight-knit, and Tate's connections in it would only continue to grow at Bennett.[9]

Tate liked being in a larger institution where she could teach more advanced students. There, as at Barber-Scotia, she would lodge on campus, which benefited her both financially and socially. The job also came with a boost in salary. The extra $600 or $700 would enable her to repay her sister for money she had sent to help her finish up at Oxford; she also would repay the funds she had been granted by the Home Society, something that baffled the women there, as she was not required or expected to do so and no one ever had. But Tate refused to be obligated financially, insisting on financial independence.[10]

Tate's intellectual intensity and her international relations background were welcomed and encouraged in her new position at Bennett. She quickly set about transforming a weekly chapel service into a public civics education program and reorganizing the history and social sciences curriculum, all while entering debates about how best to educate Black women for the modern age.

Putting on a contemporary affairs program was Tate's way of encouraging her students to stay attentive to current events. She required students to read the *New York Times* daily and then assigned them topics and helped them practice speeches or debates on pressing issues to the gathered audience. The quality of the programs and the variety of topics attracted weekly attendees from Greensboro's Black community, including the families of the college's service employees. Tate and other Black educators took seriously a democratic approach to teaching outside of their classrooms.[11]

Tate was brought to Bennett to offer classes in history and geography, but she also envisioned and directed a new social sciences "programme" (in her lingering use of British spelling) to help graduates solve civic and social problems and also to prepare some of them for graduate study in affiliated fields. Her ambitious plan was not fully realized, but it captures well her philosophy of education for Black students, which she also shared with other Black college educators. She proposed required courses in the history of civilization, ancient and medieval history, modern and contemporary European history, geography, American and European government, economics, sociology, and the history of philosophy.[12]

Tate strongly emphasized current events as part of each of those, and saw the history bachelor's degree, for example, as culminating in a senior seminar. She argued by way of illustration that "the treatment of the problems involved in the redistribution of colonies and mandates demands some knowledge of European history and imperialism, economics, geography and international institutions." Here, Tate shows her panoramic views on global politics, including the idea that imperialism could not be understood without going to its source.[13]

Perhaps her most telling proposed innovation was individual tutoring for advanced students, to include additional reading, primary research, and writing. She saw these steps, modeled on her time at Oxford, as essential to prepare Black women students at a small school like Bennett for graduate and doctoral work in the social sciences and to move beyond the idea that they could only be elementary and secondary school teachers.[14]

The question of the place of "Negro history" in her proposed program led her to theorize about the relationship between "American and Negro history." The two subjects were being taught separately at Bennett. She recommended that they be combined into a course where "we shall weave both the Negro and the white man into American life and history and truly study 'The Negro in Our History.' " She explained:

> We shall study not only the European but also the African background of American history. The Revolutionary and all our succeeding wars will present an opportunity for studying both Black and white heroes. An American Negro will help survey the site of our national capital. Reconstruction will be treated through the study of books by both white and colored authors. The literature, inventions, industrial and economic progress of both races will be interwoven. Of the two term papers required each semester in this course, one will be on a purely Negro History subject.

She saw such a combined approach as a powerful psychological corrective. At the end of the course, a Bennett student "should have lost any feeling of racial inferiority she might have had and any misconception that her race has not made a worthwhile contribution to American and world civilization."[15]

At that time, Carter G. Woodson and others were debating how best to educate Black students. Her ideas were consistent with the approach that Charles Wesley had advocated at the conference she had attended at Johnson C. Smith in 1935. But she also pursued the question of how best to teach history to Black students more generally, arguing for "less time on Alexander the Great and Julius Caesar and more on Hitler and Mussolini." In order to understand "Central Europe and Hitler's *Mein Kampf* we must know well the era of Versailles and French hegemony." She argued that appreciating "the factors involved in the Italian attack on and conquest of Ethiopia, in the Peace of Munich, in Japanese aggression in the Far East and the present Sino-Japanese conflict is impossible without a background knowledge of European history and imperialism since 1870, and especially the history of the past twenty-four years." She wanted political science courses to teach "our students how to combat disenfranchisement" and how they can become leaders in that fight.[16]

Economics should help Black students learn how "to advise our workers on labor conditions, union and bargaining problems, and how to spend their dollars where Negroes are employed" or on how to organize co-operatives and consumer unions. She also agreed with the students' complaint that they were being taught too much religion and too little on "how to fight disenfranchisement, lynching, wage inequalities, virtual peonage, and unequal educational opportunities." Tate supported the student view that Black colleges "should take the lead in the fight for Negro emancipation" by changing the way they were educating their own students.[17]

Tate's philosophy of education for Black students explicitly included ideas on how best to teach and train Black women in particular. In a speech to other Black women educators in 1937, she began boldly and in ways reminiscent of Du Bois. "The twentieth century," she wrote, "is the age of the woman and the child. . . . The whole vexed question of woman's 'sphere' has troubled the souls of men for more than a generation, and interwoven in the problem of educating the woman is the question: Does a woman's college justify itself?" Tate's answer to that question contains several broader arguments about Black college education.[18] Women's colleges could serve a special purpose by "separating young men and women when sex-consciousness is most acute," while providing controlled activities for commingling. "No sane person would attempt to check romances," she conceded, "but there is a 'silliness' that, if it does no more, vastly interferes with work."[19]

Tate was especially concerned about the role college-trained women would play in a modernizing world, and how educators could best prepare them for that. She envisioned a time when women could make a full contribution to society whether in the home or outside of it. The college woman had a growing option to not marry and to pursue a professional career, and for Tate this presented "new problems" of adjustment. She saw it as the specific mission of women's colleges like Bennett to offer "non-curricular instruction" as well as "group and individual counseling" as preparation for the psychological challenges facing women who moved into careers, whether they married or not.[20]

That article was based on a talk Tate gave at Bennett before the National Association of College Women. At the end, someone in the audience asked when it would be time for a Black women's college to be led by a Black woman. She recalled that "there was a gasp in the audience and then silence," because Bennett's president, David Jones, and his wife and her friend Susie were present. Thinking quickly, Tate answered, "certainly, after a man has built up the plant and the endowment. This brought down the house in laughter and applause." But as she later pointed out, "that is exactly what happened" when Willa Player became not only Bennett's first woman president in 1955 but the first Black woman in the United States to head an accredited four-year college.[21]

At thirty-two, Tate remained unmarried, something that may have concerned her friends. A letter from a friend in Detroit updated her on a man there who might be a prospect, writing, "you are so deserving and he seems so promising," but also suggesting, "perhaps you have met some other interesting gentlemen" in North Carolina. Tate's views and her reply to this are unknown. Her strongest expressed desires for herself remained intellectual ones, but she was beginning to wonder and read about the psychological toll of being a modern woman like her.[22]

She had a pragmatic yet visionary approach to pedagogy that recognized that a new generation of young Black educated women and men would need to stay attuned to contemporary political events, whether domestic or global. They were to be the next generation to accept the burdens of racial representation that Tate and her contemporaries already felt so deeply. Even as a newcomer to college teaching, she saw herself as entitled to participate in ongoing public debates about how best to train Black students.

Greensboro was much livelier than the small town of Concord, but legalized segregation remained as rigid. Of this, Tate says very little. She acknowledged that North Carolina was "one of the more liberal of the Southern states," but the railway station still had separate doors for white and Black. The local buses were cordoned off by race, something Tate and a white woman teacher forgot one day when they boarded and were so engrossed in conversation that they just sat down up front and continued to talk. "You know, some white people," she recalled, "you forget they're white," but the white driver had not. He spoke to them and they moved, with her friend in the white section and Tate in the one for colored, but their conversation ran on uninterrupted.[23]

When she attended theater performances in Durham, she sat in the balcony seats set aside for Blacks. But interracial exchanges for lectures and public events between the campuses of neighboring white and Black colleges were beginning. For Tate, dealing with racist policies had become a natural part of her daily life, but they still "didn't feel like the tight segregation that would exist in some places."[24]

She came to consider North Carolina her second home, because people were so welcoming and hospitable. "I have made friendships there that were like those between sisters," she recalled, remembering fondly her frequent invitations to Sunday dinners where she would eat delicious fried chicken, hot rolls, and beautiful salads, a welcome break from eating on campus at Bennett.[25] It was in doing a favor for one of her friends, however, that Tate's restless nature and sense of adventure reemerged.

Living in the dormitory had enabled Tate to save money, and while visiting in Detroit one summer, she was able to buy herself a car—something she found especially liberating. One of her friends and AKA sorors in Greensboro, Martha Sebastian, had a son who was graduating from Harvard in 1938, and Tate agreed to drive his mother to the graduation, stopping in Philadelphia along the way.[26] Her friend also knew someone who was graduating from Radcliffe, but could not get a ticket for Tate for that ceremony. Undaunted, and wanting to get inside the hall, Tate did something she was very good at—dressing for success and talking her way into places:

> I dressed very carefully. I remember every detail of what I did that morning. I had a very fine, in terms of expensive, but not showy, dark brown dress with an undercover, under slip of dark brown. I had dark brown [shoes], they were not patent leather, something like patent leather pumps with a beautiful little trim, a dark brown with flowers sort of a pitcher size hat, gloves that matched the little collar on this crisp brown dress. . . . And I had a brown bag that matched. . . . And

> then I went up to the usher. . . . and in the best English that I could command, I said, "I haven't a ticket for this ceremony, I should like very much to see it."

The student usher marched her down to a seat two rows from the podium; her friends remained seated somewhere in the back way behind her. They all laughed about it later.[27]

As she watched the awarding of the degrees, Tate paid special attention to the Ph.D.'s and the titles of their dissertations. She later recalled thinking, " 'These dissertations aren't any more significant than my B. Litt dissertation at Oxford.' So I started getting ideas." After the ceremony, she called the registrar's office and arranged a meeting the next day with the dean of Radcliffe's graduate school, Bernice Brown Cronkhite. Her meeting with Cronkhite was fortuitous for many reasons, but the first and most important was their immediate intellectual camaraderie. Tate's work at Oxford on disarmament would have been immediately legible to Cronkhite, since her Harvard Ph.D. in government, the first for a woman, had focused on international law.[28]

Cronkhite had assumed the position as graduate dean in 1934, but was only a decade older than Tate. Their meeting yielded one of Tate's longest and most consequential professional relationships, and she always called her one of her "dearest friends." Their friendship also included Cronkhite's husband, Leonard, who had been among the earliest American Rhodes Scholars.[29]

Although Tate had arrived in Cambridge expecting to drive on to Michigan to see family, she abruptly abandoned that plan as soon as she realized that there were graduate summer courses at Harvard that interested her. Of her relations with her family in this period, Tate says little. She had spent time during the summers in Michigan after her return from Oxford and visited on other occasions, staying with her sister Thelma in Detroit and enjoying an active social life there among schoolteacher friends, including outings on Belle Isle and Mackinac Island. Of all her family members, she felt closest to her sister, who was so supportive of her educational ambitions. Tate remained more emotionally distanced from her mother and father, which can be inferred by her silence on their absence.[30]

As she had before, she sacrificed her expected commitments to her family in Michigan when an appealing opportunity related to education or travel presented itself. The chance to study at Harvard for six weeks that summer was too much for Tate to pass up. Cronkhite arranged a scholarship for tuition, and one of her best friends from Oxford asked Tate to take care of her and her husband's house on Plympton Street while they spent the summer in Canada.[31]

With free tuition and now free housing, all she had to do was feed herself for six weeks. She took two graduate courses taught by Frederick Shuman, a specialist on Nazi Germany and the Soviet Union, one on international relations and another on diplomatic history, earning an A and an A-plus. Her success in the courses left her convinced, with Cronkhite's assistance, that she would find a way to return and complete work on a doctorate in government.[32]

Certainly, the relevance of the topics could not have been clearer in the global tumult of the summer and fall of 1938. Tate went back to North Carolina and delivered a series of talks at local colleges and high schools that she condensed into an article, "The Present Day International Situation," published in February 1939 in a journal aimed at Black educators. There she chastised France and Great Britain for the failure of the Treaty of Versailles, for permitting Hitler's rise to power and allowing Germany's rearmament, and, more broadly, for making a mockery of the promise of the League of Nations. Tate considered the Munich accord, which in September 1938 had ceded part of Czechoslovakia to Germany, a dangerous capitulation further enabling an eastward advancing Rome-Berlin-Tokyo axis.[33]

Tate called for a revision to the neutrality policy of the United States, which she said had left it with its "hands tied." Her greatest frustration was with the League of Nations, which had previously failed to protect Ethiopia, something she had witnessed first-hand when she visited the opening debates in Geneva on that matter before heading home in the summer of 1935. Tate seemed to place little hope in the League four years later, and her article strongly criticized it for not standing up to German, Italian, and Japanese aggression against weaker neighbors in Ethiopia, China, Spain, and Czechoslovakia. The article was her first on international issues, and an early articulation of ideas that came to form her anti-racist geopolitics.[34]

Fully committed to getting a doctorate at Harvard, Tate applied for support from the Rosenwald Foundation for a sabbatical year 1939–1940, and received the award along with other well-known Black scholars and artists including Allison Davis, Abram Harris, L. D. Reddick, William Grant Still, Lorenza Turner, and Shirley Graham. Tate sold her car and put the proceeds in Investor's Syndicate, a precursor to mutual funds, beginning a hobby at which she would excel, in part because of her mathematical inclinations and her keen understanding of economics and geopolitics. Several years later, when she sold the stock, it had increased in value five-fold, earning more than enough for her to buy a new car.[35]

With funding in hand and with Cronkhite's support, she returned to Cambridge and moved into graduate housing in Bertram Hall, to spend the year taking courses and revising and expanding her B. Litt. thesis into a doctoral dissertation. Usually she was the only woman in classes full of men. But she lived and socialized, not unlike at Oxford, in the smaller world of other graduate women at Radcliffe, who unlike her were mostly masters students.[36]

Tate received credit for some of the work she had done at Oxford, and for the two courses she had taken at Harvard the previous summer. She met the language requirements with French and German. Payson S. Wilde, a scholar of international relations and international law, served as her primary adviser; he had taken his doctorate in government there in 1931 and was Tate's exact contemporary in age. They shared an interest in contemporary world politics, and he welcomed her earlier work at Oxford on disarmament, a topic that seemed even more pertinent as war in Europe commenced.

She brought all of her intellectual strength to her preparation for her comprehensive exam, not least because of the trauma of her failed B. Litt. exam at Oxford. That failure still weighed heavily on her and caused her great anxiety. Her anxiety was not at all irrational given her new setting. She had made all A's in her classes there except for one B, a mark she resented. On the first exam in that course, she had made the highest grade in the class. When the instructor announced that by saying "Mr. Merze Tate, where is he," she surprised him when she raised her hand. On a later exam, he disputed her analysis of a legal case and judged it too detailed, and lowered her overall grade for the course. The instructor seemed to begrudge that Tate may have known more than he did.[37]

But she prevailed rather easily in the roundtable question-and-answer format of her exam, in part because she had so overprepared for it. "I can't tell you how I felt after I came out of that exam," she later recalled. "It was much more important than commencement." With that done, Tate devoted her remaining time to research at Harvard and later in Washington, as she worked on her dissertation through the end of the summer before returning to Bennett.

Meanwhile in Michigan her father's mental health, which had begun to decline as early as 1936, had deteriorated so badly that he had been committed to an asylum in Ypsilanti in February 1941. Tate's younger brother Keith, who maintained ties with their father and managed his affairs, probably made the decision to place him in a state institution during an era that deeply stigmatized mental illness and when Black people's distrust of white medical caretakers was high.[38]

Her father's mental illness only added to her discomfort and secrecy about her parents and her relationship with them. In all of her extended interviews and many profiles, she says nothing of her father, who separated from her mother when she was seven but continued to live nearby. Of her mother, she also says little, but her father's absence is absolute. His institutionalization also meant that his mental condition became a matter of public notice and public record. Later in her life, Tate would customize and fashion a family lineage for herself by celebrating her pioneer grandparents and skipping her parents' generation altogether.[39]

In spite of the turmoil in her family, Tate kept her focus on her work at Bennett and on her writing. With her usual intensity, she was able to complete a 499-page dissertation titled "Movement for a Limitation of Armaments to 1907." Its first section, "Public Opinion and the Movement for Disarmament, 1870–1898," was 120 pages long and probably was what she submitted for her B. Litt. thesis. The remainder of the work appears to be based on the large mass of material and writings that she likely had submitted originally but repurposed and updated during her year in residency, covering the long period from 1870 to 1907. In this part she traced state actors, treaties, and international conferences on disarmament, the more traditional work of diplomatic history and international relations.

She was awarded her doctorate in June 1941 at a ceremony where she replaced her Oxford ermine with a hood signifying her Ph.D. in political science, with an emphasis on international relations. Her sister Thelma and her brother-in-law James Hayes drove from Detroit to share in her joy at the honor. Tate always credited her sister's financial and emotional support and her care of their mother in Michigan as liberating her to take the time she needed to study, travel, and write. These graduation events with her were an especially poignant occasion for them. She was surprised to learn that she also was to be inducted later that day into Phi Beta Kappa.[40]

Several national press accounts noted her achievement also, with headlines such as "Miss Tate Wins Ph. D. at Radcliffe." She proudly mailed a copy of the commencement booklet to the Butler sisters at the Home Society, thanking them for making her degree possible. It became the last item added to her student file at Oxford, making it the first item to be seen, and closing the circle that had begun with her risky arrival to undertake graduate study there in 1932. Ever mindful of her own historical significance, Tate later donated a carbon copy of her dissertation to the James Weldon Johnson Collection, newly established at Yale University through Carl Van Vechten's donation of his library and archive.[41]

With the completion of her degree, Tate also finished her last year of teaching history and geography at Bennett College. She considered returning to Michigan, probably because of the press of family matters, but she was offered a job as an associate professor of political science at Morgan State College in Baltimore, and she accepted. Attached to the position came the responsibility to serve as Dean of Women, an administrative duty she did not relish, even as she dutifully moved into Harriet Tubman Hall, a very well appointed, brand-new women's dormitory with a fireplace and a baby grand piano in its common area. So after six years in North Carolina, Tate moved away from the network of friends and colleagues that she had enjoyed and would treasure even as she relocated.[42]

David Jones, Bennett's president, regretted her leaving, but he understood her ambition "to teach where the library facilities will give her more opportunity to work in the field of her specialization." Once she was in Baltimore, she seemed content for the time being. She wrote to thank her Greensboro AKA chapter for a going-away gift of a briefcase and asked to transfer her membership to the local chapter. Her social and intellectual networks from Indianapolis and North Carolina remained an active part of her life, as did connections she made at Oxford and Radcliffe.[43]

Tate settled once again into the familiar comfort of a Black academic community, but this one in a bustling mid-Atlantic city. From there, she was in easy reach of institutions essential to the life she wanted as a research scholar in diplomatic history and international relations: the National Archives and the Library of Congress, and Howard University, the campus she had kept in her sights since she graduated from college in 1927. Of her time in Baltimore, Tate offers little detail, in part because her life was quickly overshadowed by the United States entering World War II and by unexpected personal and professional developments.

CHAPTER 5

"Darker Peoples of the World"

WASHINGTON, 1942–1950

Tate was busy working on the index to her first book, *The Disarmament Illusion: The Movement for a Limitation of Armaments to 1907*, when the news flash about the bombing of Pearl Harbor on December 7, 1941, came across her radio. American entry into yet another world war meant that her dissertation topic would no longer simply be an academic concern. She was in her first term at Morgan State, but she had already tired of the disciplinary challenges of being a dean of women and living in a dormitory.

Her friends Elizabeth and Martin Jenkins, whom she had met in North Carolina, had moved to nearby Washington so he could take a position at Howard. They kept her informed of happenings on the campus and tipped her when Charles Wesley, the chair of Howard's history department and dean of the graduate school, decided to take a leave of absence to accept a position as president of Wilberforce University. Rayford Logan was appointed to serve as interim chair in history.[1]

When formal notice was given of a replacement position, Tate applied and got it. Once again, she took a calculated risk by leaving Morgan State after a year to accept a temporary position on the faculty she had long been trying to join, positioning herself there to take advantage of whatever might next come her way.

Although she did not know it, she got the job despite Logan confiding in his diary that he believed she had a "personality problem." A Harvard-trained historian of U.S. and Haitian relations, he was a man prone to strong negative views even of his closest friends, but it is not clear when or why he had formed his opinion of her. Still, after conferring with Wesley, he concluded that her superb qualifications and reputation as an experienced teacher overrode whatever reservations he held.[2]

Howard University had been in Tate's sights since 1927, when she received a teaching fellowship there but chose instead to go to Indianapolis, probably for financial and family reasons. Then, and when she arrived fifteen years later, Howard was the best and the most prominent of historically Black colleges. Established by Congress in 1867 and named for the Freedmen's Bureau commissioner and white Union soldier Oliver O. Howard, the school's origin set it apart from other Black institutions, most of which were founded by religious denominations. Its annual appropriations were insufficient to meet its needs and subject to shifting political battles, but its finances were still less precarious than other Black colleges and universities.

Open to all regardless of race, it also welcomed both men and women, as most Black institutions did during a time with many white colleges did not. Envisioned from its start to be a true university, the school had not only a college of liberal arts but professional colleges in medicine, pharmacy, and dentistry, as well as law and theology. And while other HBCUs still remained under white leadership, in 1926 Howard appointed a Black president, Mordecai Johnson, who held that position until 1960.[3]

Johnson's long tenure certainly was not without controversy, but Howard's campus also soon showed the benefits of his leadership in securing philanthropic and federal New Deal funding. A construction boom in the late 1930s dramatically expanded its physical plant. Two of the school's most iconic buildings, Frederick Douglass Memorial Hall and Founder's Library, were built then, and they still anchor the idyllic tree-lined greenspace at the center of the campus.

Howard was not only co-ed, but at a time when women were routinely excluded from academic careers, the institution was home to a formidable group of accomplished Black women who would spend most of their professional lives there. Among the first was Lucy Diggs Slowe, a 1908 alumna who co-founded the AKAs, and returned there in 1922 with a master's from Columbia to become the dean of women; she also founded and led the National Association of College Women, a group whose meetings Tate had first attended while she was in North Carolina. An outspoken national advocate for women students and teachers, Slowe clashed with Mordecai Johnson over his conservative policies; before her death in 1939, he also attacked her for living openly in a lesbian relationship.[4]

Two of the three Black women who in 1921 became the first to earn doctorates took positions at Howard—Eva Dykes, with a degree in English philology from Radcliffe, and Georgiana Simpson, in Germanic languages from Chicago. In 1930, Dorothy Porter, an alumna and graduate from Columbia's library school, assumed the leadership of the Moorland-Spingarn Research Center, where she spent the next four decades building up its extraordinary collections. After Dorothy Ferebee earned her medical degree from Tufts in 1924, the paucity of opportunities for Black women doctors in Massachusetts led her to move to Howard's Freedman's hospital. There, she practiced obstetrics and developed public health outreach in Washington and Mississippi; eventually, she would head university health services, succeed Bethune as head of the National Council of Negro Women, and become national president of the AKAs.

Marion Thompson Wright, a historian of education with a doctorate from Columbia, also taught at Howard from 1929 until her untimely death in 1962. Inabel Lindsay, a 1920 alum, came back in 1937 with her social work degree from Chicago, and later served as dean of a newly established School of Social Work. Flemmie Kittrell, with a doctorate in nutrition from Cornell, arrived in 1944; she and Tate had overlapped at Bennett, where she had been dean of women. The internationally recognized artist Lois Jones had also joined the faculty in the 1930s.[5]

These women remained in the minority and despite their training and accomplishments were largely excluded from positions of institutional power and authority. As is much better known, the faculty at that time also included many prominent Black male scholars, among them Alain Locke, the first Black Rhodes scholar and a leader of the Harlem Renaissance, the sociologist E. Franklin Frazier, political scientists Eric Williams and Ralph Bunche, the classicist Frank Snowden, dean of the school of religion William Stuart Nelson, dean of the chapel Howard Thurman, literary expert Sterling Brown, education scholar Charles Thompson, and the economist Abram Harris. In the law school, there was Charles Hamilton Houston, who devised the legal strategy that led to the *Brown* decision on school desegregation.[6]

These were just some of the exceptional faculty members and administrators assembled at Howard. The school sat at the top of a hill in the upper northeast corner of the peculiar diamond-shaped map of Washington, D.C., a capital city whose original one hundred square miles had been carved out of neighboring Maryland and Virginia. Its footprint expanded after the Civil War, but it remained a southern city, replete with segregation and discrimination.

Conditions for Black citizens there were made worse by the city's status as a special federal district, governed by congressional committees that were chaired by southern representatives. The city's residents were not permitted to vote in presidential elections until 1964, and not until 1973 were they granted limited "home rule" and allowed to elect a mayor and a city council—although they still remain under congressional oversight. In spite of ongoing campaigns for statehood rights, city residents remain without full voting representation in Congress, even though they pay federal taxes.

Black women residents and college students in the 1930s aggressively challenged segregation and discrimination with sit-ins and protests, and lawsuits. The inequities in the capital were made more manifest during the federal state's expansions under Franklin Roosevelt's New Deal. Workers drawn to new opportunities helped the city grow by a third, and much of that increase came from Black citizens whose numbers grew by 40 percent. The unseemliness of a racially segregated national capital was made even more visible with the coming of another world war in which Black citizens were again expected to serve in a segregated military and be excluded from equal opportunity in federal and defense employment.[7]

When Black activism nationwide renewed attention to the conditions of segregation and inequity in the World War II era, it was the federal government that became its target, putting the city at the center of campaigns to outlaw racial discrimination in federal and defense jobs and to end segregation in the military. A. Philip Randolph's threat in 1941 of a march on Washington led to Roosevelt's executive order ending the legalized denial of access to those jobs, but the end to a segregated military was not mandated until after the war ended.

Despite all of this, Black people poured into Washington along with others seeking new jobs created during the crisis of war. At the start of the 1940s, the city's population stood at 663,000; by 1950, it had grown to 802,000. The city remained majority white, but the numbers of Black citizens increased from 187,000 to 280,000. Even before the war, the city had long been a mecca for an educated Black elite drawn to opportunities in its still-segregated schools and in professions in law and medicine. Washington also became a much-favored destination for Black musicians, artists, and writers where the burgeoning urban community supported a vibrant cultural and literary center.[8]

This was the world of political and cultural paradoxes that Merze Tate moved into when she arrived in the city in the fall of 1942. Finding housing was not easy because of the influx of wartime workers, but Tate was lucky to have friends who invited her to live in their apartment while they were away for the year. She moved into their place on Franklin Street in the Brookland section of northeast Washington, where many faculty members from Howard lived.

She settled quickly into the communities that connected to her overlapping networks of AKA sorority members, bridge clubs, and the Black academic world of high school and college teachers she had known for more than a decade, including many from her time in Indianapolis and North Carolina who had since relocated to Washington. Thanks to her immersion in that national intergenerational community, she already knew many in the city and most on the campus when she arrived to assume her temporary position in Howard's history department.

Tate arrived, as one newspaper reported, "flush with success," with her Harvard doctorate and the publication of her first book, but at thirty-seven she was also a strong and mature woman, firmly confident in her own abilities and ambitions. She became the only Black woman teaching in the social science division at Howard, and the first in the history department. In her first quarter, and as if to confirm her versatility, Logan had her teach "Europe from the Roman Empire to 1648," "Latin America to the End of Revolutions," and a graduate course, "Problems of Modern Europe Since 1871."[9]

The attention generated by her book *The Disarmament Illusion* firmly established her reputation as a scholar. Macmillan had published it earlier in the year with an assist from Bernice Cronkhite, who had hastened it into print with a subvention from the Bureau of International Research at Radcliffe. Tate acknowledged that support, as well as that of her Alpha Kappa Alpha sorority's foreign fellowship, and faculty at Oxford and Harvard. In another clear indication of her strongest familial bond, she dedicated the book not to her mother but "To My Sister."[10]

Virtually identical to her Harvard dissertation, Tate's book was a transnational intellectual history of debates about war as a mechanism for dispute resolution, about the conflict between state sovereignty and the need for international cooperation, and about the perpetuation of historical power imbalances. The book established her as a formidable intellect with an eloquence in style and a fluency in both technical and diplomatic matters.

Tate, holding her first book, *The Disarmament Illusion,* in 1942
(Moorland-Spingarn, Howard University)

She argued that armaments were mere mechanisms or tools in ideological and political debates:

> The limitation of armaments is not a matter of mathematics nor of morals but of politics; states seek to give effect to their national policies through armaments as well as through monetary and immigration policies, tariffs and embargoes. Armament competition is inextricably interwoven with political tension, and international agreement on

armaments is possible only when the national policies of states are not in conflict.[11]

The book engaged ideas about the risks of escalating competition among nations over the strength of their arms and armed forces. But in a bold and innovative move, Tate also made explicit the links between armaments and imperialism, arguing that economic imperialism encouraged the buildup of armaments, and that their chief purpose, particularly when it came to navies, was to defend colonies.[12]

Tate examined peace congresses, churches, international jurists, interparliamentary groups, and the newly recognized "force in political life" of "public opinion," in which she included the press. But she found that there was at best only an "inchoate" movement toward limiting armaments in England, Europe, and the United States despite the flurry of meetings, writings, organizing, petitions, and resolutions on the issue over the several decades detailed in her book.[13]

In considering the participation of women in movements for disarmament she resisted the idea that they were early or especially effective advocates, and she seemed ambivalent about women's supposed maternalistic anti-war impulse. "It is only natural that women should hate war—which breaks up their homes, robs them of their sons, husbands, and support—but," she argued, "this hatred had done little by 1898 to assist the struggle for a limitation of armaments." Her consistent impulse toward anti-essentialism, which she always saw as restrictive when applied to women or to Black people, was evident in her analysis.[14]

Tate argued that peace would only come through a rational international political system, without which war was eventually inevitable. As long as powers refused to limit sovereignty or to submit to an international authority with the power to execute and enforce agreements, war remained likely. Neither the strong nor the weak had sufficient incentive to limit or reduce military capability, least of all those who had or desired empires and colonies.

The publication of Tate's book brought her immediate public notice. Published in the middle of a war and after the demise of the League of Nations, Tate's sophisticated analytical work soon generated much review attention in political science, international affairs, and historical journals, as well as in broader forums. The "disarmament illusion" of her title, perhaps alluding to the classic Norman Angell text *The Great Illusion,* had led some reviewers to expect that she would condemn pacifist "illusions." But the book demonstrated instead Tate's conclusion that it was an "illusion" that there had been any real movement toward limiting armaments by pacifists or, more importantly for her, by those holding power in armed nation-states.

Academic reviewers, including the most prominent scholar in the field, Hans Morgenthau, lauded the book as the definitive history on the subject, describing it as erudite, scholarly, and the result of untiring research. They praised her for looking beyond the state to other actors in the public debate about armament policies, although her own enthusiasm for that was limited. Many of the reviewers suggested the urgent need for the rest of the story beyond 1907, suggesting that Tate produce a second book that expanded coverage to the current era.[15]

Her book was reviewed in the leading academic journals in history, international law and politics, and political science, as well as popular publications in the United States and abroad. The variety of disciplines and reactions to Tate's work by recognized scholars accurately reflected tensions and paradoxes in the academic fields as well as her early embrace of an interdisciplinary approach.

It would take the engagement of scholars in African American studies, which consistently embraced an explicit anti-imperialism, to highlight the aspects of the book most useful for establishing links between armaments, colonization, and empire. That was made clear when the three most prominent African American historians of her day reviewed the book. Du Bois praised the quality of Tate's research and writing, but criticized her interpretation for failing to give more attention to the economic reasons for expanding armaments. This he blamed on her training, writing that "Harvard University," also his alma mater, "ignores the epoch-making philosophy of Karl Marx." Tate would not have been surprised by his views, but she admired his scholarship and had specifically requested that he consider reviewing her book.[16]

Rayford Logan hoped the book would serve as a warning "to those Pacifists whose ignorance of history or whose distortion of it helped to make World War II possible and who, unless they take a more realistic attitude toward the basic causes of war, may well precipitate a third holocaust." Like Du Bois, Logan praised the quality of Tate's work as meticulous and scholarly, assuring her "a permanent place among American historians regardless of color." Finally, Carter G. Woodson, the dean of Black historians and founder of the field of Black history, also praised Tate's analysis: "Chauvinistic doctrines, insane nationalism, and imperialistic expansion at the expense of unoffending natives in distant lands have served as enormous stimuli to the inevitable death march of these nations."[17]

Each of these reviewers brought an explicitly anti-imperialist interpretation to the question of armaments, another reminder of the early prevalence and persistence of that critique among a diverse group of Black intellectuals, including Tate. Indeed, that assessment dominates African American studies and figures in a larger Black public's political thought about the kinship between racism and imperialism. Nearly two decades ago, Robin Kelley explained that Black studies insists on an anti-racist global vision and is a field that always has been "relentlessly international and comparative."[18]

With her first book, Tate staked a clear claim on a place in those global debates, and more distinctly on explicit links between race, imperialism, and technology. This would become central to her approach to the fields of international relations and diplomatic history and among her most important theoretical innovations—her anti-racist geopolitics.

The unsettled nature of the comings and goings among the Howard faculty in this period meant that Tate's one-year temporary position had to be renewed three times, but still with no promise of permanency. Her unusual training and broad interests gave her the flexibility needed to teach European, English, and American diplomatic and military history as well as economics, international politics, political science, geography, and geopolitics. Her expertise made her very useful in filling out the curriculum, a much needed asset after Charles Wesley decided not to return to Howard, Ralph Bunche left to assume wartime duties, Harold Lewis went on leave, and the geography professor retired. When Logan himself took a sabbatical in 1944–1945, he even foisted the job of chair on to Tate, though she objected that she was not a member of the standing faculty.

The war brought many changes on campus, including new kinds of students for Tate to teach. In 1943, the Army designated Howard as the national training site for three hundred Black engineers, doctors, and dentists in the 2515th Army Service Unit under the Army Specialized Training Program (ASTP). Tate taught large classes of these young men in military history, diplomatic history, geopolitics, and geography. Most went on to active duty in the spring of 1944, with the engineering students being assigned mainly to the 92nd Infantry Division, the well-known Buffalo Soldiers combat forces deployed to Italy; smaller groups were sent to other areas in Europe and the Pacific, and some remained in the United States.

The men had been recruited from around the country, but had bonded as a unit during their training and pledged to stay in contact as they were scattered in deployment. They soon organized themselves into a group they called "The Prometheans," after the Greek god of forethought and scientific knowledge. Their intention was to remain connected during the war and to ease the transition back into civilian work and life when they returned.[19]

Tate seemed deeply affected by the work of teaching hundreds of what she called "brilliant young colored men" and then seeing them off to face the dangers of war in segregated Army units. And they formed a profound attachment to her. Tate accepted the key role as coordinator of the group for the duration of the war, minding the bankbook of their membership contributions, but most importantly serving as a point of mail contact for the soldiers. She would in turn share news from their correspondence in a newsletter that she helped produce and distribute to their key postings abroad, primarily in Italy and Germany, and the Pacific. The newsletters included personal news from soldiers, but also important practical advice on everything from taxes to veterans and spousal benefits. Tate crafted one newsletter around a detailed War Department survey of opinions on Black soldiers, something that elicited much discussion among them.[20]

Scores of letters from those soldiers flooded Tate's mail, coming not just from Europe but from more isolated postings in the Philippines and elsewhere. "When the first News Letter reached me," one wrote, "I rounded up the boys and we read it together and we had one of our bull sessions. It really brought back memories. . . . There is one person we want to thank for her patience and kindness. That person is Dr. Tate. There is only one way to state how we feel about her. . . . She's regular." The newsletter gave many of the men their first word of the whereabouts of their friends, as reported in another letter: "I devoured its contents hungrily and recalled with pleasure our short stay on Howard's campus. The joy from seeing the names of all the men is really beyond expression." One soldier, writing on behalf of "the rest of the group here in the Marianas," reported their "joy" at having received the newsletter: "It seemed to add color to this part of civilization, if it can be called such."[21]

The letters to Tate also carried news and confidences that she did not share in the newsletter, including reports of grief and trauma from losing friends or from learning that a brother in another unit had been killed. Some of the letters were from men organizing information on racist abuses against them, or letting her know of their commendations, or that they had become fathers. From Camp McCain in Mississippi, one soldier complained that although he was stationed with other Black "Ph.D.'s, lawyers, teachers," most of them remained privates because "ignorance and the ability to be an Uncle Tom seems to be a prerequisite for becoming a non-com."[22]

Tate was not compensated for helping these young Black soldiers in this way; it was not part of her temporary job at Howard. She simply honored their service by helping to provide them news of home and of one another. At war's end, she prodded Howard to honor those who had been killed in combat, saying that "the 2515th AST Unit has lost more men than any other AST Unit and most of these casualties were in the 370th Infantry of the 92nd Division." She also kept the letters the soldiers wrote to her and made sure that they would reside in Howard's archive, where she deposited them in 1945 and 1950. These hurriedly handwritten letters still capture the vibrancy and verve of these young professional Black men called to serve in a Jim Crow army.[23]

Even after the war ended, soldiers in the Prometheans maintained close ties with one another and with Tate, nourishing a union forged on Howard's campus, including in her classes on geopolitics, history, geography, and military history. They remembered how she had helped them create and maintain a sense of collective spirit, keeping up their confidence and pride in being who they were even as they were being sent off in a sacrifice of service for the good of their race as well as the country that still denied them the rights of full citizenship.

As busy as she was both as a professor and an administrator, Tate continued to research and write. She created a stark marker of her political and intellectual frame of mind when she tried without success to secure Rosenwald Fellowship funding in 1942. Shedding all pretense of scholarly restraint, Tate wrote a pithy one-page description of a project titled "The White Man's Blunders: The Twentieth-Century Sequel to the White Man's Burden." She conceptualized it as "a study of the consequences of imperialism especially as they have affected the white man and his civilization" under these chapter titles:

I. 'The White Man's Burden'
'Mission Civilisatrice' and 'Manifest Destiny'
II. The White Man Holds Weaker Peoples as Colonies and Dependencies and Thereby Corrupts His Government
III. The White Man Pushes His Industrialism Into the Phase of Imperialism and Thereby Threatens Capitalism
IV. The White Man Exports His Technics and Thereby Loses His Technical Supremacy

V. The White Man Fails to Disarm and Teaches Darker Peoples How to Arm Thereby Jeopardizing His Own Safety
VI. The White Man Creates and Then Destroys the League of Nations Thereby Re-Introducing International Anarchy
VII. The White Man Commits Fratricide Thereby Leaving the Darker Races Supreme

What she actually would have written beneath those tantalizing titles remains unknown, but in their raw form they outline a scathing critique and a fantastical scenario of the perils of colonialism for the colonizer.[24]

Tate wrote a more fully realized appraisal of colonialism and American racism in "The War Aims of World War I and World War II and Their Relation to the Darker Peoples of the World," an article in a special issue of the *Journal of Negro Education* in 1943. Written for a narrower audience of Black readers, and delivered first as a talk at Morgan State, the article defined the "darker peoples" expansively to include people in Africa or of African descent and other people of color in the Americas and Asia. She warned: "They are no longer willing to accept the white man's exalted view of trusteeship; they no longer quake at the teachings of the white man's missionaries, who bring them the white man's God but a God in whom the white man does not believe; no longer are glass beads and trinkets marvelous to them; they are much more interested in the marvels of the white man's guns."[25]

These phrases marked Tate as one who had read George Bernard Shaw's *Adventures of the Black Girl in Her Search for God* (1933), probably while she was at Oxford. She dutifully took brief notes from a section where the young Black girl argued as Tate had in her one-page description that white men would destroy themselves by their continued reliance on violence and imperialism to satisfy their greed: "I thought glass beads marvelous when I saw them for the first time; but I soon got used to them. . . . The most wonderful things you have are your guns. You use your guns to make slaves of us. . . . You will soon teach us to make guns because you are too lazy to make them for yourselves."[26]

Paying attention to injustices in Africa and India and in each imperialist empire, Tate described wage and labor exploitation, illegal land grabs, and destructive economic and political partitions. As for the United States, she reminded readers that Black Americans know "that there are elements in this country which practiced Nazism long before Adolf Hitler celebrated his first birthday and which today dominate the Federal Government and the Army and Navy." She ended by calling for a new global order with freedom guaranteed for all, and an end to vast empires. She asked: "Will the hopes of the peoples, especially the darker peoples, be realized or will the *Peace* Congress convened at the end of this global war have as its ulterior motive the division of the spoils of the vanquished and a return as near as possible to the *status quo ante bellum*?"[27]

Fearing a repeat of the politics that created the mandate system and a continuation of "the imperialist mentality" of "master and subject," Tate argued that a return to the pre–World War II status quo would not satisfy, especially since so many soldiers of color were serving in the military. She lamented that she had helped prepare the "best and brightest" of her race for the potentially fatal dangers and disruptions of military service.[28]

Although Tate had proved herself an invaluable teacher and a productive scholar, after four years she was still in a temporary position at Howard. The retirement of a faculty member in geography and one in the history department finally opened the way for her to apply for a permanent position. She applied initially for a position in the geography department, which she was qualified to assume, but in the end, with Logan's endorsement, she was hired in 1946 in the history department, the place she had hoped to land since 1927. In his letter arguing for her appointment "in the strongest possible terms," Logan lauded the caliber of her work as so high that "comment is unnecessary." Her courses drew large numbers, especially her new offerings in geography and geopolitics.

She had managed in her four years at Howard to make herself as indispensable as possible. Logan said as much, calling her "absolutely needed" for the continued success of the department and the history master's degree program, where she taught the research methods course. She finally became a professor of history, at long last garnering the respect and academic freedom that came with that distinction, still a rarity for women. She positioned herself as a diplomatic historian of international relations, a new field she conceptualized as broadly multidisciplinary. A trailblazer in this regard, she saw a reliance on many disciplines as essential to understanding global politics. This seemed especially important at a time when the interrelatedness of a world in which technological innovations in aviation and communications were shrinking the distance and space between economics and politics.[29]

Logan's commitment to hiring Tate in 1946 even meant a delay in his plan to bring his good friend and fraternity brother John Hope Franklin from North

Carolina College for Negroes to Howard. Logan had confided to Franklin that Tate had earned first dibs on the appointment. Franklin, who knew Tate from her time in North Carolina, conceded that "Merze should have the very first opportunity for a permanent appointment," while detailing his requirements for a move to Howard. When another position in history opened the next year, Franklin was hired.

Both Tate and Logan were among those at Howard who warmly welcomed their mutual friends Aurelia and John Hope when they arrived in 1947. Tate had expressed her professional support for Franklin in 1944 in a long review of his first book, one of the few she would ever review on African American history. In it, she praised him as "a young, brilliant scholar of American history," noting especially the archival work that had gone into his study of free Blacks in North Carolina. That work was "arduous," in part because Franklin had to reckon with the racist restrictions on access to the archives.[30]

Logan's joy at finally making Franklin a Howard colleague was soon overshadowed by a surprising professional disappointment. Wesley had served as both history chair and dean of the graduate school, and Logan had assumed that he too would gain the prestige of the deanship. However, he was passed over in favor of the more senior Charles Thompson, who was serving as dean of the College of Liberal Arts. In Tate's words, not getting the deanship "almost killed Logan" and, in her view, embittered him so deeply that he never got over it. That frustration became one of many that appeared to affect Logan's demeanor in the years ahead. He remained chair of their department for another two decades, until 1964. She had to contend with many shifts in his temperament, including when they shared office space for a time, an arrangement that neither could long endure.[31]

In 1947, Logan had assigned Tate, against her wishes, the task of organizing the social science division's annual conference and editing the volume of its proceedings. At war's end, of special concern to Tate and other Black scholars and political activists was whether the United Nations would engage effectively, or at all, with questions of racial inequality and colonialism. The Howard gathering focused on U.N.-designated trusts and non-self-governing territories. The large audience attending the two-day event heard talks by Du Bois, Max Yergan, the co-founder with Paul Robeson of the Council of African Affairs, and Eleanor Roosevelt, a newly appointed trustee at Howard and a member of the U.N. Commission on Human Rights. Tate prefaced the 127-page printed proceedings with a reminder that African Americans felt a deep "kinship with minorities" everywhere and that Howard's student body included many from Africa, the Caribbean, and Central and South America.[32]

Although she handled the invitations and logistics for the conference, it appears that Tate was not accorded any formal opportunity to speak at the gathering, neither to introduce speakers or to moderate the presentations or discussions. That role was reserved for male colleagues and administrators. Years later, she still complained to her dean, "I have had to do considerable work that should have been carried by the chief," specifically citing the conference, and concluding that "this delegated work relieved the chairman, allowing him time for his varied activities, but limited me in my professional research."[33]

Tate was certainly interested in the topic of the conference and knowledgeable about the mandates and the United Nations. Unlike Du Bois and Logan, she consistently refused to embrace the concepts of "trusteeships" or "mandates" as anything other than externally imposed restrictions on the sovereignty of the countries to which they were applied. That had been her view since the 1930s when she learned about and observed the League of Nations, and she saw little difference with the U.N. approach, which was built on a compromise endorsed by Du Bois and others. Implicit in that concept was acceptance of the notion that African leaders were not yet ready for self-governance or control over their own lands and resources. For her, these concepts were little more than imperialism in disguise.[34]

Tate had her own approach to international thought more generally. When she gave a talk in 1947 at Miners Teachers College in Washington, she first dismissed the conceit of the invitation by declaring that "there is *no* justification for teaching International Relations in any different way in a Negro College from the way it should be taught in a white college." The "only departure that I feel is justified is the constant reminder that the American Negro is only one of many minorities in the world and that his problem is not unique but only one phase of a much larger issue." With that phrasing, Tate aligned herself with the well-known assertion by Du Bois in 1906 that the "Negro problem in America is but a local phase of a world problem." She was convinced that strictly domestic approaches to "the Negro problem" were parochial and ineffectual.[35]

Tate then turned the talk into a theoretical disquisition on international relations and geopolitics in particular. "Power politics," she argued, could only be understood through a multidisciplinary embrace of all of the social sciences, because she found "economics, geography, political science, political philosophy, international law and geopolitics inextricably interwoven" with history:

> One cannot teach 19th and 20th century imperialism, the partitioning of Africa, of Asia, of the Pacific, of the Arctic and Antarctic regions, and the scramble for world markets and spheres of economic penetration without a background of geography. An examination of 19th and 20th century laissez-faire liberalism, leads inevitably to a consideration of the last phases of capitalism and a study of scientific socialism or Marxism; while a history of 20th century Russia and the U.S.S.R. compels one to examine Lenin's great contribution to socialism in deciphering the 'dictatorship of the proletariat' through the device of the soviet.

For Black students who might be interested already in U.S., African, and Caribbean studies, she also urged a broader view of imperialism in India and Asia.[36]

Tate reserved her longest treatment for "geopolitics," a field that captured her imagination because of her fascination since childhood with geography and maps, subjects later central to her training and teaching in global and military history. As she understood it, geopolitics was "primarily concerned with a consideration of the political state in its geographical environment," but, she warned, "the study of neither geography nor political science alone is sufficient for the understanding of geopolitics." Here, she introduced her audience to the work of the Swedish political scientist Rudolf Kjellen. She took care to distinguish the German engagement with the concept, through the Geopolitical Institute at Munich, cautioning that "the German theory of Geopolitics leads to war." But implicit in her presentation was her own conceptualization of something quite different, her concept of an "anti-racist geopolitics" that had been expressed in her talk and article in 1943. The remainder of this speech cautioned about the new demands for military bases in the air age and, more starkly, the dangers of competition over nuclear weapons.[37]

During the war, Tate had expanded her earlier work on disarmament beyond 1907, with a focus on the United States. Her second book, *The United States and Armaments,* was published in 1948 with another subvention secured by Bernice Cronkhite from Harvard's Bureau of International Research. Even in the preface, Tate's authorial voice was more assertive than in her first book, expressing a greater sense of urgency after the ferocious destructiveness of World War II. She made clear that a new arms race of extraordinary proportions and dangers would be the principal outcome of the "peace" that followed World War II. Tate also envisioned that, in order to secure its naval and air strategies, the United States would need to control the Pacific region with strategic air bases, even though many of the islands there were held by other powers.[38]

The nexus of scientific research, technological advance, and new weapons she described predicted what later came to be known as the "military industrial complex," which Tate presented as a cautionary tale for the future. Indeed, one of the hallmarks of Tate's work was her fascination with technologies used by nation-states to establish and maintain power over one another and over their twentieth-century colonial empires.[39] The somber tone of the book reflected her profound sense of pessimism about any prospect for limitation of arms. Although it did not receive as much scholarly review attention as her earlier work, this book would prove to have staying power, and it was reissued with renewed interest twenty years later, in 1969, when attention turned once again to arms limitation.[40]

Tate and her work were well known to two people working closely with UNESCO at that time, Esther Brunauer of the AAUW, who had recommended her to Oxford, and Alfred Zimmern, her adviser there. In 1948, the UNESCO liaison in the State Department invited her to be one of three to represent the United States at a six-week UNESCO summer seminar at Adelphi College, near the U.N.'s temporary headquarters at Lake Success. Tate joined participants from twenty-six other countries at what was primarily a gathering of high school teachers who were each to produce teaching materials on the United Nations and its agencies.[41]

In typical fashion, Tate went her own way and submitted a thirty-page paper titled "The International Control of Atomic Energy: A Vital Problem," in which she argued that prevailing concepts of security and sovereignty would need to be adjusted to avoid destruction and that a new international nuclear control authority was essential. She wrote: "Statesmen must constantly be kept aware that there can be no absolute sovereignty in an atomic world. The word has lost its meaning in an era where the choice is between international cooperation or international disintegration, between world peace or world destruction, between 'the quick and the dead.' " It was neither pitched at the high school level nor on topic, but it was later produced as a UNESCO pamphlet.[42]

In her first decade in Washington, Tate established herself not only as a formidable scholar but as an engaged member of the social and cultural world

Tate at the UNESCO conference in Lake Success, New York, 1948
(Moorland-Spingarn, Howard University)

of Washington's Black educated elite. The National Council of Negro Women called on her to give talks on a variety of contemporary foreign affairs topics and on the place of Black women in history and in the postwar world; she also joined Bethune's group when Eleanor Roosevelt extended an invitation to tea at the White House. She regularly attended the annual meetings of the Association for the Study of Negro History, where she was respected for her expertise in diplomatic history, including on contemporary African politics.

Tate also had been invited to join the Writers' Group, organized in 1941 to meet three times a year to discuss new writing or to host book talks. Among its members were prominent figures such as Otelia Cromwell, Owen Dodson, Georgia Douglas Johnson, and Dorothy Porter. The AKAs in Washington had welcomed her into their chapter; she worked with them on educational programming about the war and civil rights, while still enjoying the social whirl of local and annual national gatherings. She joined one established bridge club, created one of her own, dubbed "The Bridgebuilders," and started to win tournaments.[43]

Tate also socialized frequently with Howard faculty members and their wives, some of whom were also in one of her bridge clubs. Indeed, her vibrant social life depended on her being accepted into circles of married women and men in an era when marriage was a class marker and often an economic necessity for access to the world of the Black educated class. She credited her married women friends with including her in dinner party invitations and other social gatherings, never permitting her to be alone on holidays. Her status as a scholar and a professor at Howard brought her into those circles in Washington, but she had arrived already enmeshed in similar, though smaller, networks when she lived in Indiana and North Carolina.

Her reputation as a scholar spread nationally in this period. The writer Margaret Walker recalls meeting Tate in 1942 at a gathering in New York City to honor Carl Van Vechten after he founded the James Weldon Johnson Collection at Yale. Walker was "impressed by a woman she immediately saw as a model for her future," remembering the many firsts Tate had achieved by then. Others appearing on the printed program included Zora Neale Hurston, Canada Lee, and Alain Locke.[44]

By the end of the 1940s, Tate had spent more time in Washington than in any place since she left Michigan. The city and Howard had become her home base, with Detroit becoming the place where she still had her sister and schoolteacher friends when she returned from her various travels or during the summer and other breaks from work. Her tense relationship with her mother still bore the marks of earlier conflicts, worsened perhaps by long absences.

Of her connection with her father, Tate left little evidence and said nothing in her many later recollections. In 1943, he died in a mental hospital in Ypsilanti. Tate did not attend the funeral, but she did contribute her share of the costs. Decades later, she attributed her absence to being in the first year of a new temporary job at Howard, which she feared losing by missing teaching days to travel. But at some point she also was miffed to find out that her brother, after their father's mental health declined, had arranged for their father's farm to pass solely to him, depriving her of any share in it.[45]

Michigan, however, still mattered deeply to Tate. In 1947, she seemed genuinely touched and humbled when Western Michigan informed her that the school intended to award her an honorary degree. Her excitement about returning to her alma mater and accepting the honor ended up being tempered, and then postponed for a year, when her only nephew, her brother Keith's young son, died in a tragic accident. He was the only child of her immediate family; her two older brothers, her sister, and Tate herself remained childless throughout their lives. Following his death, she became too physically ill to teach summer school at Howard, evidence of how deeply she absorbed the loss, expressed once again psychosomatically, which seemed to be her way of coping with being emotionally overwhelmed.

A year later, in June 1948, she proudly attended graduation in Kalamazoo where she was honored for her achievements, by far the school's most accomplished graduate. The distinction pleased her, and she spoke affectionately of the commitment and care shown her when racial policies prevented her from being able to work in her home state as a high school teacher in 1927. She always remained grateful that faculty loaned her the money to travel to interviews until she found her first job in Indianapolis.

Toward the end of the decade Tate's mind turned to new subjects, stimulated in part by the contours of the war itself. She had tried unsuccessfully in 1947 to get a publisher's support for a "Short Military History," something she had needed for her own teaching. In 1948, she outlined in great detail a project that would trace the imperialistic history and contemporary strategies of the British, the Spanish, the Dutch, the Portuguese, the French, the Germans, the Japanese, and the Americans in the Pacific. She applied for internal funding for the project as well as support from the Rosenwald Foundation, but without success. That did not deter her from arranging with the Library of Congress for a special study space for her to begin gathering research materials.[46]

In the midst of all of this activity, Tate also demonstrated once again her ability to surprise: she turned her attention to creating two inventions, and received a patent for them. Both worked together as an internal mixing unit for electric freezers that would ease the process of making homemade ice cream. "I thought there should be such a thing, and started to see what I could do about it," she later reported. Far from being intimidated by technology, she was drawn to it.[47]

In 1949 she returned to Morgan State to be honored as its commencement speaker. Coming four years after the end of the disruption and the destructiveness of war, her speech strained for optimism and encouragement for the Black student body. "World War II was a continuation of the imperialistic power struggle of World War I, and not a war fought to set all men free," she said. She forecast that the terrain for that struggle had shifted, arguing that "the main field lies in Asia between the firm but advancing Soviet land frontier and the rim of coastal and island bases held by the European powers and the United States." She called for basic human rights for people on the African continent and urged colleges and universities to recruit and train African students as scientists, doctors, engineers.[48]

For her student listeners, she presented the fields of science, technology, and medicine as ripe for the best prepared among them. She argued that the more objective measures of competency in these fields created an opportunity for young Black people to excel, citing prominent Black scientists and medical researchers. Even the nonviolent use of nuclear energy offered possibilities for those trained in physics, mathematics, and chemistry. Not surprisingly, her vision for Morgan's students was a global one, as she encouraged them to consider working on projects in industry and agriculture in "Africa, India, China, Alaska, the Caribbean, and South America."[49]

Her speech serves as a coda and a prelude to her evolving interest in technology and science. She saw those fields of knowledge as tools not just of imperialism, but of international development as well, especially in Africa, which held so many of the raw material and mineral resources needed for modern industrialization. Her insistence was that these natural assets must be held and developed by the people of those lands, a theme that would endure in the work she was to do over the decades to come.

CHAPTER 6

"Roaming in Foreign Lands and Climes"

ENGLAND–EUROPE–EGYPT–INDIA–ASIA–HAWAII, 1950–1951

Wartime travel restrictions had kept Tate from going abroad since her return to the states in 1935, but one of the other consequences of the war was the establishment in 1946 of the Fulbright Fellows program, an initiative to foster scholarly exchanges funded by the proceeds of surplus war property. By 1948, the program was up and running and began to draw applications from scholars, including those at Howard. Two Howard faculty members were part of the Fulbright cohort of 1949: Margaret Just Butcher, a professor of English who went to France, and Frank Snowden, a historian who pioneered the study of Blacks in antiquity and who traveled to Italy. That this new federal program welcomed Black scholars from the beginning was a small but significant sign of changes wrought by Black activism during World War II, which had yielded executive orders banning discrimination in federal funding and segregation in the military. But it also marked an increasing sensitivity that global awareness of racial inequality in the United States might be countered by enabling Black Americans to serve as international representatives of the country.[1]

Tate was quick to apply to the program—first in 1949, apparently without success, and then again in 1950. She wrote on her application that she wanted to be named a lecturer in modern history, American diplomatic history, and political science at the University of Delhi. Her Howard colleague Flemmie Kittrell had already received an award to India at the University of Baroda to help establish a home economics and nutrition program there. Although the external review committee judged Tate to be the best of four history professor candidates for an assignment in India, the first year for the program there, the State Department only named her an alternate for the Fulbright. Undeterred and refusing to take "no," or in this case "maybe," as an answer, she turned to her friend Mary McLeod Bethune, who prodded the State Department to make an award to her.[2]

The award came through on October 4, a week before Tate was already scheduled to leave New York on a planned sabbatical. It was not, as she had wanted, from the university in urban Delhi, but came instead from Rabindranath Tagore's unconventional Visva-Bharati University, located ninety miles north of Calcutta in rural Santiniketan. Howard president Mordecai Johnson and William Stuart Nelson helped secure that invitation for her from the institution they had both visited recently: once again, Tate achieved what she wanted after first being told no.

Tate's Indian hosts also expected her to lecture on the history of African Americans and on the state of race relations in the United States. Since those were not topics she taught or studied, part of her last-minute rushing about included seeking books, articles, and advice from colleagues in that field.[3] Like many Black intellectuals, she resented being seen as only qualified to speak on matters related to race in the United States.

Her hosts had formed their expectations after prominent Black religious intellectuals affiliated with Howard visited India starting in the 1930s. Sue Bailey Thurman and her husband Howard Thurman traveled in India, Ceylon, and Burma in 1935 and 1936 on a "pilgrimage of friendship" sponsored by the Indian Student Christian Mission, which concluded with a visit with Mohandas K. Gandhi. Benjamin Mays, when he had been dean of the School of Religion at Howard before becoming president of Morehouse College, had traveled to India in 1937 and also met with Gandhi. A decade later, Nelson and his social worker wife Blanche had spent a year in Calcutta, in 1946–1947, under the aegis of the American Friends Service Committee; she worked with Muslim girls and he worked with Gandhi to stem violence between Muslims and Hindus after the British decision to partition the country. He had just recently returned to Howard from India again, earlier in 1950.[4]

These earlier visits are often recapitulated as part of the theological and political lineage of the civil rights movement, citing the influence of Mays, Nelson, and Thurman in introducing Gandhian concepts of nonviolence to Martin Luther King, Jr. These religious intellectuals saw in Gandhi a man whose asceticism reminded them of Jesus and whose methods against the British Empire inspired them politically. What is often underappreciated is how important India's fight for independence was for African Americans committed to anti-colonialism, coming as it did well before successful independence movements in continental Africa.

Tate differed in key respects from those affiliated with Howard who had visited India before her. She was a woman traveling alone at a time when that was rare, and rarer still in the regions where she was going. She was not sponsored by any religiously affiliated mission but went as a diplomatic historian under the aegis of a new U.S. education and cultural exchange program. Nevertheless, dutifully responsive to her hosts' requests, she prepared to meet their expectations and still do what she intended—lecture on geopolitics and international affairs and, when required, as they would also request, on Black history and contemporary domestic racial issues. She also traveled with a press pass from the Associated Negro Press, intending to serve as an international political correspondent for Black newspaper readers.

Tate purchased an around-the-world ticket for her first trans-Atlantic flight, allowing her to make many stops between the first one in London and her final destination in India. Her departure from New York on October 11 did not culminate in her arrival in Santiniketan until a month later, on November 9. Among the items she had packed for the trip were her cameras and a small dark green leather notebook embossed in gold lettering that read "Travel Diary," a gift from her friends Aurelia and John Hope Franklin.

The fifteen long, turbulent years that had passed since Tate's time at Oxford brought many changes not only to the world where she studied but to her own personal and professional life. When she traveled back to London in 1950, she saw it through a lens on world affairs sharpened by her habits of research and writing, her experiences as a Black American woman scholar, and her commitment to use her work to inform contemporary debates. Her earlier training in the seat of the British Empire and her travels in prewar Europe had been supplemented at Radcliffe during a time when she was living in the Jim Crow South for the first time. Her deep immersion in African American political culture and intellectual life in Washington had come during the consequential decade of heightened Black activism against segregation and racial inequality.

Tate saw the damage caused by the bombings of World War II and the efforts to rebuild in an exhaustive all-day tour of London before leaving for Paris. At the American Express office, she met four women students from Fisk

University in Nashville on their way to study international relations and languages in Denmark. More importantly, she also encountered Ollie Stewart, the Paris-based Black war correspondent whose articles on Black troops and the Tuskegee Airmen brought their heroic service to public attention. Stewart and Tate were both interested in Black soldiers still serving abroad after President Harry Truman's order in 1948 to desegregate the military.

There were many Black troops in Germany, and that was Tate's next stop. She boarded a train from Gare de l'Est to Frankfurt and then to Kitzingen, where she spent a week in the comfortable home of friends from Washington, Muriel and Lucius Young. He had served with the all-Black 366th Infantry after graduating from Howard, and also taught military science there. Using their home as a base, the couple and other Black families there helped drive Tate to Nuremburg, then Munich, and then through the beautiful Bavarian mountains to Berchtesgaden, the Nazi outpost that was home to "the Eagle's Nest," Hitler's former mountain retreat. Tate was curious to see first-hand the historic relics of a defeated Nazi Germany.[5]

News of a visitor from Washington brought together other Black Americans, who welcomed Tate with gatherings in her honor. Among others, she was entertained by Major Harriet West, one of two Black women to attain the rank of major in the Women's Army Corps during the war and an adviser on racial issues in the military. Her hosts made a point of serving American-style food and good champagne, Tate's favorite alcoholic drink, and their parties ended in the expected way—with bridge-playing. The extended stay in Germany permitted Tate to rest, enjoy the company of old friends, and learn more about the status of Black soldiers stationed there.

Tate reserved the mornings to write, drafting the first of nine long articles that she would publish in Black newspapers during her Fulbright year abroad. She took her press card seriously and used it to create a forum for her own political ideas on race and the military, on international affairs, and sometimes, just for a travelogue.[6]

Her time at Kitzingen inspired her to publish three exposés on abuses against Black soldiers at the installation there, which had been established in 1947 as a segregated base to train all Black soldiers who would later be posted in Europe. In three years, it had trained sixteen thousand Black soldiers and officers. The subject of Tate's reporting was the unnamed white commanding officer, whom she described as a " 'diehard' deeply prejudiced individual with the outmoded, southern conception of the Negro's place." She accused him of enacting policies of "harsh and brutal restrictions, humiliations, and injustices" that were "dictated by hatred of the Negro and contempt" of the Army's own regulations, especially in his overzealous use of the court-martial and his prohibitions on interracial dating.[7]

After detailing his violations of specific Army policies, Tate urged a campaign by the Black press and the NAACP to remove the commanding officer. Three months later, the *Afro-American* reported that the Army was disbanding the "jim crow Army post" at Kitzingen. The paper credited pressure brought from reporting done by Tate, Cliff Mackay, one of its editors, and Ollie Stewart, the war correspondent Tate had met in Paris.[8]

Tate next traveled by air to Rome so she could witness a historic event at St. Peter's Basilica: the Annunciation of the Dogma of the Blessed Virgin Mary. She waited outside the Vatican with a massive crowd of people from all over the world. Once the doors opened, "being a good cross country runner, a country girl with long limbs," she made a dash for a prime location, ending up near the altar from which Pope Pius XII spoke.[9] The long article she wrote for the *Afro-American* cast the scene both in geopolitical and deeply spiritual terms: "Here in St. Peter's was a real United Nations. Former enemies and allies sang and chanted together with only love in their hearts and joy for being present at the ceremony."[10]

The large gathering brought back memories for Tate of 1935 when she had been forced to attend a public rally where Hitler spoke, an event she contrasted with the one in Rome:

> I saw Hitler and [Julius] Streicher froth at the mouth as they worked the crowd into a frenzy of hatred for the Jewish people. Instead of a Christian chant or mass recitation of the Lord's Prayer, there was a Sprach-Choir of a hundred male voices vomiting forth an anti-Jewish credo. In place of the magnificent paintings of Michelangelo were huge placards denouncing the Jews. In place of the spontaneous cheering and waving of the pilgrims was the uniform Nazi salute of the audience as it stood and sang "Deutschland Uber Alles."

Tate explicitly credited the Vatican ceremony with giving her "the spiritual strength" for her trip to India. This is yet more evidence of Tate's evolving religious sensibilities, which included an increasingly comfortable embrace of Catholic culture and history that far exceeded a mere tourist interest in seeing the Vatican, just as had her pilgrimage to Oberammergau on a broken foot in the 1930s.[11]

Tate at the pyramids in Egypt, with Norma Todd and her daughter Cynthia (Moorland-Spingarn, Howard University)

After a brief stop in Athens, Tate headed to Cairo, where she was met on November 1 by a U.S. cultural affairs officer and also by James Todd, the supervisor of the records division at the embassy and one of the earliest Black men to serve in a consulate position. He invited Tate to stay with him, his wife Norma, and their two daughters in the Garden City district of Cairo, opposite the embassy. A delay in her flight plans caused by an airline strike kept Tate in Cairo for four days, allowing her ample time to ride a camel at the Pyramids, visit the Sphinx, and take a trip up the Nile.[12]

Tate's reporting from Cairo stood in sharp contrast to her earlier articles on the treatment of Black soldiers in Germany. She wrote with pride about Todd and his position at the embassy, noting that he and his family had been warmly received by the American and Egyptian diplomatic community, at a time when racial restrictions in the United States made this worthy of comment to Black readers.[13]

Egypt occupied a special place in the imaginations of many Black Americans, including those who had been raised on stories of enslavement and Exodus from the Hebrew scriptures. Accounts of advanced Egyptian civilizations in antiquity also were a source of racial pride and evidence of intellectual and cultural achievement that preceded European developments and civilization claims.

This was also Tate's first visit to a place that did not have a majority white population and that remained under colonial rule, although British troops began to be removed following a coup d'état in 1952. Tate's writing captures the feelings of chaos and the excitement of the juxtapositions she experienced, of ancient and modern, north and south, east and west. She also was attentive to the racial and modernizing space she encountered there:

> On the streets of Cairo one can see all types of people from the jet Black African, the Sudanese, some of whom are members of the distinguished camel corps, the bronze to brown Egyptians, and the fair Teutons. . . . Cairo, a city of contrasts, has museums . . . mosques, and Coptic monuments on every hand, and at the same time wide open squares faced by modern buildings like the one owned by Shell Oil Company.

Traveling with her hosts outside the city, first on and then alongside the Nile, afforded Tate a glimpse of rural peasant life around clusters of mud huts, of shepherds tending sheep and goats "only a short distance from the modern capitol of Cairo."[14]

When Tate traveled to the airport, she left behind the city she described as "Where East Meets West," in the headline to her article. She resumed her journey east toward Delhi, but Cairo had captured her imagination; it was a city she visited twice again in the decades to come.[15]

New Delhi's welcome for Tate was much less auspicious than what had awaited her in Cairo. No one met her at the airport, perhaps because of her repeated flight delays. She spent her first hours in India trying to find a place to stay, ending up at a YWCA. Her meeting the next day at the U.S. consulate's office with Ambassador Loy Henderson was cordial and helpful. But when she went to the office administering the Fulbright program, she discovered that in her excitement about the last-minute award, she had neglected to read its terms. Her acceptance letter clearly stated that hers was a "travel grant" only, meaning that the program paid for her airfare, but did not provide a stipend. Discomfited by the news, Tate immediately dashed off letters to the State Department asking to change her award, which they did after she mentioned that not receiving the full award might be misinterpreted as a mark of racial difference. The State Department relented. In desperation, Tate invoked race to help remedy what had been her own error.[16]

Tate made her departure from Delhi to Calcutta with an escort to the airport from the Fulbright office. A similar courtesy was extended when she arrived in Calcutta and was met by a consulate official and taken to the Great Eastern Hotel. The classic colonial-era hotel, famously referred to as "the Jewel of the East," did not impress Tate, who described it in stark geopolitical terms as little more than a "vestigial remain of British power."[17]

After meetings at the consulate office and long tussles with Indian customs officials over her suitcases, she seemed relieved to set off by train the next day for the ninety-mile trip to Bolphur and then on to nearby Santiniketan, after a month of travel. Tate welcomed her time in the first-class car as the otherwise overcrowded train left behind the bustle of central Calcutta and its busy Howrah station for the countryside of rice fields and small thatched-roof homes. The city of Calcutta would become her travel hub and a place of comfort in the small world of Americans living there, but it was Santiniketan that she called "a second home" by the time she left India in 1951.[18]

The history of Santiniketan is entwined with that of its founder, Rabindranath Tagore, the internationally renowned Bengali-born poet, writer, and philosopher. He came to global notice in 1913 when he became the first non-Westerner to win the Nobel Prize for Literature, but was already a revered figure in India from a prominent family. His exposure to western education left him dissatisfied, and he turned to the project of creating a model that departed from his English-based training, which he found rote, punitive, and distant from Indian culture.

In 1901, he established a school on land his father had acquired to use as an ashram and a retreat from Calcutta. From the start, his vision placed Indian arts, culture, dance, and music at the center of a style of teaching that harkened back to traditional cooperative Indian models that placed the student and the teacher on more equal footing. An immersion in the beauty of the natural world was at the core of his approach, represented there even today in open-air classes (except in the rainy season).

The school was formalized in 1931 as Visva-Bharati, distinguished by its admission of students regardless of sex, nationality, race, creed, religion, caste, or class. The school was embraced by those working for Indian independence; Jawaharlal Nehru sent his daughter Indira to school there for a year in the 1930s, and Gandhi later visited Tagore at the school in 1940. After Tagore's death in 1941, his son Rathindranath became its leader; in 1951, after independence, the college-level program was affiliated with the state-supported University of Calcutta, but preserved its original infrastructure and grounds and its distinctive approach to educating students.[19]

When Tate arrived at the train station in the small town of Bolphur, Anil Chanda, the principal at Visva-Bharati, welcomed her, taking her and her belongings over the two-mile ride to the campus at Santiniketan. Once there, Chanda took her directly to a simple one-story building that housed four visiting scholars in separate rooms. On her first day, Rathindranath and his wife Pratima Tagore invited her to Uttarayan, their on-campus home. They hosted a tea with Chanda and another visiting professor, sitting on their veranda overlooking the beautiful gardens. It was an ideal start because her social and intellectual life there would revolve around conversations with faculty and the steady stream of visitors to Santiniketan from around the world.[20]

Tate's first impressions of the new surroundings go unnoted in her diary. Her entries moved from a tentative "unpacked trying to get used to my new home" to the willed certainty of "feeling at home." But when a State Department official in New Delhi later wrote to see how she was doing, Tate typed him a letter on Visva-Bharati letterhead describing her warm welcome while also detailing her living conditions in very blunt terms:

> My room, which has a cement floor, is furnished with a wardrobe, a desk, a book rack, and a bed made of seven nice hard boards covered with a mattress one-quarter of an inch thick. . . . The windows have no glass, only bars and blinds which, of course, when closed admit no light or air. Insects, lizards, mice, etc., come and go, mostly come.[21]

Her letter listed several small things that would improve her living conditions (mosquito netting, a small stove to cook and to heat water, a reading lamp, and curtains), but her overall tone was polite gratitude, not complaint. "Much more significant are the historic, international, intellectual, and spiritual aspects of Visva-Bharati," she wrote. "I consider myself very fortunate to have been invited here, to be among those privileged to have been invited here, to be among those privileged to reside in Rabindranath Tagore's abode of peace."[22]

To her credit, Tate voiced no public criticisms or complaints about the physical challenges of living in Santiniketan, either then or later. Her austere rural childhood in Michigan may have best prepared her for the isolation of Visva-Bharati. Her adaptability and embrace of Santiniketan earned her special respect there. "The few Americans who have lectured here and at other Indian institutions," she reported, "it is alleged, arrived by motor car, delivered their lecture, perhaps stopped for tea, hastened away to catch a T. W. A. or Pan American plane for the United States, and then wrote a book on India."[23]

The campus library still holds evidence of Tate's presence there. The college's official paper of record, the *Visva-Bharati News,* printed a long, laudatory description of her "brilliant record of academic success," referring to her as "Dr. Miss Merze Tate." The article also captured the complex expectations visited upon her during her time in India, based not on gender but on color, race, and nationality. It noted that Tate was to teach modern European history, international relations, and diplomatic history, but that she delivered her inaugural lecture on "Negroes in America." What she said in the lecture was described neither in the article or by Tate, and for sure the topic would not have been her first choice. But the interest in African American history had been made clear to her before she arrived and that sentiment prevailed.[24]

Tate continued to be integrated into the social and cultural life at Visva-Bharati. She had come to appreciate the sophistication of the faculty there, calling them "the most distinguished scholars in India" and noting in particular her admiration for the influential artist Nandalal Bose. Lectures by visiting scholars were frequently followed by tea or dinner, as visitors from Turkey, Calcutta, Indonesia, Tibet, and China passed through during her first few weeks. Not unlike at Howard, the Faculty Wives club invited her to join their frequent social gatherings, often dinners with especially delicious meals (unlike the food served by the college) and lively conversation. Ranee Chanda and her husband Anil often had her join them for meals in their home, along with a visiting teacher from France, a woman who lived in the same faculty compound as Tate.[25]

Tate's arrival during Diwali, the festival of lamps, commemorating the new moon of Kartik, delayed the start to her teaching until after her inaugural lecture, but when she began to offer a twice weekly seminar in international relations, it proved to be a popular and well-attended class. Most of her students were political and social science majors in their third and fourth years. Equipped with maps and extensive visual aids that she had brought with her, Tate's skills as an excellent teacher attracted not only students but also staff and other faculty members who came by, she said, "to see the show." Tate's quick engagement with the community in Visva-Bharati earned her notice and praise in the institution's annual report: "We could have hardly made a happier choice. Dr. Tate has been conducting regular classes in International

Relations and History and her lectures have proved very popular with teachers and students interested in the subject."[26]

Tate's accounts of her extended stay permit an insider's glimpse of aspects of Indian religious and cultural life rare for an American visitor, joining in evenings of outdoor music, going to a moonlight picnic with her students, and sitting in a glass mandir, or temple, for a divine service. The cultural highlight of Tate's first term included not only Diwali but the annual Visva-Bharati convocation festivities, which drew twelve thousand dignitaries and visitors from villages near and far. Driven to write as a way to process what she encountered, her rich descriptions capture the energy and excitement of the three-day celebration:

> There were scholarly meetings and teas and two musical soirees at the Tagore home. Village dances, dramas, and music went on in the open air without respite for three days and nights. A fireworks display took place on two evenings. There was a merry-go-round and a ferris wheel made of wood and propelled by human power. At night the steps of Scholars Block where I reside were covered with sleeping villagers who used the flower beds for a W.C. Ox dung was everywhere but, of course, carefully gathered, shaped into pancakes, and dried for fuel. The whole affair was a big event and jolly good fun.

It may have been fun, but in her private travel diary, she also noted, perhaps more tellingly, "Dancing and music continuous. Head swimming."[27]

On Christmas Day, Tate joined thousands making their way out of Santiniketan after the festivities ended. She struggled through the crush of the large departing crowd at nearby Bolphur station and "succeeded in being pushed into a first-class carriage of the Calcutta Express," where twenty-eight passengers traveled in a space intended for six, "but," she reported, "we managed." She arrived safely and in time for Christmas tea and dinner in Calcutta with Elizabeth and Wilson Hume; he was executive secretary of the YMCA operations in India, Ceylon, Burma, and Pakistan. Their spacious house set back in a gardened courtyard at 5 Russell Street was in the heart of Calcutta's "White Town," which also included the American consulate office and the nearby shopping and restaurant district on Park Street.[28]

But she was not long to stay in Calcutta, as she intended to spend the break between Visva-Bharati's terms doing what she loved best: traveling. Her obsession with seeing as much as possible would take her all over India, including many regions rarely visited by Americans. Some of the highlights of her travels afford a glimpse of the worlds she was encountering and the post-independence political period she was witnessing.[29]

Tate's first flight took her to Nagpur, in the Deccan plateau, where she boarded a train for Wardha to be driven to Sevagram, where she spent two days at Gandhi's ashram. He had been assassinated just two years earlier, which created a haunting absence. But his earlier visits with African American theologians and religious scholars Johnson and Nelson remained strong in the memories of those who welcomed Tate. "At both Sevagram and Wardha I had to speak on the Negro in America and sing Negro spirituals. President Johnson and Dean Nelson visiting before me made my lot extremely difficult in India," she noted wryly in her diary.

The emotive power of Black religious music, especially the spirituals, is undeniable; one of its first formal performances in India came during a visit by the Fisk Jubilee Singers in the late 1890s. Indian visitors to the United States would have been exposed to the tradition too, and certainly by the time of Tate's arrival in the 1950s, recordings and radio broadcasts had brought the music to international attention. Sue Bailey and Howard Thurman sang "Were You There When They Crucified My Lord?" at Gandhi's request when they had visited in the 1930s. But when the Nelsons visited, they had refused to sing, and instead they read hymn lyrics aloud. Tate was not immersed in the Black church milieu as were those who preceded her, but she tried to politely comply with the requests of her hosts.[30]

Tate left Wardha on an overnight train trip to Aurangabad, where she stayed in the posh Nizam State Hotel. Renewed, she walked all over the city and then took a bus tour of the historic and visually spectacular Buddhist caves at Ellora and Ajanta. She also found time to shop in the showrooms of a local silk factory and bargained for a dark red sari.[31] Off on yet another overnight train journey, the austerity of Santiniketan and of Gandhi's ashram receded even further as she made her way to Hyderabad, a place she called "the rich Muslim city on the Deccan." She was welcomed there on New Year's Day and hosted by the family of Nawab Mehdi Nawaz Jung, a prominent Indian official, who lived in the "the Beverly Hills of Hyderabad," Tate's analogy for the Jubilee Hill section of the city.[32]

Certainly food was one of the clearest indicators for Tate of the vast differences in status, caste, and privilege that she encountered in India, but so were certain other Western social conventions. "At the Secunderabad Club duplicate bridge was played," she explained, and "the hosts and the guests were

Tate in India, center on the couch, 1951 (Moorland-Spingarn, Howard University)

nawabs, rajas, chief ministers, members of India's United Nations delegation, directors of banks, railway lines, airlines, officers in the army, etc." However polite a guest Tate proved to be, she did not hold back in the game she loved and played competitively; she and her partner won every rubber. Though she does not say it, she was likely the only woman playing, as the game there was largely the province of men.[33]

From Hyderabad, Tate flew to Bangalore, known, as she noted, as "the garden city of India."[34] She gave a public lecture on the evening of January 4 to an overflowing audience of more than two hundred people at the Indian Institute of Culture, sponsored by the University of Mysore. She had been asked to speak on "Negro Life and Culture." In her private diary, she described how she once again "had to sing Negro Spirituals."[35]

A train trip to Mysore for two days made for what Tate described as the "most exciting part" of her first extended travel in India. But what she was captivated by was the transformed beauty of Mysore into the "City of Lights," as it had come to be known. She traveled to "Krishnaraj Sagar (a great hydroelectric and irrigation project)" and stayed at a modern hotel overlooking the dam and exquisite Brindavan Gardens, acres of colorfully illuminated fountains, accompanied by music. She was enchanted by the scene, which to her surpassed Versailles.

The combination of technology and beauty seemed almost to have overwhelmed her keen visual sensibilities even on a trip full of so many other architectural and natural wonders. But she also saw the scientific development as key to what she hoped could "happen all over India in a decade or so," that the brilliantly illuminated villages "wreathed in a chain of lights" might serve as a model for bringing electricity to more villages throughout India.[36]

Once back in Bangalore, Tate flew on to Madras where she stayed with Indian government officials and was entertained at luncheons and dinners. There was "good and tasty food" and the "conversation on politics and government problems was always spicy and enlightening." She did observe the posting of guards to protect against uninvited communists, which her hosts informed her were "rather vociferous in South India."[37]

Tate also met with Mildred and Lawrence Burr from Chicago; she referred to him in a letter as "a colored American serving in the Y.M.C.A." who has "made a fine reputation in India." The Burrs had been sent to India in 1946, so by the time Tate met them, he had with great difficulty established his work with the poorest boys, many of whom lived on the streets. Tate dispatched an article to the *Afro-American* that lauded Burr's work and leadership in South Asia.[38]

After a period of rest, recovering, and writing at Santiniketan, she left by train to Benares for two months of travel across India, and later to Ceylon (now Sri Lanka) and Burma (now Myanmar). Her first stop was at Benares Hindu University, where she delivered two lectures, both on the subject she came prepared to teach: the meaning and scope of geopolitics. Welcomed by members of the departments of political science, history, and geography, she proudly reported that she drew four hundred or more to each of her lectures. After the lectures, she toured the ancient Buddhist capital Sarnath, then on to Lucknow, the capital of Uttar Pradesh.

The next day she delivered a lecture titled "Negro Family Life" at Isabella Thoburn College and met faculty from the University of Lucknow, despite feeling unwell and suffering from fever and digestive distress. An overnight train took her on to Delhi where she stayed at a Quaker center, but with worsening health, she agreed to receive cholera injections. Tate regained strength enough to resume sightseeing and bargaining for gifts, including a Kashmir shawl and more scarves. An early train to Agra the next day brought her to the architectural magnificence of the historical Agra Fort and the Taj Mahal, where she spent a "restful and easy afternoon" and later returned to see it by moonlight.[39]

Over ten days of travel and sightseeing, Tate had moved through such a vast and dizzying array of spiritual, political, and historical sights and experiences that it is difficult to imagine how she processed all she was seeing and feeling. After a full day and night of writing and resting in Delhi, she boarded an overnight train for a long ride across western India, destined for Baroda (Vadodara). There she had tea with her Howard colleague Flemmie Kittrell at the University of Baroda and met some faculty members, but did not lodge with her, opting instead for a government guest house where she was able to catch up on her writing.

She headed off by train again, this time to Bombay (Mumbai) on India's far west coast. She met with faculty at the University of Bombay, "several Rotarians," and "numerous missionaries." India's largest city and the frenzied travel schedule seemed to exhaust her, and by the end of three days there she was only able to write in her diary: "quite tired."[40]

Exhausted or not, she rallied in time to make her February 27 flight from Bombay to Madras, the city she had first visited in January, but this time she had been invited to address the geography department at the University of Madras. Over the course of her stay, she lectured on the topics she felt most well trained and eager to do: "Meaning and Origin of Geo-Politics," "Lessons of Geo-Politics," and "Factors of World Power." She found the city, and especially its Marina Beach, beautiful, and she seemed happy for the privacy of staying at the Ambassador Hotel. She also had time for another conversation with Lawrence Burr, whom she had met on her earlier visit.

The extended travel was taking a toll on Tate, and she began having difficulty hearing because her ears had not recovered from a recent flight. That did not stop her from leaving India on March 4 for Ceylon, flying from Madras to Columbo. In Horana, she lectured at Sri Palee College, a school founded by Wilmot Perera, whose fortune had come from rubber and tea estates and production. The family hosted Tate overnight and drove her back to Colombo, where news of her visit generated a press conference, a radio interview at the Air Ceylon broadcasting station, and many meetings, luncheons, and teas, including with educators at the University of Ceylon and at a women's Methodist college.

A press report of Tate's visit to Ceylon captured attempts to categorize the visiting American woman professor. Noting that the "Negro Professor is expert on international affairs, cooking and bridge," the *Times of Ceylon* also emphasized that "cooking is one of versatile Professor Tate's many interests," that she was an expert on Chinese cooking, and had won awards for her "Lemon-lime-

Tate at a lecture in Rangoon, 1951 (Moorland-Spingarn, Howard University)

pineapple chiffon pie." The newspaper also reported that Tate was an avid traveler who liked to "see the sights for herself. She is a keen photographer and carries two rather expensive cameras with her."[41]

Burma also had always been one of Tate's intended destinations while in India, just as it had been for Sue Bailey Thurman and Howard Thurman during their visit in the 1930s. With help from the United States attaché to Burma, Tate was accorded courtesies that she very much appreciated and believed she was entitled to receive. It also meant that her visit was well publicized beforehand, generating a nonstop schedule of dinners, lunches, and teas in her honor. The local newspapers ran extensive coverage of her talk in the U.S. Information Service library, from which one can glean both the level of excitement over hosting a "distinguished American Negro educator" and the content of her lecture.

Under the title "Geopolitics: Definition and Scope," Tate introduced the concept of geopolitics as one of the newest ways of thinking about international relations and foreign affairs. As she often did when discussing the topic, she warned away from German misappropriation of the term. She emphasized instead certain predictions based on its concepts, including the centrality of base acquisitions for military superiority in an air age, the growing importance of regional economic agreements, and the rise of coalitions of small nations against the threat of any single large national power.

In her view, studying geopolitics could aid in pursuit of peaceful solutions instead of only being invoked in pursuit of war. One reporter explained that Tate's analysis covered more than geography or political shifts: "Changing technologic conditions would also alter the situation, particularly in the exercise of power, because advances in the speed of communication and in the techniques of industry would necessarily cause variations in the power position of particular countries." This presentation captures her ongoing theorizing about the relationship between technological advances and international political imbalances.[42]

Tate spent early April in Santiniketan, beginning preparations for her departure from Visva-Bharati as the term neared its end. She had time with her friends and colleagues but busied herself largely with writing her valedictory lecture, "An Alien Looks at India," although its content remains a mystery.

Tate apparently remained very popular with her hosts in Santiniketan. The *Visva-Bharati News* reported that the officials, staff, and students gathered to give her a warm sendoff: "Miss Tate has endeared herself to everyone by her charming manners during her stay at Santiniketan, which she described as her 'second home' in her farewell address. We wish all success to her in future life." Elsewhere in the paper, among a list of new books added to the Visva-Bharati Central Library were those that Tate had contributed when she left: several American diplomatic history and international studies texts alongside Gunnar Myrdal's *American Dilemma* and Rayford Logan's *The Negro and the Post-War World,* reminders once again of the bifurcated nature of her Fulbright year's intellectual legacy. Those books remain still in the college's catalog.[43]

In the clearest evidence of the Tagore family's fondness and respect for Tate, they invited her to escape the summer heat of West Bengal by visiting their mountain retreat in the village of Mongpu in the hills of Darjeeling, what she called Tagore's "retreat from his retreat." Nestled in the Himalayas near the Nepal and Tibet borders, the location offered Tate respite, quiet good company during her week-long visits away from both the temperatures and the exorbitant pace of her usual traveling schedule.

At the very end of her time in India, Tate's extended excursion to the cooling weather of Kashmir brought her most important political encounter in

India. When she had visited Rangoon, Tate and Adeline Babbit, one of the Fulbright scholars who had hosted her, discovered that they both wanted to visit Kashmir, so they agreed to make the trip together. Flying into Kashmir was tricky and often delayed by snow even when temperatures in Delhi hit 100 degrees. When they flew into the narrow mountain passage to the Kashmir valley, she later wrote, "it looked like the wings would scratch the edge of the pass" as the plane began its dramatic descent.

Once they arrived at Dal Lake, Tate and Babbit rented a houseboat, which became Tate's home for six weeks, and Babbit's for a month. The two women settled into the leisurely life in the large community of boats on the lake, served by merchants paddling up to them and selling their wares. She and Babbit spent their days exploring the floating gardens or the beautiful terraced gardens along the lake, and taking excursions on narrow waterways off the lake. Tate was able to read and write, too, during what was one of the more restful and happiest periods of her time in India. Her friendship with Babbit, who was based in Hawaii, would endure over the decades to come.[44]

Avoiding the heat of India by traveling into its highlands was a luxury, although a popular one for tourists like Tate as well as for India's elite families. On her flight, she had noticed an elegant, beautifully dressed woman smiling at her across the aisle, looking as if she wanted to speak. Tate took the initiative, politely prompting this exchange: " 'Madame, you remind me so much of your ambassador, Madame Pandit in Washington, D.C.' She smiled. She said, 'I'm her sister.' And I said, 'Well, we entertained her at Howard and she received a degree at my university.' " The ambassador to the United States from India was Vijaya Lakshmi Pandit, whom Howard had awarded an honorary degree to in 1949, and later became the first female president of the United Nations General Assembly. Tate's conversation was with her younger sister Krishna Nehru Hutheesing, a writer who, along with her husband, Gunottam, had been jailed during the fight for Indian independence.

The sisters' brother was Jawaharlal Nehru, the prime minister of India, who later also flew in for Kashmir Day celebrations, bringing his daughter Indira with him. The family spent the day with the governor on a large boat moored in the middle of the lake. Their presence generated a great deal of excitement, including in Tate, who was able to take many photographs of the prime minister water skiing off the back of a speedboat.

Relying on her *Afro-American* press card, Tate gained access to the formal events to be held that evening in Srinagar, succeeding in getting seats for Nehru's speech, which she received in advance in English and Hindi. At the dinner that followed, Tate found herself seated next to Indira, with whom she conversed during the meal, including about Santineketan. She quickly dispatched an article to the *Afro-American* detailing Nehru's speech about unsettled political relations with Kashmir. She described his temperament as that of "a friendly and gracious man" and "a scholar, a statesman, and an idealist," explicitly rejecting notions that he was a "rabble-rouser" by way of defending his position of Cold War neutrality.[45]

Tate returned to Calcutta in July and prepared for her final departure from India and went through a round of farewell luncheons, teas, and dinners, sponsored by the U.S. consulate and by Indian, English, and American acquaintances in Calcutta. When she left, she also received a friendly sendoff from "the immigration, customs, health and currency control officials at Dum Dum Airport," men who had come to know her very well through her frequent flights in and out.[46]

Her departure on July 23 was far more decorous than her arrival in Delhi nine months earlier, for she had been accorded "V.I.P" status and was assisted personally through each administrative stage at the airport. After all she had seen and done, the usually composed Tate seemed emotionally overwhelmed to be leaving India and starting the homeward leg of her journey.

> When at last the time came to board the plane, when we walked out to the designated gate, I beheld an unaccustomed sight. Looming before us in the 23:30 o'clock darkness were gleaming white steps with glittering gold letters spelling out at the top NEW YORK and descending on the back of each step the words: LONDON, ISTANBUL, BEIRUT, KARACHI, DELHI and CALCUTTA. In the utter exhaustion from a grueling day, the first dazzling words, "NEW YORK," dazed me. Was it true that after ten months of roaming in foreign lands and climes that I would again return to my country, even if flying away from it in the opposite direction? Would this swift twentieth century method of transportation bring me safely home? For an instant I stood transfixed. Then the young Indian by my side inquired: 'Did you forget something?' This question brought me back to reality and I moved forward to mount the white and gold steps for home.

Aboard the Pan American Clipper Yankee Ranger, Tate found herself enthralled by the "cross section of the world" represented among the passengers on the flight. In that moment, she imagined herself as part of an international, cosmopolitan traveling public. Early commercial international flying was still a novelty and conjured an intimacy and passenger familiarity later lost as the number and size of flights expanded. But getting "home" would have to wait until after Tate's planned stops in Asia, which added another six weeks to her time away from the United States.[47]

Usually a very calm traveler, Tate was quite anxious as her flight headed toward Bangkok. In her rush to leave Calcutta, she had not had time to inquire about a visa. Luckily, once she reached out to the Fulbright program office in Bangkok, an old friend whom she had studied with at Radcliffe, Ambhorn Japhani Meesook, instantly recognized Tate's name. Meesook had recently left her position in the Thai Ministry of Education to work with the new Fulbright program.[48] After Tate's plane landed, the American consulate and Fulbright offices in Bangkok arranged for her to be treated as a "V.I.P." on the receiving end of her trip.[49]

Through a constellation of connections, Tate found that her time in the bustling international city of Bangkok was filled with a busy schedule of meetings with educators and scholars, outings for music and entertainment, and daily luncheons, teas, cocktail parties, and dinners in her honor. Having become accustomed to the limited food choices in India, she was palpably enthusiastic about the quality, quantity, and diversity of Thai cuisine.

Tate met with Fulbright teachers and scholars as well as Thai educators and professors. She delivered lectures on Santiniketan to the Siamese Association of University Women at Chulalongkorn University and to teenage girls at the Wattana Wittaya Academy and presented a slide show on her travels to the YWCA. The topics of geopolitics and "the American Negro," staples of her time in India, did not seem to be among those requested or offered. Her hosts in Thailand did not have expectations about Black American visitors, probably because there had been so few.

Guided sightseeing by her many hosts, featuring a private tour of the Royal Palace, took Tate to many of the city's most beautiful temples, including Wat Arun and Wat Po, the gigantic Sleeping Buddha, the Courts of One Thousand Buddhas, the Temple of the Emerald Buddha. She spent a day on a boat exploring the many small residential canals off the Chao Phya River, culminating with a stop at the Royal Boat landing, which housed the colorful, elongated, ornate, glistening gold boats reserved for royal ceremonies.[50] Tate attributed the vibrancy of Thailand and its people to the fact that it had not suffered the foreign subjugation or colonization that India and other countries had.

Always eager for new travel opportunities, Tate extended her planned ten days in Thailand for another week so she could fit in a weekend trip to Angkor Wat, the abandoned ancient temple compound deep in the Cambodian jungle. She joined a group of travelers who chartered a small plane for a weekend flight for the three-hundred-mile trip. There she explored the twelfth-century architecture enclosed by a rectangular moat, which reflected the carvings and colors of its enormous sandstone walls containing both Hindu and Buddhist motifs. Tate was transfixed by the remote four-hundred-acre site, especially its sculptures and buildings with "saffron-robed Buddhist priests" treading from "one chamber of worship to another."[51]

The vastness and complexity of the architecture, set down in the middle of an impenetrable jungle, stunned Tate, who appreciated it as both an artistic and a technological achievement of an advanced ancient non-Western civilization: "In its glory it was perhaps the largest city in the world. Rome had fallen, Paris was a village, London only a 'mart of traders'; Angkor rivaled Carthage in size and population and Babylon in might." Even for the well-traveled Tate, the majesty of Angkor offered deeper lessons: "Here, in one of the remotest spots on earth, one of the world's greatest civilizations left behind it not the riches, jewels, pomp and grandeur of the rulers, but the warmth, ingenuity, artistry, beauty and philosophy of its people impressed into enduring monuments of stone." Tate's juxtaposition of the architectural wonder and genius of those who built Angkor with western cities reflected an anti-colonial critique similar to the one that Aimé Césaire later made in 1955 about the cultural achievements of the Vietnamese before the arrival of the French.[52]

At the time of Tate's visit, Cambodia was in transition to independence from its former status as a protectorate. Tate was critical of the jarring presence of French colonialism, represented even in the group's lodging in Le Grand Hotel, where the "graceful entrance resembles the approaches to chateaux in the Rhone valley." The architecture of this, "a spot as French as any in France," with luxury products on sale, and "the dinners of seven and eight courses with three or four meat plates," contrasted starkly with what she had seen even in the best hotels in India. "Chic French women in parties that had come to Angkor from Saigon," she wrote, "were startling to eyes accustomed to staid English women, missionaries and simply dressed Americans in India, Ceylon, Burma and Thailand."[53]

Two years later, in 1953, Cambodia would free itself from over a century of French rule. Only then would the country regain control over this commanding example of Khmer architecture, a heritage site that was so valued that it remained on the country's flag through shifting regimes as it still does today.

After her return to Thailand from Cambodia, Tate moved on to her next destination on August 9, flying to Singapore where she lodged at the Fort Canning Street YWCA. Once again, Tate's travel observations are laced with her analysis of the particular kind of imperial vestiges she found there, this time British rather than French. Overall, Tate found the city a disappointment because it so resembled a "western metropolis and might well be in England or western Europe," offering nothing unique or distinctive to her well-traveled eyes. "After visiting fabulous Siam," she noted, "this 217 square mile island seemed drab and colorless, hardly worth a reel of Kodachrome film."[54]

Tate lectured at a business and women's professional club, which in turn generated dinner and sightseeing invitations. Absent the rich social calendar in Bangkok, Tate took many of her meals at the YWCA, and was especially disappointed by the lingering British influence on the menus there. "Here in lush, tropical Singapore, the spice depot and entrepot of the world," Tate observed, "in an institution with Malayan and Chinese cooks, the watery stew, the insipid vegetables, and the flat omelette might just as well have been prepared in dreary London or Liverpool. . . . The British Government may be retreating politically, the British Empire may be crumbling, but wherever Britannia reigns or has reigned, John Bull still impresses indelibly upon the cuisine."[55]

The YWCA was unusual in other respects, as Tate found herself the only American there: most of the rest of the women were not tourists but stenographers or clerical workers on salaries so limited that they could not afford to live elsewhere—most even returned there for lunch. She found herself intrigued by the world of women she encountered daily: "The residents were English, Scotch, Irish, Australian, Canadian, Indian, Pakistani, Ceylonese, Burmese, Malayan, Chinese, Indonesian, Guinian, Jamaican, French-Indo-Chinese, Japanese, and various mixtures of all these, such as Anglo-Indian, Anglo-Chinese, Anglo-Malayan, and Franco-Chinese."

She observed that in the voluntary seating arrangement in the dining room the white British gathered at one table and none of the others ever crossed to it. Tate analyzed this arrangement in global political terms:

> The Malayans, Chinese, Indians, Indo-Chinese, and Ceylonese always sat at a middle table and formed certainly the most interesting, fascinating, and 'colourful' group. (I choose this table.). Anglo-Malayans and Anglo-Indians, like in society, had no particular place and scattered themselves about the room.

In this seating, Tate saw reminders of a pattern she knew all too well from her home country, here reflecting persistent divisions in the region.[56]

When Tate boarded the Pan American Clipper "Kit Carson" en route to Manila on the night of August 12, she called herself a "weary pilgrim." The half-full flight allowed for a restful night on her sleeperette. As she drew the curtains around her, she realized that she was the only woman passenger on board.[57]

Once she arrived, she lectured at the Philippine Woman's College and at the Philippine Christian College and also met with several Fulbright scholars living in the city. Manila had suffered the effects of bombardment during the war, but evidence of reconstruction and rehabilitation was now plentiful. Tate saw this development as an indication of the country's growing economic dependency on the United States, and she feared long-term dangers in this for the Filipino people. She noted especially the consequences of the Trade Act of 1946, which included a stipulation "that puts American citizens on a footing of equality with Philippino [*sic*] citizens in the acquisition of title to land and the right to engage in exploitative and industrial activity."[58]

Tate astutely observed that this conferred on the United States even greater economic power, compounded by military bases on the islands. She recognized how the bases there and elsewhere would be a key component of American-style imperialism, a prescient analysis of the centrality of military bases to U.S. international expansion. This would not have been news to Tate or other Americans with military family members who served, then and now, on bases around the globe.[59]

Tate observed that "American businessmen, advisers, industrialists, and experts" were already a dominating presence, and not a positive one. "One characteristic of Americans has made such a deep impression on the Filipinos," she reported, "that they use the appellation 'American' for any intoxicated man whether European, American, Oriental or Filipino." She spoke of the Philippines as a "young devastated republic" with several competing internal claimants on its political future, including the Hukbalihap ("People's Army Against the Japanese") Movement, which had opposed both the Japanese and the landowning class during the war. The group had been labeled and dismissed as communist, but Tate cautioned that "the peasants themselves know little of Marxism. They are simply men sick of exploitation and injustices and they do not care what outsiders call their leaders."[60]

Tate traveled next to Japan, after a stopover in Hong Kong where she stayed just long enough to be hosted at a luncheon by an American cultural affairs official and to change into her more formal traveling suit before being ferried to the airport for the flight to Tokyo. Tate had secured an invitation to visit occupied Japan from a Howard colleague who was on a Fulbright at Utsunomiya University. She also had a contact on General Douglas MacArthur's staff, a woman who had facilitated a visit by a group of Japanese women to Washington where they were hosted at Howard by Tate. These business and professional women returned the favor and kept her busy touring Tokyo, seeing Kabuki theater, and having tea.[61]

Although she had a long list of Black soldiers serving there, they were prevented from hosting her due to severe housing shortages, but she was able to see some of them. Among them was Major John Martin of the Japan Logistical Command headquarters, whose family took care of her between visits to Gifu, Osaka, and Kyoto. Just as she had done in Germany when she visited Black troops, Tate wrote an article for the *Afro-American* detailing what she saw as racially motivated mistreatment in Japan. In this case, she brought attention to Lieutenant Colonel Harold Lofton, who had been passed over as post commander, a slight that was eventually rectified later.[62]

Spending time in Hawaii had always been part of Tate's plan for her Fulbright year. Babbitt's friendship also paved the way for an invitation to address the Hawaii Pan-Pacific Women's Association, a group dedicated to educating and improving the status of women across the Pacific Islands and in mainland Asia.[63]

But it was the presence of Black military families that provided an avenue for Tate to more fully explore Hawaii. It was there that she met the Thompson family, Allen and Frances, husband and wife, who both were young Black military officers, he in the Army and she a nurse, first in the Navy and later the Army. Having spent time in the Washington area, they eagerly welcomed news of a professor visiting from Howard. It was with their help, especially from Frances, that in just four days in the islands, Tate frenetically saw as many of them as possible.[64]

Like Tate, Frances had what she calls the "travel bug," shaped by her father's vivid recollections of his service abroad in World War I. Shared experiences of seeing the world and living in other cultures gave Tate and the Thompsons much in common at a time when access to international travel was far more limited than it is today. They would form one of her closest and longest friendships in the decades to come, bonding as deeply as family.[65]

Hawaii was her final stop before returning to the west coast of the United States. Arriving from Asia rather than the United States led her to conclude that the Hawaiian islands, often referred to as a crossroads in the Pacific, remained far more eastern than western, and in ways quite different from Cairo, where she had written about "East meeting West" at the start of her Fulbright year. Indeed, it was her time visiting the islands that convinced Tate that the comprehensive study of imperialism in the Pacific she had proposed in 1948 could start at home. She would focus on the history of the U.S. conquest of Hawaii, which she marked not at its annexation, but earlier, in the 1820s, when New England missionaries arrived.

That epiphany would lead her into an extraordinary period of intellectual exploration of Hawaii and, eventually, the wider southwestern Pacific region, including Australia and New Zealand, and beyond. Her extensive travels through war-torn Europe to Cairo and throughout India and Asia equipped her with a nuanced understanding of the consequences of the presence of British, French, and United States governments and corporations in those regions.

In those and other ways, her exhaustive on-the-ground travel experiences and interactions with an unusually wide variety of people shaped her international thought. Her time abroad reinforced her rejection of an overly simplistic anti-communist Cold War politics, and her embrace of the complex histories of imperialism in India, Hawaii, Asia, and the Pacific, including among those external nations then posturing for power in those regions. Tate's Fulbright year also kindled her thinking about the need for an expansive unifying theoretical intervention examining the links between race and the ever-evolving technologies of modern imperialist expansion.

Her extensive written accounts of her time away and her itinerary are exhausting even in abbreviated form. One can only imagine how physically, mentally, and emotionally demanding the trip was for a forty-six-year-old woman traveling alone in regions where the familiar comforts of home were often lacking. The year stands as a testament to her intellect, courage, and toughness. Tate's time abroad owed itself to her willingness to study and embrace cultural differences and to depend gracefully on the hospitality of strangers.

Tate, center, on her return to Washington from her Fulbright year abroad, 1951 (Moorland-Spingarn, Howard University)

Tate also had skillfully exploited the privileges of being an American traveling under official U.S. sponsorship of a nascent Fulbright program. This came at a time when fundamental privileges of citizenship were still denied her and other Black citizens at home. She experienced this as a fact and not a mere irony.

When Tate's Pan Am flight landed in Los Angeles on September 10, a group of her AKA sorors met her at the airport to welcome her back to her home country and her familiar networks of Black American women after nearly a year's journey around the world. She lingered long enough to be feted by and to give a talk to members of the local chapter of "The Links," the Black women's social service organization.[66]

She then took a flight across the continental United States, breaking her journey in Detroit where she saw her sister and brother, and also gave a talk to the local chapter of her sorority, Alpha Kappa Alpha. When she arrived in Washington, she was met by friends at the airport and was later welcomed back by Mordecai Johnson, Howard's president. Tate had arrived just in time for the new academic quarter. She would then experience the tumultuous world of 1950s international and domestic racial and gender politics, viewed from her home in Washington and on the campus of Howard University, but now informed by an extraordinary year of travel that she always claimed was a highlight of her life.[67]

CHAPTER 7

"Challenges of Our Age"

WASHINGTON, 1951–1958

Dressed in her full academic regalia, with her distinctive white ermine hood from Oxford, Tate processed side by side with Flemmie Kittrell into Howard's Rankin Chapel for the official opening of the 1951–1952 academic year on October 9. Mordecai Johnson, the university's president, told the audience that Howard was a "world-minded center of intellect and culture." As proof, he emphasized its high proportion of international students and the growing number of faculty and students who taught or studied abroad. He had chosen three speakers coming back from time away in foreign countries: a Nigerian student who reported on his research in the Caribbean, Flemmie Kittrell, and Tate, both to speak on their times in India.[1]

Tate's triumphant return to Howard was eclipsed by the surprising news that in her absence, Rayford Logan had appointed her to serve as department chair without notifying her or getting her approval. His good news, that he had won a Fulbright to Paris for 1951–1952, was bad news for her. When she tried to refuse the appointment, she was told that she had to do the work anyway. She complained to her deans that for the second time the position of chair "had been forced on me against my will," reminding them that she had done the job a decade earlier before she was even a permanent faculty member.[2]

Howard, which was always co-ed, deserves credit for opening its faculty to women at a time when few colleges and universities did. But institutional power remained in the hands of men, as department chairs, deans, and the president. Tate's primary complaint was that the men showed favoritism to one another in decisions about hiring, salary, course scheduling, summer teaching, administrative duties, and so on. If salary were "based upon academic preparation, honors, degrees, experience, publications, travel, prestige, and the publicity and glory a professor brings to Howard University and not upon personal, fraternal, and difference-in-sex considerations," Tate argued, she would stand "second to none of the regular members, and in some instances surpass the head of the department."[3]

She acknowledged that the "saintly approach would be for me to accept silently and supinely an inferior status and salary and still carry the heaviest burdens," but nothing in her personality or her temperament or history of advocating on her own behalf led her to do that. She also continued teaching a wide variety of courses, explaining at one point that while others taught in only one field, she had taught twenty-five different courses, including "European, English, American, Diplomatic, and Military History, International Politics, Political Science, Geography, and Geopolitics."[4]

Compounding Tate's resentment was the fact that her salary was less than that of others in the department, that she would receive no additional compensation for taking on the position of chair, and that there was inadequate administrative support. She argued that men in the department with fewer publications made more than she did, and yet were not being burdened with additional duties. She made clear to her dean that she "would not quietly accept a status and a salary in the department inferior to that of any other member, except its chairman." Tate refused to continue as chair unless the deans adjusted her salary and provided secretarial assistance. After some small accommodation was reached, she agreed, albeit unhappily, to serve the year as chair.[5]

Tate continued teaching her wide variety of courses. She taught economics to Joseph Stevenson, who came to Howard as an undergraduate in the 1950s. He recalls that Tate came very well prepared for her lectures, and that you had to take lots of notes; she was helpful to students, but she also assigned a lot of work and had very high grading standards. Joseph Harris, another undergraduate at that time, also learned the discipline to take copious notes because her lectures and discussions were so full of information. If a student performed well, she was quick to offer praise, but less committed students were scared away.

Like Stevenson, Harris soon served overseas in the military. After being drafted into the Korean War, Harris returned to Howard to begin graduate work in history; she encouraged him to study colonialism in the Pacific—advice he did not take, choosing to work with Logan instead. She did not hold that against him, later recommending him when he left Howard to work on his doctorate. His time at Howard was the start of his own exemplary academic career as an Africanist; two decades later, he would return as a faculty member himself, and as Tate's colleague and final chair.[6]

Tate began work on what she called a "geopolitician's" analysis of her year in Asia after her former mentor and professor Nancy Scott prodded her to write quickly while details were still fresh in her mind. Attacking the project with her usual obsessive intensity, Tate produced a one-hundred-page documentary-style account of her homeward journey from India through Asia and to Hawaii: part travelogue, part astute political analysis that reiterated her own evolving concept of anti-racist geopolitics.[7]

Writing during the time that the United States was engaged in the Korean War, Tate places the conflict in its broader regional context. She highlighted the emergence of a "New Asia" whose leaders shared a "concept of Asia's inherent right to political independence," where any disagreements among them went to the structure that would best support that freedom. She condemned French colonialism in Indochina, British colonialism in Malaya and Hong Kong, the nationalism of Chiang Kai-shek, and American interventions as all being incompatible with the new Asia and argued that each created real danger.

> At the present time the United States is supplying considerably more aid to the French forces in Indo-China and to the army and police in Thailand than we should like to see China send to those countries. Chinese intervention in Southeast Asia is far more likely to take the form of smuggling in troops and supplies than of overt invasion. Just what degree of concealed intervention on the part of either side will be considered an act of war?

This analysis presages United States engagement in the region in Vietnam soon to come.

Outlining the tensions in disputes within and between Tibet, Nepal, India, Burma, Malaya, Korea, and Japan, she cautioned against overconfident long-range political forecasts for the region. The scarcity of adequate food and housing for millions in the region rendered many susceptible to the promises of communism. The military and internal social policies of the United States, she argued, had overtaken its own ideals, now identified primarily with "racial discrimination, guns, tanks and atomic bombs."

Without humanizing its actions and attitudes toward "people who differ from us," the United States, in her view, could never claim higher moral integrity. It was racial discrimination especially that diminished that claim. "Stay-at-home Americans are unaware of the great damage to the democratic cause through our delay in extending freedom and equality to all men," she concluded. The "artificial prestige of the white man has vanished," she warned.[8]

Even though she sent her report to Fulbright officials at the State Department, she did not censor or hold back on her views about the damage caused by her home country's own failings and unjust policies at home and abroad. Tate conveyed a vivid and sharp historical and contrarian geopolitical understanding of a region rife with Cold War fears of communist and Western encroachment. When she shared her analysis with colleagues and mentors, including those in the field of international relations at Harvard, she received laudatory comments for her work, as she had from inside the State Department.[9]

Her travels in India and Asia, and her lectures there and in the United States, had also convinced Tate that those regions of the world were understudied and misunderstood during an era when they had emerged as a new center of global conflict and potential power. In 1952, she developed an ambitious new course, "Asia and the United States Since 1945," which would remain in her teaching rotation for years to come. In the space of the classroom, she could exercise intellectual control while educating a younger generation about the region she now saw as pivotal in global politics.

The course was characteristically comprehensive. She construed the "East" widely, made up of Near, Far, and Middle. The syllabus examined U.S. interests in Japan, China, Korea, Formosa (now Taiwan), India, and Pakistan, and then turned to Southeast Asia, which included Indochina, Indonesia, the Philippines, Thailand, and Burma. The class concluded with what she called the "oil" countries of Iran, Saudi Arabia, and Kuwait, and finally, Egypt. Tate's teaching brought together disparate sources about quite different countries. The assigned readings incorporated textbooks on individual countries where available, but she was forced to rely heavily on primary sources, various government and public policy reports, as well as current journals and newspapers.

Tate ended the syllabus with this quotation from Adlai E. Stevenson: "You can shoot Communists, but you can't shoot poverty, ignorance and Communism." She once again flagged her resistance to the dominant framing of the Cold War era, amplified in a concluding section headed "Weaknesses and Mistakes." Tate remained convinced that an appreciation of specific conditions and policies in contemporary Asia was crucial to understanding global politics, and the twenty pages of terms and readings reinforced that for her students.[10]

Early in 1953, Tate acted on her thinking and submitted to her dean, then William Stuart Nelson, an outline for an Asian Studies program to be established at Howard, a proposal that did not succeed. Had she been successful, Howard would have been early to enter a field of study that could also have modeled an approach that originated from intellectual currents and political impulses quite different from the Cold War anti-communist framing of later area studies programs, whether about Asia or elsewhere. Tate's approach would have been more expansive and would have rested instead on her anti-imperialism and her anti-racism.

Tate's mission as a scholar had always embraced teaching about international affairs to Black audiences and in a wide variety of venues. This included not just her published academic writing, but her many appearances at Black colleges, women's clubs, churches, and sorority gatherings. That was the Black civic sphere that welcomed her, eager to celebrate her achievements and to learn from her. She hoped the tales of her travels would encourage others to see the world for themselves. Beginning that fall and continuing over the months to come, she traveled to deliver lectures and show her films and slides from her time in India and Asia.[11]

At several churches in Washington and other cities, she often gave a talk with a tantalizing title, "Missionary Work and the Future of Indian Christianity," but whose content remains a mystery. Her talks about India in other more public forums were better covered in Black newspapers. More frequently, she delivered one titled "India in Transition," which explained that country's complicated political importance to the future of global politics while outlining its internal challenges.

Hers was also a politically optimistic presentation, as she explained her support for Nehru's vision for the country, concluding that India was destined for world leadership, economically and politically. She reassured her audience that Nehru was drawn to neither communism nor domination by Western powers, a nod to ongoing Cold War debates about India's political neutrality. Tate proudly portrayed Nehru and Ambassador Pandit as part of the "emergence of statesmen, other than white, who are able to take their places in world affairs and carry on with ability, dignity, and 'savoir faire.' " For her they were both exemplars of the "darker peoples of the world" newly showcased on the global stage.

Tate in 1951, dressed in a sari
(Moorland-Spingarn, Howard University)

But she also felt compelled, once again, to clarify that Nehru was "no stooge" for communism or Western powers, but a leader committed to independence from both. Tate would reiterate that analysis on a radio interview in Baltimore conducted to honor the AKA's annual boule, emphasizing that Nehru was walking a "tightrope" to avoid allegiance with either power. She also told her audiences that "the number one question in all India is the existence and cause of racial discrimination in America, prompted chiefly by Russian propaganda." She was not denying the truth of the allegations from the Soviet Union, but rather pointing to the international political vulnerability that segregation and racial injustice created for her home country.[12]

She also enlivened her account by describing the beauty and diversity of India and the hospitality of its people, reassuring her audiences that it was safe for women to travel there. In some cases, she illustrated her lectures with slides and film she had shot herself.[13] Her most extensive set of talks took advantage of Howard's spring break in 1952 when she traveled back to North Carolina, the state she had called home nearly twenty years earlier. Her colleagues at seven institutions—Bennett, Barber-Scotia, Johnson C. Smith, Palmer Memorial, North Carolina College, Meredith College, and Shaw University—all invited her to lecture on their campuses about her Fulbright experience. The time in North Carolina made for a very special homecoming for her in the Black southern community that had first welcomed her from Oxford.

For her Bennett College talk, she not only dressed in a sari, but demonstrated how to unwrap and rewrap it, to the discomfort of the school's president, David Jones. The students told her afterward that "they thought he was going to lose his mind when I started to demonstrate how to put on a sari."[14]

At the same time that she was thinking about global affairs, Tate engaged on several fronts with dramatically shifting domestic racial politics. Even before the *Brown* decision in 1954, she was concerned about the potential impact of school desegregation on Black schoolteachers and principals. She had not been a high school teacher since 1927, but she had never left the social networks of her teacher friends in Indianapolis, North Carolina, and Washington. Many of her AKA sorority sisters or members of their families also worked in elementary and secondary schools.

She expressed her fears about the prospect of school integration in Washington to leaders of the American Friends Service Committee, a Quaker group that, among other organizations, was working to eliminate segregation in the capital, where there was still a white and a "Negro" school division. A newsletter from the organization in 1952 had described the problem of overcrowded Black schools while enrollments in white schools had declined drastically, but with no attendant shifting of needed teachers or resources into the Black schools.

The group argued for an integrated school system as the remedy. This prompted Tate to write in support of desegregation but not without linking race, power, and economics:

> I am opposed to any system of so called integration that displaces trained and professional Negroes. That is what has happened in practically every instance of integration to date. Therefore, your project

> administered by a biased School Board—such as that in the District of Columbia—harbors certain hidden dangers for my race. After all, the Friends Service Committee will not be the administering agent. Seldom does a majority group capitulate without an ulterior motive which in the long run serves its economic interest to the detriment of the minority.[15]

Tate was not alone in her views. Distrust of white-administered desegregation plans for public schools left many teachers and others in Black communities with similar qualms. For her and them, support for the ideal of integration was not the issue, but rather how desegregation was to be implemented and by whom—a prudent critique at a time when power over funding and teacher pay and placement still remained in the hands of the very same white people who had so adroitly administered segregation. She had pledged in her letter to attend and speak out at future school board meetings as these discussions continued in Washington, something she could do without fear or risk, in contrast to friends who were paid by the D.C. school system.

Much less crucial and more quotidian aspects of shifts in segregation policies also figured in Tate's leisure life. Black bridge players in 1932 had formed the American Bridge Association (ABA), which worked to promote the game in Black communities through a national, regional, and local structure paralleling the all-white American Contract Bridge League (ACBL). Bridge gained more popularity and visibility as Black women formed social clubs to play what was viewed as a challenging and respectable card game, unlike those associated with vices and questionable venues.[16]

More advanced Black players like Tate also wanted to compete in rounds of officially sanctioned games that were controlled by the ACBL. Undoing the national policy would require Washington-based Victor Daly, the ABA's president, to engage in aggressive public relations tactics and solicit backing from supportive white allies, among them Albert Morehead, the prominent bridge columnist for the *New York Times*. Morehead's posting of his usual "Sample Deal" in a column featuring Black players made his most effective argument against the racial bar. In it, he reported "a bridge hand played recently by a prominent Negro player, Victor Daly of Washington, D. C. He held the South hand and his partner, North, was Miss Merze Tate, a professor at Howard University in Washington." Any bridge player following the formulaic and familiar symbols and language of bidding and play would be able to judge the excellent quality of the two Black players.[17]

It was shrewd to highlight the D.C. duo because the Washington Bridge League, a local unit of the ACBL, was among those most resistant to lifting racial restrictions. As Daly put it, the nation's capital was "that northern city with the southern exposure" and the white league was among those holding fast to the racial bar. It was not until 1967 that the national ACBL adopted a bylaw banning racial discrimination.[18]

Daly, Tate, and other Black bridge players also knew well the greater gravity and larger dangers of the ongoing struggles in the 1950s, whether in the Supreme Court or Montgomery or Little Rock. Under the banner "Sit Down for Bridge so that They may Sit Down to Eat," the organization raised money to support "the wave of protests by students which is sweeping the South" and to make contributions to the NAACP, the United Negro College Fund, and the National Urban League. Daly, however, cautioned clubs in "unfriendly areas" not to name their effort the "NAACP Benefit Fund," but rather to simply call it a "charity" fund, apparently a necessary act of political self-protection.[19]

Tate also would have been painfully aware of the racial politics of the city in which she lived even as she moved easily between the several worlds in the still-segregated city, spaces that rarely converged except on special occasions. One of those was an AKA scholarship fund-raising fashion show in 1954 that Tate organized. She brought in models from the Grace Del Marco Agency in New York, the most prominent Black agency, to put on a showcase at the Willard Hotel featuring seven different "scenes" of styles and occasions.

But, never missing an opportunity to teach about her field, Tate then narrated a Parade of Nations with a second set of "models" representing twenty-seven countries. Those women were drawn from her network of female staff at embassies and consul's offices, supplemented by international students at Howard. The use of fashion for fund raising came into even greater popularity when the traveling Ebony Fashion Fair premiered in 1958.[20]

Tate also worked closely with Radcliffe alumni in Washington, helping to raise money and host educational programs. For that, Radcliffe awarded her its Graduate Chapter Alumna Award in 1955. Cited for her scholarship and teaching, she was also especially pleased to be recognized for "her services in Europe and in the Orient as a worthy ambassador from the academic community of the United States."[21]

While her focus remained on her work, Tate's relationship with her family in Michigan seems to have continued to be fraught. When an uncle was killed in a farm accident in the spring of 1953, she did not attend his funeral, much

Tate in 1952 (Moorland-Spingarn, Howard University)

to the disappointment of her family, although she did send money to help with expenses. Her sister Thelma typed a long letter describing the large crowd at the service and explaining that their entire family had been there—and that everyone asked where she was. The "sad part" of their uncle's death, she wrote, was that he "had never been converted": he was not a church member, which she believed deprived him of the possibility of salvation or of being reunited with family in heaven.

This reflected the urgency of Thelma's religious concern, but also the suddenness of his death was a reminder that anyone's time could come to an end quickly. In that spirit, she closed her letter with a plea that her younger sister "patch up differences" with their mother, who at seventy-seven seemed "frail" and "weak"—"do like the rest of us just listen. For after all what difference does it make as we each have to live our own lives. Make her a little happier maybe."[22]

Myrtle Tate also wrote to her daughter, by hand and in pencil just as she had done when she had inquired after her at Oxford in 1935. Her account of the funeral was much more dramatic, calling it an "awful day" made worse because it "rained and the wind blew in almost hurricane blasts." She ended by reminding her daughter that "the old saying is when rain falls in a new grave another will follow shortly." Leaving no room for wonder, she ended, "it may be me," signing "From Mother." Religion or religious differences played a role in the family tensions even as her mother remained pained generally by Tate's absence and refusal to conform to expectations.[23]

Heeding her sister's plea, Tate soon spent more time in Michigan, teaching that summer at Wayne State in Detroit and in 1955 at Western Michigan. She also usually attended the annual Old Settler's reunions in August, when the descendants of the families that had come in the 1800s gathered. A relative in Washington would drive her there, and when the weekend concluded with a Sunday morning church service, Tate would wait outside in his car, reading.[24]

Developments on Howard's campus continued to consume most of her time. Red-baiting and questions of academic freedom generated both anxiety and debate, as Howard's status as a federally funded institution meant faculty members were subject to loyalty oaths. The university devoted its annual social science division conference in 1953 to the topic of academic freedom at a time when so many were targeted by the red scare of the period, and not just those in federal employment. One of the greatest threats to faculty members such as Tate who studied international affairs or those engaged in global political networks was the possibility of passport suspension, a tactic deployed with devastating effects on well-known political figures like Du Bois and Paul Robeson. Closer to home, FBI interviews with Rayford Logan about his early political affiliations unsettled him very deeply, as did the State Department's decision at one point to grant him only a one-year renewal of his passport after discovering his affiliation as a younger man with an organization it deemed suspicious.[25]

Tate's advice to colleagues fearful of an FBI interview was to tell the truth and sign the loyalty oath, a pragmatic approach well suited perhaps only for those like her who had not engaged in certain kinds of political activism or affiliated with organizations now subject to heightened scrutiny. The FBI had conducted an extremely thorough investigation of Tate in 1950 when she applied for work with Voice of America, made moot by her 1951 Fulbright award to India. But the thoroughness of that review reveals how diligently the agency searched for signs of suspect political activity.

Agents in every domestic location she had ever lived conducted extensive interviews with employers, friends, neighbors, teachers, colleagues, and even her hairdresser. She was found to be of stellar character and reputation, much admired with no questions of loyalty or security risk, and no affiliations with "suspicious" people or organizations, and she had clean credit and police records everywhere she had lived. The only redaction in the report concerns what appears to be her father and her mother's separation.[26]

The portrait of Tate that emerges from the report is remarkably congruent with the life she often recounted, and the one affirmed in archival records about her, both those she created and those she never saw. Methodically tracing her associations in Michigan, Indianapolis, North Carolina, Boston, Maryland, and Washington, the forty-page FBI report provides a narrative account of the first forty-five years of her life. Its agents reached back to her childhood in Blanchard, where her family was remembered by their postmaster and a local banker who attested to their excellent reputation.

Over and over again, those questioned by the FBI called Tate brilliant, an excellent teacher and scholar, a well-liked and respected woman of exceptional drive and ability, and highly regarded by all who knew her. Her mentor and friend Bernice Cronkhite at Radcliffe revealed that she had recommended Tate for the presidency of Spelman College. The only unenthusiastic word in the report came from someone at Howard who referred to her as "eccentric." Many years later, Tate requested and saw the report herself, but she would have known without seeing it that no suspicions had been raised by the process. Still, her strong political views about racism in the United States and global imperialism were no secret to anyone who read her academic and press publications.[27]

The only red flag in her file concerned not Tate but Payson S. Wild, a professor of hers formerly at Harvard, who, the report revealed, had been under surveillance since 1946 for his membership in a political organization judged to be a communist front. He was effusive in his praise of Tate, and told the FBI agent that "although she wanted most of all to help her people, she was not a vociferous crusader by any means" and that he saw her as "one of the outstanding women of her race." But suspicions of him, for which he was hounded publicly, did not attach to his former student who had listed him as a character reference.[28]

In addition to the threats from Cold War domestic surveillance, the prospect of the desegregation of higher education figured in a recurring debate at Howard about the objectives of a college program at a Black institution. A proposal in 1954 argued that Howard should "prepare the student to meet the special problems peculiar to the Negro; to strengthen his ability to function as a member of a minority group and as a member of American society," and "increase the general store of knowledge with particular emphasis upon the American Negro and the darker races in other parts of the world."[29]

In some ways, this presaged debates that raged in the decade to follow, not only about how to best train Black students, but about the place of Black studies—an issue that would trigger student protests. Not surprisingly, Tate proposed instead that there should be less concern with race and "the Negro." She suggested instead a stress on the "political and cultural aspects of world affairs with particular emphasis upon the part the darker peoples are playing in international relations." Here again, she opposed what she thought was a provincial approach to race in the United States.

Tate also feared that it would have the potential effect of limiting the academic ambition for Black students precisely at a time when there were small signs of increasing opportunities. She also argued that for students who suffered from "intellectual isolation" and an "inferiority complex," a broader view of the world was essential. She also seemed to fear that too much attention to race and its inequalities would weaken their will to fight through barriers, as she had done, or worse, risk having students use racial discrimination as an excuse for underachieving. She and her generation of Black people felt they had coped with racism through fierce determination, and she feared this tenacity would be lost.[30]

This was consistent with ideas about race she had expressed earlier, but her approach also reflects the thinking of a non-Americanist scholar arguing for a more global approach to race and inequality, one that would make her own work and interests relevant in any curricular shifts to come. Perhaps as well, Tate had in mind Black students like her, those whose intellectual interests by both discipline and geography might not touch directly on domestic racial issues, or even political ones.[31]

Of the continuing challenges Tate confronted in this period, gender inequality clearly animated and angered her. Although Howard had a very accomplished group of women faculty members when most colleges excluded women, power and leadership remained in the hands of men who ruled the departments, schools, and the president's office. Beyond concerns about salary, she was most affected by decisions about coveted summer teaching slots. Because Tate's primary research venues were in Washington, having to leave interfered with her scholarly productivity, including the time and effort spent trying to get a summer placement elsewhere, and often without success.[32]

Tate also took deep personal offense at what she saw as unfairness in the treatment of women at Howard. But in these complaints, she was never alone or speaking only for her own needs. She joined women colleagues to stand up for policies that were "equitable, honest and humane," especially for the many part-time instructors. But their efforts, she wrote, were often "overridden either by higher authorities or by sheer force of numbers," as women remained in the minority. Women faculty, instructors, and administrative staff, as she saw it, were "humiliated, discriminated against, and are the most neglected group of employees at Howard University."[33]

Deference was never part of her personality, and Tate continued to fight publicly against those inequities for decades, but never just for herself. The association of women faculty and professional administrators, the Women's Faculty Club, continued to provide an inclusive forum for organizing and support for the extraordinary group of accomplished Black women at Howard. As one of the few women full professors, Tate was in a more protected position to deploy her prominence to help raise gender issues. When the College of Liberal Arts in 1955 established a committee on the status of women, Tate chaired its subcommittee on salaries, and fought to get departments to provide detailed information on gender differences in salaries, promotions, rank, and tenure, but without success.[34]

Tate took notice in 1957 when the university launched its own offensive on the treatment of women faculty at Howard. She clipped and saved a three-page *Howard Bulletin* article with a title that encapsulated, perhaps unintentionally, the tensions around gender and women faculty members: "GENTLER SEX PLAY INTEGRAL ROLE: At Howard Women Make Up 25 Percent of Faculty." Touting its history of always admitting women students as evidence of its commitment to gender nondiscrimination, the article also highlighted that Howard employed far more women faculty members and in higher rank than other colleges and universities in Washington.

However, the claim that a quarter of the "faculty" was female was based on a definition that included instructors and assistants. Those women made up more than half of the 118 named, and the unfair conditions they faced had provoked specific denunciation from Tate and other women faculty. Here the university tried a sleight of hand to use those instructors to inflate its numbers as part of its claim of being progressive on both gender and racial grounds (through its comparison with neighboring white institutions).[35]

The women faculty at Howard did, however, constitute one of the largest groups of highly educated professional Black women in the country. The article included short profiles of its distinguished women faculty members, drawing attention to its one female school dean, Inabel Lindsay of the school of social work, along with the holders of the positions of dean of women and the director of the health service. Beautifully illustrated with thirteen photographs, including one of Tate, the university essentially congratulated itself for the quality of the women who served it, letting their prominence accrue for its benefit while deftly silencing and deflecting ongoing complaints about pay inequity and the absence of women in powerful administrative positions. Tate's own virulent protests over gender inequity at Howard would persist for the duration of her career there, and indeed were an enduring feature of her tenure.[36]

India and Asia still loomed large in Tate's mind, and she expressed that in her many book review essays in this period. On the pages of the *Journal of Negro Education* and the *Journal of Negro History,* she evaluated a variety of genres of books about Southeast Asia, including novels, memoirs, essays, travelers' and reporters' accounts. All published between 1954 and 1957, her essays constitute a revealing body of work attesting to the wide range of her interests but also her political ideas about that region. The proliferation of works on India and Asia available in the United States in this period attracted interest from a Black reading public keen to learn about contemporary developments there.

Tate brought her own views on race and gender in the United States to writings on prohibitions on sexual relations across caste, religious, and racial boundaries in India. She reviewed a small collection of essays by Manmatha Nath Chatterjee, a European and American-educated scholar who had taught social sciences for three decades at Antioch College. Pointed attention to Chatterjee's comparisons of caste and racial restrictions on intermarriage reflected that she thought the readers of the *Journal of Negro History* might find that especially interesting.

In the book, Chatterjee argued bluntly that the crux of the race issue was that "the in-groups have always sought to protect their women folk from falling into the hands of the out-groups." Tate detailed his contrast of Brahmin caste prohibitions with what he called a "K. K. K. method" where a dangerous double standard applied, depending on whether the "inter-mating" involved a white man and a Black woman or a Black man and a white woman. Chatterjee criticized both systems as wrong and based on irrational misconceptions of race. Tate agreed, concluding that the race question was so charged with emotions that it "does not seem to be solvable by intellectual means," leaving unanswered what might work instead.[37]

Two novels that Tate reviewed carried this theme forward. Both featured tragic stories of mixed marriage, one across racial lines and the other religious differences. *The Bombay Meeting,* an ambitious work by Ira Morris, fictionalizes an international gathering of writers, a cast of dozens whose travels and observations about the problems of modern India form the backdrop for an affair between a white American man, like the author, and what Tate describes as "the beautiful, fragile, tortured Shakuntala Clubwalla, a Hindu woman who saw her family massacred in the partition troubles and thereafter existed in a mystical world of melancholia." This coupling and its representation of the search for a way for West and East to achieve an equal partnership also did not seem to capture Tate's imagination.[38]

Tate's essay on a historical novel by UNESCO's India specialist Khushwant Singh described its vivid depictions of the Punjab massacres in 1947. The novel portrayed Mano Majra, a fictional village stop on the railroad between Delhi and Lahore, as a place of peaceful coexistence among Hindus, Muslims, and Sikhs, before the rupture of Partition and desperate attempts to escape the murder and mayhem that followed. Another affair, this one between a Sikh peasant and a Muslim weaver's daughter, helps drive the plot, which ends with death, heroism, and more death. Of that Tate said no more, but she commended the novel for capturing well both "the flavor of India" and the "turbulence connected with independence and partition." The book had a long afterlife of many printings and also served forty years later as the basis for the critically acclaimed Hindi film *Train to Pakistan* in 1998.[39]

Tate's lack of interest in the romantic plotting of the novels is not surprising. She remained most engaged by depictions of the complex cultural and political worlds in India, based on her reading as a scholar and her experience in Southeast Asia in 1950 and 1951. The pairing of men and women from different representative divides may have seemed overly simplistic to her, even though it is a well-worn literary device. Du Bois even deployed it in his 1928 novel *Dark Princess,* which featured the symbolic political union between a Black American man and an Indian princess, a coupling that left no role for either the Indian man or the African American woman in this imagined brown and Black global alliance.[40]

Tate's essays about the accounts of Americans who had traveled and spent time in India fit more comfortably with her own interests and experiences. She was quick to express her disappointment in a book by the respected journalist Robert Trumbull who, starting in 1947, had spent seven years as the India correspondent for the *New York Times.* Tate was familiar with his reporting, and used it in her course on Asia, but she was less impressed with his book, "wishing it were more comprehensive and more penetrating." Tate disagreed with his negative assessment of India's policy of neutrality, admonishing instead that "Indian thinking does not lie in terms of a great crusade of communism or anti-communism." She asked rather: "Is it not to the world's interest and, consequently, to our own to have a great democratic country capable as serving as a bridge between the East and West?"[41]

When Eleanor Roosevelt returned from a five-month tour of the Middle East and Southeast Asia in 1952, she also wrote a book that was part travelogue and part political primer. An invitation from Nehru had prompted the trip, but it also came after a Pakistani official accused Roosevelt's work at the U.N. Children's Emergency Fund of privileging the needs of white European children over those in Asia. Tate's review of the book emphasized again the familiar political trope that Roosevelt also stressed when she argued that the country was in the best "position to foster the growth of good will and understanding between East and West." Underlying this repeated trope of India as a "bridge" seems instead to be an imperative that the country serve more as an ideological barrier or buffer between the West and its fears of communism in the region.[42]

It is not surprising that Tate's review of Roosevelt's book was upbeat. She had met the former First Lady on several occasions, including at Howard and the White House, and she especially appreciated that she had spoken at Santiniketan. Still, Tate placed Roosevelt's account in the category where she believed it belonged, commending her for writing "an informative book for the general reader and as first class entertainment for the armchair traveler." Between this line of praise and appreciation was Tate's implicit critique that, for all of her commitments and abilities, Roosevelt was still not an expert on the region, or a scholar like Tate.[43]

Tate presumed that those who had studied the history and geopolitics of Southeast Asia before spending time there were in the best position to write about it. That was clear when she reviewed three books by Black American men who had been commissioned to travel and write about Southeast Asia and the meeting of Afro-Asian nations at Bandung. She brought to the task all her knowledge and her disapproval that these men had been chosen despite what she saw as their lack of expertise. She also criticized the underlying State Department policy of sending Black men to Southeast Asia in a clumsy attempt to use their "Negro" status to defuse communist criticisms of racial inequality in the United States.

From the very first sentence in her review of J. Saunders Redding's *An American in India,* Tate made clear her disappointment with his "dismal" account of his journey. Tate argued that Redding was so unprepared for his trip that he could only see India through "western spectacles" and that he could never escape his status as a "Negro" sent to defend American racism. He had missed the "true excitement and stimulation of India," she charged, including its idealism. Tate criticized his use of the word "native" to describe Indians, a people she defended as having freed themselves from "imperialism, overlordship, and master-servant relationships" and who now were "independent and liberated from western domination."[44]

Tate strongly supported Nehru's vision of the country's path forward, in particular his devotion to non-alignment, choosing neither the West nor communism. The harsh tone of her review also revealed her own deep investment in India and its depiction by visitors, especially those who emphasized its staggering levels of poverty and dispossession.

The journalist Carl Rowan made a State Department–funded trip to Southeast Asia in 1954, and it had just ended when he was asked to return to Indonesia to cover the Bandung meetings. His subsequent book, *The Pitiful and the Proud,* described both trips. She found him less constrained than Redding by racial self-consciousness and less rattled by communist challenges, but still showed little sympathy for his complaints of exhaustion from having to defend his white countrymen. She also criticized his report for being marred by his personal and intimate feelings, faulting him for treating his fears of "snakes, lizards, and neutralism" on the same level. Of the portion of the book that described his time at Bandung, she highlighted his report of Nehru's speech claiming Africa as a "sister continent."[45]

When Tate turned to Richard Wright's book on Bandung, *The Color Curtain,* she of course knew of him. Yet she found Wright's reporting to have come through the limited eyes of a "Black Boy," a reference to Wright's book with that name. Tate did not hesitate to chide him.

> Consequently, Mr. Wright's report suffers from his lack of knowledge of international and Asian affairs and from his own deeply imbedded race consciousness. The author over-emphasizes the color angle and attributes to Asians and Africans a 'miraculous unity' that is non-existent. The Conference did not represent the consolidation of a Peking-Delhi-Cairo Axis directed against the West nor was it a manifestation of the solidarity of the colored peoples of the world against the white.[46]

Again, this illustrates how an anti-racist geopolitics, in her mind, differs from a limited provincial view of racialized political identities. For these Black writers, accustomed to their status as members of a non-white minority, the power of the gathering turned in part on its novelty as one of the first conferences of its kind, as Tate herself had noted, and by the presence of leaders from African nations. But to call the conference an "Afro-Asian" gathering, as was to be the case, may itself have been misleading in that the Asian nations, including the one where it was held, outnumbered the others and dominated the meeting.

Tate agreed that the real import of the meeting was that distinguished Asians and Africans spoke for themselves rather than having to listen to white westerners "claiming the right to speak for and to dispense of the destinies of others." But her analysis moved swiftly from the value of symbolic significance to more practical follow-up questions. She remained more the pragmatic realist and skeptic than idealist, and she was not partial to utopian hopes.

Yet her assessment of longer term significance and progress was tempered by her own geopolitical expertise and orientation. That left her dubious that color and shared oppressions would easily translate into unified collective power. In the end, she remained, as she had been at least since her days at Oxford, pessimistic about meaningful alliances among independent sovereign nations, including those from Asia and Africa.

Her training and understanding of the history of attempts at more formal coalition building among sovereign nations, whether at the League of Nations or the United Nations, had left her keenly aware of the challenges even with the presence of formal structures and large budgets. She did endorse the ideas contained in the meeting's final communiqué, which called for cooperation among those assembled, greater control of their own natural resources, and an end to Western control of the shipping industry.

If the West did not heed the meeting's call to its moral conscience, Wright cautioned, then the USSR was patiently waiting to fill the void, having the advantage of no "record of racial practices." That view had been at the center of Tate's very first review of a book about India, Krishnalal Shridharani's *Warning to the West,* in 1943, which called on the United States to lead the way to alliances with Asia, but only if it could shed its notions of white supremacy.[47]

Others at the meeting criticized it for other reasons. Marguerite Cartwright, a Black journalist and faculty member at Hunter College, also attended what she called the "Asian-African" conference and later published an article that "lamented the fact that there were no women represented among 600 delegates at Bandung." She also challenged the anti-communist Cold War lens that framed Adam Clayton Powell's account of his time there.[48]

The respected Black journalist Ethel Payne, after spending two years living in Japan, also traveled to the conference in her job as a reporter for the *Chicago Defender.* The headline of her article, "African Nations Play Minor Role at Bandung," reflected her view that the leaders of Asian nations had dominated the gathering and the road to an easy alliance of Asian and African nations was not a given. Like Tate, she questioned whether a shared history of colonialism was enough to unify in the long run. These contrarian analyses have been neglected, illustrating again how difficult it was for Black women's ideas to be taken seriously, especially about international affairs.[49]

Tate's many review essays in the 1950s placed her ideas in important public debates about political relations among the "darker peoples of the world," including African Americans. Her willingness to stake out her own positions also shows how intellectually unintimidated she was by prominent Indian and Black male writers, including the internationally well-known Wright. Her publications also reveal her ideas about race, gender, color, and caste in Indian politics and reiterate her rejection of the reflexive Cold War anti-communist lens of the 1950s. Tate's writing in that decade widens the frame of international political debates, emphasizing her own ideas on race, gender, imperialism, and anti-communism.

Tate's essays on India and Southeast Asia ended there, marking the culmination of a decade of travel and reading. But even as she wrote, she had begun her work on the parts of the world that were farther south and in the Pacific, the region she had identified as her next area of study. The epiphany that her Pacific imperialism project could center on Hawaii now included attention to the colonizing ambitions of larger islands toward their smaller, less-populated but economically valuable neighbors. When she could, she read and worked in archives obsessively, amassing material from the Library of Congress, the National Archives, the State Department, and Harvard and the University of Michigan.

But she still would need to travel for research again—this time to archives and libraries in Hawaii and the southwest Pacific region. Racial restrictions denied most Black scholars access to the outside financial support needed to take a full year of leave, or in her case, to travel internationally. Desperate to do that, Tate had tried without success for another Fulbright at the Asian Studies Institute at the University of the Philippines or at Madras University in India.

Tate expressed her frustrations that faculty members at Howard who wished to be productive scholars needed to receive more institutional support. Never hesitant to ask for what she needed and for what she believed she deserved, whether at Western Michigan or Oxford or Howard, the fifty-two-year-old Tate took her case for additional release time directly to President Mordecai Johnson. "In addition to teaching fifteen hours with eight o'clock and Saturday classes (last year evening classes also)," she explained, the "only full day that I have for writing is Sunday; consequently, I have not attended church since last summer." Deploying every argument she could, she also said that she would soon suffer a "physical collapse" if she was not granted relief. She begged for reduced teaching and more research leave for professors who wished to publish, making a case on behalf of several other faculty members, including her friend the Africanist William Hansberry, "who has material of inestimable value that should be made available for posterity."[50]

That is how she was able to take a sabbatical in 1957–1958 and return once again to the Pacific, the region that had captured her imagination a decade earlier and became the focus of her intellectual work in the decade to come.

CHAPTER 8

"A Weary Researcher"

HAWAII–FIJI–AUSTRALIA–NEW ZEALAND–ASIA–EUROPE–USSR, 1958–1960

"While fashion wise men and women debate the pros and cons of the sack dress," the *Chicago Defender* reported in the spring of 1958, "Miss Merze Tate serenely chose three to wear in the tropics on her Pacific safari which will end in her circling the globe for the second time before returning home." That lede was an odd teaser for a long article about an extended scholarly research trip that also included a complete recapitulation of her career and achievements, likely supplied by Tate herself. More important, the full extent of her years of quiet research and writing on Hawaii and the Pacific was clear from the article's report that she planned to gather yet more materials for two already drafted manuscripts, "The United States and Hawaii to 1898," and "Australia's and New Zealand's Interest in the Pacific."[1]

Tate arrived in Honolulu on April 1 after a nine-hour flight. She had received leave, but in the absence of research or travel support, she paid for the trip herself. Word of her plans spread among the Black soldiers and sailors she knew who were stationed there, as well as those she knew through her network of Fulbright friends and Howard connections. The news of her research visit soon reached the University of Hawaii faculty, who helped her find housing; she ended up as a house guest with the family of Allan Saunders, the dean of the College of Arts and Sciences. Losing no time, she started to spend her days working at the university library, the archives of Hawaii, and the Hawaiian Mission Library. But her evenings and weekends were spent sightseeing, socializing, and playing bridge.[2]

Tate's idyllic routine in the spectacular beauty of Hawaii came to an abrupt halt in early May when she received word from Detroit that her sister Thelma, who had been diagnosed with cancer earlier in the decade, had taken seriously ill and was not expected to survive. Tate at first planned to return, but then simply froze in place with a psychological conflict between her love for her sister, her fears of arriving to see her suffer and die, or already dead, and her desire to complete her long-awaited research trip. But somehow, Tate managed to get herself on a Pan-American plane and return to Detroit, where she witnessed not a death, but what she called "a tremendous improvement." She then flew back to Honolulu.[3]

As she had done before, however, Tate relied on an occupied mind and travel as psychic and physical escape. After Hawaii, she traveled to Fiji, Australia, and New Zealand. In weekly letters to her Detroit relatives, Tate always inquired after her sister, but then sought to distract them with detailed accounts of her adventures. She described for them the racial and class complexities on Fiji:

> The Fijians are a dark—not a Black—people with thick bushy hair and seem to cultivate the bushy hair do—men and women. The Indian, imported . . . to work on the sugar plantations are fecund and now outnumber the aborigines. From indentured servants they have become land owners, shop keepers, merchants, government officials at the lower level (of course the Englishman, New Zealanders and Australians are on top), while the Black or dark Fijian is the laborer, servant, a few have government posts.[4]

From New Zealand, she reported to her family on important discoveries in her archival work, and regaled them with descriptions of the scenery from her four-hundred-mile trip by land from Auckland to Wellington. The bustling city of Sydney and its large and well-administered libraries and archives satisfied Tate before she left for Melbourne, Darwin, and Brisbane—her last stops before beginning the frantic rush of a homeward journey that took her through Indonesia. In Jakarta, she stayed again with her friends the Todds, the African American diplomatic family that had hosted her in Cairo in 1950.[5]

Tate pushed on to Bangkok, Karachi, and New Delhi to see old acquaintances. She then made what she called a "hazardous trip through the crisis-torn Middle East," where she did sightseeing in Baghdad, Damascus, Beirut, Cyprus, and Ankara, and eventually, Istanbul, Vienna, and Paris. In Paris, she spent four or five days reading at the Bibliothèque Nationale, hosted by a Black American family.[6]

She traveled next to London and the British Museum and the British Public Record Office, with her way eased by a letter from the consulate's office in Washington. By the time she returned to New York and then on to Washington in mid-September, Tate had been away from the city for nearly six months. A promised plan to go see her sister before classes started had to be dashed, she says, because she arrived too close to the start of the term to make the trip to Detroit.[7]

Her sister Thelma's health continued its decline that fall term. After Thanksgiving, her condition took what Tate called "three downward turns" before it became clear that cancer would soon end her life. Tate spent her Christmas vacation in Michigan with her family. Thelma died the next spring, and she was buried on Palm Sunday, 1959, in the family's section of the Pine River Cemetery. This was a grievous loss for Tate, whose sister was the family member she was closest to, and the one whose emotional and financial support had sustained her through college and when she was stranded at Oxford. In Tate's absence, her sister managed her financial affairs, helped care for their mother, and welcomed her in her home in Detroit.[8]

The timing of one of Tate's most privately held decisions may have been in reaction to her sister's death. On June 10, 1959, she converted to Catholicism through a "profession of faith" and "conditional Baptism," a designation for those who cannot recall or are uncertain if they were ever baptized before. With her prodigious memory, Tate more likely was embarrassed to admit that she might never have been baptized, something hinted at in one of her sister Thelma's letters after the sudden death of their uncle who had not been "saved."

Taking the name "Mary Merze Tate," she joined St. Anthony of Padua, a predominantly white neighborhood parish church in the Brookland section of Washington near Catholic University, the Basilica, and the Franciscan Monastery of the Holy Land. Her "patrini" were old friends from her time in Indianapolis, Iva and Tilford Davis. Tate had sponsored a tea for them when they were married in St. Rita's Catholic Church in Indianapolis and had remained close to them through the years. Her Catholicism was shared with her very close military family friends Frances Thompson and Muriel and Lucius Young.[9]

More than that remains a mystery. She does not appear to acknowledge directly her Catholicism in any of her expansive recollections, although she often credits "Providence" for the fortuitous turns in her life that had enabled her to succeed professionally. Evidence of her faithfulness rests in her archive at Western Michigan, where among items taken from her home after her death are her well-used rosary and the original instructional pamphlet that had come with it.

Indeed, her affinity for the Catholic church seems to have preceded her formal decision by decades and may account for her excitement to see the pope and to witness the Annunciation of the Blessed Virgin Mary at the Vatican in 1950 on her way to India, something she recounted with vivid detail. It also makes more significant her reporting on the arduous journey she made through Nazi Germany for the pageantry at Oberammergau while still using a cane to walk after her bike accident at Oxford.

As a scholar of European history, Tate necessarily understood the complexities of Catholic religious history, including the rich Anglo-Catholic traditions at Oxford, a place where the academic terms are marked by the liturgical calendar and the plentiful sounds of sacred music are inescapable and inviting. At some point, both her intellectual and religious sensibilities may have drawn her to the Catholic church's monuments to faith, and eventually, to the faith itself and the comforts of its rituals and liturgy for believers, especially in her own times of personal crisis. She was later confirmed at St. Matthew's Cathedral in Washington and remained a member of St. Anthony's and supported it financially for the rest of her life.[10]

The other decision Tate made after her sister's death was to build herself a home. She had bought land in the late 1940s in the Brookland community in Washington near where she had lived in an apartment for seventeen years. Located close to Catholic University and in easy reach of Howard, the neighborhood had attracted Black middle-class families including those of Ralph Bunche and Rayford Logan. She had acquired four adjoining lots in the late 1940s even though she suspected that the land was under a racially restrictive covenant that the owners ignored to settle a complicated estate. The property looked across the street into the block-long wooded Civil War–era Fort Bunker Hill Park, guaranteeing that it would be protected from development and remain a quiet and secluded street. Her neighbors on that block were all white, and many also attended St. Anthony's.

Despite many inquiries from developers over the years, she had refused to sell the property, reserving it for when she had time to build her "dream house." Tate engaged the prominent Black architect Lewis Giles to design and construct the house. She had wanted the property because it came with a southern exposure that would bring ample natural light all year round. With a large bay window in the living room to capture the view, the spacious brick rambler also included a garage and a separate garden-level apartment. She planned to rent that out to male graduate students or staff from Catholic University or Howard because she thought the presence of a man coming and going would increase her safety as a woman living in a house alone—something far less common then than now.[11]

After living in Washington since 1942, she finally had created for herself a space suited for her to work and write at home. She also designed it with a large enough kitchen and dining area for entertaining friends with bridge parties and dinners, which she did with the same obsessive attention to detail that she brought to her scholarship. Her home displayed mementos from her travels, along with her photo albums and scrapbooks. Over time, she planted azaleas, roses, and other flowers and shrubs that would flourish in Washington's southern climate, eventually adding what she called a "memory" or a "friendship" garden on the west side of the house. By either name, she included plants to honor or memorialize others or given to her by friends. When the house was completed and Tate moved in, it became the place she called home for the rest of her life.

Tate's urge to travel did not cease after her sister's death. If anything, travel may have taken on even greater emotional urgency for her, especially if it combined research and leisure. She was fortunate that funding from external academic sources was slowly beginning to be awarded to Black scholars. For three years, she had applied for an American Council of Learned Societies grant even though her friends kept saying they would not give it to "a colored person." But that did not stop her: "I just kept applying to see how many times they would refuse me." Finally, on the third try, she received support in 1959 for summer research in London and became one of the first Black scholars to receive an award. Her friend and former colleague John Hope Franklin, who had served on the society's advisory board, first told her that the award was coming her way.[12]

She had completed most of the research for her project since her earlier visit by using other sources, but she still used the grant to leave the country just a few months after her sister was buried. She flew on June 21 from New York to Amsterdam, Copenhagen, Oslo, Stockholm, and Helsinki to see parts of the world new to her. Relying on contacts through the AAUW, she reached out to women who advised her on lodging but also showed her around and invited her to meals and concerts. In Norway, she stayed with Pat Shaw Iverson, the daughter of her Washington friend Esther Colpitts Shaw, who was very happy to host someone who could share memories of her mother, an English teacher. Tate made a trip on her own to see fjords, but since she was the only Black person on the boat, people took pictures of her as she was trying to photograph the scenery.[13]

Her nearly two weeks in Scandinavia ended in Helsinki, where she joined at her own expense a seventeen-day guided bus tour to Russia, with stops in Leningrad, Novgorod, Kalinin, Moscow, Smolensk, and Minsk. The Kansas-based Maupin Tours in 1956 had become the first company to offer trips to the Soviet Union after World War II and had received a great deal of publicity for it. Tate was among the earliest tourists to sign up, even though she rarely joined guided group tours because of the expense and her preference for solo travel, but this was the best way to visit the Soviet Union at the time.

The cities were of great interest to her but so were the many smaller provincial towns between Leningrad and Moscow. She was impressed that so much of the extraordinary historic architectural grandeur had not been destroyed during the revolution but had been preserved and reused as museums and for educational purposes. The historical and cultural sites had special appeal, but she also enjoyed a provincial circus and the more spectacular Moscow circus.[14]

When the tour stopped in Moscow, Tate was in the lobby of the Hotel Ukraine when she saw a "nearly seven foot tall" Black man:

> I looked at him and he looked at me. Now this is in the heart of the U.S.S.R. I walked over to him and I said, "I'm Professor Tate from Howard University." He said, "I'm a member of the Harlem Globetrotters. We played here last night." Of course, they had had a good game; they had won. He said, "They brought us bouquets of flowers." That was the Russian way of showing their appreciation. He said, "We didn't know what to do with them."

The team was on its first ever tour of the Soviet Union and had been greeted by Nikita S. Khrushchev at Lenin Central Stadium. One of the team members was a young Wilt Chamberlain, and the player she was speaking with could have been him.[15]

Tate crossed the border at Brest and made her way across eastern Poland to Warsaw, the final stop on her tour. From there, she moved on as a solo traveler to Vienna, and then into Germany, where she combined research and sightseeing. She worked in libraries in Munich, Augsburg, and West Berlin, perhaps researching the history of Germany's Pacific territories. She made time to take tours of Berlin sponsored by the U.S. Army, and bus trips to Ludwig's Castles and Garmisch in Bavaria. She returned to Oberammergau, where she had seen the Passion Play in the 1930s.

After a stop in Paris to work again in libraries and archives there, she finally went to London, where the Public Record Office proved to be "the richest source" for her project, which she would have known from her work in the city the previous summer. By the time of this ACLS grant, her need to do research other than in London was limited, but she bought the roundtrip ticket with the grant, using her own funds to tack on other places she wanted to visit.[16]

The most important archives for her work remained in Hawaii, but getting back there was a much more difficult and expensive proposition. The next summer, a research award of two thousand dollars from the *Washington Evening Star* allowed her to return to Honolulu, where she spent six and a half weeks in the archives and libraries she had begun mining for materials in 1958. She hired two typists there to reproduce the texts of documents and newspaper articles she selected, a time-saving requirement in the era before photocopying. As always, she had prepared for the trip by alerting both military and academic connections there when she intended to arrive.[17]

Tate was by then working simultaneously on two book-length projects, the new one on the United States and Hawaii to 1898 and the completed one on Australia's and New Zealand's expansionist aims in the Pacific. With her research completed, what she most wanted to do was to stay home and write. In 1961, the Rockefeller Foundation's director of social sciences, Kenneth Thompson, an international relations scholar and an admirer of her earlier work, suggested that she apply for a grant for her Australia and New Zealand project, which he saw as pathbreaking. Tate was reluctant because, as she told him, she was still annoyed that the foundation had refused to help fund her 1958 travels to the Pacific, which she had paid for herself.

But she later reconsidered, and applied, writing him in obsequious maudlin tones that for "a weary researcher, struggling against innumerable difficulties, your letter came like water to a famished traveler in a desert." One of the solicited reviewers of her application, C. E. Carrington, professor of British Commonwealth relations, Royal Institute of International Affairs, referred to her as "he," but his review of her proposal was laudatory, citing the need for work by other than "provincial" Australia and New Zealand scholars to explore exactly what Tate proposed and in the context of British imperialism in the Pacific amid international rivalries. "The history of British imperial policy elsewhere than in Africa between about 1867 and 1897 has been largely neglected, and this is the period of the partition of the Pacific Islands and of South East Asia."[18]

While emphasizing that her application succeeded on the strengths of her record and the project's potential, one of her recommenders suggested that it also would be good for "race relations" for the foundation to fund a "Negro." This would have bothered the prideful Tate, but it was reflective of that moment in the early 1960s. She received a two-thousand-dollar award that allowed her to remain in Washington in the summer of 1961 and devote her time to writing rather than teaching summer school.[19]

Even before she received the Rockefeller funding, she had begun to submit articles for publication and make inquiries about placing her expected book manuscripts. This process would prove challenging at a time when Black scholars still struggled to have their work accepted by many academic journals and publishers. The field of scholarly publishing remained a white, male-dominated bastion.

Placing work by women professors also was still difficult. To her request to an academic publisher for advice on the preferred length of a manuscript submission, Tate received this reply: "The only reasonable answer to that question was given by a man who said that the length of a manuscript should be like that of a woman's skirt—short enough to be interesting, long enough to cover the subject."[20]

Early in 1960, Tate tried to interest publishers in her book manuscript on the long history of United States relations in Hawaii, a more relevant topic after the islands became a state in 1959. Hawaii and the Pacific, however, did not seem to be of enough interest, or suited for west coast or Hawaiian publishers. Presses also told her that her work, which she was proposing as a two-volume book, was too long, too detailed, and too dense.

Tate had gotten similar complaints and critiques of her earliest scholarly work at Oxford. This was probably a fair and accurate analysis—habits of mind and research patterns are difficult for a scholar to break or transform. She gathered so much material from her years of obsessive and comprehensive research and reading that she routinely had this problem. The solitary intensity of her engagement with the material also made it very difficult for her to have the distance needed to eliminate the excess, especially in early drafts. Her self-centeredness did not permit her to place herself in the reader's place or overcome her own fascination with her archival finds and material.

All writers need editors, and Tate also lacked a network of peers in her fields to help judge what should stay and what should go. This was a consequence of the exclusion and marginalization of Black men and women from the professional scholarly organizations. She was left to solicit advice from publishers and tried to follow it when her earliest inquiries suggested that she edit her manuscript down by at least by half. She also was given conflicting advice on whether to publish parts of her work in journals, but after the rejection of the book manuscript, she seemed to decide to do both—continue to edit the manuscript and pull out parts that did not fit and solicit journals to publish articles. She knew that she had enough material to do both without duplication of argument or coverage.[21]

Tate's collection of rejection letters from journals preserves all the ways she was told "no" over and over again. Repeatedly, she was complimented on the quality of her research and writing, but was still declined because of questions of fit or audience, the work's importance, or its over-specialization for an American scholarly market. Length and density sometimes remained problems too, even though Tate wrote in lively clear prose.

Even as her work was rejected, Tate remained undeterred and became more creative about where to place her writing. Her studies bridged diplomatic history, international relations, and economic history in ways that trespassed and defied disciplinary boundaries. Her interdisciplinarity preceded its acceptance or more general use in academic work. Finally, her attention to imperialism and race in Hawaii and the southwestern Pacific was both novel and politically challenging.[22]

Because she wrote on a wide range of subjects, she pursued many different kinds of journals, including some outside the United States. Her persistence paid off. From 1959 to 1968, she published twenty-seven academic articles based on her research about Hawaii and the southwestern Pacific, a prolific output by any measure. Her work appeared in a variety of prestigious journals in history, political science, and religion in the United States, Australia, New Zealand, and Canada.

Tate's large body of scholarship on the region remains the largest and most important of her academic career. Her groundbreaking work was published throughout the 1960s, when other scholars were more receptive to the arguments and ideas she made about imperialism, especially as practiced by the United States. Her scholarship rested on her prodigious research and writing skills, and her arguments and interpretations also were bold and innovative.

It was many decades before other scholars offered as "new" the kinds of interventions that she had already advanced.

Unlike her writing on disarmament, Tate's innovative ideas on the Pacific do not lend themselves to easy summary because of their reach and range. Several specific areas of interest clearly emerge from her large oeuvre on the Pacific. She highlighted the multigenerational role of New England missionaries as tools of imperialist intervention in Hawaii. She also set the early debates over the United States annexation of Hawaii and British Commonwealth acquisitions in the South Pacific in the context of slavery and race relations. And she created a diplomatic history of Hawaii and the southwestern Pacific that charted intra-regional imperialist ambitions and cast the region as terrain for important shifts in Anglo-American and British Commonwealth relations. Tate's articles cover topics that supplement her ongoing work on book-length manuscripts.

Over the course of eight articles in five journals, Tate analyzed the New England Presbyterian and Congregational missionary families working from 1819 in what was then known as the Sandwich Islands, which they saw as a "religious frontier" that extended westward the closing frontier later conceptualized by Frederick Jackson Turner. Many of these early families were headed by elite white men trained at Princeton and Yale. She detailed how missionaries learned the language, invented a way to convert it into Roman characters, translated the Bible and educational textbooks into a written Hawaiian language, established a printing operation to produce Bibles and textbooks, and then built schools, and taught, trained, and converted teachers.[23]

Although she portrayed the early missionaries with predictable sympathy for their educational work, she also viewed them as leading actors in a story of American imperialism over peoples of color abroad. She linked religious exploration and state diplomacy in the nineteenth century, arguing that the powerfully connected Hawaiian mission joined church, state, and economic interests in advancing the shift to a sugar plantation economy. Their mission relied eventually on an alliance between the American Board of Commissioners of Foreign Missions, the Boston Board of Trade, and later the Hawaiian Club of Boston—an example of the holy trinity of religion, the state, and business.[24]

Tate used an innovative generational approach, revealing how in time the largest landowners and the ruling business class on the islands were the sons and grandsons of those early missionary families. Those children were not educated alongside the children native to the islands, but were sent instead to a new network of private elementary and secondary schools modeled after New England preparatory schools. Those schools trained members of a business and professional class that also included some of the children of the islands' Christianized families. The descendants of those private preparatory schools still exist; President Barack Obama graduated from one of the oldest of them, the Punahou School, founded in 1841.[25]

Tate also highlighted that the educational system the missionaries established for the island's peoples served as the vocational training model employed at Hampton Institute, and later, through its graduate Booker T. Washington, at the Tuskegee Institute. Her analysis of two generations of the Armstrong family demonstrated very effectively how this happened. Richard Armstrong, a Pennsylvania schoolteacher, served the Sandwich Islands Mission in the 1830s, eventually working for the project for seventeen years before becoming the minister of public education for the Hawaiian kingdom.

His son Samuel became a general in the Union Army and served as director of the Freedmen's Bureau and later as founder and principal of Hampton Institute, bringing new ideas about the civilizing influence of vocational training as practiced by his father in Hawaii. Tate then drew a line of influence from Armstrong to Hampton to Booker T. Washington to Tuskegee Institute to Gandhi, who, she argued, "adopted the idea of manual training for the basic education program for India." Another of Richard Armstrong's sons, William, trained as a lawyer and served the Hawaiian sovereign government as attorney general and in other posts; later, in New York, he represented those who were clamoring for the U.S. annexation of Hawaii in 1893.[26]

As much as Tate had declared herself not a historian of domestic racial issues, it was impossible to avoid them in nineteenth-century United States political history, even if one focused on international expansion, and as she came to see it, perhaps especially so. She was also not immune to insights from her position as an African American, especially at a time when the civil rights movement and national politics, and scholarly and popular attention to race, were becoming so much more prevalent. But she also was influenced by her graduate students and their interest in race, in some cases co-writing articles with them as a way to gain publication credits for them.

Among her earliest publications on Hawaii were articles concerned directly with slavery, or rather with the question of whether slavery was to be instituted in Hawaii after annexation or if some temporary importation of slave labor would be possible. That question persisted even after the Civil War, transformed into a debate about whether free southern "colored labor" could be shipped in to meet the demands of a growing sugar industry.

In these ways, Tate argued, the ongoing political crossfire about slavery and its extension or abolition figured in the early annexation debates as did ideas about the export of free Black laborers to the islands. She explained how the British deployed the history of race relations in the United States as a reason to oppose its annexation of the islands. Annexation advocates in the 1850s were predominantly in the "southern slave holding states," raising the "possibility of the islands becoming a slave state." Some missionaries also initially opposed talk of annexation because of their abolitionist beliefs. The end of the Civil War would shift these concerns.[27]

Ideas about race and racial groups drove these discussions, Tate explained. The association of Hawaiian sugar planters, for example, opposed the idea of sending Black Americans to the islands, arguing that "native Hawaiians are a different race entirely, and are capable of becoming assimilated in all the branches of modern civilization with Anglo-Saxons; but, with negroes as a class—never." Tate emphasized public debates about the fears of interracial mingling between Blacks and native Hawaiians. Sereno Bishop, a prominent Presbyterian missionary, argued that slavery had only partially redeemed the descendants of Africans from "debasement," that the islands would "deteriorate like the population of Hayti," and that "Hawaiians needed breeding up, and not down." At the same time, the United States, Tate noted, did not want Hawaii to be overrun by Chinese immigrants, or by the British importing Indian "coolies."[28]

These debates in newspapers and official accounts seemed to have caught Tate by surprise. That she chose to write about it is also a measure of how personally and politically offended she was by what she and her graduate students found in her historical research. In quoting a newspaper article that called twenty-one Black people brought to the islands from Tennessee "a happy brand of negroes," she added an explanatory comment in her citation footnote: "White Americans generally believe that all Negroes are 'happy' all the time. . . . However, several educated American Negroes moved independently to the territory of Hawaii in the early half of the twentieth century and achieved distinction, holding judgeships and other government positions, as well as diplomatic appointments." With that corrective, she sought both to challenge a persistent stereotype held in white American minds, using her knowledge about the history of Black people in Hawaii to do so, and to impose a class distinction.[29]

Tate extended her exploration of slavery and race to frame debates accompanying imperialist interventions in the region by Great Britain. She came to understand this political and diplomatic history through her close reading of government correspondence and sessional accounts in London and in Australia and New Zealand. From that research, she wrote an account of how kidnapped Polynesians from other islands were among the early laborers brought to the island of Fiji. "Blackbirding," as it was called, was practiced by the British but also tolerated by the French, "who looked upon 'kidnapping,' or 'la traite,' as an offense of no importance."[30]

But Tate viewed this practice through the history of slavery, seeing it as a "new traffic in human beings" that reproduced "the horrors of the 'middle passage,' " adding that those captured were "detained by force, cruelly flogged, and sometimes killed if they tried to escape." She emphasized that "women and young girls were forcibly taken from their husbands or relatives and often found themselves at the mercy of the savage crews of the ships engaged in the kidnapping." The practice "broke up patterns of family life, labor, and warfare," she argued, and "contributed to the disintegration of native life." This is an indirect but powerful example of how standpoint enriches scholarship when it brings out comparison and juxtaposition that are fruitful and that other scholars might overlook.[31]

Elsewhere in the Commonwealth, Australia's interventions into eastern New Guinea generated debates over the appropriate manner of empire to deploy, revealing racial ideas embedded in Britain's imperial history. Tate cited a British official, Sir Arthur Gordon, who argued that it was "undesirable to assume, unasked, the sovereignty of several millions of savage and semi-civilized people, because . . . England has already Black subjects enough," suggesting instead that the governance model used in India might work better. New Zealand officials, she wrote, opposed the idea of joining a federation among neighboring islands out of fear that it would "open the most racially pure country in the South Pacific to a flood of island immigrants, including even Indians from Fiji." Richard Seddon, whom Tate called "New Zealand's imperialist premier," feared that annexation of Fiji would leave his country overwhelmed and outnumbered by a "colored population," at one point asking "how many *niggers?*" Britain instead made Fiji into a Crown colony in the 1870s, a status that quieted the debate, at least for then.[32]

As if to reference those earlier fears of racial intermingling in New Zealand, Tate concluded her article on race and racism in the South Pacific this way: "This concern over the 'shadow of the coloured races' was not unfounded, for despite the meagerness of New Zealand's acquisitions and her nineteenth century racial purity, her Minister of Island Territories, in a conference with Merze Tate in July 1958, revealed that every fourth New Zealander has an island relative." The American example of concealed and often coerced interracial sexual relations did not seem far from her mind, just as it had surfaced in her earlier analysis of similar fears in India, though framed differently in terms of caste and religion.[33]

Just as in the 1940s, when she first published work on World War II and the "darker races," Tate turned to the *Journal of Negro History*, the *Journal of Negro Education*, and the *Journal of Religious Thought* which welcomed her early work on race and imperialism in the Pacific, including her spate of articles on the role of missionaries in Hawaii. In those forums, which reached a predominantly African American readership, Tate laid out her research in a clear and passionate prose that linked her work to an expanding model of Black studies advanced by publications based at Howard and in Washington. For those readers, Tate's work in the early 1960s would resonate loudly. Tate had tried twice without success to interest the *Mississippi Valley Historical Review* (the predecessor to the *Journal of American History*) in the articles on race and slavery in Hawaii, but was told that her work did "not seem to make a sufficiently important new contribution to justify acceptance in the *Review*."[34]

Tate's travels across the region helped shape her views as did the heightened activism of the modern civil rights movement's renewed attention to the history of slavery and racism in the United States. Her vivid descriptions and observations in her letters to her family had emphasized the reinforcing hierarchy of race, class, and nationality in Fiji, in particular. But her understanding of British imperial relations with African colonies and certainly with India, where she had lived earlier in the decade, also informed her analysis. Undergirding her work on the region was a sympathetic portrayal of the plight of indigenous people, whom she depicted as being treated as "commodities" to be moved about, displaced at the will of more powerful external nations.

Tate's final argument in her articles on Hawaii and the southwestern Pacific relied on the diplomatic history of the region as evidence of shifts in Anglo-American relations. She maintained that over a fifty-year period in the nineteenth century, Britain shifted its suspicion of United States engagement in

Hawaii to an acceptance and welcome of its move toward annexation. "Although not clearly recognized at the time," she concluded, "and certainly not by Australia and New Zealand, the annexation of Hawaii without a single protest or annoying question from Great Britain—despite considerable 'twisting of the lion's tail'—illustrated the growing identity of interests between her and the United States and served as the first symbol of Anglo-American understanding or rapprochement which was to become a significant factor in international relations in the twentieth century."[35]

As one of several examples, she singled out the views expressed in 1898 by Sir Cecil Spring-Rice, the prominent British foreign officer who had served as ambassador to the United States. In a letter to Henry Cabot Lodge written after the Senate approved a joint resolution for the annexation of Hawaii, Spring-Rice explained that "I don't believe that England, the island, is strong enough, or will remain comparatively strong enough to defend English civilization alone— . . . And I welcome any step which America takes outside her continent because it tends to the increase of the common good." In this way, Great Britain had come to see the United States as, in Tate's words, "a future great sea power, a kindred people, and a potential ally" in the Pacific region.[36]

Tate's journal articles on the evolution and significance of Anglo-American relations in the Pacific earned her international professional notice. The *Pacific Historical Review,* the journal of the west coast branch of the American Historical Association, awarded her its Louis Knott Koontz Award in 1963 for her article on Great Britain and the sovereignty of Hawaii. The versatility of Tate's skills as a researcher, scholar, and writer made her work relevant to scholars in several disciplines and regions, including Hawaii, the Pacific, and the British Commonwealth.

Tate also gained notice at the largest professional historical organization, the American Historical Association, in the early 1960s, a time when its annual conferences still remained slow to recognize African American and female scholars and the field of "Negro" history. She had been invited to provide commentary on a 1962 session on historical aspects of the problem of disarmament chaired by Hans Morgenthau, the venerable international relations scholar who had reviewed her first book on that topic. The panel focused on atomic weapons, and included Alice Kimball Smith, best known for her writings on the Manhattan Project. Tate's remarks complemented Smith's work on international control of atomic energy, but she made her own argument about the necessity for scientists themselves to engage in public policy and political advocacy. The following year, Tate was invited to be a member of the program committee that was chaired by Hilary Conroy at the University of Pennsylvania, with whom she shared intellectual interests about disarmament and Asia studies. He assigned her the task of organizing the sessions on United States diplomatic history.[37]

Tate's earlier work on disarmament also regained popular attention when efforts to limit nuclear testing emerged in the early 1960s. When the United Nations announced efforts to curtail the spread of nuclear weapons testing, women's international peace groups organized delegations to observe the start of negotiations in Geneva, in March 1962. Black newspapers announced that Coretta Scott King and Tate were among those selected to go. But Tate had some reservations about the organizers, Women's Strike for Peace, and judged their approach to the subject naive and uninformed. "Many of these ladies' organizations about limiting armaments and war no more, and so on," she would say, "they just don't know the facts." She resented that they had assumed she was a pacifist simply because she had written about disarmament, a misperception that would have been clear if they had actually read her work.[38]

The white women organizers also offended her personally and struck her as too controlling: "I could tell from those ladies that they wanted to possess me." In an unusual move for someone usually eager to travel, Tate withdrew from the trip after having lost patience with the trip's organizers. She broke completely with them, but still sent them materials that she hoped would "relieve them of some of their illusions or disillusions."[39]

With that done, Tate pivoted back to the Pacific, the region that would continue to occupy her mind for the rest of the 1960s.

CHAPTER 9

"A Modern Scholar"

WASHINGTON, 1960–1972

"A medieval monk might isolate himself from the world and devote all his waking hours to his writing projects," Tate once wrote, "but a modern scholar finds this impossible and also undesirable." She engaged a busy social and political life in Washington, and also kept in touch by mail with many others across the country and around the world. Her voluminous social correspondence is full of cards and letters thanking her for entertaining or for gifts or for notes of encouragement to friends recovering from loss or illness.[1]

Her new house served her well as she hosted bridge luncheons and elaborate dinner parties, when she could repay the hospitality always shown her by friends in Washington and beyond. Among her most frequent visitors were James Allen Thompson and Frances Thompson, the military officers who had first met her in Hawaii. The Washington area was their home between postings and after retirement, permitting a deep friendship that lasted for the rest of their lives.

Tate and the Thompsons often socialized together with Lucius Young and his wife, Muriel, another prominent Black military family. They had hosted Tate on her travels in Germany, and he also served as a professor of military science at Howard. They had in common their extensive travels, and a love of bridge. Tate, Frances Thompson, and the Youngs also shared their Catholic faith.

Tate, 1960s
(Zhang Collection, Western Michigan University)

Tate was a splendid cook and hostess, often showcasing cuisines from her travels around the world and presenting them on beautiful table settings from Tibet. Frances and Allen Thompson remembered many parties at Tate's home where they met other friends of hers such as Ethel Grubbs, and fascinating guests like Benjamin O. Davis, Sr., the Army's first Black general. Dinners would be full of talk of contemporary domestic and world politics, but they would always conclude with bridge, where the Thompsons witnessed Tate's mastery in good-natured competition.

Tate was considerably older than the Thompsons, and Frances recalls her "taking them under her wing" from their first meeting. She was impressed by Tate's intellectual generosity, saying that she "did not hoard her knowledge, but passed it on to others." At the same time, she never "flaunted" her education, but was very gracious and "down to earth," with a great sense of humor.

Over the years, their friendships were sustained during their postings by frequent letters back and forth with the woman they came to call "Sis." The letters tapered off when the couple returned to the Washington area, where they eventually retired and continued the relationship in person.[2]

When the Thompsons later had two children, Allene and Jay, they too joined family gatherings with Tate, known to them as "Auntie Merze." As a military family, they moved around a lot, so they were accustomed to the need, in Allene's words, to "make family where ever they were." Holiday and other gatherings were at their home or the Youngs' or Tate's house, full of beautiful things gathered from her many travels. She and her mother would take long walks with Tate in the gardens at the nearby Lourdes Grotto, where Tate would describe "where else in the world she had seen these particular species of flowers and plants."[3]

Allene remembers that Tate was "a marvelous cook" and a fun hostess, but it was their "quiet times" together that meant so much, just sitting on her porch or looking out her back window at her garden. Tate liked to hear her read and also encouraged her to talk and tell stories. She would stay over on occasion and sleep in what she called "the blue room," which was full of gorgeous white French provincial furniture. Tate brought back a colorful child-sized chair for her from Mexico and kept it in her house for her to use when she visited. Allene began a stamp collecting hobby when her Auntie Merze would send her stamps from around the world.

For her brother Jay, Tate's home was a fascinating place, because it was full of books, photographs, art, and unusual objects she had collected in her travels. Her cooking impressed him, too, because "nothing she did was ordinary, bland, or common," including the bacon she fried especially for him in the shape of a curlicue. But it was her "kind spirit" that meant the most to him; as he grew older, she would listen patiently as he "talked to her for hours." The family also made good use of Tate's prized parking spot at the Library of Congress when they would all go to see Memorial Day or Fourth of July fireworks from Capitol Hill.[4]

It is easy to imagine the spirited conversations about contemporary events that Tate had with her friends the Thompsons and the Youngs, both well-traveled military families with broad understandings of international and domestic politics. Tate, her colleagues at Howard, and her friends in Washington witnessed first-hand the political turmoil of the 1960s: the political assassinations, U.S. escalations in the Vietnam War (where Allen Thompson served as he had in occupied Japan and Korea), and the protests against it, including controversies over the disproportionate number of Black and poor soldiers sent to fight.

Tate donated money and attended the March on Washington in 1963. She supported the civil rights movement and its aims to end legalized segregation and discrimination just as she had done as a teenager speaking from the stage in Battle Creek High School, and as reflected in her corpus of writing in academic journals and books, and in her reporting from abroad. The influence of all that was happening politically is expressed most clearly in her scholarship, which even more explicitly linked race and slavery to her interpretations of imperialism in the Pacific. That is where she thought she could best make a difference, as a scholar and a teacher.[5]

Early in 1963, editors at Yale University Press completed a review of her draft on the United States and Hawaii, suggesting revisions that would improve the chances of publication. They were impressed by the significance of the work and by her balanced presentation of what they knew would be a controversial reinterpretation, written in a style that was "clear and cogent." But they were vexed by Tate's lifelong tendency toward too much content and dense detail, recommending that the work be reduced by at least a third or half. By June 30, Tate had resubmitted, and when the new version still needed additional editing, she successfully solicited five hundred dollars from Howard University to pay for a suggested outside editor.[6]

When that editor recommended even further reductions, Tate willingly complied, balking only when she feared that the press was trying to tone down the political arguments of her work. "Is it intended that I omit the intrigues or all that is incriminating," she wrote, "and present a missionary's history of the Hawaiian Revolution of 1893?" This is a reminder of the originality and political pointedness of her research and arguments as she moved away from a state-sponsored perspective. The "missionary" view was also that of the business elites as they were conjoined in a reinforcing enterprise.

Reassured that her "point of view" would remain intact, Tate worked intensely on the revisions and resubmitted the reduced manuscript that fall. She also had interested Yale in a second volume focused on the earlier history of United States engagement in Hawaii, essentially the half of the original manuscript she had been asked to remove. For Duke University Press, she continued to work on a third manuscript, focused on the ambitions of Australia and New Zealand in the region in the context of British policy in the South Pacific.[7]

While churning through work to be published, Tate's responsibilities as a teacher and the travails of Howard's history department continued unabated. By the early 1960s, the department faculty had shifted in small but important ways. John Hope Franklin had left for Brooklyn College in 1956 and Elsie Lewis had been hired to teach United States history the year of his move; Chancellor Williams joined the department in 1961, pioneering there his work on ancient and pre-colonial African history.

Importantly, the international relations faculty in 1956 had hired Bernard Fall, the renowned journalist and scholar of Southeast Asia and Vietnam. Fall wrote more than a hundred articles in popular venues and six scholarly books criticizing the failed French military experience in Indochina, and the United States interventions in Vietnam. His intellectual interests aligned closely with hers, and she admired and respected him as a scholar and a friend. Fall's work was supported in part by the Rockefeller Foundation, where Tate had suggested that he be funded.

Fall remained an active and popular member of the faculty until his untimely death from a land mine during a trip to Vietnam, one of six he made between 1953 and 1967. Tate's recounting of the shock of his death and the grief she felt remained a poignant episode in her oral interview a decade later. His presence at Howard may also help explain why Tate kept her academic focus on the particular parts of the Pacific she was studying, while recognizing the importance of Fall's work and his enormous influence in his writings on contemporary events in Indochina.[8]

Tate continued to train graduate students in the history department, including some she helped prepare for careers in academia. Among them was the prolific historian and prominent political activist Mary Frances Berry, who remembers Tate for her teaching of historical methods and that she was an absolute "role model for research at the Library of Congress." Tate showed her that being a "scholar" began with relentless in-depth archival research, forcing her students to expand "the possibilities of what they could see and do" on their own.

Berry remembers that Tate was very professional with her students and did not coddle them. But she encouraged and supported those willing to do the hard work she expected from them. Berry also remembers Tate's brilliant teaching of the unfolding Cuban missile crisis in 1962, broadening the narrow Cold War framing to conclude that the United States was in the wrong.

In manner and affect, Berry saw Tate as one of a group of strong and independent Black women at Howard. Tate suffered there professionally because she refused to subscribe to any gender conventions of female deference to men, including her male colleagues at Howard. Her training at Oxford and Harvard and her publication record rivaled and exceeded those of the men she worked with, which was rarely acknowledged or respected.[9]

Howard graduate students interested in a Ph.D. would earn a master's degree but seek admission to a doctoral program at a white institution, as did Berry. The *Brown v. Board of Education* decision in 1954 had led to a move toward desegregation of higher education, which brought attention to the scarcity of Ph.D. training for Black students. The ongoing political ferment also hastened federal and foundation support for Ph.D. training at Howard. Between 1955 and 1960, four natural science departments there were funded to add the higher degree.

Tate joined her colleagues in 1962 in supporting the creation of a history Ph.D. after reassurances that additional faculty would be hired. Indeed, over the next two years, six new faculty members were added in the fields of Russia, Latin America, the United States, modern Europe, Africa, and China. That brought some relief from teaching burdens on the current faculty but also added the labor-intensive work of overseeing doctoral training and dissertations.[10]

When Winston Langley, later a professor of political science and international relations and provost at the University of Massachusetts, Boston, arrived at Howard for graduate study in 1965 from Jamaica, he found not only that Tate understood his British-modeled educational background but that she was the "only one at Howard with a vision of the world that complemented his." He appreciated that she had such a broad understanding of global politics and colonialism at a time when the teaching and study of history and international relations were "far more compartmentalized." For him, "she was an interdisciplinarian before there was interdisciplinarity" in part because of the "breadth of her interests and training."[11]

Like Berry, he remembered her "impeccable dedication to methodology" in the use of primary documents, teaching him that historical research should be as rigorous as the "exacting requirements of the natural sciences." She helped him as a student to secure his own research desk at the Library of Congress, something he treasured. Students who worked with her, he said, had to be "very committed," because she required a "lot of written work," far more than other professors. In her classes, Langley observed that she "lectured wonderfully" in discussions that were "littered with the latest developments in the field" with her fluidly "shifting from one source to the next."[12]

Langley recalls that he "found out about her on his own," as other professors did not routinely send students to Tate. She seemed to him to be outside the male faculty networks, which led him to sense a certain loneliness for her at Howard. When he tried to add her to his graduate committee on political science and international relations, the department refused his request. Even as a student, he appreciated how difficult Tate's position at Howard must have been. Her work on disarmament and diplomatic history was "not a woman's world in her time or even today" but one that in his view was such a "male dominated area" that she has yet to receive recognition for what she achieved.[13]

Tate and Langley shared an interest in international law and political economy, and she urged him to stay focused on his own work. He took that to heart and continued to publish widely despite his administrative responsibilities. His dissertation had focused on relations between India and China in the post–World War II era, and his later writing spanned global studies, women's rights, and human rights, with a recurring focus on relations between China and the United States. One of the most useful things he also learned from her was how to draw maps from memory. His only regret from his time as Tate's student is that he did not follow her advice on using his training to invest in the stock market as she had prodded him to do.[14]

Rayford Logan chaired the history department for two decades until 1964, an extremely long tenure under the best of circumstances. His conflicts with Tate, over everything from classroom assignments to access to typing assistance to summer courses to curricular decisions, worsened over the years. At a time without formal grievance procedures and other protections, in dueling letters to the dean, she complained about what she viewed as his unfair and unprofessional treatment, and he detailed how she remained in defiance of him. He had tried to block or divert Tate's Rockefeller grant and seemed to resent the other small summer funding opportunities that were coming her way for her work on the Pacific. Their relationship had deteriorated to the point that they seemed to communicate primarily via formal typed letters, often copied to the dean.[15]

Tate was by every measure a strong, opinionated, independent woman, with an iron will and a determination to do what she thought was best for herself and for her students. She was never shy about asking for what she wanted and thought she deserved, whether in college, at Oxford, in India, at Radcliffe, or Howard. That is why she complained relentlessly in writing, defended herself in person, and refused to cooperate with Logan if she thought she was in the right. In other words, she fought back.

Logan's personal feelings about her (and many others in his life) are well documented in a source that we have access to but she did not: his copious diaries. To read his daily inner monologues is to enter the mind of a man who is generally angry, bitter, and often paranoid, a pattern that seems to worsen over time. But it is difficult to overstate the way in which his abusive descriptions of his feelings about Tate are offensively misogynistic, and repeatedly full of gender-specific profanity and name-calling. It is not clear what Logan knew of Tate's religion, but in his diary he also espoused virulently anti-Catholic sentiments, writing that the Church was the greatest threat to liberties of the American people, pledging to vote against Eisenhower because he had visited Cardinal Francis Spellman, and wondering if his passport would have been suspended for a year if he had been Catholic.

Tate was not the only faculty member or person about whom Logan had strong negative views or interactions. He absolutely detested Mordecai Johnson, Howard's president, and requested that he not be allowed to speak at his funeral. Logan devoted a section of his draft autobiography to "My Trials and Tribulations with President Mordecai Johnson and Professor Merze Tate" and blamed both for causing him to have a heart attack. Even his private feelings about those he called his closest friends, including his much younger fraternity brother John Hope Franklin, were fraught with jealousy, resentment, and fury. He attributed Franklin's success and his move to white institutions to the fact that he was dark-skinned, unlike Logan, who could have passed for white; he admired Franklin, who named his son after him, but also confided that he was "just a bit too aggressive." He resented Ralph Bunche's Nobel Prize and considered Benjamin Mays to be overrated, calling a talk he had given "pure ham and corn."

But it is one thing to be jealous and hypocritical, and another to hold an increasingly irrational hatred of Tate, over whom he exerted his authority, however petty, as department chair for two decades. In speaking later about how poorly she was treated at Howard, she emphasized that she survived by refusing to be embittered or to let hatred dominate her mind and her life. Tate publicly directed her complaints about gender discrimination and inequities at Howard at the pattern and practice of a male-only patronage system from which women were excluded, not naming Logan or any one person by name.

Tate somehow persisted in doing what professors do—she taught, she researched, she wrote—and she spent time enjoying her life with her friends, playing bridge, and traveling. As important, her sense of self led her to adamantly refuse to see herself reduced to being a victim, whether from racial discrimination or gender-based harassment from Logan. That's how she survived the emotional toll from the constant battling with Logan, a struggle well known to their colleagues and her friends.

Logan's stepping down as chair in 1964 and his retirement two years later coincided with the emergence of new leadership, including some younger women who would make special efforts to express respect for Tate's work at Howard and her scholarly achievements. Elsie Lewis, hired after Franklin's departure in 1956, became Logan's immediate successor, soon to be followed by Lorraine Williams in 1970. Tate celebrated these appointments and felt liberated after serving so long under Logan's rule as chair. Many years later, well after Logan's death in 1982, she was given the opportunity to speak about him to his biographer. She simply declined.[16]

At nearly sixty, Tate's physical energy and mental stamina remained strong. But early one evening in January 1964, a teenage boy rang her doorbell to alert her, he said, that someone suspicious was in her yard behind her house. When he suggested that he come in so they could walk through the house to investigate, Tate resisted and offered instead that they go outside around the corner of her house. Once they were in her yard, he turned on her, stabbed her viciously in the back, and ran away.

Fortunately, two passers-by saw her and had neighbors call an ambulance, which rushed her to the nearby Catholic Providence Hospital. She lost so much blood that she was in severe shock, her blood pressure had plummeted, and she could barely breathe because one of her lungs was filled with blood. Death seemed so near that a priest administered the Catholic rite of extreme unction to her. Desperate, doctors attached her to a thoracic pump, which over the next week removed half a gallon of blood, and helped save her life.[17]

"Intruder Stabs Howard U. Professor," the *Washington Post* reported the day after the attack, calling her condition "critical" and describing her attacker as "a Negro in his late teens wearing a dark jacket." With that report and others to follow, news of Tate's stabbing and her "poor" condition generated outrage and a tremendous outpouring of sympathy and support from friends at Howard and in Washington, and later, from those around the country and overseas. The Radcliffe Club of Washington organized a blood drive to help replenish supply after she required so many blood transfusions. Even after she was able to return home, she had to be hospitalized again for another twelve days, as surgeons tapped her lungs repeatedly to suction out fluid buildup, a process she found even more painful than the installation of the thoracic pump.[18]

Although she lived alone, Tate did not suffer from lack of care, thanks to the community of friends she had cultivated among her AKA sorors, bridge clubs, and Howard colleagues. Close women friends, including Frances Thompson, stayed with her, cooked for her, hired a private nurse, and saw her back and forth to doctors. After the attack, colleagues at Howard taught her classes and otherwise tried to relieve her of worry and responsibility.

But when the dean wrote in March to offer her a leave of absence for the remainder of the term, Tate refused, saying she was on the road to recovery and intended to return after spring break. A fall in her bathroom that fractured two ribs had delayed an earlier return. Still, her stoicism, refusal to show vulnerability, and singlemindedness about her work remained fully in place.

> Since I have microfilm from the Archives of Hawaii waiting for me in Founders Library and three rare books from the Honolulu Public Library on reserve in the Library of Congress—all ordered before the accident—and a manuscript sent to Duke University on December 21, 1963, returned for condensation by about one-half, I have plenty to occupy me. My conscience would not permit me to work on these and not meet my obligations to my students, all of whom I taught last semester.[19]

With that Tate showed once again that her reflexive response to trauma, this time from "the accident," was to keep her mind busily engaged with reading and writing, and with teaching. She marshalled her prodigious powers of concentration as if to erase both the physical pain and psychological scars from the nightmarish violent attack that nearly ended her life at her "dream home." Once again, she summoned her physical and emotional toughness and habits of denial and persistence to see her through. Her obsessiveness about work turned it into an escape and a refuge from other realities, even those as intimate as her own physical suffering, pain, and fear.

At the end of that year, after she had fully recovered, Tate hosted a lavish formal "thank you" luncheon for eighty guests at the DuPont Plaza Hotel, an event that ended with bridge games. Seated on the dais at the head table alongside Tate were, on her right, Mary Bunting from Radcliffe and on her left, Norma Nabrit and Elizabeth Jenkins, old friends and the wives of the presidents of Howard and Morgan State, respectively. She remained especially grateful to the doctors and nurses she credited with saving her life, inviting her surgeon's wife to the luncheon and showering the nuns at Providence Hospital with gifts of tempting sweet treats during Lent.

At some point, Tate had methodically compiled a five-page listing of each person who had helped her, with a description of how she knew them and how they had helped care for her, listing everything from cards, flowers, and food to free use of a vacation cottage on the Chesapeake during her recovery. This was her practice, to compile and to write and to document, as if the act of doing that calmed both her mind and her emotions.[20]

Despite the attack in her yard, Tate's home on Perry Street provided the solitude and quiet she needed to recover and to write. But she and her neighbors were taken aback when at the end of that year, the District of Columbia School Board included their block as a possible site for a new school for mentally disabled children, in part because of the park where they could easily play. The city proposed eminent domain over the entire block, a proposal that Tate said was "a greater shock to me than the stabbing." She rallied to help organize the neighborhood's opposition, meticulously preparing a document detailing why many other sites would be much better.

Tate also helped solicit letters and testimony to argue for a disparate religious impact on Catholic institutions in the neighborhood while also extolling the virtues of her "harmonious integrated" block (although she was the only Black resident). Skillfully deploying both religion and race, along with the usual fears of traffic woes, Tate's effort convinced the school board to remove their block from the list. Once again, as with her appeals about her Fulbright grant, she would use race to achieve a desired end, even as she resisted the idea of using it as an "excuse" or to ask for preferential treatment.[21]

The spate of personal bad luck that had begun with the stabbing in 1964 continued in the years that followed. She was not spared the increasing perils of urban living, at one point having her purse snatched and later her car stolen. Even the isolation offered by the wooded park across the street that had drawn her to buy the lots in the 1940s had by the end of the 1960s become an attractive nuisance as a haven for petty criminals, including some seeking to sell or buy drugs.[22]

Tate had refused the offer of a leave from teaching after her stabbing, but when Howard generously granted her $3,500 in summer research money that year, she took it. She was due a sabbatical in 1964–1965 and had tried to secure outside support for the year. But getting none, she took leave at half pay so she could continue working on her research and writing projects.[23]

Finally, after five years of trying, she succeeded in placing an article coauthored with a graduate student on atomic testing after World War II by the United States in its "strategic area" of Bikini in the Pacific. That testing required permanent dislocation of islanders, something avoided in the much more limited testing conducted in Nevada. She questioned whether "strategic" status entitled the United States to exercise wanton disregard for the danger and threat to the health of Bikini and neighboring islands.

That action, in an allusion to her earlier work on disarmament, caused "disillusion" for "those to whom the words 'colonialism' and 'imperialism' have sinister connotations." She argued that it mattered little whether the international legal relationship to a more powerful nation was that of "strategic area," "trust territory," "Crown colony," or "mandate," as all forms so diminished the sovereignty of the weaker partner. In this way, Tate also distinguished herself from those, like Du Bois and Logan, who had accepted the compromised concepts implicit in both the earlier League of Nations "mandates" and the U.N.'s later embrace of "trust territories." For her, the explicit power imbalance persisted regardless of the label applied.[24]

In good news, Yale University Press agreed to publish her book on Hawaii, supported once again by a small subvention from the Bureau of International Research at Radcliffe, marking the end to the fund that had sponsored her work and that of other women authors. In bad news, Yale declined to publish her second volume on Hawaii, saying that its list could not make room for both.[25]

Meanwhile, Duke also passed on her manuscript on Australia and New Zealand, a consequence she believed of her failure to cite the unrelated work of scholars from those countries who had been asked to review it. Tate's editor at Yale also then reviewed that third manuscript, all 768 pages of it. After once again being told that her work needed to be cut by half, Tate set about doing that. When Robin Winks, the Yale scholar of the British Empire, critiqued her manuscript, he suggested to the press that she add a new chapter on imperialism. She also grudgingly did that, only to have a different reader suggest later that it be deleted, a not uncommon occurrence in academic publishing.[26]

At wit's end, Tate made clear that she had no objection to removing it. Although she had spent a summer writing it, she never saw it as relevant or essential to her book. She explained that she had little interest in "theories" of imperialism: "This is not my field. I detest dialectics, I have no time to waste on polemics, and do not give a _ _ _ _ about the difference between Hobson's, Schumpeter's, Kautsky's, and Lenin's concepts of imperialism. I am concerned over what was sought and actually acquired in the imperialist struggle." In a letter to her archivist friend in Wellington, she was even more blunt, writing that Winks simply wanted to impress that he "knows far more about the subject than the writer" and that imperialism was his "pet subject," citing his edited collection from 1963, *British Imperialism: Gold, God, Glory.*[27]

Finally, in 1965, Yale's prestigious history list included Tate's book, *The United States and the Hawaiian Kingdom: A Political History.* She had managed to complete her work on it by the end of the year in which she was stabbed. She also succeeded in placing her related second volume with Michigan State University Press, which published it in 1968 as *Hawaii: Reciprocity and Annexation.* Because the original manuscript was separated, the two books had some overlap, but for the most part the second book was the detailed prehistory that she had been asked to remove from the first. When read together, one sees both the reach of her intellectual ambition as well as the consequences of her obsessive devotion to research and detail.[28]

As always, she followed her own intellectual convictions, not those of others. Her work on Hawaii began with the earliest recorded encounters between the Hawaiian islands and an American ship in 1789. With meticulous attention to detail, but a lively narrative style, Tate rendered that long prehistory with precision and verve. Although the outcome of the story was obvious, Tate situated the United States' justification and annexation in the broader context of its relationship with others interested in the region, especially Great Britain. Her books became a standard treatment of the long back story to the annexation of Hawaii in 1898 and its transformation into a "near colonial" status from that time until statehood in 1959.

Tate's approach was consistent with the methodological expectations of diplomatic history while also presenting bold interpretations. One of her aims was to refute what she saw as a bias in the existing historical accounts toward those she called the "annexationists." For her, the history of the United States' long involvement in Hawaii, which she dated from the missionary work of the 1820s onward, cleared the way for the eventual success of the annexation drive and had broader significance. She also explicitly called her book "An Economic Interpretation of the Hawaiian Revolution."[29]

"The Hawaiian controversy was more than a partisan issue," Tate wrote; "it actually initiated the great debate in American history over the merits of imperialism." This is an argument that countered the idea that the later

Spanish-American War at the turn of the century marked a shift in U.S. acquisitions of extraterritorial lands and people. For her, it had begun much earlier in Hawaii.

The political and economic engagement there was a prelude to the eventual acceptance of the idea that the country would extend its holdings beyond its continental borders, bolstering its assumption of Great Power status. In doing this, Tate repositioned Hawaii as the site for the earliest debates about American colonialism, one of her most important innovations. By the 1890s, broader support for territorial expansion emerged in debates about the Panama Canal and other acquisitions, such as the Philippines and Puerto Rico following the Spanish-American War. The impulse to conquer and control was present in all of these examples, but for Tate, Hawaii had been a proving ground for the convergence of economic, political, and military interests that drove these later actions.[30]

Telling the story of the nineteenth-century struggle for Hawaii's lands and strategic location through compelling portraits of many actors in a long drama, Tate paid attention to the missionaries, ruling Hawaiian royal family members, private sugar plantation interests, the press, and key public and private officials from the United States and elsewhere. She also attempted to counter the notion that annexation was welcomed or supported by native Hawaiians and their leaders. She presented a great deal of evidence to disprove claims that the United States was forced to act to keep the islands from being taken over by Great Britain, France, or Germany.[31]

Her original articles on race and slavery in Hawaii had been published first in journals aimed at Black readers, after she had tried placing them elsewhere. But she reemphasized that work here, and referenced her own articles repeatedly. She had no reservations about making her racial analysis a central part of her larger work.

In her second book on Hawaii, Tate told the detailed history of the political process and public debates over the trading relationship between the United States and the Hawaiian kingdom, primarily around sugar production, shipping, and imports. Ironically, this book, excerpted from her original manuscript, has greater coherence than the first, which suffers from a feeling of hasty incompletion because it had emerged out of the once conjoined larger narrative.

The "how" of the eventual takeover became clear to Tate during her reading of state archives and public sources in Hawaii, London, and the United States. "The propertied class," she wrote, "owned nearly all the real and personal estates, and conducted nearly all the substantial business. This group—not the native Hawaiians—controlled the combination of labor and capital which organized the industry and commerce and provided much of the revenue of the archipelago."[32]

Tate emphasized again that the sugar planters were able to evade responsibility for instigating revolution by placing the blame on the queen instead. She also detailed the falsification of the claims and the slanderous sophisticated public relations effort launched to cover up the real reasons for deposing the last ruling monarch, Queen Liliuokalani, in the so-called Revolution of 1893, but which Tate called a "bloodless coup d'état." She wrote: "Defamation of her character and an exposé of the rottenness of the monarchy were resorted to as a means of achieving the desired end." Tate seemed especially invested in exposing what she saw as an illicit political move and in redeeming the reputation of the last royal, whom she likely saw as a woman of color wrongly accused and demeaned.[33]

She challenged the notion that increased economic links to the United States accrued benefits to native Hawaiians, countering arguments that they would also prosper "under the 'trickle down' economic theory." Referring to the reciprocity treaty that had been in place before annexation, she explained that after six years in effect, "not one Hawaiian of pure blood in all the Islands owned or operated exclusively a sugar or rice plantation." She explained that "rice cultivation was almost exclusively in the hands of the Chinese. Cattle ranches are largely operated by the Portuguese. . . . The thousand little shops, bakeries, restaurants, and laundries were the property of the Chinese, Portuguese, and other foreigners."[34]

With her articles and two books, Tate had stepped boldly into the field of Hawaiian and Pacific studies while advancing arguments about American imperialism, race, and religion. Her work attracted scholarly attention for several reasons. Her wealth of articles had established her expertise as did her publication with Yale, but some of the attention was a product of the mid-1960s political milieu as well as her fresh interpretative paradigm.

Walter LeFeber, a prominent liberal diplomatic historian, called the work the best single-volume history of Hawaiian-American relations and the one most attuned to congressional and presidential politics. Harold Whitman Bradley, a historian of Hawaii, reviewed both books for the *American Historical Review* and called her work skilled and "definitive," saying that it could not be ignored. Other Hawaii specialists compared her favorably to the well-respected Ralph Kuykendall, who devoted his career to Hawaiian history.[35]

None of these reviewers, however, made any mention of Tate's own contextual arguments about race or enslavement, labor or the Civil War, all of which were intrinsic to nineteenth-century "frontier" politics. Yet these aspects of her work did headline two newspaper interviews with Tate during a summer 1965 visit to Hawaii. Her status as a Black woman historian also featured prominently in the pieces alongside photographs of her. Tate sought once again to deflect the role of her race in her work: " 'I don't let race warp my point of view,' she added. 'If I find race relevant to my writings, I don't hide it. But I don't blow it up either.' "[36]

Another article emphasized that she was both "a leading woman historian and a leading Negro historian," labels that Tate was reported to "dislike," preferring "to be judged solely on her merits as 'a historian.' " She also declined to comment on the civil rights movement, "explaining politely that 'I am a historian, not a sociologist,' and that it is not her field." That would be her retort in 1968, after her second book was published, when a Hawaii newspaper editor wrote to arrange an interview about "the contributions of Negroes to Hawaii."[37]

This tension between one's identity, work, and political obligations was a recurring one among Black writers, artists, and scholars as diverse as Langston Hughes, Du Bois, and Zora Neale Hurston, with a rekindling in the Black arts movement of the late 1960s. Sometimes expressed in questions, for example, about whether one was a "Black artist" or an "artist," the place of race in the creative process became entangled with debates about the powers and limitations of racial representation. In Tate's view, to label her professional status or her work by race was to restrict it or raise questions about her objectivity and competence.

Yale University Press signaled its continued commitment to Tate and her book by nominating it for the Bancroft Prize and considered doing it for the Parkman Prize as well, two of the most prestigious history book awards. She later reported repeatedly that she was told by white colleagues on Howard's faculty that the Bancroft Prize committee had decided she was to receive the award only to hear later that an unnamed historian had objected vehemently, an account that is difficult to verify. Even for a Black woman scholar to have been nominated in 1965 was a distinction, but the "first" she wanted did not come her way or accrue to Howard or Radcliffe, as she had wished. It took another three decades for a Black scholar to win the award, David Levering Lewis in 1994; not until 2012 would a Black woman, Tomiko Brown-Nagin, receive the honor.[38]

Even without the prize, Tate's first book sold very well and had gone into a second printing after its first year. Her many articles and the two Hawaii books further enhanced Tate's reputation as a scholar of the Pacific. After 1965 and into the 1970s, she regularly reviewed books on Asia and the Pacific in academic journals, including the *American Historical Review* and the *Journal of American History,* among others. She deployed her expertise in those reviews, once noting in a favorable reading of the young Paul Kennedy's book on Anglo-German-American relations and Samoa that he could have benefited from research in the National Archives for New Zealand, as she had done. But she welcomed his attention to the history of the "new imperialism" in the region, the topic she had begun to explore in 1948.[39]

Tate never found a way to publish her book on Australia and New Zealand, although she was able to publish several articles from that work. Her revisions of the third manuscript also dragged on due to editorial staff changes at Yale University Press, which she believed doomed the project's publication there; a final rejection came after three years of review delays and additional revisions. As a sign of conflicting shifts in the field of history, one reader argued that as "a historical account of European penetration into the Pacific it is old fashioned" while another criticized her attention to race as a "value judgment" that was "out of place in a scholarly work." It is true that her methodology and sources were associated with traditional diplomatic history, but, as the second comment confirms, her questions and her contrarian arguments were not.[40]

After years of research, writing, and revising, Tate refused to accept that her manuscript on Australia and New Zealand's ambitions toward their island neighbors was never going to be published. When Yale said no, Tate took the manuscript to Harvard University Press, which sent it to New Zealand for review by Angus Ross, the premier scholar in the field. He confirmed the significance and originality of the work and commended it for "the concept of a history covering Australian and New Zealand interests 'from the tropics to the pole' and from the beginning of British settlement to the present." His eighteen-page report complimented her research and recommended the manuscript for publication after revisions to reduce excess materials, a not unusual review outcome. Still, the book never made it into print, even though she continued to work on it into the 1970s. Later, she even divided the manuscript in two, with one on Australia and the other on New Zealand, but still without publication success.[41]

As for Hawaii, she had gathered material to capture the drama of the Hawaiian monarchy by writing a biography of Kamehameha IV, the young king whose life ended tragically at age twenty-nine. Tate had found much to admire in him, including the health care plan he instituted, while noting his opposition to annexation; he also sought closer connections to Great Britain and the Anglican church as a defensive strategy. When she was unable to interest publishers in a biography, she converted her account into a 780-page fictionalized rendition, titled *Uneasy: The Life and Times of Kamehameha IV.* She also was not able to bring that to print despite eventually adopting a Hawaiian pseudonym, hiring an agent, and making appeals for the editorial attention of Jacqueline Kennedy Onassis at Doubleday. Creative persistence remained one of her most consistent characteristics even when she was exploring genres far afield from her training.[42]

The culmination of her work in the Pacific came later, in 1973, when Howard University published a collection of twenty-seven of her articles as *Diplomacy in the Pacific.* Tate proudly claimed the volume as her "fifth book," seeming to compensate for the repeated rejections of her other manuscripts. A review of the book highlighted the articles from a decade earlier on race and slavery, topics that earlier critics had greeted with silence. With that, Tate's quarter century of research and prolific publishing on Hawaii and the Pacific came to a close. There, as elsewhere, her conceptual reach was ahead of its time, but also exceeded her ability and willingness to cater her research and writing into forms acceptable to academic publishers.[43]

Tate's family in Michigan required more time and energy in the decade after her sister's death. She had become more dependent on her three brothers and sisters-in-law in Michigan who helped care for their aging and ailing mother. Tate helped financially and also had designated her older brothers and their wives as her beneficiaries out of concern for her mother's well-being. She expressed her appreciation through gifts sent to two of her brothers who lived in Detroit and one who had retired and was living in Mecosta, closest to their mother.

But relations between daughter and mother still seemed strained, as if the emotional distance between Michigan and Washington could not be bridged. "Dear Mother," Tate wrote plaintively in 1962, "I hope you enjoyed your birthday and Mother's Day gifts I sent. Herschel writes quite often and says the neighbors at the corner are looking in on you and that all goes well so far. I have been in bad shape with a slipped disc in my spine, but am improving somewhat. . . . Drop me a line when you feel like it." When their mother soon was no longer able to live in her own home alone, the family resorted to paying someone to live with her, an arrangement that also proved unworkable over time. Her brothers and their wives then began alternating having her stay with them in Detroit or Mecosta.

By the time Myrtle Tate turned ninety in 1965, her mental health was in serious decline. At one point, Tate had agreed to have her mother come to Washington as an escape from the harsh Michigan winters, but her condition deteriorated so quickly that travel was no longer possible. When her senility made it difficult for her to live safely at home with them, her children faced the dreaded decision of whether to put her in an institution and how to pay for it. This was an era when, as her son Herschel explained, families feared that "they have to drug them and tie them in chairs and I don't want to see that happen to her. She has worked to [*sic*] hard and sacrificed to [*sic*] much to let that happen to her."[44]

But the next year, with her condition more than they could handle, her family agreed to place her in a care facility in Mt. Pleasant, with some state financial assistance, which their proud mother who viewed Social Security as charity would have detested. Tate also helped pay for her care and traveled to Michigan to visit her.[45]

In March 1969, Myrtle Tate passed away, ten years after her older daughter's death. An obituary that her remaining daughter Merze helped write commended her deep Christian faith and her "gifted talent in recitations and readings." Descendants from the Lett and Cross families and from a wide community circle of longtime friends and neighbors attended, officiated, provided music, and served food at her funeral services. The carefully crafted family history deftly obscured that Tate's mother had been married twice, as if even in death, their family's public image needed protection.[46]

This decade in Tate's life ended in the way it had begun, with loss and grief, first from her sister's death in 1959 and then her mother's in 1969. But it also had been filled with professional fulfillment and recognition. A month after her mother's death, Tate received word that she had been selected as the winner of the Isabella County Native Daughter Award. Recounting her humble beginnings on a farm and her many achievements since, the chair of the award committee said, "It is almost incredible that this long and impressive career started in the village of Blanchard and circled the globe. This is one Native Daughter of whom we can all be very proud."

Photographed smiling, seated on a couch, wearing a business suit, and holding an open copy of *The United States and the Hawaiian Kingdom,* Tate appeared confident, relaxed, and ready for whatever was to come. But race and place still mattered in Michigan, where "Native" referred to those like her who were born there, but not to the Saginaw Chippewa peoples living on the nearby Isabella Indian Reservation.[47]

Age did not diminish Tate's appetite and ambition for new projects. In 1970 she turned sixty-five, an age when many begin to think of slowing down or retiring. Despite her complaints about salary inequities at Howard, her financial future was secure, even as she continued to represent herself as "a poor single woman" with no one to help support her.

She continued to keep quiet, however, about the extent of her large investments in the stock market, which she had begun while living in North Carolina in the late 1930s. Spotting promising opportunities based on her extensive newspaper reading and her understanding of economics, international relations, and geopolitics, Tate had for decades bought low, held, and reinvested proceeds from stocks, watching them split and multiply and split again. She deployed prominent brokers first in Detroit and then in Washington to manage her holdings, but she remained firmly in charge of her portfolio. Colleagues and students would overhear her in her office at Howard making calls to buy and sell stocks, but no one knew that her holdings were so substantial.

Although she always had been very generous in gift giving to friends and family, she also had a lifelong habit of saving money and meticulously accounting for her own spending, as her travel diaries and grant reports often detailed. "I do have to watch every Penny," she once explained, "in order to have dollars to make more dollars." Over time, those saved, well-invested dollars multiplied enough to permit her to think about benefiting others while also building and preserving her own legacy.[48]

It is not surprising that she wanted to help Radcliffe, where she had earned her doctorate and which had provided subventions for the publication of three of her books. She remained active in alumni affairs and was especially grateful that the Washington chapter had organized a blood drive for her benefit in 1964 after she was stabbed. But in deciding what to do, she recalled as well the crucial financial support she had received from the AKAs and from Oxford when she was most desperate.

With all that in mind, she decided to donate $100,000 to create the first graduate fellowship at the then Bunting (now Radcliffe) Institute in her name. She wanted the award to be open to all women, with no preference for race, nationality, or subject of study, and that it also be available to international students, who, like her, might find themselves otherwise unable to complete their work. She hoped that the funds might "mean the difference between

Alumna Recognition Award winners, Radcliffe, in 1979; Tate is at far right, with Adrienne Rich next to her (Moorland-Spingarn, Howard University)

success or failure—or even life or death—to the student," and "change the course of her life," which is how she thought about her AKA fellowship and her Oxford degree.[49]

The money for the gift came over several years, but she contributed enough up front to enable the first award from the Merze Tate Fellowship to be made the next year, in 1972. Those substantial early portions came from her holdings in Hot Shoppe (later Marriott) stocks, purchases she had made while closely following the travel and tourism sectors. But her expected contributions for the fellowship represented only a small portion of her portfolio of mutual funds and at least thirty-six other stocks. She proposed to Radcliffe's treasurer that those holdings also could be designated for the institution's benefit, if he could help structure her will or a trust so that her older brothers, should they survive her, would receive lifetime proceeds, with the remainder going to the institution.

After sending a draft will to accomplish that and a year of being promised action, Tate became insulted that she was not being taken seriously as a potential donor. At one point she wrote to Radcliffe president Mary Bunting suggesting that she "light a firecracker or a Molotov cocktail" under the treasurer. Finally, exasperated, she concluded that he, "accustomed to dealing with estates involving millions of dollars, could not be bothered with my holdings" and she should rethink her offer to make a gift of her entire estate.[50]

Radcliffe's loss was Western Michigan University's gain. The school considered her among its most outstanding graduates, having awarded her an honorary degree in 1947. Tate had maintained close ties with faculty and administrators there over the years, often corresponding frequently with favorite professors. When she approached officials about her wish to endow scholarships, three senior administrators flew to Washington to meet with her in her home, where they sat in the living room and, over a lunch she had prepared, drafted an appropriate will and a revocable living trust agreement that she later signed in August 1973.

With that, Tate set in motion a plan that eventually would endow fully funded undergraduate scholarships based on need and merit, but not reserved for Black or female students. Tate's warm relationship with Radcliffe continued despite the shift of her projected estate assets to WMU. Even after she completed her pledged amount for the fellowship, she continued to contribute over the years but always designated that her funds should go to support the graduate Merze Tate Fellowship.[51]

Even as she was preparing for the transition from teaching to retirement, Tate remained committed to her students, including her earlier students such as Mary Frances Berry and Winston Langley, who would become professors themselves. Among a later cohort was Lester Brooks, who still recalls: "The first thought that comes to me when I hear the name, Merze Tate, is how awestruck I was in her presence. She was so well-known, well respected, and I had read her scholarship." He especially admired the "dignified manner" in which she carried herself, which also influenced his decision to become a "serious student" and then a professor himself.[52]

One of her last students was Lydia Lindsey, a Howard undergraduate who also took her history master's degree there in 1974. She remembers Tate's commitment to rigorous methodological training but also how her advancing age had not dimmed her attention to fashionable self-presentation, including always being well-coiffed and with manicured nails. Tate's recommendation years later helped her to be admitted for doctoral work on Jamaican immigrant women workers in Birmingham, centering the plight of black women in Black British studies and discussions of British imperialism.[53]

As Tate faced the end of her career at Howard, she most coveted a Distinguished Professorship, which she viewed as a much-deserved recognition based on her publications, international reputation, and decades of service to students and the institution. But in 1971, Rayford Logan was permitted to come out of retirement to claim that honor, which must have seemed especially unfair to her as a still active member of the faculty. Although at some point her dean did recommend that she receive that distinction, it was never awarded to her. She believed then and for the rest of her life that had she been a man, with the same record, the honor would have gone to her then or even earlier. She would later include this disappointment as further evidence of the "deep humiliation" and "financial loss" she suffered as a woman professor at Howard.[54]

Tate's decades of work at Howard and as a scholar did not go unnoticed by others, however. History department chair Lorraine Williams highlighted Tate's career as part of an event in 1970 honoring the department's senior professors. An associate dean, Annette Eaton, took the opportunity to thank her specifically for her example as a woman professor. Tate's presence, she wrote, "provides the inspiration, the strength, the courage to continue the fight against the prevailing atmosphere of paternalism." Citing her productivity as a scholar, Eaton praised her as a "model for us to copy" and "a standard to be kept before our eyes as we shape our own careers." When her collection of articles on the Pacific was published, her junior colleague Michael Winston wrote to thank her for "her example of devoted scholarship," adding that "I am not unaware of some of the trying circumstances that you have worked under" and that his admiration for her "as an historian is all the greater."[55]

When Allison Blakey joined Howard's history faculty straight out of graduate school in 1971, Tate was among his most senior colleagues. He saw her as a "kindred academic" because he was a Black scholar trained as a Russian historian. It was in teaching Black students there that he was pushed to research people of African descent in Russia and Europe, similar to the way that her students' interests in the 1960s influenced Tate's work on race and slavery in Hawaii and the Pacific. Arriving as she was coming to the end of her career, he recalled that she was viewed as a legend as a scholar but by then she struck him as an isolated, private, and emotionally guarded person. He was sympathetic to how difficult it must have been for a woman of her generation to achieve so much in fields where there remained few women and few Black academics.[56]

Retirement from Howard University began for Tate in 1974, but she was permitted to teach until 1977, a courtesy extended to her and others to maintain income for a few extra years. Even before she neared the age of retirement, she had begun to think about her own legacy, not only as a philanthropist, but as a woman who had led an unusual life of travel, scholarship, and teaching. Her many adventures as a world traveler and accomplishments as a scholar always stood at the center of how she wished her life to be celebrated and remembered.

In 1969, Logan published *Howard University: The First Hundred Years, 1867–1967,* an official 656-page institutional history. He also used his account to settle some old scores; he wrote in detail of Mordecai Johnson's unfair treatment of Lucy Slowe as a way to criticize the former president. Logan devoted much attention to individual faculty over the years. Yet Tate, with whom he had worked since 1942, appears in the book only in a photograph on a page with three other "distinguished professors" and in the appendix in a bibliography of works by Howard writers.[57]

That erasure from Howard's official institutional history provided Tate with even greater incentive to find ways to document her own life, including her presence at the university, her career, and her travels. Being a devoted researcher, she knew that creating and curating an archive was the best way to preserve the evidence that a future researcher would need to resurrect the story of her life and her work. So, with the help of Dorothy Wesley Porter, she began contributing her papers, her scrapbooks, her photographs, her films, and her bridge trophies to Moorland-Spingarn in 1973, a process she would continue with Michael Winston, Porter's successor.

In the final decade of her academic career, the campaigns for racial and gender equality in the 1960s and 1970s began to have some ripple effects in the profession Tate had joined in 1935. The historian William Freehling of the University of Michigan wrote in 1970 to ask her help in finding a "man," a "qualified Black Scholar to teach our courses in Afro-American history." Tate did not mince words, writing, "may I say that if we knew of an available bona fide one we would secure him for our history department. Most of those 'moveable' are pretenders."[58]

Tate herself had begun to receive entreaties from predominantly white institutions as they began to search for Black faculty, but these opportunities seemed to have little appeal to her. One colleague and friend raised the possibility of a position on the west coast after her retirement, but she demurred. University officials elsewhere asked if she would be interested in being considered for a position as a chancellor or dean or vice president of academic affairs. She had never expressed an interest in administrative work and that had not changed, but she also understood well the larger political shifts under way.

When the Woodrow Wilson fellowship program specifically invited her to apply for funding, she commented to a friend that the "reason may be that I neatly fit the requirement of minority representation in two ways—by my color and my sex." Bowdoin College approached her about sharing her work on "the Black experience," but in typical fashion Tate did not hold back in declaring that although she was "colored," her specialty was "in history—diplomatic history, international relations and political science" and that her doctorate from Harvard was in government.[59]

Just as she had seen the evolution of political attacks on racism, Tate also witnessed the coming of women's suffrage and campaigns for liberation and greater opportunities, including in her own profession. A number of women historians were just beginning their careers as she was contemplating the end of hers. The AHA Committee on Women Historians reached out to Tate in 1972, inviting her to appear on a panel titled "Life Styles for Women Historians: Past and Future" at the annual meeting in New Orleans. Tate gave that meeting a plaintive critique for the paucity of Black men and women scholars in the largest association in the white-dominated history profession.

> The ratio of Negroes to others—as usual—was small, not much over 1 per cent, and far from 10 percent. From random observation, I would estimate that not more than 25 to 35 Negro members were present [out of 3,000]. . . . In the panel discussions on American Diplomatic and European Diplomatic History, I was the only person of color present and in the case of the one on which I participated, 'Life Styles for Women Historians,' there was only one other in the large audience [Mary Frances Berry].

Whether in a room full of white men discussing diplomatic history, her chosen subfield, or in a room full of white women coming into the profession, Tate's status as a senior Black woman historian remained a mark of her exceptionalism, but also of her long struggle to be a scholar.[60]

Nell Painter, then an assistant professor at the University of Pennsylvania, approached Tate a few years later and asked her to help fix the "lily-white aspect" of the Berkshire Conference of Women Historians, whose panel offerings ignored Black women. As a member of the conference's programming committee, she asked Tate to present a paper on "Black women" from some aspect of her research. In a handwritten postscript, Painter admitted that she did not expect Tate to do that, explaining that "I'd be very proud to see you at the Berks, just to show them a thing or two. You'll forgive me if I bask in your reflected light—we share the same alma mater. I'm a Harvard Ph. D. 1974. My hat's off to you, madame."

Tate's reply in declining was her usual formulaic proclamation that she was too busy with too many unfinished projects and teaching. What she did not add was her usual curt reminder that the requested subject was not her specialty, perhaps a small courtesy to a newly minted, energetic young Black woman historian.[61]

CHAPTER 10

"The Sinews and Arteries of Empire"

AFRICA–WASHINGTON–AFRICA, 1972–1976

When student activists mounted a takeover of Howard's campus in 1968, Tate had complained about disruptions for faculty and administrators. But she was not unsympathetic to the curricular changes the students were demanding. "Last semester, with students clamoring for courses on Africa," she later reported, "I concluded: 'If you can't beat them, join them.' " She created a new course called "Imperialism in Africa" that also served as a forum for "avid" freedom of expression where students could "air their views and let off steam." The class, she said, "proved popular and interesting" not only for students at Howard but some from other colleges in the city.[1]

Tate referred to herself as part of "the middle generation," who "look askance at student demonstrations here and abroad" and "deplore the damage and the militancy, and wonder what will happen to this world in turmoil." She complained that Howard student protesters had destroyed the prized large maps that she used in her teaching and had fought to have the department buy. Casting campus shutdowns as the work of a "vociferous and militant minority," she commended other students who through "sheer will power and brilliance" stayed focused on their academic work.[2]

So even as she supported the larger political aims of the student protests, she remained uncomfortable with their tactics. As someone who devoted herself to education and building institutions like Howard, it pained her that new "radicals" from a younger generation disrupted and threatened to destroy what she saw literally as part of her life's work.

New offerings in both African and Black American history had formed the core of the students' demands. Both fields had their own histories at Howard. Two early titans of studies of early African civilizations, William Hansberry and his student Chancellor Williams, had both held positions in the history department, but not without stirring controversy there and in their scholarly fields. Hansberry had arrived in 1922 and established a popular African studies program despite deep skepticism there about his pioneering work on ancient and medieval African civilizations. His time on the faculty ended with his retirement in 1959. Williams had joined the faculty in 1949 and also was a scholar of early African civilizations, whose groundbreaking books on African antiquity had begun in the 1960s, with the best known, *The Destruction of Black Civilization,* published in 1971, five years after his retirement from the university.

Of the two, Tate had most enjoyed a warm working relationship with Hansberry, whom she admired, although she repeatedly prodded him to publish the multivolume work he could not bring to completion in his lifetime. She sympathized with him over what she saw as his unfair treatment at the hands of Rayford Logan and others who discounted his knowledge, exacting revenge by delaying and denying him advancement in the department. Logan repeatedly had refused to recommend him for any grant or a full professorship.

It was Tate, who in her role as acting chair in 1951–1952, recommended and enabled the Hansberry family to spend a Fulbright year in Ethiopia and Egypt. She was good friends with his wife Myrtle, an AKA soror, and remained so after her husband's death in 1965. At a long overdue Howard University tribute to Hansberry in 1972, Tate praised him as a "scholar, teacher, and advisor *par excellence*" who had "pioneered half-a-century ago in a field which has since become popular," calling him a " 'prophet without honor' in his own country," signifying what was also true—that she believed that Howard had treated him very poorly. But she saw as the larger tragedy that Hansberry had not been enabled to convert his vast knowledge and "files, files, and more files of notes, pictures, maps, graphs" on Africa into the six volumes he had conceptualized, despite her repeated entreaties and suggestions.[3]

Tate's own intellectual interest in Africa was not new, as demonstrated in her earliest anti-imperialist writings. She also had published ten long essays in the 1940s and 1950s about books on contemporary Africa, even while she was also writing about India, Asia, and the Pacific. Tate rejected false distinctions between the plight of Black South Africans and Black Africans under Belgian and German rule; to her, they all suffered under "ruthlessness and brutality" and color bars that robbed them of their most productive land and natural resources. Citing the "grotesque disproportions" of the ruling white minorities, she rejected the designation by one writer of South Africa as "a white man's country." That, she wrote, was designed merely to "tickle the ears of white men" who embraced a "Pan African Idea" that would extend that logic to the whole of Black Africa.

She also bemoaned Italy's "Fascist Colonial officials" in Ethiopia, Eritrea, and Somalia. She did not limit her criticism to "arrogant Saxon exploitation," but raised questions about the ways that East Asian, Chinese, Japanese, and other merchants also subjugated native Africans—a critique similar to one she had made about Native Hawaiians. She argued that Africans deserved basic rights and living wages and that Africa should be treated as "more than an area for tropical development."

As for the British, Tate dismissed the notion that their empire in Africa no longer existed, rejecting the idea of a "Commonwealth of Nations" as mythic. More generally, and unlike others including Bunche, Du Bois, and Logan, she consistently bemoaned the U.N. mandates there as little more than a new "cloak for imperialism." She feared that the continent would simply be subject to even greater exploitation in an age of growing global economic interdependence. The availability of uranium in the Congo, for example, made it vulnerable to nations such as the United States that needed the rare mineral for atomic weapons.[4]

Starting in the early 1960s, Tate had tried repeatedly to live and teach in Africa, without success. In 1963, Hansberry strongly recommended her for a visiting professorship at the new University of Nigeria, where he was revered, not least because Nnamdi Azikiwe, the first president of the country, had been a student of his at Howard. Hansberry wrote of Tate that in her intellectual range and "by the yardstick of international reputation," she was Howard's "most distinguished scholar." The university offered her a position, which she eagerly accepted, but in the end officials were unable to secure what they considered adequate housing for her despite her protestations that she required little, citing her time living and traveling in India.

Still intent on being on the African continent during her upcoming 1964–1965 leave year, she tried through the American embassy to secure a position at Haile Selassie University, but that too failed. The State Department then solicited her for a Fulbright to Uganda, an opportunity she welcomed enthusiastically, but that also did not materialize in time. Tate also had pursued an affiliation in Nigeria through a new program at Michigan State University, also without success.[5]

When Tate decided to offer her new course, she explained that "although Africa is not my specialty, international relations is," and she approached it by building on her deep knowledge of comparative European imperialism—not just in Africa, but in India, Asia, and the Pacific as well. After scrambling to pull together appropriate reading materials, she concluded that a textbook on external interventions into Africa was "urgently needed" and successfully applied for university research funds so she could write one. In an expansive narrative outline of nineteen chapters, Tate's proposal repurposed her jettisoned chapter on theories of imperialism from her Pacific project.

Her outline captured once again what had most interested her from the very start of her scholarly career: the "how" of imperialism, or the tools and technologies deployed to establish and maintain power. She used pithy one-word section headings, "exploration, penetration, exploitation, appropriation, conquest, and partition," to be applied expansively to every region and each imperial power. Concluding with the emergence of independent states, she argued vehemently against mandates and trusteeships as antithetical to sovereignty and as modern forms of external control.

Envisioned as a methodical charting of the history of British, German, Spanish, French, Portuguese, and Italian powers on the African continent, her comprehensive conceptualization of her research interests, as in the Pacific, would have required a tome or two for each. Habits of mind and intellectual proclivities are difficult to change, even as she shifted geographic focus, but not her methods of research and writing. The fields she worked in were understudied, so she often saw the need for both original research and teachable synthesis, goals that are at odds or difficult to produce in one treatment, since a monograph would suit one purpose and a textbook the other.[6]

Tate continued to rework and expand the draft of the textbook over several years, informed by her classes. She told a friend that "vociferous Black power students are serving as guinea pigs," while also admitting that they were making very helpful suggestions. She relied on primary sources to teach as she struggled to find scholarly material that was not dated or propaganda. As if the ambitious scope of the project she had in mind was not enough, she also imagined a sequel, to be called "Nationalism and Africa," which would cover the period after the emergence of independent nations, presaging in some ways concerns raised in more recent scholarship. It was also her intention that the proceeds from her work on Africa would fund a scholarship for history majors at Howard, to honor the students who were pushing her teaching and scholarship in new directions.[7]

The textbook proposal was but a glimpse of her much broader intellectual trajectory on Africa. Reminiscent of the technological faculties she had displayed in her work on disarmament and atomic energy and testing, this project about Africa also was soon reshaped by her lifelong fascination with trains and railroads. She had ridden them across the United States, England, Europe, and India. But her specific interest had been piqued by an article in the *International Railway Journal* in 1962, which she likely read at the Library of Congress. That long essay, "Africa: New Railways for New Nations," was a detailed narrative and technical description of every contemporary route by country with costs and corporate involvement.[8]

By 1972, she had added a chapter to the textbook proposal, "Railways: Sinews and Arteries of Empire," which outlined what she saw as a new manifestation of imperialism: alliances between emerging nation-states and international corporations, including those based in the United States. Focused on mineral extraction and transport to large new ports, the new railway lines—which supplemented the extant colonial railway systems—also moved laborers en masse from their homes to mining operations all over the continent. Tate sketched out and mapped the growing presence of these new projects as the second part of a history of colonial railway systems in Africa, a topic she addressed in her teaching. Her approach to the march of global capitalism into Africa rested on her keen observation that patterns of extraction dictated the paths of railway development in Africa.

So even as she was still writing on the Pacific, she was already thinking about her next big research project. This came even before she made her repeated attempts to spend 1964 and 1965 in Africa, where she hoped to begin research to supplement what she could do from sources available in the United States. Not being able to travel to Africa in the 1960s obviously had not prevented Tate from making progress on her project about the increasing engagement of large international corporations there. When her travel plans were thwarted, she began to explore other ways of gathering the information she wanted, including by corresponding directly with large international corporations engaged in building or expanding railway networks that terminated at huge new seaports. But she did not reveal that she intended a highly critical evaluation of the impact of those economic interventions on Africa and Africans.

Finally, in 1973, Tate was able to visit Africa, at her own expense after not being able to secure financial support; in 1976, she returned on a funded research trip. Those two journeys came as she was entering the seventh decade of her life and the twilight of her professional career, adding what she saw as another set of adventures to her lifetime of international travel and research.

Her ability to make those trips required her to navigate the complexity of contemporary domestic, African, and international politics and diplomatic relations, which she did in quite contradictory ways. So much of her travel over the years had depended on her ability to move from one safe harbor to another, from one trusted official or friend of a friend or institution to the next. On these two trips, her reliance on that formula revealed dramatic changes under way in Africa, as well as the perils of privileging the personal over the political at a time when the relationship between the two was unsettled and changing.

Like her trip to the Pacific in 1958, Tate's plans to go to Africa over Howard's 1973 winter break were nearly overtaken by the death of a sibling, this time her older brother Theo. She managed to attend a service for him in Michigan on December 9 and still make her planned departure from New York the next day. Her month-long trip would take her to Monrovia, Kinshasa, Salisbury, Nairobi, Dar es Salaam, Addis Ababa, and Cairo, a typically hectic schedule made possible by planes large and small taken from city to city.

Tate's project on railroads in Africa was so ambitious that she had to split it into two parts, as was often the case with her work. The first part focused on the history of colonial railways, and she had been able to conduct much of that research through the holdings of the Library of Congress. The more contemporary portion required on-the-ground research as she investigated the giant corporations working with African states to build new railroads and ports for mineral extraction.

Liberia was one of the countries most relevant to a project that examined the workings of the iron ore company LAMCO, a Liberian, American, Swedish conglomerate that in the mid-1950s had built a rail line linking the Nimba mining region to the shipping coast. She hoped as well to gather information on the Chinese-funded Tanzania-Zambia railway project then under construction. The new line would link the port at Dar es Salaam to Zambia's copper belt, ending that landlocked nation's dependence on the white-ruled states of Rhodesia and South Africa for transport.

In planning this trip, Tate followed what she had first learned during her 1950 Fulbright year in India, relying on foreign embassy officials in Washington and State Department representatives posted in the countries she planned to visit. She would correspond with U.S. embassy officials in the countries and request assistance or advice on lodging as a woman traveling alone; in some cases, she would be invited to stay in the official residence or near the consulate office. For the research she intended to do, she also had requested basic engineering and financial information from the companies involved and arranged tours of their facilities.

Liberia was Tate's first stop, and she spent five days there. She went to services in Monrovia at the First Methodist church, with beautiful stained glass and the familiar hymns "The Old Rugged Cross" and "Who So Ever Will May Come." She wrote in her travel diary that it "reminded one of home," odd phrasing that captured her distance from the poignancy of the familiar. Perhaps "home" was Michigan, where her brother had recently been buried, or Washington where she lived. She was struck by one difference between the Methodist church at home and in Liberia: "Apparently Women's Lib has had some influence on Monrovia. A woman read the Scripture. And a woman helped collect the regular and the second collection—for the poor and needy—collection. Often at home ladies [only] collect the missionary pennies."[9]

The highlight of her time in Liberia was a first-hand observation of the giant LAMCO operation that linked the Mount Nimba region by rail to the Monrovia port. Company officials arranged for a tour of their facilities and provided more information on the intricacies of the operation, and she also met with government staff. Fascinated as always by engineering and construction, Tate marveled at the complexity and sophistication of the operational requirements needed to extract and then move iron ore by rail from mine to ship.

LAMCO's enormous physical presence and separate residential compound led her to refer to it, like the Vatican, as a "state within a state," a distinct self-governed area for international employees and their families that made living in Africa "comfortable," with a separate water supply, and fresh food and vegetables shipped in from Lebanon. Here Tate's astute observations foreshadow the concept of an "enclave economy," a term that later became dominant in the analysis of precisely this kind of foreign investment in resource-rich countries in Africa, as well as in South America and Mexico.[10]

The remainder of Tate's time in Africa reverted to the pattern in most of her travel history, darting from place to place and hoping to see as much as possible in the shortest amount of time. She took in the natural beauty of Tanzania and Kenya, including views of Mount Kilimanjaro and Mount Kenya, which dazzled her, before spending time in Nairobi and Dar es Salaam.

But she was most moved by what she called "the grand climax of her journey," eight days seeing the historic and sacred sites in Ethiopia and the modern city of Addis Ababa.

After a guided tour "from Queen of Sheba Country to Addis," Tate reverted to her familiar form of manic visual description of all she saw, with the same child-like enthusiasm she had for the pictures in *Zig-Zag* travel story books. "There I did a five-day historical tour of ancient and medieval capitals," she wrote, "including: Axum, the birthplace of Ethiopian civilization, the three thousand year-old capital of the Queen of Sheba, with standing and fallen obelisks and steles—stairways for the souls of the dead—massive pylons and monuments." Her account combined her interest in history and the beauty of both the natural world and technological innovation. She was just as impressed with Addis Ababa. "That modern capital surprised me," she reported, as she described its royal palaces, Haile Selassie University, City Hall, the ultramodern Telecommunication Building that housed the Organization of African Unity, St. George's Cathedral, the Grand Mosque, and the "Merkato," the "largest open market in Africa."[11]

Tate's time in Ethiopia, Kenya, and Tanzania was made much easier by the extension of hospitality from Black American officials serving there. During her two weekends in Addis Ababa, she was hosted by Daisy and John Withers, the director of the Agency for International Development in Ethiopia. Similarly, in Nairobi she was welcomed by Frenise Logan, a U.S. cultural affairs officer; Tate knew his wife, Mary, from Bennett College.

Beverly Carter, the American ambassador to Tanzania, made arrangements for Tate's visit there over Christmas, providing lodging and meals for her at the ambassador's official residence. He knew of Tate's "distinguished" career, reminding her that he had great respect for her "play at the bridge table" and that his wife Carlyn had taken a history course from her at Howard in the 1940s. In coordinating Tate's visit, Carter wrote to Logan in Nairobi that he had "long admired her contribution in the field of History and current affairs. She is an unusual person." No one would dispute that, regardless of his particular meaning, lost in the flat tone of formal State Department correspondence.[12]

The most curious and concerning aspect of her trip, however, came from her decision to visit Victoria Falls, the largest waterfall in the world. It is not surprising that Tate would want to see and photograph this magnificent natural wonder, which flows from the river separating Zambia and what was then called Rhodesia, now Zimbabwe. It is possible to view the falls from the

Zambia side of the river, but she was determined to see the more spectacular view from the Rhodesian side.

Tate continued to have relationships with embassy officials in Washington, including being on friendly terms with Eileen Fox, a clerk and bookkeeper at the Rhodesia Information Offices in Washington. Fox not only provided information on Victoria Falls, but also arranged to have a member of the Office of Foreign Affairs meet her there and take her to Salisbury so she could visit the National Archives and historical sites.

Tate was fully aware of the politically sensitive nature of Rhodesian and U.S. relations, and the reasons for it. She was savvy enough to ask on entry that her passport not be stamped so as to raise no questions when she traveled later to Kenya and Tanzania. But that did not stop her from accepting the hospitality and conveniences extended to her, which included a dinner in her honor hosted by the foreign affairs department. A mixed-race gathering of Blacks, whites, and southeast Asians, it included several professors from the university and other officials.[13]

She did do some research in the archives, but it is highly unlikely that she described her project on railways as the study of the "sinews and arteries of empire." Her trip had dual aims, to gather research and to see the spectacular beauty and landmarks of central and southeastern Africa. Her hosts in Rhodesia had helped with both, and she left saying to them that she wished she would be able to visit again. But later, to a contact in Liberia, she wrote, "what a fine dose of brain washing," as if her duplicity had succeeded in getting her something she needed and that otherwise would have been unavailable.[14]

Her return to New York from Africa was marred by a January snowstorm that delayed her arrival in Washington. But as was her pattern, she self-congratulated for an otherwise safe trip. "Thus I made the five weeks journey without a bruise, sprain, insect bite, headache, or one day's illness," she wrote to a friend, "but I was arrested and detained briefly for photographing a downtown section of Cairo and was released just in time to catch the flight to Beirut." The delay cost her several other intended stops—in Tunisia, Algiers, Casablanca, Rabat—but she seemed to have seen plenty to satisfy her intellectual curiosity and her sense of adventure.[15]

After returning to Washington, Tate continued to research the railways project and to pepper corporate and government officials for more detailed information on the financial and engineering aspects of their operations. She was gathering information not just from LAMCO about its operations in Liberia, but also about the other mining and port projects then under construction. Her ambition was to show how the alliances between international conglomerates and national governments simply masked another kind of imperialism that robbed Africa of the true value of its vast mineral and other natural resources.[16]

Tate's research habits meant that this project, like her work on Hawaii and the Pacific, expanded exponentially even after she had split the work into two parts, one on the history of the "colonial railways" and the other on the vast expanse of the newer "mineral railways." Living in Washington aided Tate's exhaustive research habits, because she had such easy access to the Library of Congress, the National Archives, embassy libraries, and the resources of university libraries at Howard and elsewhere. In a mind that thrived on complexity and excessive detail, these combinations made it difficult for her to gauge when enough was enough.

After her winter break trip to Africa in 1973, Tate immediately began to search for ways to return. She wanted to do elsewhere on the continent what she did in Liberia: interview corporate and government officials about projects, gather additional materials available only there, and see these railway, seaport, and mining projects for herself. Only this would satisfy her compulsion for thoroughness and first-hand knowledge.

The constraints imposed by her Howard professorship lessened after she retired in 1974. A new regime of more sympathetic administrators, especially Lorraine Williams, took her work on this project seriously. However, when she had applied for travel funding earlier, one of them made the mistake of telling her that although her submission was stellar, the priority was to support younger scholars. At seventy-one, she now saw age as an additional category for discrimination against her. After she complained that had she been a man of any age her work would have been funded, the university eventually awarded her a grant, which enabled her to purchase a special forty-five-day airfare for a return trip to Africa, in May 1976.

Tanzania and Kenya were return trips for Tate as she worked through contacts made and sustained from her earlier trip to make arrangements for lodging and logistics. But there were three additions. She traveled to Zambia and concluded her visit with a stop in Lagos, spending the longest amount of her time in South Africa, where she was hosted for two weeks by its Public Relations Department.

South African officials generally were suspicious of Black Americans seeking to travel to their country, often making it difficult for them to get a visa.

But she had spent the three years since her first trip to Africa cultivating a relationship with two prominent officials at the South African embassy in Washington. She also had initiated a constant stream of correspondence for information with officials in the companies she was researching and wished to visit. Tate believed that having been hosted by Rhodesian officials in 1973 was seen as a factor in her favor, too.

That decision three years earlier to travel to Rhodesia, mired in international sanctions against its white minority rule, was puzzling enough politically for someone whose work from the 1940s on had advanced a strong anti-racist and anti-imperialist critique. Her trip to South Africa seemed a continuation of her compulsion to satisfy her research and travel urges even though the apartheid regime was anathema to her and most Black Americans; this was true even before the emergence of the Free South Africa Movement in the 1980s led in part by her former student Mary Frances Berry. Tate's genuinely fervent belief in the importance of documenting and warning of the looming threat from African re-colonization through global capital investments served as self-justification for her subterfuge and for overriding her own longstanding political commitments.

When she applied for the visa and had to list her publications, she assumed that since her work was not overtly about "race relations," it would ease the way for her. Her visa was approved in one day, because, she said, "I was safe." Certainly, South African embassy officials also would have recognized the public relations value of a visit by a Black American scholar from Washington. Tate took an odd pride in the fact that nothing about her triggered any fear that she intended any harsh political critique, although her proposals as shared with Howard and with the Woodrow Wilson Foundation emphasized her anti-imperialist analytic frame for the project.[17]

Tate referred to her two trips to Africa as a "safari," defining the word to mean "a journey for a purpose," and she seemed comfortable having more than one aim. She enjoyed the benefits of the courtesy and care the government extended to her, which included access to corporate and state leaders and extended guided tours of the facilities she longed to see first-hand. But in her preparations, Tate was very mindful of the racial politics she was entering.

In making plans for the leisure time she would have over two weekends in Johannesburg and Cape Town, she wrote to Stanley LePere, a "colored man" known by her friend Theresa Danley to show visitors around, asking if he knew "any Coloureds—especially women leaders" who might want to meet with her. She asked to attend services at "a Coloured Church" in each city, as well as to be able to visit "settlement" areas outside of Cape Town. But her curiosity had its limits, as her practicality and scholarly aims also left her cautious: "Obviously, since I am the invited guest of the South African government, which is being most gracious on my behalf, I do not want to become involved with so-called 'Radicals,' and thereby jeopardize the success of my trip to see mineral railways and harbours."[18]

Johannesburg was her first stop in Africa after flying from New York and changing planes in Dakar. On her first day there, LePere and his wife drove Tate to parks and sights nearby. That Sunday, she wrote in her travel notes, she went with them "to the multi-racial St. Mary's Cathedral in the heart of Johannesburg, met the Black Dean [Desmond] Tutu, appointed Anglican Bishop of Lesotho, and several liberal whites. Sightseeing in the city, through the Indian section, and to several nearby beautiful suburbs; had dinner at the LePere's flat; called on several coloured couples in a more affluent coloured section, drove a short distance into a deplorable 'Black Township.' "[19]

Tate wrote to friends that when she congratulated Tutu on his recent elevation to bishop, the forty-five-year-old anti-apartheid activist, who had been dean of St. Mary's for only a year, explained that he had been reassigned because the church "wanted to strangle him" by removing him from the city and assigning him instead to an area with twenty-five white parishes and a smaller number of Blacks. Among the "liberal whites" she met was Helen Joseph, the labor and anti-apartheid activist whose story of her work and detention under house arrest Tate detailed in her travel jottings.[20]

The next day the "official" part of her visit commenced, bringing all the benefits over the next two weeks of being the state's guest. Staying in luxury hotels and accompanied by one woman official after another, she was driven or took trains or was flown by small private planes to visit Pretoria, Durban, Cape Town, and the big rail-to-port projects at Richard's Bay and Sishen-Saldanha Bay. She met with company officials and engineers and was able to observe the massive construction projects that had drawn her there.

But even under careful shepherding, Tate's powers of observation were keen to the presence of non-white people, including the staff who waited on her at planned gatherings at corporate headquarters or in restaurants. At one railway station Tate noticed an old locomotive and train used to transport Blacks out of the city at night. "They were just running in all directions, hundreds of Blacks to catch this train, because you see," she recalled, "they're not permitted to live in the city. They live out in the Black area. We could have been crushed if we didn't get out of the way, you see, by the horde of people catching that last train after the work day, to get to their own area, on the outside of Pretoria."[21]

One of the traveler's highlights came on a jarringly different kind of train. At the very end of her time in South Africa she was able to ride on the famous luxury line, the Blue Train, from Pretoria to Cape Town. Her status as an American permitted certain privileges, but the fact of her color in highly racially regimented public spaces still carried risks and limitations when she was on her own. So intent was Tate on traveling on the Blue Train that she had asked her friend at the Rhodesia Information Office in Washington whether it would be possible even if she had to accommodate herself to color restrictions: "If there is any difficulty on account of my being colored about meals en route, I would carry a box lunch and a thermos." Her seatmate on the train was not South African but a British woman, probably pre-cleared to be comfortable sharing meals with her.[22]

In Cape Town, Tate had asked to meet with Erika Theron, a social scientist and head of a commission on the status of coloreds whose report later would bear her name. Theron had visited Howard and met with Franklin Frazier and Inabel Lindsay, the dean of the School of Social Work. Tate also was taken to visit new developments designed for colored families and filled with American-style rambler homes. The political purposefulness of these visits was not lost on Tate, as she also noted that in Cape Town she saw "slum areas" being "cleared of 'Coloureds' and Asians, to make way for high rise flats for whites," and that they were being forced to move to new compounds fourteen miles outside the city.[23]

Zambia was on Tate's itinerary because she still was trying to gather more information on the Tan-Zam Railway, but after meeting with a government official in Lusaka, she came away thwarted because he seemed to know less or would reveal less than she already knew from her years of research. But she also wanted to visit Livingstone so she could see the Zambezi River Falls from that side, having done it on the other side in Victoria Falls in 1973. She would be able to see the famous railway crossing over the gorge there, which she considered a feat both of British engineering and "empire building."

Her sense of adventure had not waned, and she set out alone from the Hotel Intercontinental on the edge of the park to cross "a swinging narrow wooden bridge engulfed in mist" and then scrambled "down slippery rocks through an entangled palm and rain forest to arrive at the valley level below the bridge and near the boiling pot to photograph the scene." Getting back up was extremely difficult, and sent her to bed afterward, but "it was worth the tremendous effort and utter exhaustion," she wrote. In a rare expression of emotion, Tate found herself "sad—disquieted" by the political differences between Zambia and Rhodesia that divided a formerly unified land of rich mineral deposits, pastoral farmland, and stunning natural beauty that she believed could have made for "a paradise on earth."[24]

Tate's return visit to Tanzania included a trip to the Tan-Zam Railway station and the busy shipping harbor. She also did research in the Railway Archives, where she put her German to use on the development of the colonial lines before World War I. Mary Ida Gardner, a prominent African American YWCA official, showed Tate around, taking her to Coral Coast beach, dinner, and her church.[25]

A one-day excursion via airplane to Zanzibar brought Tate face to face with the history of the African slave trade, and the Cathedral of Christ built on the site of the old whipping post: "At the northeastern extremity of the island is a slave cave hewn from the basic rock and formerly used to confine slaves shipped to the nearby coast, as well as those who labored on plantations in the vicinity. From this cave slaves chained together were marched miles to the Zanzibar market." Here one senses Tate feeling an emotional connection to Africa as a Black American. Her persistent claim of being the "granddaughter of pioneers" had not broken the chain of connection to both enslavement and Africa.[26]

"Beautiful, modern Nairobi" remained a favorite city for Tate. She revisited her friends Mary and Frenise Logan, who remained at the American embassy. Tate attended some social events there, and Mary Logan later called her presence "vivacious." She had a lunch with AAUW members at the university, but she remained focused on her research. "I also managed to travel to Kisumu, the terminal of the Kenya Uganda Railway on Lake Victoria Nyamza, through the Great Rift Valley," she wrote, "and now can better understand some of the construction problems of the first railway in East Africa."[27]

Tate's last stop would be Lagos. After flying from Nairobi, her arrival in the bustling West African city was unsettling for her, not least because, unlike her usual pattern, she knew absolutely no one there. She was taken aback by the noise and bustle, and fared badly in her choice of hotel, which she felt was both unsafe and unsanitary. After visiting the archives of the Nigerian Railway, she left for Ibadan, which she found beautiful, more spacious, and better suited for her. There, she enjoyed time with Doris Hull, a former graduate student and librarian from Howard, who was at the university library, which Tate also enjoyed exploring.[28]

After a long, overcrowded Pan-Am flight on June 21 from Lagos to New York, Tate concluded her forty-three days in southern, eastern, and western Africa. She was relieved when she finally made it back to Washington, grateful to be able to say, "But I survived."[29]

Even before her travels to Africa, Tate had begun to write about the colonial railways there and the new ones being planned. When she decided to share more of her work on Africa, she turned to the professional gathering space that had been the most nurturing and hospitable in her long career, the annual meetings of the Association for the Study of Negro Life and History. She had started to attend the meetings in the 1930s, and it remained a place where she presented a variety of her ideas about Africa.

Tate had offered comments on a paper in 1972 about the history of the Italo-Ethiopian War, a subject she felt so strongly about that in 1935 she had traveled to Geneva to witness the League of Nations' opening debates on the conflict. Starting with the 1974 annual conference, she delivered "The Tan-Zam Railway: A Symbol of Nationalism Vs. Imperialism," the first in a series of three papers drawn from her larger project. She argued that the "costliest move toward economic independence" for African nations involved creating transport routes and infrastructure for international trade, whether by rail or roads or ports, or all three. She described the alliance between Kenneth Kaunda of Zambia and Julius Nyerere of Tanzania, in which both men envisioned a route to the Indian Ocean for Zambia that did not cross white-ruled Rhodesia or Mozambique, allowing the country to "to turn her back on her white southern African neighbors and forge new links with Black East Africa." Refused railway funding support from the United States and the World Bank, Kaunda and Nyerere turned to China in 1970 for what was "the largest foreign aid project in Africa's history."[30]

James Spady, a Black independent scholar and journalist in Philadelphia, was so taken by the presentation that he reached out to thank her for "such a cohesive, analytical, and interpretative work," which could only come from her "interdisciplinary approach." Having read her many articles and books, he said this was her best work, and that "the power of your brilliant scholarship had never shone through so brightly." He asked, "How did you ever become an authority on mineral resources? It is no wonder that some people arrogantly view you 'as some kind of a freak.' " He predicted that her scholarship would serve as a model for generations to come.[31]

She delivered a second paper in 1975, "Iron-Ore and Liberia's Future," based on her first trip to Africa. One of her recurring questions was whether Africans, in Liberia or elsewhere, would be trained to take over the new large-scale enterprises or earn fair wages for their labor. "I should like to write more than 'under the trickle down economic theory of what is good for the Republic of South Africa is good for the "Coloureds" and Blacks,' " she wrote to a South African company official in 1974, as if daring him to correct her.[32]

Tate also uncovered the early presence of Americans in exploitive economic explorations in Africa. "American Pioneers in the Congo," her 1976 paper, exposed "the role that American generals, lieutenants, adventurers, geologists, topographers, financiers and industrialists played in the early exploitation and development of Leopold's Independent Congo State and the Belgian Congo." That was based in part on research she had done years earlier in Belgian archives but was a continuation of her work documenting late nineteenth-century American imperialism, before the usual received starting point of the Spanish-American War—just as she had done with her work on Hawaii. Her papers were received with standing ovations, she would later recall.[33]

But it was the enormous African railroad project that would remain Tate's focus for the decade to come. The colonial railways project had twelve chapters, moving both chronologically and geographically, starting with the construction of the first railways on the continent—in Egypt and the Sudan—and then methodically through the rest of southern Africa, the Congo, Kenya and Uganda, Tanzania, Togo and Cameroon, Angola, Niger, Liberia, French west and equatorial Africa, Tunisia, Morocco and Eritrea, and, finally, Ethiopia. Tate intended to use this history to argue, in her own shortened version: "Railways as Proof of 'Effective Occupation'/Railway and Port Concessions as Prelude to Annexation/Railways Cheaper and More Efficacious than Guns." She also outlined the "Effects on Africans: Their Livelihood, Loss of Land, Training, Health and Welfare, Migration, Mobility and Tribal Bonds."[34]

Presenting railways as "invasion and occupation instruments," she returned once again to her ideas about race and the technologies of imperialism that she had developed first in her work on armaments and mechanization of war, and later on missionaries and education in Hawaii. This remained her theoretical approach, an anti-racist geopolitical conceptualization that grew out of the versatility of her training and teaching in diplomatic history, geography, political economy, geopolitics, and international relations; her research languages, including German and French; her access to the Library of

Congress and the National Archives; and, her decades of global travel for research and pleasure.

The manuscript containing all this work, titled "Mineral Railways in Africa: Their Impact on National Economies," was in her mind a necessary contemporary sequel to the colonial project. Looking at new and proposed railways, she emphasized that Africa's vast and varied natural resources and mineral wealth was now the overriding economic justification that would join nationalist interests and those of international corporations, with newer railways terminating at massive new deep-sea port developments. She saw in real time an expanding modern-day manifestation of an old pattern, but still offering much for outsiders and little for African workers. She believed that the economic disadvantages of emerging independent African nations rendered them vulnerable to the globalized international corporate imperialism of the so-called post-colonial era.[35]

Enthusiastic and undaunted by the size of these two projects, Tate relished the complexity and challenge she was imagining into being. "If nothing is ventured, nothing is won. Since I am a pioneer—a granddaughter of pioneers from New England and Ohio who homesteaded in Michigan, I am prone to venture. Otherwise, I should not be dealing with mineral railways in Africa, which classifies me as a 'freak' in the minds of some gentlemen." Seemingly oblivious to the ironies of that claim for one studying the colonializing railroad ventures she intended to document, Tate hunkered down for the enormous amount of work needed to see this project through.[36]

The civil rights–era resurgence of interest in Black history created new sources of funding and a ready audience among African Americans for Tate's work. If her timing was good in that way, it was bad in another. For decades, her solo travel life had depended on personal and professional connections, especially those forged at Howard and in Washington's world of embassies and foreign service staff. Her trips to Rhodesia and South Africa as a guest of the government did not sit well with some colleagues at Howard who believed she had let herself be used for propaganda purposes despite her view that she was able to use the visit to advance her anti-imperialist research project.

Tate remained stubbornly resistant to the way that ideas about the personal and the political had shifted in that period. In what she saw as an act of appreciation, she asked that the South African and Rhodesian staff who had arranged her visits to their countries be invited to an affair honoring her at Howard. Her colleague Harold Lewis then tipped off what she called some "activist students" about her request. She seemed caught off guard and miffed when, under threat of protests, the invitation was withdrawn the day before the event. She confided all this to her friend John Hope Franklin, writing "what a pity courtesy and kindness cannot be separated from politics."[37]

For a woman who had been ahead of her time in so many aspects of her life and work, at seventy-two Tate found herself now out of step with the strategy of more overt activism against racist imperialism in Africa, a political history she had researched, taught, and condemned for more than three decades. So she did not disagree with the goals, which still leaves this as one of the most perplexing decisions, because it veers so sharply from her strident writings on race and imperialism. Her willfulness and her ambitious devotion to her work and her reliance on networks of personal relations blinded her to her own compromises, which her critics could see much more clearly.

But she saw a greater, overriding purpose in her travel research for her project on international corporate capitalism's pursuit of African mineral and other resources. And once she had made up her mind about that, it was not in her character to do anything but find a way to see that through, even though she knew the political transgressions required. The trips also gave her one more opportunity to be accorded the treatment she believed she deserved as an internationally recognized American professor and scholar who believed, as she had said about her friend and colleague Hansberry, that she was also a "prophet without honor" in the country to which she had returned.

CHAPTER 11

"Living History"

WASHINGTON–CAMBRIDGE–MICHIGAN, 1976–1996

After six weeks in Africa, Tate returned to Washington in June 1976 to find a letter waiting for her from Matina Horner, the president of Radcliffe, asking for advice and help with a new Black women's oral history project at the Schlesinger Library. The subject captured Tate's interest, but not without skepticism. "Although I am not an enthusiastic advocate of oral history," she replied, "which, from its use in the Pacific Islands and in Africa, leaves something to be desired, perhaps the scholarly and energetic Letitia Brown can convince me of its value for the particular project in view."[1]

A decade younger than Tate, Brown had earned her doctorate in history from Harvard in 1966, pursuing a long and busy teaching career at Howard, and in 1971 becoming the first Black faculty member at George Washington University. She launched and helped secure funding for what was expected to be a two-year project to ensure that Black women were among those whose history would be preserved at the Schlesinger Library. With funding from the Rockefeller Foundation, Brown envisioned oral history interviews with women who had begun their civic and professional work during the 1930s and whose lives had contributed to the betterment of Black communities.

Out of respect for Brown and the potential significance of the project, Tate soon made the easy trip in July from her home in Brookland to Capitol Hill to attend the first Advisory Committee meeting, a location arranged by Representative Yvonne Braithwaite Burke, a committee member and her

AKA soror. Tate knew most of the others there, including both Elsie Lewis and Dorothy Porter from Howard; Margaret Rowley had come from Atlanta University, and Muriel Snowden from Boston. Marcia Greenlee had been chosen by Brown to serve as a research fellow on the project.[2]

That meeting was the only one Brown attended, as cancer cut her life short the next month. The death of Brown, a woman ten years her junior, seemed to heighten Tate's own resolve to help see the project through. The will to push it forward would come from the surviving committee members, the Black women who were soon approached to be interviewed, and administrators at the Schlesinger, especially Ruth Hill, a Black woman librarian and oral history coordinator there.

Tate needed no further convincing of the significance of the work to be done after a lifetime of complaining about challenges, especially gender disparities, facing Black women. So, uncharacteristically, she said "yes" even in a moment when she was eager to use her recently acquired research to complete two manuscripts on colonial and mineral railways and while she was still trying to place her two completed books on Australia and New Zealand.

Tate brought to the project her usual intensity, which she focused on helping to build the list of potential interviewees. She had expansive ideas about which Black women's lives to include, listing women who were not college educated, or in professional work. She suggested, for example, a Black woman who operated the elevator at the Library of Congress, someone who had pulled herself up from poverty and whom she had come to admire during all the time she spent there over three decades as a researcher. She thought about trying to find women who were not on the East Coast, including more from the Middle West. She also suggested women like her friend Elizabeth Jenkins, the wife of Morgan State's president, who sacrificed her own professional goals to support her husband's.

Ida Van Smith, a former student of hers at Barber-Scotia, made the list for her work as a pilot, flight instructor, and head of a flying club for Black children. She recommended interviews with Yvonne Burke, Shirley Chisholm, Cardiss Collins, and Barbara Jordan, all then in Congress. If the project expanded its reach into the ranks of younger women, Tate had a long list ready for that, too, including Mary Frances Berry, whom she called one of her "most brilliant students." In the end, funding woes meant that only seventy-two women were interviewed, but they captured a wide diversity of work and service.[3]

At first a skeptic about oral history methods, Tate soon approached the project with the zeal of the recently converted as she realized the opportunity it offered to preserve histories of Black women's lives. She had come to see her involvement with the project as the capstone of her own career as a Black woman scholar.

Tate was only one of two Advisory Committee members who were also interviewed as part of the project, and the only member who also chose to conduct interviews. One of her concerns was that the group of younger women who were being assigned as interviewers might not elicit the most comfortable conversations with older, accomplished, and more reserved Black women. So she took it upon herself to train and serve as an interviewer, working as others would from a list of suggested topics about family background, childhood, education, and more probing topics.[4]

The seven interviews Tate conducted proved as revealing about her as about those she interviewed, coming at a time when she had begun to reflect on her own life and legacy. They provide an important glimpse of Tate engaged in conversation, released from the solo voice of her own mind on the printed page. Recorded on cassette tapes, the interviews also preserve Tate's soft lilting voice, a stark contrast to her bold scholarly voice captured over six decades of talks, speeches, articles, books, travelogues, and letters.

The women Tate interviewed were chosen by her, and she had recommended and encouraged each of them to participate. Susie Jones and Frances Williams had come from the earliest periods in her life: sisters she had met in St. Louis when she interviewed with their father for high school teaching positions in 1927. She was later reunited with both, Jones at Bennett College and Williams in Washington. A second set of sisters, Dr. Lena Edwards and Mary Edwards Hill, also had come into her life in Washington. Eva Dykes, Dr. Dorothy Ferebee, and Flemmie Kittrell all had faculty or administrative connections to Howard. Tate had first overlapped with Kittrell at Bennett; Dykes had left Washington in 1944 just after she had arrived, but they had been members of the Roundtable Club, a literary group.

In late 1977, Tate flew in quick succession to Greensboro, St. Louis, and Huntsville to conduct interviews, and was driven to New Jersey for another; she was able to conduct three in Washington, doing one each in 1977, 1978, and 1979. Her willingness to do this was a measure not only of her apparent conversion to the methodology of oral history but her commitment to preserving the legacy of other Black women through narrative archival evidence. So she approached the work as a protective friend, colleague, and admirer, but also as a scholar and historian working to preserve what she called "living history."[5]

The women Tate interviewed had led quite different and very fulfilling professional lives: they included two doctors, two social workers, and three professors. All were born in the 1890s and were at least a decade her senior, except for Kittrell who was almost her contemporary and, like Tate, had grown up in a rural area and had not come from a formally educated family. Tate the interviewer was unwavering in her graciousness and politeness, and her ability to recede and listen, interrupting usually only to clarify or redirect.

Her voice is that of the woman acknowledged repeatedly by her many friends, preserved in her own archive in decades of thank you notes, cards, and personal letters. The interview exchanges captured her kindness, generosity, empathy, and willingness to spotlight others. The sessions easily slide in and out of conversations among old friends, varying only in degrees of familiarity and intimacy, but all palpable with Tate's admiration and appreciation for the complex lives these Black women had created for themselves in the century of Jim Crow and segregation.

Tate gently probed family histories, an often fraught exercise among Black people of earlier generations. "It might be well if we would start with your roots," she began, "since roots are now so important in people's lives," referencing Alex Haley's recent book and miniseries. For each woman, the interviews reveal complicated kinship routes out of slavery. And for each, the quest for education was the pivot on which all else turned, whether the woman was born in Kentucky or Virginia or North Carolina or Washington. Of the women, three had remained unmarried and without children like Tate; those who had wed spoke of reconciling their own professional ambitions with their roles as wife or mother. For women of a generation that regarded personal questions as taboo even among friends, these interviews brought much of what was considered private into public view.[6]

Initially the differences between herself and the women she interviewed seemed to capture Tate's attention. All but Kittrell had been born into the educated Black elite; the others were from families whose parents or sometimes grandparents were college educated. These women represented the social world Tate inhabited as an adult but not the one in which she was born.

With Susie Jones, Tate returned with nostalgia to her own days as a thirty-year-old woman at Bennett where Jones served alongside her husband David, who was the president. She had wanted to interview Jones as a way to highlight the often unacknowledged work and professional sacrifices of women who partnered in the work of their more publicly recognized husbands. But she also wanted to pay homage to Bennett, where Jones and her husband had warmly welcomed her to the campus community in 1936.

Sounding self-conscious of the tape recorder at first, Tate began as she would all of her interviews, by noting the date and time, and by describing her physical surroundings. The two women reminisced about how the Jones family had hosted Grace Hadow, her principal from Oxford, during her U.S. tour in 1938. Tate, whose memory for details remained robust, reminded Jones that the visit was capped by a Nathaniel Dett choral program in Hadow's honor in the college chapel. Perhaps it also was such a vivid memory because that visit was the last time Tate saw Hadow, who died suddenly two years later.[7]

The conversational interview covered many topics, including Jones's political work with other Methodist women. When Tate asked her about the contemporary women's movement, Jones agreed that "the struggle for racial equality and the struggle for women's rights have been two parallel struggles in American life." Under Tate's gentle prodding over photographs, the by then widowed Jones also spoke about the recent death of her eldest son, a painful loss she called "shattering." Jones thanked her for enabling that conversation and for the comfort in her grief that came from "for the first time" looking at her "life as a whole," quoting Howard Thurman on the concept of "the therapy of memory." When Tate later interviewed the early civil rights activist Frances Williams, Jones's younger sister, they too spoke of the "peace of mind" that came from looking back over time in a structured way as one neared the end of one's life.[8]

Among the questions the project suggested were ones about the impact of race or sex on the women's lives, and, with some of the women, Tate deftly used those lines of inquiry to satisfy her own long interest in just that topic. The formidable Dorothy Ferebee, an obstetrician, the former head of health services at Howard, former AKA basileus, and successor to Bethune at the NCNW, did not hesitate in answering that "sexism was a very common practice, and still is; that women are not recognized, regardless of their qualifications; they're not given the kind of acceptance and recognition to which they're entitled." She argued that to succeed women usually needed a "champion" to advocate for them, either a man in power or a more senior woman.[9]

Ferebee also was quite frank about her unhappy dentist husband's resentment of her success and his failed attempts to have her leave work and stay at home, which she dismissed as an "irritation." The two later divorced. Although her interview had been delayed by illness, Ferebee's strength and power seemed undiminished in the long conversation, which she dominated from start to finish. But even she, under Tate's soft questioning, was reduced to a touching quietude when describing the photograph of the christening gown used by her granddaughter that had been worn first by her and then by her deceased only daughter, all three of whom shared the first name Dorothy.[10]

Tate's conversation with Flemmie Kittrell shed the formality of those with much older women and those with whom she was less well acquainted. Close in age, the two women not only shared time as colleagues at Bennett and then at Howard, but they had mutual experiences as never married, childless, avid solo international travelers. It took eighteen months for Tate to locate the retired Kittrell for the project, as she had been away in Europe and India, where she would soon return.

Lovely reminisces of travel occupied much of their time, with Kittrell referring to herself as "an international girl" and a "world citizen" as they shared stories of water markets in Thailand, time spent on houseboats in Kashmir, trips to Africa, Japan, and Hawaii, and the differences between New Zealand and Australia. Kittrell also sympathized with Tate for traveling to Rhodesia and then as the guest of the South African government to complete her research: her own travels to both countries had come in the late 1960s but under USIA sponsorship.[11]

At interview's end, the two women warmly pledged to continue their friendship and, as Kittrell put it, their "fellowship intellectual wise." She no longer kept a home in Washington but invited Tate to visit her in Gloucester, Virginia, where she planned to spend her retirement years. One key difference between the two women was that Kittrell voiced no complaints about Howard, citing the men there who had supported her in her work, a sentiment Tate left unchallenged although her own experience felt quite different.

She did this out of respect for Kittrell, who had been recruited personally by Howard's president and promised a new home economics building, something that was eventually brought to fruition. Kittrell's field, one ceded to women, may also have offered a more unfettered route for her hard work and commitment to be received and recognized. By all accounts, she was a beloved and respected figure at Howard, feelings seemingly shared by Tate.[12]

Tate's most revealing conversation came when she flew to Huntsville to visit Eva Dykes, the interviewee she knew least well. Born in 1893 into a well-educated Washington family, Dykes held both a bachelor's degree and a doctorate from Harvard. She was one of a trio of Black women to break into the ranks of the Ph.D. in 1921. Trained in English philology, Dykes had left a position on Howard's faculty in 1944 to teach at Oakwood College, a Black Seventh Day Adventist institution in Alabama—a decision she made as a devout Adventist. Tate remained deeply private about her own faith, giving no hint of it even in her interviews with the sisters Lena Edwards and Mary Edwards Hill, women whose lives and careers were molded by their family's deep commitment to Catholicism. Yet she seemed moved by Dykes's faith commitment, one that had her leave Howard and Washington, places Tate had worked so hard to reach, for a small and then unaccredited religious institution in the Deep South.[13]

The most taciturn of those Tate interviewed, Dykes left plenty of time for her to ask some of the suggested questions often skipped with the other women. Demurring when asked if her race had hindered her, Dykes was more forthcoming when Tate asked how sex had affected her salary or status compared to a man with a Harvard degree. Dykes explained that salary had never been a motivator for her, but she confirmed that women at Oakwood were paid less than men with the same credentials. When she asked an administrator why, she was told "well, you are a woman," even though she explained that a loaf of bread cost her the same as it did a man. "That accounts for the women's lib now," Dykes told Tate, "and the efforts of many other groups of women." She added that she thought that "women's lib is doing a good work . . . very good work."[14]

That analysis was not new to Tate, who had been arguing against gender discrimination and salary inequities all her career, but what was more surprising was that she also asked Dykes whether she felt a "void in your life because you didn't marry or have children." She deflected, emphasizing that she would only have married within her faith, but it was Tate who answered what was obviously a question she had asked herself. "I know from my own experience, though, that you have many students who are, in a sense, your children, that you have touched their lives in some way, and they tell you about it."[15]

Tate had made a similar point in 1974 when a younger white woman wrote of her envy of "ladies like yourself, who have been able to live such interesting and varied lives and pursue their own intellectual interests." Tate had responded philosophically and poignantly: "Twentieth century women apparently are in a dilemma. Those who have a home, children and a career—like you—are the fortunate ones, yet you aspire for even more. Those who have only a career long for a family. You have five children, who are a reflection of you. I have had five books published (hope for two more to come from the press), which are in a sense a reflection of me. They will be in world libraries for many years to come. But I have no immediate family, which is a status not to be envied."[16]

She broached the sensitive topic of loneliness with Dykes indirectly, asking, "you generally have engagements on Thanksgiving and Christmas?" They both expressed gratitude for holiday invitations, which they credited to the thoughtfulness of their women friends. When Dykes revealed that her father and mother had divorced when she was very young, she also emphasized that she had never felt what Tate referred to as "the trauma of separated parents." Dykes explained that her father, her mother, and her stepfather all remained "good friends," interacting in what later came to be known as a "blended family."

Tate was intrigued by this concept of a "friendly" divorce, something that seemed by her silence to have been at odds with her own childhood experience. These exchanges with Dykes were one of the few times that Tate revealed feelings of vulnerability, here about being unmarried, childless, and living far from family, but also, without saying, still carrying within herself the trauma of her parents' relationship, without acknowledging it even in the intimacy of the moment, or at least not on the record.[17]

Again, Tate pushed the conversation forward, asking "how do you feel about the ending of life here on earth?" Dykes's faith meant that she wanted "to be ready when I die," and that she did not fear or dread death. Neither did Tate, explaining, "I've been near it, that is, clinically dead, and extreme unction in the Catholic church is beyond anything you can imagine." This is one of the few times Tate publicly revealed her Catholicism. "Yes," said Dykes, as Tate called herself "fortunate" to have survived, while also saying that "death can be beautiful." She added, "I hope I don't die in a flaming airplane, or under a great deal of steel and metal on a train or plane, but I'm hoping I can drift away."[18]

Death had marked the start of the project and marred its completion, too. Dorothy Ferebee, whose interview in December 1979 had been delayed by illness, died less than a year later, in September 1980, and Flemmie Kittrell died of a heart attack the next month. Tate attended their services in Rankin Chapel, and sent copies of the homilies and funeral programs to the Schlesinger. The day before her funeral service, Ferebee's AKA sorors attended her four-hour open-casket wake where she lay dressed in pink, one of their colors, as each of 150 members all wearing white placed a twig of ivy on her coffin. Their "Beyond the Ivy Wall" ceremony concluded with them singing the AKA anthem joined in clasped hands around the chapel. It is unclear whether Tate attended or participated in the ceremony, but the open coffin and the emotion of the ceremony probably would not have suited her.[19]

She was at the funeral service the next day when the federal cabinet secretary Patricia Roberts Harris, a former Howard student and administrator, delivered the eulogy for Ferebee, praising her as an exemplar for Black women, one who worked under "the double handicap of race and sex," including at Howard where the "virus of sexism limited her." Harris was the first Black woman appointed to the Cabinet, in 1977, and she used similar language then in a note to Tate thanking her for being "a role model for all of us who were Howard students."[20]

At Kittrell's memorial in Rankin Chapel, where she and Tate had marched in tandem when they returned from India in 1951, the celebrant described her life as one of service to her race and the larger world. Tate had already begun to plan for how she wished to be remembered, but the coming of these two deaths so soon after her long, lively conversations with both women could not have left her unaffected. She worked closely with Ferebee's grieving son and daughter-in-law to edit the transcript of the interview. For Ferebee, Kittrell, and the other women she interviewed, Tate wrote generous profiles that were placed at the front of each bound transcript; at the back of each was a brief biography of Tate.[21]

Tate's own interview for the project did not begin until 1978, and from the start it was clear that the parameters of the format she had so skillfully deployed proved much too restrictive to capture the life she had lived and wished to record. Theresa Danley, a Washington friend who also interviewed others in the project, tried to guide Tate through what should have been highlights of a busy, well-traveled scholar's life. After five days of recording, already exceeding the typical day or two of other interviews, for some reason, the interviewing ended.

They did not resume recording again until two years later, in early December 1980. In that long interim, Tate apparently had continued to marshal supporting evidence of her life. Coupled with her still prodigious memory for visual detail, her in-depth political knowledge of every place she had visited, her collections of photographs and awards, Tate's narrative compulsiveness consumed an additional seven days on tape, in part because as she aged, her tendency toward long digressions only increased, becoming more akin to a heavily detailed stream of consciousness. She wore down the polite and patient Danley into a faltering state of resignation.

Even with portions lost, Tate's interview became the longest in the project, yielding what are now cited as twenty-five audiotapes, next to the two or three

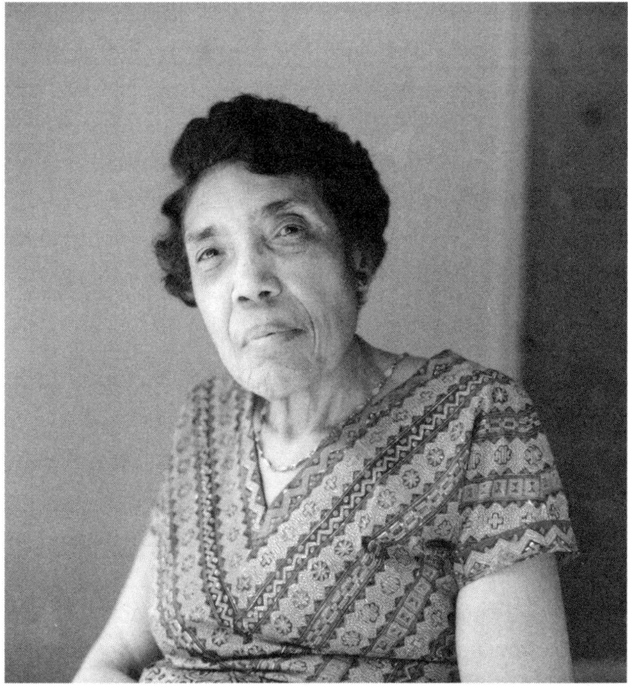

Tate in her Black Women Oral History Project photo, 1984
(Zhang Collection, Western Michigan University Archives)

needed for most others. The project of transcribing the interview also became a prodigious undertaking, as did her editing of it, a corpus estimated to be six hundred or more pages of raw original transcript. That process remained incomplete, which may explain why, ironically, Tate's interview was not included either in the bound volumes or in the later published interviews.[22]

Tate applied her compulsion for detail and comprehensiveness to the primary documents of her own as she tried firmly to frame the narrative of her life. Her near photographic memories provide a rich visual recapitulation of her childhood, her friendship networks, her many travels, but also of what brought her joy and how she worked as a scholar and teacher. Still, as was her habit as a researcher and a writer, Tate's brilliance at gathering and processing masses of information brought with it an inability to know when enough was enough, including in her own interview.

The Black Women Oral History Project became and remains one of the most important collections in Black women's history. In 1984, a celebratory traveling exhibit and book, *Women of Courage,* featured stunning new color photographs of some of the women in the project, including Tate. She made sure those she interviewed were included, but she did not particularly like her own picture, thinking that she had not looked her best because she recently had been ill. When the interviews were published for wider circulation, Tate saw her work in "living history" become what would be her last writing to make it into print. As she neared her eighties, her mind remained busily engaged but her memory and her body had begun to betray her.[23]

Howard University remained Tate's intellectual home even as she worked on the Radcliffe oral history project. In 1976, former Howard student Joseph Harris had returned to the university's history department. At his job interview, he remembers that she warmly embraced him and told him how glad she was to welcome him back. Harris had left Washington in 1956 but found on his return that the rigidly segregated city he remembered had "opened up" in the intervening two decades.

After he assumed the position as her department chair, he continued to have a good relationship with her as he began to have conversations with her about her retirement plans and her own legacy. By then she had given funds to Radcliffe and Western Michigan. When he approached her to "see if she would support some kind of donation to Howard," she replied that "no one had asked her." She then endowed the Merze Tate Seminar in Diplomatic History, following an example set by Logan at his retirement.[24]

Put into effect immediately, the annual event brought in speakers with foreign service experience or international expertise to address a wide range of topics, including human rights, southern Africa policy, relations between Africans and Arabs, foreign aid policy, refugee crises. Among those invited were Ambassador Mabel Smythe and Senator William Proxmire, as well as two of the men whose families had hosted her in Africa: Beverly Carter, then U.S. ambassador at large, formerly in Liberia and Tanzania, and John Withers, former U.S. AID director in India, Ethiopia, and Kenya. For the inaugural lecture in the series she made sure that several of her favorite and best students were invited, including Mary Frances Berry and Howard professor Babalola Cole; she also requested her longtime friends Ethel Grubbs, whom she considered a "big sister," and Beatrice Scott, who as Supreme Basileus had supported her fellowship to Oxford in 1931. This also was the event where she invited, and then disinvited, the staff representing South Africa and Rhodesia.[25]

Tate was also still working on her books on Africa, securing a contract for both manuscripts in 1982 with Howard University Press. But as she aged, it seemed that her inability to stop revising or to edit down masses of materials worsened. Even after she submitted copies of the "finished" manuscripts, the frustrated editor at the press was begging her to stop changing them. The two manuscripts were never published, and no complete copy of either made it into her Howard archive.

Her two manuscripts on the Pacific also were never published, although she continued to work and rework them, taking some solace that many of her ideas on the region had been captured in the collection of her articles on those subjects in 1973. As late as 1978, she also was still trying to place her converted fictionalized account of a Hawaiian king.

Tate seemed to be working even more frenetically than usual as she tried to beat the clock: she had so much left to do in the time remaining in her life. One of her understandable fears was that she too might become senile or lose her mental acuity, as had been the case already for both of her parents and one of her half brothers. During this time, back in Michigan, her younger brother Keith had been diagnosed with Parkinson's disease, and her remaining older half brother Herschel was suffering from loss of sight and the beginnings of memory loss. She had begun to have problems with her own eyes, evidenced by the steadily enlarging size of her looping cursive script and by the District of Columbia's decision to restrict her to daytime driving.

Yet, in her public presentations in this period, Tate remained poised and prepared as she enjoyed events that honored and acknowledged her life and work. She attended ceremonies where she was awarded honorary degrees from Bowie State in 1977 and Lincoln University in 1978. Although she had retired, Tate continued to receive attention from Howard for her career and accomplishments. The history department, in conjunction with the 1977 annual meeting of ASALH, honored six of Howard's "distinguished" faculty, Tate, Logan, Lorraine Williams, Chancellor Williams, Charles Wesley, and John Hope Franklin.

Especially meaningful to her was an event at the Moorland-Spingarn in 1977 when the Prometheans formally installed their archives, a collection that had begun with the materials and their letters she had donated in 1945 and 1950. During the ceremony, which also honored the eleven soldiers lost in battle, Tate spoke about her connection to the "300 brilliant young colored men" whose lives were interrupted to serve in a segregated Army. To laughter, she

Tate at installation of Prometheans Archive, Howard University, 1977 (Moorland-Spingarn, Howard University)

reminded them that as editor of their newsletter, it was her job to share their "bits of *appropriate* and I emphasize appropriate poetry and clean jokes."[26]

More seriously, she expressed her gratitude that when she nearly died from stab wounds in 1964, their national president was at her bedside the next morning at nine, soon followed by a beautiful floral arrangement. The men's appreciation of Tate extended beyond the Howard event, as they honored her at their annual reunion dinner in 1980 with a "Promethean Plaque of Honor" and remembered her again at their fiftieth anniversary gathering in 1993.

Even though the editing on her Black Women Oral History Project transcript was never completed, Tate's meticulous preparation for that interview seems to have been put to good use when Joseph Harris produced a long, glowing profile for the magazine of the Graduate School of Arts and Sciences in 1981. Twenty-five pages long, including nearly thirty photographs tracing her life from infancy, the article did the autobiographical work that she had tried to achieve through her many days of being interviewed. She apparently edited and re-edited drafts of the article along with Harris, until he finally froze it in print.[27]

The life Tate represented there began and ended with her time at Oxford, concluding with just a snippet from the poem she had written aboard ship in 1932. Her photograph from the *Women of Courage* project graced the magazine's front cover, where preview text framed Tate as "a brilliant Afro-American woman whose creative and productive work as a diplomatic historian" had won praise from national and international authorities. It was a laudatory article throughout, an exhaustive recounting of her long lifetime of travels and achievements.

Her own hand in the article was plainly manifest in its relentless march through time with details both from the narrative recollections of her interview with Danley as well as from documents that were or would soon be in her archive at Howard, where she continued to donate papers. In these ways, Harris wrote a second-person account that she could easily have narrated, though quite immodestly, in the first person.[28]

Tate tried out a shorter version of her life history in the third person when she delivered the same speech on two different occasions, the first in 1981 when she traveled to Colorado Springs to accept the distinguished alumnus award from the national association representing state universities, and later, in 1984, at the dedication of a new computer center she had endowed at WMU. As in the Howard profile, she placed her family in the history of the Homestead Act of 1862, while portraying her younger self as a brilliant student who succeeded every place she landed, at WMU, Columbia, Oxford, Radcliffe. She characterized her financial contributions to educational institutions as expressions of gratitude for their support "in a color and sex discriminating society." Crediting Howard for much of the income that made her generosity possible, she also quickly reminded listeners that her salary had suffered at the hands of the men in power through actions that were "at times unconscious and at other times deliberate, nefarious and malevolent."[29]

Tate's engagement with WMU had only deepened after 1976, when she became a charter member of its fund-raising board, which brought her back to Kalamazoo, including for the golden anniversary of her 1927 graduation. She continued to increase her financial gifts to WMU, using some of her stock holdings to set up a new irrevocable unitrust and to endow a Merze Tate Medallion Scholarship for undergraduates.

It was during this period that she met Karen Stone, a young white 1978 WMU accounting graduate in northern Virginia, who began to serve as Tate's adviser for her increasingly complicated tax returns; they also served on the WMU Foundation board together. Fascinated by Tate's accounts of her many travel adventures, Stone often invited her to spend time with her family in Alexandria, picking her up from her home in Brookland. Later, Tate raised questions about what would happen to her financially in case of prolonged illness, and received reassurances from officials at WMU that it would see to her care.[30]

Tate was entering a bittersweet period in her life. While accolades and celebrations came her way, she also grieved the loss of old friends and family members. Martin Jenkins died suddenly in 1978, soon after the passing of William Stuart Nelson, for whom she wrote a moving tribute. She had first met both men and their families in the 1930s in North Carolina. Tate had witnessed the loss of Howard colleagues Mordecai Johnson in 1976, Kittrell and Ferebee in 1980, and Rayford Logan in 1982.[31]

Her longtime Radcliffe friend and colleague Bernice Brown Cronkhite lived to be ninety, dying in 1983. Susie Jones passed away in 1985. Blanche Nelson and Norma Nabrit, close women friends she had first met in North Carolina in the 1930s, died in 1988. Tate continued to support other friends who were hospitalized, showing up to feed them or sit nearby. For nearly two years, she helped care for one of her closest friends, Ethel Grubbs, who suffered a debilitating stroke and died in 1981. When her colleague the artist Lois Jones returned from burying her husband Pierre in Haiti, Tate organized a large group of friends and a reception at the airport for her.

Her family in Michigan continued to dwindle, with her younger brother Keith dying at seventy-six in 1983; she did not attend his funeral, citing her own health and the difficulty of travel. But their relations had been strained since he had their senile father transfer his farm to him, effectively, in Tate's view, depriving her of an entitled half share. Her older half-brother Herschel died in 1987, and a sister-in-law in 1989, ending her closest surviving links to her home in Mecosta County.[32]

Still, Tate's life in retirement remained busy socially and professionally. She said "yes" when Nathan Huggins asked her in 1981 to serve on the board of the newly created Du Bois Institute at Harvard. At Howard, she continued to host her seminar series, bringing in the scholar Akira Iriye in 1982 for "War, Peace, and Culture in 20th Century U.S.-East Asian Relations."[33]

The Bridgebuilders, a club Tate had founded in 1946, honored her in 1987 with a party, calling her "a Diamond of a Lady." Members who had gathered on the first Friday of every month for decades wrote remembrances which they collected in a scrapbook, forming a modern version of a nineteenth-century friendship album. They attested to her skills at the bridge table, but also to her graciousness to players not as skilled, her "spirit of friendly, witty camaraderie," and her learnedness. They teased her that for as long as they had known her, she was always working "TO MEET A DEADLINE," a claim common among scholars. One friend crafted "A Salute to Merze—brilliant scholar, renowned writer, arts devotee, world-wide traveler, excellent bridge player. Discriminating hostess. Delightful companion, loyal friend—charming, versatile, scintillating—may all the fine things that you deserve continue to fill your life."[34]

Tate still enjoyed the many cultural offerings in Washington, including going in 1985 to see the poet laureate Gwendolyn Brooks at the Library of Congress, thanks to a lift from her younger Howard colleague and literary scholar Claudia Tate, since she was no longer allowed to drive at night. Although born four decades apart, the two Howard scholars shared in the excitement around the explosion of attention to Black women writers in the late 1970s and 1980s, including the younger Tate's now classic *Black Women Writers at Work.* The historian Sharon Harley also recalls that Tate had attended the launch of the pathbreaking anthology *The Afro-American Woman,* part of the emergence of the new field of Black women's history, in 1978.[35]

Having lived long enough to witness this development, Tate approached it with her usual intellectual intensity. Under the label "Black Women," she had started in the 1960s to amass her own collection of clippings on that topic well before her later role on the Black Women Oral History Project. She made note of a program at Radcliffe in 1973, "The Black Woman: Myths and Realities." Continuing her habit of close daily newspaper reading, Tate was especially attentive to the work of two prominent Black women journalists at the *Washington Post,* Jacqueline Trescott and Dorothy Gilliam, saving their three-part front-page series "The New Black Woman" in 1986. They examined the challenges for Black women who were "mold-breakers" in many professional fields and who, under the title "Mixed Rewards of Success," also had to contend with the stresses of expected family duties, motherhood, and tensions with Black men. These were exactly the same issues Tate had raised in her earliest writings in the 1930s on how best to educate and support professional Black women.

Tate seemed to take special pride when the *Washington Post* ran an article in December 1985 about D.C. native Susan Rice's selection as a Rhodes Scholar or when the *Radcliffe Quarterly* announced in 1981 that Linda Perkins, a Black woman scholar of gender and education, had received a fellowship there.

Tate's international focus remained in place as she also clipped articles on African women and female circumcision, the work of Bishop Tutu's daughter Mpho, and the U.N. Decade of Women.[36]

Her unfinished scholarly work also still continued to occupy her, but as she neared her eighties, declining health and grief slowed her, as she explained repeatedly in letters to administrators at Howard and WMU. To her former chair Lorraine Williams, she confided that she had "been ill and undergoing treatment," and "in addition, lost my brother in Detroit in July." The next year she wrote WMU officials: "If I survive the many pressures on my time and strength, I hope to update five manuscripts and index one already under contract before the loss of eyesight and death."[37]

Doctor's appointments for her eyes, dental work, and physical therapy sessions for curvature of the spine consumed her time and interrupted her thinking. "I am now going three times a week for therapy," she complained, "which leaves very little for hundreds of problems and scores of requests, shopping for food, care of the house and yard and work on manuscript." She feared that the pressures she felt about her work were about to drive her "nearly insane, with only three to four hours sleep during the night."[38]

Celebrations of her life and work as a scholar continued to lift her spirits. Harvard extended a special invitation and she flew to Boston to receive recognition at its 350th anniversary celebrations in 1986. That same year, Howard University awarded her an honorary degree, calling her "one of America's outstanding diplomatic historians" and thanking her for "distinguished service" to the institution and its students; the choice of words may have assuaged some of the hurt Tate felt at never having been named a Distinguished Professor. Photographs from the event show her animated and engaged in conversation over a meal with the other recipients, Cicely Tyson, Sammy Davis, Jr., and the publisher John Johnson.

Yet Tate's stubborn hand showed itself in the citation's description of her many travels: "You have been the guest of LAMCO, the largest mining company in Liberia, of the Foreign Affairs Department in Rhodesia, and of the Government of South Africa." She persisted in believing that her acceptance of the trip was justified by her scholarly research needs, hoping here to have the last word on that controversy from the previous decade. But the trip also had come to mean so much to her because, as she may have suspected at the time, it became her final experience as an international traveler.[39]

In 1991, the American Historical Association, whose annual meetings had left Tate feeling so alone, honored her with its Scholarly Distinction Award.

Credit for that goes to the African American historian Roslyn Terborg-Penn, who as chair of the AHA Committee on Women's Historians led the drive for the honor, with the support of her former colleague and chair Joseph Harris and the newly created Committee on Minority Historians.

Tate also lived to see her philanthropy put to good use. Support for graduate students at Radcliffe brought her annual reports about the women who had received funding from her fellowship. From WMU, undergraduate students who received a Merze Tate Medallion Scholarship wrote to thank her for making a college education possible for them. She continued to make small gifts to other institutions, including Bennett College and Teachers College. But Michigan remained on her mind.

Her largest and most significant gift came in 1990 when she donated $1 million to WMU to create a new Merze Tate Student Academic Endowment Fund, an unrestricted gift for student assistance. Tate's overall support for her undergraduate alma mater totaled nearly $2 million, the equivalent of $9 million today. When she was interviewed in the *Detroit Free Press* about her gift, she said, "I don't understand what all the commotion is about," explaining that her attention was elsewhere: "I'm working on three different projects now." When news of her gift was reported, Agnes Cummings Haywood wrote from Michigan to congratulate her, but also to say that Tate had made her wedding dress. Her letter, among the last to be added to Tate's Howard archive, was a poignant reminder that as a young woman with very little money, she had earned some cash as many Black women before had done—working as a seamstress, a craft her mother had taught her.[40]

At eighty-five, Tate had lived long enough to see the fruits of her generosity, to be recognized by her profession and educational institutions, and to enjoy celebrations with those she had socialized with for many decades around dinner and bridge tables. In all these ways, she enjoyed accolades often offered only after one's death. But, as she told Eva Dykes, she was unafraid of that nearing eventuality and had prepared herself to face it.

In a letter addressed to "The Only Undertaker, Funeral Director, Remus, Michigan," Tate inquired in 1985 about "the approximate cost involved in picking up a wrapped casket—mine, Merze Tate's at the Northwest Airlines airport in Grand Rapids, and transporting it to Pine River Cemetery." After carefully describing the cemetery's location, she explained where her grave should be opened: "It would be in the plot of Mrs. Myrtle Tate, where also lies Mrs. Thelma Hayes, Theo Cross and Ernestine Cross, and Isaac Flowers."

Despite the seriousness of the task, Tate apparently had not lost her dry wit. "Obviously, I cannot provide the exact date, as I have not yet died," she wrote. Ever cost-conscious, she emphasized that she was also comparing prices with a funeral home in Detroit.[41]

Always practical, independent, and accustomed to taking care of herself, Tate feared that there would be no one left in Michigan to see to her burial there, the home she designated as her final resting place. It was likely the loss of her sister-in-law Ernestine Cross in 1985 that had triggered Tate's letter—she was the family member who had helped manage her affairs after the death of her sister in 1959. Even though she had one brother still alive at the time of her letter, his health slowly deteriorated before his death in 1987; his wife and her remaining sister-in-law would soon follow in 1989.

Around this time, Tate's memory began more and more to travel through time as she began to re-experience in real time events and places from her long life. This time travel came and went, but became more frequent. But she also was aware that her mind could become confused and that her memory was unreliable. She eventually was diagnosed with early stages of dementia. She continued, however, to be able to enjoy the pleasures of the present, including musical, theatrical, and literary performances. But in conversation, with growing frequency, she would reveal herself to be reliving adventures from a long life of travel and intellectual adventures as if they too were in the recent present.

When it was no longer safe for her to live alone, Karen Stone acted on behalf of the WMU Foundation to arrange for round-the-clock care. A nurse and her family moved in with Tate, cooking and caring for her, taking her to doctor's appointments, and also to social and cultural outings and weekly mass at St. Anthony's. After a lifetime of being alone and living in her own mind, Tate enjoyed the safety and comfort of others while being able to remain in the home she built for herself in 1960, surrounded by her papers and books, scrapbooks, and travel mementos.

The Thompson family had continued to be close to her over the years and remained steadfast friends, helping as she became less able to care for her house or to entertain and cook as she had when she was younger. Their son Jay went to Howard in 1985 and made his home in the Washington area. He appreciated her care for him as a young man when he decided to follow his gifts as a jazz guitarist. He says that she "changed my life" by pushing him to do the necessary hard work to be able to take pride in whatever he did, making him a "better person" for it. Tate encouraged him to study with the toughest member of the music department at Howard, the Oxford-trained Ph.D. Doris Evans

McGuinty, and he credits the two women with pushing him hard to elevate his understanding of music. He also remembers how Tate's quiet Catholic faith grounded her as she aged, although he says that she was religiously private and never dogmatic.

His sister Allene followed her parents into military service after graduating from West Point. Despite her travels and deployments, she also remained close to Tate, writing back and forth while she was away, but also visiting whenever she returned to the area. Of the last visit she remembers with Tate, she recalls hugging her, holding her close, and feeling a physical fragility that surprised and saddened her because it differed so much from the strong, vibrant, energetic woman she knew as Auntie Merze.

Both of the Thompson children remember that among the most important gifts they received from Tate were Marriott stock certificates, which she started giving them when they were about ten. She taught them how to follow the stock market and about the value of investing for the long term. Both of them followed her advice and both credit that stock with helping them make the down payments to become first-time homeowners.

In the summer of 1996, Tate suffered a heart attack at home and was rushed to nearby Providence Hospital, where she was pronounced dead. More than thirty years had passed since she had first been administered extreme unction there after her stabbing in 1964.

"Diplomatic Historian Merze Tate Dies at 91," read the *Washington Post* headline for an article that recounted her time on Howard's faculty, named the titles of all of her books, detailed her Fulbright year; described her several degrees and her positions at Barber-Scotia, Bennett, and Morgan State; noted her Phi Beta Kappa membership; and lauded her philanthropy. The account read as if Tate could have written it, and in its last line, it repeated what she herself had long realized: "She leaves no immediate survivors."[42]

Tate had carefully laid out her wishes for her funeral. A traditional mass was said at her parish church, St. Anthony's, where she had been a member since 1960. Members of the Prometheans served as pallbearers and the Bridgebuilders Club helped with the repast. Her funeral drew a crowd of friends, neighbors, and colleagues from Howard. Allen Thompson delivered a eulogy and his son Jay played music, as Tate had requested. His daughter Allene was away on active duty at the time but learned later that Tate had bequeathed her the little Mexican chair that she would use with her own children.[43]

Tate's printed funeral program ended with language she often had used to narrate her family's history: "Merze was born among the pine trees of

Michigan. She grew up in a frame house built from pine lumber. She attended a grade school built of the same pine timber which stood near a grove of pine trees. Merze will be laid to rest in a pine coffin in Pine River Cemetery near Blanchard, Michigan."

Tate's colleague Joseph Harris remembers the starkness of the plain pine coffin but he also found it fitting because she was "not a lavish person." When he saw it, he remembered her joking with him about how the students at Howard were driving new Oldsmobiles, but she had never owned anything but a less expensive Chevy. It was as if in this most personal of final choices, she also expressed the faithful humility of her own mortality.[44]

As she wished, Tate's body was flown back to Michigan, accompanied by Stone, and driven to the cemetery in Rolland Township. There, so many in her family had been laid to rest, including her parents, her sister and brothers, as had the family neighbor, Vernie M. Fish Smith, who had helped deliver her. The interment ceremony drew some from Detroit but most came from nearby surrounding communities. For some, the gathering was the first time they learned that she was Catholic. The final pages of the funeral guestbook were filled with the surnames of the Black families who called themselves Old Settlers—Guy, Lett, Cross—names also engraved on tidy rows of weather washed headstones laid out in a spacious field of summer's lush green framed by darkened stands of tall pines.[45]

Afterword

When I drove on to the main street of Blanchard, Michigan, in the summer of 2015, the first thing I saw was the new sign outside the Tate Memorial Library, recently renamed to honor Merze Tate. Inside was an extraordinary exhibit of photographs chronicling her long professional life and her many world travels. I stopped at Pine River Cemetery, and found her headstone resting alongside her family. Nearby, the homestead where Tate was born is still part of an isolated rural landscape, but verdant in the middle of the farming season. I headed south, back to Grand Rapids where I had stayed the night before. Days earlier, I had flown there and headed farther south still, to Kalamazoo to read through her archives at the sprawling campus at Western Michigan University, now home to 24,000 students.

It would have pleased Tate to have a library named in her honor, as fitting a tribute as any for a scholar who had been a child whose imagination was fed by her love of reading. This renaming should be credited in part to the work of Sonja Hollins, a Black WMU alum who discovered Tate's story in researching the history of Black students at the school. Miffed that she had graduated from the university without having learned about Tate, she has worked since then to honor and memorialize Tate in the place she called home. Hollins founded the Kalamazoo-based Merze Tate Explorer's Club in 2008, an organization that mentors Black girls to go to college and places Tate's example and the opportunity to travel at the center of its work.

In 2020, WMU approved the establishment of its Merze Tate College, an alliance of services and programs. Her endowed Medallion merit-based scholarships still provide full funding for selected students. That and other recognition have begun to come Tate's way. At Oxford, the faculty of history named its seminar room in her honor, and when her college, St. Anne's, built a new library, they named its student study space after her. The American Political Science Association named its award for best dissertation for her.

In the course of working on this book, I have spent time in the places central to Tate's life story, including Howard University where she had an office in Douglass Hall. Her brick rancher in the Brookland section of Washington still stands on a short block of houses facing the wooded park across the street, and bordered on one end by a Franciscan monastery as it was when she lived there.

When I lived at Oxford in 2018–2019, Tate was on my mind daily as I walked and worked in a historic infrastructure and witnessed traditions preserved at their core exactly as they were when she was there in the 1930s. I sat in the same college chapels and performance halls listening to organ and choral music just as she did, and walked through the same gardens, watching punting on the Cherwell. But I was also painfully aware of how different my experience was in most other ways, in particular how the privileged conditions I worked in were so different from those for her as she struggled to earn her Oxford degree.

Tate's time traveling in India and Asia in her Fulbright year was a key influence in her later work. In February 2019, I flew from London to Doha to meet a colleague for a trip to Kolkata. We followed the same route by train from there to Bolphur and then on to Santiniketan. To arrive there now is still to enter a tree-filled campus where the original buildings remain, despite expansions in the school's mission and footprint over the decades. Most of what Tate saw remains, including the building where she lived and the houses where she socialized, all connected by tree-lined pathways of red clay bordered by mounds of marigolds. At its center is the Mandir, or temple, walled by stained glass with a marble floor, but still used as a gathering space for quiet and meditation each morning and evening, and for Wednesday services.

Kolkata is much expanded and modernized, but the footprint of the section of the city where Tate interacted with Indian officials and other Americans remains home to consulate offices as well as the house where she stayed with the Humes family. The cacophony of sounds and sights of the city includes the powerful visual pageantry of Hindu traditions and Muslim calls to prayer. The architectural remnants of the British Raj also remain ever present as part of the built environment that she encountered as well.

Tate made many trips to and through Hawaii to conduct her meticulous research at the Hawaiian Historical Society. On my first trip there, the length of the journey from the west coast of the United States makes indelible its enormous distance from this continent. There had to have been powerful incentives, both military and economic, before and after the air age, to mount and maintain a presence there from occupation to annexation to statehood.

Following Tate's trail to these places and Thailand helped me reckon with their importance to her and her work, but also to try to make better sense of her obsessive need to travel and explore. The power of that desire and her need to meet it remains a central and sometimes enigmatic feature of her long life, and a vexing one for me as her biographer.

Tate would also be especially pleased that digital technological innovations in recent decades have made access to her printed work, especially her articles, a mere keyboard search away. This means that students and scholars are much more likely to have her work available to be read, taught, and critiqued. Many of her pressing intellectual concerns about nuclear arms limitations, race and post-colonial conditions, and the technologies of international corporate imperialism remain as relevant today as they were during her lifetime, and in some cases even more so. And if the yield of the Google Alert on her name is any indication, notice of her and her scholarship is spreading here and abroad.

As my work on Tate's life has now come to an end, I will dismantle the space in my own home where I assembled the disparate archival evidence of her life and published works. The expanse of the project required a room of its own, which I intend to reclaim. While I am relieved to have reached the end of this work, I will be happier still to escape the blue-lit screens of digital materials and drafts, to pack up the shelves of notebooks and books, and empty the cabinets of file folders accumulated over a decade of work. I will take down the many maps I needed to keep track of her travels, and the photographs of her that have surrounded me as I worked to fashion a narrative out of the collected remnants of her extraordinary life. What I have learned about her and her bold and irrepressible spirit now rests between the covers of this book.

APPENDIX

Published Works by Merze Tate

BOOKS

The Disarmament Illusion: The Movement for a Limitation of Armaments to 1907 (New York: MacMillan, 1942).

The United States and Armaments (Cambridge: Harvard University Press, 1948).

The United States and the Hawaiian Kingdom: A Political History (New Haven: Yale University Press, 1965).

Hawaii: Reciprocity or Annexation (Lansing: Michigan State University Press, 1968).

Diplomacy in the Pacific: A Collection of Twenty-Seven Articles on Diplomacy in the Pacific and Influence of the Sandwich (Hawaiian) Islands Missionaries (Washington, D.C.: History Department, Howard University, 1973).

PAMPHLETS

Trust and Non-Self-Governing Territories: Papers and Proceedings of the Tenth Annual Social Science Conference, April 8–9, 1947, Howard University (Washington, D.C.: Howard University Press, 1948).

The International Control of Atomic Energy: A Vital Problem (UNESCO, August 1948).

ARTICLES

"The Justification of a Women's College," *Bulletin of Bennett College* (December 1937), 12–16.

"A Proposed Social Studies Programme for Bennett College for Women," *Quarterly Review of Higher Education Among Negroes* 5, no. 2 (April 1937): 14–16.

"The Teaching of Social Sciences in Negro Colleges," *Journal of Higher Education Among Negroes* (1938).

"Some Suggestions For Improving the Teaching and Materials of History," *Quarterly Review of Higher Education Among Negroes* 7, no. 2 (April 1, 1939): 143.

"The Present Day International Situation," *National Education Outlook* (February 1939): 14–16.

"The War Aims of World War I and World War II and Their Relation to the Darker Peoples of the World," *Journal of Negro Education* 12, no. 3 (Summer 1943): 521–532.

"The War Aims of World War II and Their Relations to the Darker Peoples of the World," *Morgan State College Bulletin* (June 1943): 4–15.

"The Challenges of Our Day," *Morgan State College Bulletin* (September 1944): 6–12 (commencement speech delivered on June 6, 1944).

"Teaching of International Relations in Negro Colleges," *Review of Higher Education Among Negroes* 15, no. 3 (July 1947): 149.

"More Light on the Abrogation of the Anglo-Japanese Alliance," *Political Science Quarterly* 74, no. 4 (December 1959): 532–554 (with Fidele Foy).

"Sandwich Island Missionaries Train a Native Pastorate," *Journal of Religious Thought* 18, no. 1 (Winter–Spring 1960): 33–39.

"British Opposition to the Cession of Pearl Harbor," *Pacific Historical Review* 29 (1960): 381–394.

"The Early Influence of the Sandwich Island Missionaries," *Journal of Religious Thought* 17 (1960): 117–132.

"Hawaii's Program of Primacy in the Polynesia," *Oregon Historical Quarterly* 61 (1960): 377–407.

"The Australasian Monroe Doctrine," *Political Science Quarterly* 76, no. 2 (June 1961): 264–284.

"The Sandwich Island Missionaries Lay The Foundation for a System of Public Instruction in Hawaii," *Journal of Negro Education* 30, no. 4 (Autumn 1961): 396–405.

"Sandwich Island Missionaries: The First American Point Four Agents," *Annual Report of the Hawaiian Historical Society* (1961): 3–19.

"Hawaii's Early Interest in Polynesia," *Australian Journal of Politics and History* 7 (1961): 232–243.

"Canada's Interest in Trade and the Sovereignty of Hawaii," *Canadian Historical Review* 44 (1962): 20–42.

"Slavery and Racism as Deterrents to the Annexation of Hawaii, 1854–1855," *Journal of Negro History* 47, no. 1 (January 1962): 1–18.

"The Sandwich Islands Missionaries Create a Literature," *Church History* 31, no. 2 (June 1962): 182–202.

"Decadence of the Hawaiian Nation and Proposals to Import a Negro Labor Force," *Journal of Negro History* 47, no. 4 (October 1962): 248–263.

"Great Britain and the Sovereignty of Hawaii," *Pacific Historical Review* 31, no. 4 (November 1962): 327–348.

"The 'Grand Crisis' for the Sandwich Islands Mission and the Year of Decision," *Journal of Religious Thought* 20 (1963–1964): 43–52.

"Sandwich Islands Missionaries and Annexation," *Journal of Religious Thought* 20 (1963–1964): 137–145.

"The Myth of Hawaii's Swing Toward Australasia and Canada," *Pacific Historical Review* 33, no. 3 (August 1964): 273–293.

"The Question of Development and Nationhood in New Guinea Since World War II," *Journal of Negro History* 56, no. 1 (January 1971): 43–53.

"Effects of Nuclear Explosions on Pacific Islanders," *Pacific Historical Review* 33, no. 4 (November 1964): 379–393 (with Doris Hull).

"Hawaii: A Symbol of Anglo-American Rapprochement," *Political Science Quarterly* 79, no. 4 (December 1964): 555–575.

"Slavery and Racism in South Pacific Annexations," *Journal of Negro History* 50, no. 1 (January 1965): 1–21 (with Fidele Foy).

"Australian Interest in the Commerce and the Sovereignty of Hawaii," *Australia and New Zealand Historical Studies* 11, no. 44 (April 1965): 499–512.

"Twisting the Lion's Tale Over Hawaii," *Pacific Historical Review* 36, no. 1 (February 1967): 27–46.

"U. S. Diplomacy: Influence of Sandwich Island Missionaries and the ABCFM," *Oregon Historical Quarterly* 68 (1967): 53–74.

"Nauru, Phosphate, and the Nauruans," *Australian Journal of Politics and History* 14 (1968): 177–192.

"Recent Constitutional Developments in Papua and New Guinea," *Pacific Affairs* 44, no. 3 (Autumn 1971): 421–427.

"Australia and Self-Determination for New Guinea," *Australian Journal of Politics and History* 16 (1971): 246–259.

REVIEW ESSAYS

"American Bigotry: History of Bigotry in the United States, by Gustavus Myers," *Journal of Negro Education* 12, no. 4 (Autumn 1943): 655–656.

"Krishnalal Shridharani, Warning to the West," *Journal of Negro Education* 12, no. 4 (Autumn 1943): 654–655.

"Fightin' Oil (review of 'American Oil at War,' by Harold Ickes)," *Journal of Negro Education,* 13, no. 2 (Spring 1944): 201–203.

"Middle America, Charles Morrow Wilson," *Journal of Negro Education* 13, no. 4 (Autumn 1944): 524–525.

"The Voice of Norway, by Halvdan Koht and Sigmund Skard," *Journal of Negro Education* 13, no. 4 (Autumn 1944): 525.

"The White Man's Pan African Idea" (review of Lewis Snowden, *The Union of South Africa*), *Journal of Negro Education* 13, no. 1 (Winter 1944): 76–79.

"Whites and Blacks on South Africa" (review of Selwyn James, *South of the Congo*), *Journal of Negro Education* 13, no. 1 (Winter 1944): 72–76.

"The Free Negro in North Carolina, 1790–1860, by John Hope Franklin," *Journal of Negro Education* 13, no. 1 (Winter 1944): 70–72.

"A Realistic Peace, review of *The Gentlemen Talk of Peace,* by William B. Ziff," *Journal of Negro Education* 14, no. 4 (Autumn 1945): 594–596.

"The Twenty-Ninth Annual Meeting of the Association for the Study of Negro Life and History," *Journal of Negro Education* 14, no. 1 (Winter 1945): 122–125.

"Twentieth Century China, review of *China Looks Forward* by Sun Fo," *Journal of Negro Education* 15, no. 1 (Winter 1946): 70–72.

"How and Why the War Was Won" (review of *The Winning of the War in Europe and the Pacific,* by General George C. Marshall), *Journal of Negro Education* 15, no. 1 (Winter 1946): 55–63.

"Will We Have Peace, review of *Foreign Policy Begins at Home* by James P. Warburg," *Journal of Negro Education* 15, no. 1 (Winter 1946): 72–75.

"Foundations of World Organization: A Political and Cultural Appraisal, by Lyman Bryson; Louis Finkelstein; Harold D. Lasswell; R. M. MacIver," *Journal of Negro Education* 21, no. 4 (Autumn 1952): 499–500.

"Somaliland Under Italy's Heel," *Journal of Negro Education* 21, no. 4 (Autumn 1952): 497–499.

"Africa, A Study in Tropical Development," *Journal of Negro Education* 38, no. 3 (July 1953): 335–339.

"Out of Confusion by Manmatha Nath Chatterjee," *Journal of Negro History* 39, no. 3 (July 1954): 220–221.

"Imperialism in Disguise," *Journal of Negro Education* 23, no. 4 (Autumn 1954): 447–449.

"Life with the Nehrus" (review of Nayantara Sahgal, *Prison and Chocolate Cake*), *Journal of Negro Education* 23, no. 4 (Autumn 1954): 443–444.

"Who Are South Africans," *Journal of Negro Education* 23, no. 4 (Autumn 1954): 444–447.

"The Awakening East," review of Eleanor Roosevelt, *India and the Awakening East, Journal of Negro Education* 23, no. 1 (Winter 1954): 61–63.

"A Personal Report on An American Negro in India," review of Saunders Redding, *An American in India: A Personal Report on the Indian Dilemma and the Nature of Her Conflicts, Journal of the Negro Education* 24, no. 2 (Spring 1955): 130–132.

"Looting Land with Love," review of Hallam Tennyson, *India's Walking Saint: The Story of Vinoba Bhave, Journal of Negro Education* 24, no. 4 (Autumn 1955): 454–456.

"The French Minority in Canada," *Midwest Journal* 7, no. 2 (1955): 187.

"Review of Richard Wright's *The Color Curtain:* A Report on the Bandung Conference," *Journal of Negro History* 41, no. 3 (July 1956): 263–265.

"A Fascist Land of Hate and Fear, 'Through Malan's Africa,' by Robert St. John," *Journal of Negro Education* 24, no. 4 (Autumn 1956): 452–454.

"A Report on India," review of Robert Trumbell, *As I See India, Journal of Negro Education* 25, no. 4 (Autumn 1956): 412–413.

"The Punjab Massacres of 1947: Review of Mano Majra by Khushwant Singh," *Journal of Negro Education* 4, no. 25 (Autumn 1956), 410–411.

"The Bombay Meeting, by Ira Morris," *Journal of Negro Education* 25, no. 1 (Winter 1956): 47–49.

"Life of the Kikuyu," *Journal of Negro Education* 26, no. 4 (Autumn 1957): 484.

"The Pitiful and the Proud by Carl T. Rowan," *Journal of Negro History* 42, no. 1 (January 1957): 65–67.

"China: New Age and New Outlook, by Ping-Chia Kuo," *Journal of Negro Education* 26, no. 4 (Autumn 1957): 484–486.

"One Man's Africa, by John Seymour," *Journal of Negro Education* 26, no. 4 (Autumn 1957): 483–484.

"W. E. B. Du Bois: *A Study in Minority Group Leadership,* by Elliott M. Rudwick," *Journal of Negro History* 47, no. 3 (July 1962): 205–207.

"The United States and the First Hague Peace Conference, by Calvin Dearmond Davis," *Political Science Quarterly* 79, no. 3 (September 1964): 462–464.

"American Epoch, A History of the United States Since the 1890s, ed. by Arthur S. Link," *Journal of Negro History* 49, no. 4 (October 1964): 269–270.

"American Activities in the Central Pacific, 1790–1870: A History, Geography and Ethnography Pertaining to American Involvement and Americans in the Pacific Taken from Contemporary Newspapers etc., by R. Gerard Ward," *Journal of American History* 54, no. 3 (December 1967): 646–647.

"The United States and the Washington Conference, 1921–1922, by Thomas H. Buckley," *Annals of the American Academy of Political and Social Science* 395, Students Protest (May 1971): 195–196.

"Buddhism in Hawaii: Its Impact on a Yankee Community, by Louise H. Hunter," *American Historical Review* 77, no. 5 (December 1972): 1413–1414.

"The Disenchanted Isles: The Story of the Second Revolution in Hawaii, by Theon Wright," *American Historical Review* 78, no. 3 (June 1973): 745.

"*Don Francisco de Paula Marin: A Biography,* by Ross H. Gast; *The Letters and Journal of Francisco de Paula Marin,* edited by Agnes Conrad," *American Historical Review* 79, no. 1 (February 1974): 222–223.

"*The Diaries of Walter Murray Gibson, 1886, 1887,* by Jacob Adler," *American Historical Review* 79, no. 2 (April 1974): 597.
"Dr. Hyde and Mr. Stevenson: *The Life of the Rev. Dr. Charles McEwen Hyde,* including a discussion of the Open Letter of Robert Louis Stevenson, by Harold Winfield Kent," *American Historical Review* 79, no. 3 (June 1974): 884–885.
"The Warrior King: *Hawaii's Kamehameha the Great,* by Richard Tregaskis," *American Historical Review* 79, no. 5 (December 1974): 1627.
"The Children of Pride, ed. Robert Manson Myers," *Agricultural History* 49, no. 2 (April 1975): 457–458.
"The Samoan Tangle: A Study in Anglo-German-American Relations, 1878–1900, by Paul M. Kennedy," *Pacific Historical Review* 45, no. 1 (February 1976): 144–145.

NEWSPAPER ARTICLES

"Finds Army Dictator Rules Negro GIS in Germany with Brutal Fist," *Chicago Defender,* November 4, 1950.
"Officer Thumbs Nose at Army," *Afro-American,* November 4, 1950.
"Tells Plight of Negro Officers at Kitzingen," *Chicago Defender,* November 11, 1950.
"Royal Welcome Given Visitor to Infantry Base in Germany," *Afro-American,* November 25, 1950.
"Howard University Professor Tells of Her Intriguing Visit in Egypt, Oriental Crossroads 6,000 Miles Away," *Afro-American,* November 25, 1950.
"Pilgrimage to Italy: Dr. Merze Tate Meets U.S. Artists in Rome," *Afro-American,* December 2, 1950.
"Visit the Pope," *Afro-American,* December 16, 1950.
"India Likes Afro," *Afro-American,* July 7, 1951.
"Scholar Pandit Nehru Impresses H. U. Visitor: Held Idealist Statesman Prime Ministers Friendly, Gracious," *Afro-American,* July 21, 1951.
"Boys Leader a Hit in India: Oklahomian's Fame Spreading in Orient, *Afro-American,* July 21, 1951.
"Our Baptist Missionaries in India," *Afro-American,* September 1, 1951.
" 'Incomparable' Col. Harry F. Lofton: Slated Belatedly to Head Army School He Founded," *Afro-American,* September 15, 1951.
"Wife's Faith, Officer's Return Is Strange Story," *Afro-American,* September 22, 1951.

BLACK WOMEN ORAL HISTORY PROJECT, INTERVIEWER AND EDITOR

Susie Jones, July 11, 1977.
Flemmie Kittrell, August 29, 1977.
Frances H. Williams, October 31–November 1, 1977.

Lena Edwards, M.D., November 13–14, 1977.
Eva B. Dykes, November 30–December 1, 1977.
Mary Edwards Hill, April 4, 1978–August 9, 1978.
Dorothy Boulding Ferebee, M. D., December 28 and 31, 1978.

Sources

Howard University
- Moorland-Spingarn Research Center
  - Merze Tate Papers
  - Rayford Logan Papers
  - Alpha Kappa Alpha Collection
- University Archives
  - Prometheans
  - Department of History
  - Writers Club

Harvard University
- Schlesinger Library Black Women Oral History Project Files

Western Michigan University
- Zhang Legacy Collections Center
  - Merze Tate Collection
  - Nancy Scott Clippings File

Library of Congress
- Rayford Logan Papers

Oxford University
- Bodleian Library
- Alfred Zimmern Papers
- Rothermere American Institute Library
- St. Anne's College Archives

Visva-Bharati University, Santiniketan
    University Archives and Library
United States Indian Education Foundation, Delhi
    Merze Tate Fulbright Reports, 1950–51
University of Arkansas, University Library
    Special Collections, Fulbright Scholar Grantee Directories
Yale University
    Beinecke Rare Book and Manuscript Library
    University Archives, Yale University Press Papers
Columbia University
    University Archives
Schomburg Center for Research in Black Culture
    Victor Daly Papers
Duke University
    John Hope Franklin Collection
University of Michigan
    Bentley Historical Library
    Thomas M. Spaulding Papers: 1901–1969
Hawaiian Historical Society
    General Collections
University of Otago, New Zealand
    Archives, Angus Ross Papers

INTERVIEWS (BY TELEPHONE)

Mary Frances Berry, 5/12/2015
Allison Blakely, 5/31/2022
Joseph E. Harris, 11/17/2020
Ruth Hill, 5/5/2015
Sonja Hollins, 8/12/2020 and 6/30/2015 (in person)
Winston Langley, 6/19/2020
Lydia Lindsey, 12/9/2022 (in person)
Allene Thompson Martin, 10/13/2020
Inez Smith Reid, 5/2021
Joseph Stevenson, 9/2019.
Karen Stone, 12/9/2014 and 5/22/2020
Allen Thompson, 12/17/2014
Frances Thompson, 9/2021
Jay Thompson, 12/22/2020
Michael Winston, 6/23/2020

Notes

PREFACE

1. Barbara D. Savage, "Professor Merze Tate: Diplomatic Historian, Cosmopolitan Woman," History Department, University of Pennsylvania, 2011, and an abbreviated version with the same title, in *Toward an Intellectual History of Black Women,* ed. Mia Bay, Farah Jasmine Griffin, Martha S. Jones, and Barbara D. Savage (Chapel Hill: University of North Carolina Press, 2015).
2. Patricia Owens and Katharina Rietzler, eds., *Women's International Thought: A New History* (Cambridge: Cambridge University Press, 2021); and Patricia Owens, Katharina Rietzler, Kimberly Hutchings, and Sara C. Dunstan, eds., *Women's International Thought: Towards a New Canon* (Cambridge: Cambridge University Press, 2022).
3. Cheryl Wall, "Black Women and the Pleasures of Intellectual Work," *Southern Journal of Philosophy* 59, no. 1 (March 2021): 16–27.
4. Wall, "Black Women and the Pleasures," 22, 23–24.
5. Fannie Barrier Williams, "The Colored Girl," *Voice of the Negro* 2, no. 6 (1905): 400–403; Deborah Gray White, ed., *Telling Histories: Black Women Historians in the Ivory Tower* (Chapel Hill: University of North Carolina, 2008); Wanda A. Hendricks, *Fannie Barrier Williams: Crossing the Borders of Region and Race* (Urbana: University of Illinois Press, 2014), 152.

INTRODUCTION

1. "Hinman Contest Held Last Night—Merrill Bramble for the Boys and Merze Tate for the Girls, Were the Winners—Big Crowd Was Present," *Battle Creek Enquirer,* 5/1/1921; "Able Orations Won in Contest," *Battle Creek Enquirer,* 5/15/1921.

2. Tate was quoting the abolitionist Wendell Phillips, "A Hero of the Black Race," lecture delivered in New York and Boston, December 1861, and widely reprinted, including in *A Library of American Literature from the Earliest Settlement to the Present,* ed. Edmund Stedman and Ellen Hutchinson (New York: Webster, 1891).
3. Dorothy Porter to Tate, 5/11/1973; Tate to Michael Winston, Director, Moorland-Spingarn Research Center, 1/21/1975, 7/24/1978; Vernie Merze Tate Papers, Howard University (hereinafter cited as "MT/HU"), Finding Aid, Tate Papers, October 2011, Manuscript Division, Howard University.
4. That remained the case despite early notice given her by Roslyn Terborg-Penn and Darlene Clark Hine. *Black Women in America: An Historical Encyclopedia,* volume 2, M–Z, ed. Darlene Clark Hine, Elsa Barkley Brown, Rosalyn Terborg-Penn (Bloomington: Indiana University Press, 1993), 1141–1142.
5. Francine Wilson, *The Segregated Scholars: Black Social Scientists and the Creation of Black Labor Studies, 1890–1950* (Charlottesville: University of Virginia Press, 2006); Jeffrey Stewart, *The New Negro: The Life of Alain Locke* (New York: Oxford University Press, 2018); David A. Varel, *The Scholar and the Struggle: Lawrence Reddick's Crusade for Black History and Black Power (*Chapel Hill: University of North Carolina Press, 2020) and *The Lost Black Scholar: Resurrecting Allison Davis in American Social Thought* (Chicago: University of Chicago Press, 2018); Bruce Kuklick, *Black Philosopher, White Academy* (Philadelphia: University of Pennsylvania Press, 2008); Genna Rae McNeil, *Groundwork: Charles Hamilton Houston and the Struggle for Civil Rights* (Philadelphia: University of Pennsylvania Press, 1983); Charles P. Henry, *Ralph Bunche: Model Negro or American Other* (New York: New York University Press, 1999).

CHAPTER 1. "HER OWN STORY"

1. *Isabella County Enterprise,* Mt. Pleasant, Michigan, 2/17/1905.
2. Tate, Black Women Oral History Project (hereinafter cited as "BWOHP").
3. Tate, BWOHP, Certified Copy of Record of Birth, Vernie Merze Tate, State of Michigan, County of Isabella, Mt. Pleasant, Mich., Merze Tate Collection, Zhang Legacy Collections Center, Western Michigan University (hereinafter cited as "MT/WMU").
4. Tate, BWOHP; Irma Guy, "Pioneer Days in Isabella County, Michigan," *Negro History Bulletin* 23, no. 5 (February 1960): 102; *The Old Settlers: A Nation Within Itself* (Remus, Mich.: OSRW, 2013); U.S. Census reports and other federal and state records confirm the family's origins in Hocking County, Ohio, and their relocation to Michigan. Charles Lett, Myrtle Tate's father, was born in 1830 in Ohio (U.S. Census, 1850, 1860), registered for the Civil War draft in 1863 in Michigan, enlisted in Michigan 1st Infantry Regiment in October 1863, and mustered out in 1865 to Charleston, S.C. By the Census of 1870, he was living in Millbrook, Michigan. His sister Lucinda Lett Flowers, who helped raise Myrtle, followed a similar pattern, born in Ohio, leaving Hocking for Millbrook, Mich., by the Census of 1870. For this and other public records research, thanks to Natalie Shibley. Also see George K. Hesslink, *Black Neighbors: Negroes in a Northern Rural Community* (Indianapolis: Bobbs-Merrill, 1967).

5. *The Old Settlers;* U.S. Census. Charles Tate, Myrtle's husband and Merze's father, was born in Ohio in 1864, and relocated to Rolland, Michigan, by 1880. Myrtle Tate was born in Millbrook, Michigan, in 1875; her mother Susan died shortly after in Mecosta County; Susan E. Lett, death, 6/1/1875, "Michigan, Deaths, 1867–1897," Millbrook, Mecosta, Michigan, Department of Vital Records, Lansing, page 202. Myrtle Cross filed for divorce from her first husband, Edward Cross, on 8/29/1900 on grounds of non-support; Michigan, Divorce Records, 1897–1952; Myrtle and Charles Tate, married on 9/23/1901, Michigan, Marriage Records, 1867–1952, Isabella County, Michigan Department of Community Health, Division for Records and Health Statistics. Ages of children and their locations are found in U.S. Census reports for 1900, 1910, 1920, 1930, 1940.
6. Tate, BWOHP; Tate interview in "Mainly About Folks," *Battle Creek Enquirer and News,* 10/11/1953.
7. Marah Ellis Ryan, *Merze: The Story of an Actress* (Chicago: Rand, McNally, 1888); Nina Baym, *Women Writers of the American West, 1833–1927* (Chicago: University of Illinois Press, 2011), 233, 299.
8. Tate, BWOHP.
9. Tate, BWOHP; *The Old Settlers.*
10. Tate, BWOHP.
11. Tate to Attorney William M. Graves, Detroit, n.d.; Roy Zingery, Register of Deeds, Isabella County, to Tate, 9/27/1952, MT/WMU. Plat Maps, Willits Farm Atlas of Mecosta County, Michigan; Millbrook Plat Map; Wheatland Plat Map; Millbrook Business Directory; Rolland Township Isabella County Plat Map; Atlas and Farm Directory of Isabella County, Michigan: compiled from county records and actual surveys, 1915, Standard Map Company, Michigan County Histories and Atlases.
12. *Isabella County Enterprise,* 6/6/1913, 8/15/1913, 6/19/1914, 5/26/1916, 1/5/1917; Tate, BWOHP.
13. Tate, BWOHP.
14. The Boston children's author Hezekiah Butterworth published this popular series from 1879 to 1895, each a large volume with delicate drawings. Titles included *Zigzag Journeys in the Orient,* and *in Europe, in Classic Lands, in The Occident, in Northern Lands, in Eastern Lands, in India, in Australia, in The Mediterranean, in The Levant, in The Sunny South, in The British Isles,* to cite a few of the eighteen volumes. I first encountered the books in a library exhibit of them during a research trip to Western Michigan University, and they matched Tate's detailed descriptions of them.
15. Tate, BWOHP.
16. *Isabella County Enterprise,* 6/5/1914; Tate, BWOHP.
17. Tate, BWOHP.
18. Benjamin C. Wilson, *The Rural Black Heritage Between Chicago and Detroit, 1850–1929: A Photograph Album and Random Thoughts* (Kalamazoo: Western Michigan University, 1985), 124; Marie Dusenberg, *A History of Negroes in Battle Creek* (Battle Creek: Willard Library, 1952); *The Paean,* Battle Creek High School Yearbook, 1921, Battle Creek, Michigan (author's possession).
19. Tate, BWOHP; U.S. Passport Application for Kathryn C. Glass, issued 5/12/1921, noting intent to travel from New York to England, Scotland, France, Italy, Switzerland, Holland,

Belgium; National Archives and Records Administration (NARA), Washington, D.C., NARA Series, Passport Applications, January 2, 1906–March 31, 1925; Ancestry.com; U.S. Passport Applications, 1795–1925 [database online]; Kathryn Glass, arrival July 10, 1923, from London, New York, Passenger Lists, 1820–1897, Records of U.S. Customs Service; Glass, departure from London to New York, 6/30/1923, United Kingdom, Outward Passenger Lists, 1890–1960. Again, for assistance with U.S. Census and genealogical research on Tate's family, thanks to Natalie Shibley.

20. *The Old Settlers.*
21. Tate, BWOHP.
22. Letter to Tate from Helen (Smith) Kaiser, Chicago, 1/4/1968, MT/HU.
23. *Blanchard Banner,* n.d., "Former High School Student Making Good," MT/WMU.
24. Tate's college was first known as Western State Normal School; the name was changed to Western State Teachers College in 1927. It became Western Michigan College of Education in 1941, then Western Michigan College in 1955, and finally Western Michigan University in 1957. I refer to it as "Western," "Western Michigan," or "WMU."
25. *The 1927 Brown and Gold: The Student Annual of Western State Normal School,* author's possession.
26. "Nancy E. Scott," Faculty Record and Clipping Files, WMU; Courtesy Sharon Carlson, Zhang Legacy Collections Center, Western Michigan University.
27. Scott, "The Effects of the Higher Education of Women Upon the Home," *American Journal of Sociology* 32, no. 2 (September 1926): 257–263; "Be She Wife or Old Maid, Co-Ed Called the Best—Educator to Defense of College Girls," *Chicago Daily Tribune,* 9/30/1926.
28. Tate, BWOHP.
29. Letter to Tate from Mrs. Mae Guy, The Dardanel Art Club, Battle Creek, Mich., January 28, 1925; "Western Student Is Awarded Scholarship," *Western Herald,* n.d., MT/WMU.
30. Tate, BWOHP; Jeffrey Mirel, *The Rise and Fall of an Urban School System: Detroit, 1907–1981* (Ann Arbor: University of Michigan Press, 1993).
31. Tate, BWOHP.
32. "Negress Wins School Honors," *Christian Science Monitor,* n.d., MT/WMU; "Lansingites Get W. S. N. Diplomas," *Lansing State Journal,* 6/13/1927.
33. Letter to Tate from Henry W. Shoe, Park School, Willow Grove, Pa., March 2, 1927, MT/WMU.
34. Mirel, *Rise and Fall of an Urban School System,* 55–58, 62. Thanks to Elizabeth Todd-Breland for advice on the history of education in Michigan.
35. Kevin Boyle, *Arc of Justice: A Saga of Race, Civil Rights, and Murder in the Jazz Age* (New York: Macmillan, 2004).
36. Calvin Enders, "White Sheets in Mecosta: The Anatomy of a Michigan Klan," *Michigan Historical Review* 14, no. 2 (Fall 1988): 59–84; Craig Fox, *Everyday Klansfolk: White Protestant Life and the KKK in 1920s Michigan* (Lansing: Michigan State University Press, 2011); JoEllen McNergney Vinyard, *Right in Michigan's Grassroots: From the KKK to the Michigan Militia* (Ann Arbor: University of Michigan Press, 2011), 201.

37. Tate, BWOHP.
38. Mirel, *Rise and Fall of an Urban School System,* 187.
39. Tate, BWOHP.
40. Tate, BWOHP.
41. Dean D. W. Howard, College of Liberal Arts, Howard University, to Tate, 6/29/1927, MT/HU.
42. Tate, BWOHP.
43. Tate, BWOHP.

CHAPTER 2. "DISTINGUISHED COLORED MEN AND WOMEN"

1. Emma Lou Thornbrough, *Indiana Blacks in the Twentieth Century* (Bloomington: Indiana University Press, 2000); Richard B. Pierce, *Polite Protest: The Political Economy of Race in Indianapolis, 1920–1970* (Bloomington: Indiana University Press, 2005), 3, 6, 7, 10–12, 14; Thornbrough, "Breaking Racial Barriers to Public Accommodations in Indiana, 1935 to 1963," *Indiana Magazine of History* 83 (December 1987): 301–343.
2. Thornbrough, *Indiana Blacks in the Twentieth Century,* 15, 21, 25, 27, 29, 31; Darlene Clark Hine, *When the Truth Is Told: A History of Black Women's Culture and Community in Indiana* (Indianapolis, 1981). Also see Jack S. Blocker, *A Little More Freedom: African Americans Enter the Urban Midwest, 1860–1930* (Columbia: Ohio State University Press, 2008); Earline Rae Ferguson, "The Woman's Improvement Club of Indianapolis: Black Women Pioneers in Tuberculosis Work, 1903–1938," *Indiana Magazine of History* 84 (September 1988): 237–261.
3. Thornbrough, *Indiana Blacks in the Twentieth Century,* 5, 50.
4. Thornbrough, *Indiana Blacks in the Twentieth Century,* 53; Thornbrough, "Segregation in Indiana During the Klan Era of the 1920s," *Mississippi Valley Historical Review* 47, no. 4 (March 1961): 594–618; Thornbrough, "The History of Black Women in Indianapolis," in *Indiana's African-American Heritage: Essays from Black History and Notes,* ed. Wilma L. Gibbs (Indianapolis: Indiana Historical Society, 1987), 68–92. Also see Mark David Higbee, "W. E. B. Du Bois, F. B. Ransom, the Madam Walker Company, and Black Business Leadership in the 1930s," *Indiana Magazine of History* 89 (June 1993): 101–124.
5. Tate, BWOHP.
6. Tate, BWOHP.
7. "Miss Marshall Is Hostess to the Nines," *Indianapolis Recorder,* 9/14/1929; "Les Pierettes Open Season with Bridge and Dancing," *Indianapolis Recorder,* 9/23/1929; "Miss Merze Tate Hostess to Club," *Indianapolis Recorder,* 1/24/1931; "Pretty Party," *Indianapolis Recorder,* 4/11/1931; "Week-end Visitor Is Entertained," *Indianapolis Recorder,* 2/7/1931; "Davis-Marshall Nuptials Colemnized [*sic*] at St. Rita's Roman Catholic Church," *Indianapolis Recorder,* 6/20/1931.
8. Tate, BWOHP.
9. "Club Calendar," *Indianapolis Recorder,* 11/16/1929; "Clubs Have Resumed Active Work After Vacation Season," *Indianapolis Recorder,* 10/12/1929; "Y.W.C.A. Notes," *Indianapolis Recorder,* 5/10/1930.

10. Letter to Tate from D. B. Waldo, President of Western Michigan Teacher's College, 4/8/1929, with her handwritten reply at the bottom; Waldo to Tate, 9/16/1930, with report on an Attucks student; MT/WMU.
11. Tate interview, BWOHP.
12. Tate interview, BWOHP.
13. Transcript, Teachers College, Columbia University, Merze Tate Papers, St. Anne's College Oxford (hereinafter cited as "Tate/Oxford").
14. "Study Abroad: Miss Merze Tate," *Pittsburgh Courier,* 6/27/1931; "In Europe: Miss Merze Tate," *Chicago Defender,* 8/8/1931.
15. Tate, 1931 Travel Diary, MT/HU. Thanks to Tsitsi Jaji for translation assistance.
16. Tate, 1931 Travel Diary, MT/HU. On African American travelers abroad in this period, see Farah J. Griffin and Cheryl J. Fish, eds., *A Stranger in the Village: Two Centuries of African-American Travel Writing* (Boston: Beacon, 1998); Keisha N. Blain and Tiffany M. Gill, eds., *To Turn the Whole World Over: Black Women and Internationalism* (Urbana: University of Illinois Press, 2018).
17. Tate, 1931 Travel Diary, MT/HU.
18. D. J. Markwell, "Sir Alfred Zimmern Revisited: Fifty Years On," *Review of International Studies* 12 (1986): 279–292; Tomohito Baji, "Zionist Internationalism? Alfred Zimmern's Post-Racial Commonwealth," *Modern Intellectual History* 13, no. 3 (2016): 623–651; Patricia Owens and Katharina Rietzler, "Polyphonic Internationalism: The Lucie Zimmern School of International Studies," *International History Review,* published online, 2/15/2023, DOI 10.1080/07075332.2023.2177321 (https://doi.org/10.1080/07075332.2023.2177321); Frank Moorhouse, *Grand Days* (London: Picador, 1994), *Dark Palace* (Sydney: Vintage, 2001), and *Cold Light* (New York: Random House, 2011).
19. Tate, 1931 Travel Diary, MT/HU.
20. Tate, 1931 Travel Diary, MT/HU; Papers of Sir Alfred Zimmern (1879–1957), Bodleian Archives and Manuscripts, University of Oxford.
21. Tate, 1931 Travel Diary, MT/HU.
22. Tate, 1931 Travel Diary; Paulette Nardal, "A Negro Woman Speaks at Cambridge and Geneva," *La Revue du Monde Noir,* n.d., 40–41, gallica.bnf.fr.
23. Tate, 1931 Travel Diary. Stonequist later published *The Marginal Man: A Study in Personality and Culture Conflict* (New York: Scribner, 1937). He also married Lucie Zimmern's daughter Edith in 1924.
24. Zimmern Papers, Bodleian Library, Oxford; "Moving Image: Lorenza Jordan Cole interviewed by Bette Yarbrough Cox," https://calisphere.org/item/c8cfe06fb249f9c329b943cd0fa27db7/Cole and https://archive.org/details/calauem_000192.
25. Tate Travel Diary, 1931, MT/HU.
26. Tate Travel Diary, 1931, MT/HU.
27. Tate Travel Diary, 1931, MT/HU.
28. "The Social World," *Indianapolis Recorder,* 11/7/1931.
29. "Travel Club to Take Cherry Blossom Tour, Easter to Capital, Washington," n.d.; "Travel Club Is Encouraged by Louis Ludlow, n.d., MT/WMU. News of the Travel Club became a recurring feature in the *Indianapolis Recorder,* under a "Travel Club" banner, with articles written and submitted by Tate.

30. Marjorie H. Parker, *Alpha Kappa Alpha Through the Years, 1908–1988* (Chicago: Mobium, 1990).
31. "Questionnaire, Foreign Fellowship—Alpha Kappa Alpha Sorority," MT/HU.
32. "Winner, Miss Merze Tate," *Chicago Defender,* 1/16/1932.
33. "Travel Club of Crispus Attucks High School, 1932, Cherry Blossom Tour"; "Travel Club Has Interesting Tour," n.d., MT/WMU.
34. Tate, "Should Colored Children Travel?" *Indianapolis Recorder,* n.d., MT/WMU.
35. "Parents Give Party for Teacher," n.d., MT/WMU.
36. "Indiana Students Visit Howard Univ.," n.d.; "Bicentennial Visitors," *Afro-American,* n.d.; "Merze Tate Takes Group to Capital," n.d., MT/WMU.

CHAPTER 3. "SAIL TO THE FUTURE"

1. Marion Paton Terpenning (Mrs. W. A.) to AAUW, 4/17/1932, MT/Oxford. Walter Terpenning, who taught sociology and economics at Western, shared his wife's views on Tate, writing in 1942 of their "high expectations" of her, crediting her with "great energy and endurance, native ability that amounts to genius, great ambition and determination, and a fine, cooperative spirit"; Walter A. Terpenning, Professor of Economics and Business Administration, Albion College, to AAUW, Committee on Fellowship Awards, 12/9/1942, MT/HU.
2. Letters to AAUW: Hattie Edwards, AKA, Basileus Alpha Mu Omega Chapter, 4/5/1932; D. C. Shilling, Professor of Political Science, WSTC, 4/13/1932; Bertha S. Davis, Dean of Women, WSTC, 4/18/1932, MT/Oxford.
3. Letters to AAUW: Nancy E. Scott, Professor of European History, WMU, 4/15/1932; Francis W. Hornbeck, Michigan AAUW, 4/22/1932; Smith Burnham, Western, to AAUW, 4/18/1932; F. Lee Benns, University of Indiana, to AAUW, n.d., MT/Oxford.
4. Letter to Grace Hadow, Society of Home Students, from Esther Caukin Brunauer, AAUW, 6/1/1932, MT/Oxford. Two applications were sent with recommendations; a third applicant was advised to apply directly; "Report to the Committee on Selections for Oxford on Contents of Committee's Files, List of American Women Recommended and Accepted by Oxford University, 1928–1948," AAUW Microfilm Reel 104, 437. Thanks to Katharina Rietzler for retrieving.
5. Hadow's Notes on Tate's application, n.d., MT/Oxford.
6. Hadow letter to Tate, 6/25/1932, MT/Oxford.
7. Letter to Tate from Maudelle Bousfield, Alpha Kappa Alpha Sorority, Chicago, 5/16/1932, MT/HU; Tate letter to Hadow, 7/26/1932, MT/Oxford; Tate, BWOHP; admission ticket, 1932 Olympics, MT/WMU.
8. Letter to Tate from Hadow, MT/Oxford.
9. Tate cable to Hadow, 8/18/1932; R. F. Butler cable to Tate, 8/23/1932; Butler cable to Tate, 8/24/1932; Tate cable to Hadow, 8/28/1932; Tate letter to R. F. Butler, 9/4/1932, MT/Oxford.
10. Tate, BWOHP.
11. "Sails," *Chicago Defender,* 10/15/1932.
12. Janet Howarth, "Women," in *The History of the University of Oxford,* volume 8, *The Twentieth Century,* ed. Brian Harrison (Oxford: Oxford University Press, 1994), 346–374.

13. Helena Deneke, *Grace Hadow* (London: Oxford University Press, 1946); *Oxford Dictionary of National Biography,* entries on Grace Eleanor Hadow and (Christina) Violet Butler; M. Reeves, *St. Anne's College, Oxford—An Informal History* (printed by St. Anne's College, 1979); *The Ship* (yearbook of the Society of Oxford Home Students, Old Students Association), St Anne's Archive, Oxford; George Smith, Elizabeth Perez, and Teresa Smith, *Social Enquiry, Social Reform, and Social Action: One Hundred Years of Barnett House* (Oxford Department of Social Policy and Intervention, Barnett House, 2014); C. V. Butler, *Barnett House, 1914 to 1964: A Record for Its Friends* (Printed for Private Circulation, 1964).
14. Letter from Tate to Hadow, 10/11/1932; Hadow to Tate, 10/21/1932; Tate to Butler, n.d., Tate/Oxford.
15. Tate, BWOHP.
16. Tate, BWOHP.
17. Tate, BWOHP.
18. Gbemi Rosiji, *Lady Ademola: Portrait of a Pioneer: Biography of Lady Kofoworola Aina Ademola, MBE OFR* (Lagos: EnClair, 1996), 25–30. Ademola's account of her years at Oxford had been published earlier as "The Story of Kokoworola Aina Moore, of the Yoruba Tribe, Nigeria," in *Ten Africans,* ed. Margery Perham (Evanston: Northwestern University Press, 1963; reprint, 1971), 323–343.
19. C. V. Butler to Tate, 11/23/1932; Tate to Butler/Hadow, n.d., Tate/Oxford.
20. C. V. Butler to Tate, 11/23/1932, Tate/Oxford.
21. Butler to Hadow, n.d., Tate/Oxford.
22. Mrs. Gairdner to Hadow, n.d., Tate/Oxford.
23. Hadow to Gairdner, n.d., Tate/Oxford; Tate, BWOHP.
24. Tate to Hadow, n.d., with Hadow note, "admitted as B. Litt Probationer—subject Disarmament," Tate/Oxford.
25. Tate to Hadow, 6/17/1932, Tate/Oxford.
26. Tate, BWOHP.
27. Tate, BWOHP.
28. Letter from Tate to Hadow, 10/4/1932, Tate/Oxford; "Certificate," University Registry, Oxford, 25th November 1933, Miss M. Tate, Tate/WMU.
29. Tate to Hadow, 11/21/1933, Tate/Oxford.
30. Tate to Hadow, 11/21/1933; Hadow to Tate, 2/28/1934; Tate to Hadow, 2/28/1934; Mrs. E. C. Brunauer, AAUW, to Hadow, 4/21/1934; Letter from Phelps-Stokes Fund to Hadow, 2/27/1934; Hadow to Jones, Phelps-Stokes Fund, 3/2/1934; Hadow to Tate, 3/7/1934; Thomas Jesse Jones, Phelps-Stokes Fund, to Hadow, 3/20/1934, Tate/Oxford.
31. "Merz [*sic*] Tate Is Awarded B. Litt. at Oxford," *Pittsburgh Courier,* 6/20/1934.
32. Tate to Hadow, 6/15/1934, Tate/Oxford.
33. Tate to Butler, 6/20/1934, with notes, Tate/Oxford.
34. Tate, BWOHP.
35. Tate, BWOHP.
36. Tate, BWHOP; James Shapiro, *Oberammergau: The Troubling Story of the World's Most Famous Passion Play* (New York: Vintage, 2001); *Snead's Guide: The Passion Play at Oberammergau, 1930: The Complete English Text of the Play* (London: Ernest Benn, 1930). Thanks to Judith Weisenfeld for her help on Oberammergau.

37. Hadow to Tate, 7/11/1934 and 7/25/1934; Tate to Hadow, 7/19/1934 and 7/20/1934; London School of Economics and Political Science to Tate, 7/15/1934; Tate to Hadow, 8/1/1934, Tate/Oxford.
38. Tate to Hadow, 10/9/1934; Hadow to Tate, 10/12/1934, Tate/Oxford.
39. Zimmern to C. V. Butler, 11/5/1934, Notes to file, 11/5/1934, Tate/Oxford.
40. Coate to C. V. Butler, 11/16/1934 and 11/19/1934, Tate/Oxford.
41. Coate to C. V. Butler, 11/16/1934 and 11/19/1934, Tate/Oxford; University Registry, Oxford, 12/1/1934, Tate/WMU; *Oxford Dictionary of National Biography,* Agnes Headlam-Morley; Rosiji, *Lady Ademola,* 29.
42. Tate to Hadow, 1/20/1935; Hadow to Tate, 1/21/1935; Tate to Hadow, 12/12/1934; Hadow to Tate, 12/14/1935; E. H. Banner, The Gentlewomen's Employment Association and Ladies' Work Society, to Hadow, 2/12/1935 and 5/16/1935; Hadow to Vice Principal Butler, 3/19/1935, Tate/Oxford.
43. Myrtle Tate to Oxford, 4/16/1935, with note on April 26 response in script, Tate/Oxford.
44. Tate to Hadow or Butler, n.d.; Headlam-Morley to V. Butler, 4/26/1935. Tate/Oxford.
45. Headlam-Morley to V. Butler, 4/26/1935, Tate/Oxford.
46. Note to file, Hadow, n.d., Tate/Oxford.
47. Minutes, Board of Faculty of Social Studies meetings, 1928–1945, 5/4/1934, 10/26/1934, 11/30/1934, 6/14/1935, Bodleian Library. Thanks to Patricia Owens.
48. Hadow to Tate, 6/14/1935, Tate/WMU; Zimmern to Butler, n.d.; Headlam-Morley to Butler, n.d., Tate/Oxford.
49. Tate to R. F. Butler, 6/20/1935, with Butler's margin notes indicating Tate's deceptions, Tate/Oxford.
50. Tate to Hadow, 7/5/1935; Hadow to AKA, 7/5/1935; Hadow to Tate, 7/5/1935; Tate to Hadow, n.d., Tate/Oxford.
51. Daniel S. Papp, ed., *As I Saw It,* by Dean Rusk, as told to Richard Rusk (New York: Norton, 1990), 78–80; Eric Williams, *Inward Hunger: The Education of a Prime Minister* (Markus Wiener, 2006), 53.
52. Tate, BWOHP.
53. Tate, BWOHP.
54. Tate, BWOHP.
55. Tate, BWOHP; Certificate, August 22, 1935, Deutsches Institut Fur Auslander an Der Universitat Berlin, Tate/WMU. Thanks to Katherina Rietzler for translation.
56. Tate, BWOHP.
57. Tate to Hadow, 9/3/1935, Tate/Oxford.

CHAPTER 4. "A NARROW LIFE, BUT A RICH ONE"

1. Tate, BWOHP.
2. Barber-Scotia College, "Our History" (2023), https://b-sc.edu/our-history.
3. Lucy D. Slowe, "Higher Education of Negro Women," *Journal of Negro Education* 2, no. 3 (July 1933): 352–358; Linda M. Perkins, "Lucy Diggs Slowe: Champion of the Self-Determination of African-American Women in Higher Education," *Journal of Negro History* 81, no. 1/4 (Winter–Autumn 1996): 89–104; "7th Meeting of Race Women's

Deans Ends at Wilberforce," *Norfolk Journal and Guide,* 3/28/1936; " 'Women's Deans Not Lady Cops,' Dean Slowe," *Chicago Defender,* 4/4/1936; Perkins, "The National Association of College Women: Vanguard of Black Women's Leadership and Education, 1923–1954," *Journal of Education* 172, no. 3 (1990): 65–75; Stephanie Evans, *Black Women in the Ivory Tower, 1850–1954: An Intellectual History* (Gainesville: University Press of Florida, 2008).

4. Tate, BWOHP. This association was the predecessor to the current Association of Social and Behavioral Scientists.
5. Tate, "Three Years in England," *Ivy Leaf,* 1936; "AKA Fellowship Recipient Completes 3 Years of Intense Grad Study," *Norfolk Journal and Guide,* 1/11/1936; "Prominent Women Speak to AKA Group," *Norfolk Journal and Guide,* 1/4/1936; "Foreign Fellowships," *Baltimore Afro-American,* 1/11/1936; "S. Atlantic Region Host to 18th Boule of AKA Sorority," *Afro-American,* 1/4/1936.
6. Stanley Warren, "The Monster Meetings at the Negro YMCA in Indianapolis," *Indiana Magazine of History* 91 (March 1955): 57–80.
7. "Oxford Grad—Miss Merze Tate Entertained by Host of Friends," *Indianapolis Recorder,* March 28, 1936, MT/HU; Warren, "Monster Meetings at the Negro YMCA." After Tate's appearance in 1952, the next women to appear were Eleanor Roosevelt, Irene Gaines, president of the National Association of Club Women, and the writer Lillian Smith.
8. Deidre Bennett Flowers, "Education in Action: The Work of Bennett College for Women, 1930–1960" (dissertation, Columbia University, 2017).
9. Tate, BWOHP; "Bennett College Adds 8 to Faculty," *Afro-American,* 9/5/1936; "Bennett College Faculty Increase for New Term," *Philadelphia Tribune,* 9/3/1936.
10. Tate, BWOHP.
11. Tate, BWOHP.
12. Tate, "A Proposed Social Studies Programme for Bennett College for Women," *Quarterly Review of Higher Education Among Negroes* 5 (April 1937); "Bennett Curriculum Put in Four Divisions—Tate to Chair Social Sciences," *Greensboro Day News,* 6/1937.
13. Tate, "A Proposed Social Studies Programme"; "Bennett Curriculum Put in Four Divisions."
14. Tate, "A Proposed Social Studies Programme"; "Bennett Curriculum Put in Four Divisions."
15. Tate, "A Proposed Social Studies Programme."
16. Tate, "Some Suggestions for Improving the Teaching and Materials of History," *The Quarterly Review of Higher Education Among Negroes* 7, no. 2 (1939); Carter G. Woodson, *The Mis-Education of the Negro* (Washington, D.C.: Associated Publishers, 1933); Charles H. Wesley, "Guiding Principles in the Teaching of Social Sciences in the Negro Colleges," *The Quarterly Review of Higher Education Among Negroes* 3, no. 4 (October 1935).
17. Tate, "Some Suggestions for Improving the Teaching and Materials."
18. Tate, "The Justification of a Women's College," *Bulletin of Bennett College* (December 1937): 12, 14. The speech was given on 3/26/1937 before the fourteenth annual convention of the National Association of College Women in a session held at Bennett; Linda M. Perkins, "The National Association of College Women: Vanguard of Black

Women's Leadership and Education, 1923–1954," *Journal of Education* 172, no. 3 (1990): 65–75.

19. Tate, "The Justification of a Women's College." These questions on gender and higher education were being discussed more widely; Perkins, "Do Men and Books Mix? Women, College, and Romance," *Educational Researcher* 21, no. 8 (November 1992): 29–33.
20. Tate, "The Justification of a Women's College"; Tate quoted in Beatrice Hinkle, "Woman's Subjective Dependence Upon Man," *Harper's Magazine* 164, no. 980 (1932): 193–205; Kate Wittenstein, "The Feminist Uses of Psychoanalysis: Beatrice M. Hinkle and the Foreshadowing of Modern Feminism in the United States," *Journal of Women's History* 10, no. 2 (Summer 1998): 38–62.
21. Tate, BWOHP.
22. Fannie to Tate, October 7, 1936, MT/HU.
23. Tate, BWOHP.
24. Tate, BWOHP.
25. Tate, BWOHP.
26. Tate, BWOHP.
27. Tate, BWOHP.
28. Tate, BWOHP; Bernice Brown Cronkhite, *The Times of My Life* (1982); "In Memory, Bernice Brown Cronkhite, 1893–1983)," *Radcliffe Quarterly* (September 1983): 31.
29. Tate, BWOHP.
30. Tate, BWOHP.
31. Tate, BWOHP.
32. Tate, BWOHP.
33. Tate, "The Present Day International Situation," *National Educational Outlook Among Negroes* (February 1939): 14–16; Letter from S. E. Duncan, Principal, Washington High School, Reidsville, N.C., to David R. Jones, 10/5/1938; Letter from Immanuel Lutheran College, Greensboro, N.C., to Tate, 10/13/1938; Letter from Werner Lawson, North Carolina A & T, to Tate, 10/27/1938; Letter from A. Heninburg, North Carolina College for Negroes, to Tate, 11/1/1938, MT/HU.
34. Tate, "The Present Day International Situation"; Barbara Dianne Savage, "Beyond Illusions: Imperialism, Race, and Technology in Merze Tate's International Thought," in *Women's International Thought: A New History,* ed. Patricia Owens and Katharina Rietzler (Cambridge: Cambridge University Press, 2021), 266–285.
35. "Rosenwald Fellowship Grants for 1939," *Chicago Defender,* May 6, 1939. On the car, BWOHP. Parts of Investor's Syndicate were later acquired by American Express, and today the descendent company is Ameriprise Financial.
36. Tate, BWOHP.
37. Tate, BWOHP.
38. Tate to Attorney William M. Graves, Detroit, n.d.; Roy Zingery, Register of Deeds, Isabella County to Tate, 9/27/1952, MT/WMU.
39. Tate to Attorney William M. Graves, Detroit, n.d.; Roy Zingery, Register of Deeds, Isabella County to Tate, 9/27/1952, MT/WMU.
40. Tate, BWOHP; Tate, "Movement for a Limitation of Armaments to 1907," Harvard University Archives.

41. "Miss Tate Wins Ph. D. at Radcliffe," *Baltimore Afro-American*, 6/28/1941; *Norfolk Journal and Guide*, 6/28/1941; *Chicago Defender*, 7/5/1941; Radcliffe Graduation Program, 1941, Tate/Oxford. On the copy of Tate's dissertation in Van Vechten Collection, thanks to Sandra Markham, Beinecke Rare Book and Manuscript Library, Yale University, via email 1/31/2011.
42. "Merze Tate Fort Custer Hostess," *Pittsburgh Courier*, 9/20/1941.
43. Letter, David Jones, 7/5/1941, MT/HU; Tate, to Beta Iota Omega, AKA, 10/23/1941, and Tate to Esther Holloman, Greensboro, 10/23/1941; "Morgan Girls Living in $150,000 Dormitory," n.d., newspaper clipping; "Dr. Merze Tate in Position at Morgan," n.d., newspaper clipping, Tate Scrapbook, WMU Archive; "Morgan Gets 4 Teachers, New Dean," *Baltimore Afro-American*, 8/30/1941.

CHAPTER 5. "DARKER PEOPLES OF THE WORLD"

1. Tate, BWOHP.
2. Rayford Whittingham Logan Papers, Manuscript Division, Library of Congress, "Diary," 9/5/1942; postal telegram from Logan to Tate, 9/9/1942, MT/HU; Tate, BWOHP. Caroline Ware also was appointed to a temporary position, but she soon moved to the School of Social Work.
3. For the official history, see Rayford Logan, *Howard University: The First Hundred Years, 1867–1967* (New York: New York University Press, 1969).
4. Linda Perkins, "Lucy Diggs Slowe: Champion of the Self-Determination of African-American Women in Higher Education," *Journal of Negro History* 81, no. 1 (Winter–Autumn 1996): 89–104; Perkins, "The National Association of College Women: Vanguard of Black Women's Leadership and Education, 1923–1954," *Journal of Education* 172, no. 3 (1990), 65–75.
5. Linda M. Perkins, "The Black Female Professoriate at Howard University: 1926–1977," in *Women's Higher Education in the United States*, ed., Margaret A. Nash (New York: Palgrave MacMillan, 2018); Janet Sims-Woods, *Dorothy Porter Wesley at Howard University: Building a Legacy of Black History* (Charleston: The History Press, 2014); Allison Beth Horrocks, "Good Will Ambassador with a Cookbook: Flemmie Kittrell and the International Politics of Home Economics," dissertation, University of Connecticut, 2016; Diane Kiesel, *She Can Bring Us Home: Dr. Dorothy Boulding Ferebee, Civil Rights Pioneer* (Lincoln: University of Nebraska Press, 2015); Walter G. Daniel, "A Tribute to Marion Thompson Wright," *Journal of Negro Education* 32, no. 3 (Summer 1963): 308–310; Graham Russell Gao Hodges, ed., *Marion Thompson Wright Reader* (New Brunswick: Rutgers University Press, 2021); Rebecca VanDriver, *Designing a New Tradition: Lois Mailou Jones and the Aesthetics of Blackness* (University Park: Pennsylvania State University Press, 2020); Catherine Johnson, "Eva Beatrice Dykes" and "Georgiana Simpson," in *Black Women in America: An Historical Encyclopedia*, volume 1, A–L, and volume 2, M–Z, ed. Darlene Clark Hine, Elsa Barkley Brown, Rosalyn Terborg-Penn (Bloomington: Indiana University Press, 1993), 372–373, 1038–1039.
6. Kenneth R. Janken, *Rayford W. Logan and the Dilemma of the African-American Intellectual* (University of Massachusetts Press, 1993); *Charles H. Wesley: The Intellectual Tradition of a*

Black Historian, ed. James L. Conyers, Jr. (New York: Garland, 1997); Jeffrey Stewart, *The New Negro: The Life of Alain Locke* (New York: Oxford University Press, 2020); Charles P. Henry, *Ralph Bunche: Model Negro or American Other* (New York: New York University Press, 1999); Genna Rae McNeil, *Groundwork: Charles Hamilton Houston and the Struggle for Civil Rights* (Philadelphia: University of Pennsylvania Press, 1984); Dennis Dickerson, "William Stuart Nelson and the Interfaith Origins of the Civil Rights Movement," in *Churches, Blackness, and Contested Multiculturalism: Europe, Africa, and North America*, ed. R. Drew Smith, Williams Ackah, and Anthony G. Reddie (New York: Palgrave Macmillan); Louis Ray, *Charles H. Thompson: Policy Entrepreneur of the Civil Rights Movement, 1932–1954* (Madison: Fairleigh Dickinson University Press, 2012); Jonathan Holloway, *Confronting the Veil: Abram Harris Jr., E. Franklin Frazier, and Ralph Bunche, 1919–1941* (Chapel Hill: University of North Carolina, 2002); Zachery R. Williams, *In Search of the Talented Tenth: Howard University Public Intellectuals and the Dilemmas of Race, 1926–1970* (Columbia: University of Missouri Press, 2009).

7. Mary-Elizabeth B. Murphy, *Jim Crow Capital: Women and Black Freedom Struggles in Washington, D.C., 1920–1945* (Chapel Hill: University of North Carolina Press, 2018), 140–148; Chris Myers Asch and George Derek Musgrove, *Chocolate City: A History of Race and Democracy in the Nation's Capital* (Chapel Hill: University of North Carolina, 2017), 251.
8. Asch and Musgrove, *Chocolate City*.
9. Tate, BWOHP; Tate to Logan, 2/24/1938; Logan to Tate, 4/6/1938; Telegraph, Logan to Tate, 9/9/1942, MT/HU; "Merze Tate Takes Post at Howard," *Chicago Defender*, 10/3/1942; "Dr. Merze Tate," *New York Amsterdam News*, 10/2/1942; "Dr. Merze Tate at Howard University," *Pittsburgh Courier*, 10/3/1942.
10. Tate, BWOHP; Tate, *The Disarmament Illusion: The Movement for a Limitation of Armaments to 1907* (New York: Macmillan, 1942); Savage, "Beyond Illusions," 266–285.
11. Tate, *Disarmament Illusion*, 346.
12. Tate, *Disarmament Illusion*, 348, 351.
13. Tate, *Disarmament Illusion*, 351–352, 358, 162–163.
14. Tate, *Disarmament Illusion*, 83–84.
15. Louis M. Sears, "Review," *The Annals of the American Academy of Political and Social Science* 224, no. 1 (November 1942): 201–202; W. Arnold-Forster, "Review," *International Affairs Review Supplement* 19, no. 10 (1942): 532–533; J. Wesley Hoffmann, "Review," *The Journal of Modern History* 15, no. 1 (1943): 62–63; William O. Shanahan, "Military Problems," *The Review of Politics* 5, no. 3 (1943): 387–392; Elton Atwater, "Review," *The American Journal of International Law* 36, no. 4 (1942): 742–743; Hans J. Morgenthau, "Review," *The Russian Review* 2, no. 2 (1943): 104–105; Pitman B. Potter, "Review," *The American Political Science Review* 36, no. 5 (1942): 973; Julian P. Bretz, "Review," *The Mississippi Valley Historical Review* 30, no. 1 (1943): 89–90. The book was also reviewed in London in *The Guardian*, 9/18/1942, 3.
16. W.E.B. Du Bois, "Scholarly Delusion," *Phylon* 4, no. 2 (1943): 189–191; Tate to Du Bois, May 22, 1942; Du Bois to Tate, May 28, 1942, W. E. B. Du Bois Papers, Special Collections and University Archives, University of Massachusetts Amherst Libraries.

17. Rayford Logan, "No Peace for the Pacificist," *Journal of Negro Education* 12, no. 1 (1943): 92–93; C. G. Woodson, "Review," *Journal of Negro History* 28, no. 2 (1943): 251–253.
18. Robin D. G. Kelley, " 'But a Local Phase of a World Problem': Black History's Global Vision, 1883–1950," *Journal of American History* 86, no. 3 (1999): 1045–1077.
19. Tate, BWOHP; "Origins of the Prometheans," 10/11/44, "Correspondence Folders"; "2515th Service Unit, Army Specialized Training, Howard University, Washington, D.C., Student Training Regulations"; Tate, Remarks, "Installation of the Archives and Memorial Dedication of the Prometheans, Inc., n.d.; all in "Prometheans Inc., Records," HU; Tate, "Prometheans Newsletter" (August 1944, December 1944, October 1945), Digital Howard@Howard University.
20. Tate, BWOHP; "Origins of the Prometheans," 10/11/44, "Correspondence Folders"; Tate, Remarks, "Installation of the Archives and Memorial Dedication of the Prometheans, Inc., n.d.; all in "Prometheans Inc., Records," HU; Tate, "Prometheans Newsletter" (August 1944, December 1944, October 1945), Digital Howard@Howard University.
21. Tate, BWOHP; "Origins of the Prometheans," 10/11/44, "Correspondence Folders"; Tate, Remarks, "Installation of the Archives and Memorial Dedication of the Prometheans, Inc., n.d.; all in "Prometheans Inc., Records," HU; Tate, "Prometheans Newsletter" (August 1944, December 1944, October 1945), Digital Howard@Howard University.
22. Tate, BWOHP; "Origins of the Prometheans," 10/11/44, "Correspondence Folders"; Tate, Remarks, "Installation of the Archives and Memorial Dedication of the Prometheans, Inc., n.d.; all in "Prometheans Inc., Records," HU; Tate, "Prometheans Newsletter" (August 1944, December 1944, October 1945), Digital Howard@Howard University.
23. Tate to Mordecai W. Johnson, 6/19/1945, Prometheans, Inc., Archives, HU. Tate's role with the Prometheans is noted in Lopez D. Matthews, Jr., Ph.D., *Howard University in the World Wars: Men and Women Serving the Nation* (Charleston, S.C.: History Press, 2018), 52–57. The group disbanded in 2011 because of declining and aging membership.
24. Tate, "THE WHITE MAN'S BLUNDERS: The Twentieth Century Sequel to the White Man's Burden"; Letter to Tate from William Haygood, Julius Rosenwald Fund, 12/23/1942, MT/HU.
25. Merze Tate, "The War Aims of World War I and World War II and Their Relation to the Darker Peoples of the World," *Journal of Negro Education* 12, no. 3 (1943): 521; Tate, "Speech—The War Aims of World War I and World War II and Their Relation to the Darker Peoples of the World," *Morgan State College Bulletin* (June 1943), Tate/HU.
26. Bernard Shaw, *The Adventures of the Black Girl in Her Search for God* (New York: Dodd, Mead, 1933), 39; Tate, handwritten notes, *The Adventures of the Black Girl in Her Search for God,* MT/HU.
27. Tate, *War Aims,* 529, 532, 521.
28. Tate, *War Aims,* 529, 532, 521.
29. Logan to Dean J. St. Clair Price, 6/6/1945, Rayford Logan Papers, Howard.

30. John Hope Franklin to Logan, 1/31/1946, Logan Papers, HU; Tate, Review, "*The Free Negro In North Carolina,*" *Journal of Negro Education* 13, no. 1 (Winter 1944): 70–72; Tate, BWOHP.
31. Tate, BWOHP.
32. Tate, *Trust and Non-Self-Governing Territories, Papers and Proceedings of the Tenth Annual Conference of the Division of Social Sciences, The Graduate School, Howard University, April 8th and 9th, 1947* (Washington, D.C.: Howard University Press, 1948).
33. Tate to Dean J. St. Clair Price, October 29, 1951, MT/HU.
34. On decolonization debates, Sam Klug, "Making the Internal Colony: Black Internationalism, Development, and the Politics of Colonial Comparison in the United States," Ph.D. diss., Harvard University, Graduate School of Arts and Sciences, 2020.
35. Tate, "Teaching of International Relations in Negro Colleges," *The Quarterly Review of Higher Education Among Negroes* 15 (July 1947): 149–153, 149; Kelley, "Local Phase," 1054.
36. Tate, "Teaching of International Relations in Negro Colleges," 149.
37. Tate, "Teaching of International Relations in Negro Colleges," 150.
38. Tate, *The United States and Armaments* (Cambridge: Harvard University Press, 1948), 273–274.
39. Tate, *The United States and Armaments,* 273–274.
40. E. Atwater, "Review," *Annals of the American Academy of Political and Social Science* 258 (1948): 141–142; William M. Boyd, "Diplomacy and War," *Phylon* 9, no. 3 (1948): 279–281; Child, C. J., "Review," *International Affairs,* 25, no. 1 (1949): 114–115; W. Henry Cooke, "Review," *Pacific Historical Review* 18, no. 1 (1949): 150–152.
41. Glenda Sluga, *Internationalism in the Age of Nationalism* (Philadelphia: University of Pennsylvania Press, 2013), 1.
42. Merze Tate, "The International Control of Atomic Energy: A Vital Problem," pamphlet, 1948, 3, 19, MT/HU.
43. Tate, BWOHP; Letters to Tate from NCNW, 1/16/1945, 3/12/1945, 3/7/1945, 5/8/1945, 11/22/1946. On AKA Boule luncheon panel "Human Rights, Our Unfinished Business—Civil Rights," Tate to Luther Jackson and William Savage, 12/3/1948; John Hope Franklin added to panel, ASNHC, 10/1946, Philadelphia, Tate on panel on "Present Day Africa," MT/HU; "Minutes," The Writers Club, Inc., Moorland-Spingarn, HU.
44. "James Weldon Johnson Literary Guild Dinner to Honor Carl Van Vechten," *New York Age,* 11/21/1942; Maryemma Graham, *The House Where My Soul Lives: The Life of Margaret Walker* (New York: Oxford University Press, 2022), 244.
45. Tate to Attorney Willie M. Graves, Detroit, n.d.; Tate to Attorney Joseph Brown, Detroit, n.d., WMU Archive.
46. Letter to Tate from Prentice-Hall Inc., 6/9/1948; Memo from Tate to Logan, 3/18/1948; Letter to Tate from Willard Webb, Library of Congress, 3/16/1948, MT/HU.
47. "College Honor Graduate Invents Icebox Device," 1948, scrapbook, MT/WMU. See Merze Tate, U.S. Patent 2446066 A, "Mixing Unit for Refrigerators," filed 12/23/1943, granted 7/27/1948, Google patent search by Natalie Shibley.
48. Tate, "The Challenges of Our Day," *The Morgan State College Bulletin* (September 1949): 6–7. The commencement address was 6/6/1949, MT/HU.
49. Tate, "Challenges of Our Day," 9.

CHAPTER 6. "ROAMING IN FOREIGN LANDS AND CLIMES"

1. "Conference Board of Associated Research Councils Committee on International Exchange of Persons, Fulbright Awards by Academic Years, American Citizens," University of Arkansas, University Library, Special Collections, Fulbright Scholar Grantee Directories.
2. Tate, "Application for USG Grant, Conference Board of Associated Research Councils Committee on International Exchange of Persons," 5/17/1950; "Recommendation Concerning Miss Merze Tate," 8/16/1950; "Merze Tate," United States Indian Educational Foundation (USIEF) Files, Delhi. Thanks to Adam J. Grotsky, executive director, USIEF, New Delhi, for providing these materials and Tate's reports on her time in India, via email, 12/14/2018; Tate to William Stuart Nelson, Mysore, India, 7/10/1950; William Stuart Nelson Papers, Howard University, with thanks to Dennis Dickerson; Tate to Bethune, 10/7/1950, MT/HU; Tate interview, BWOHP.
3. Howard P. Backus, chief, Fulbright Programs Branch, U.S. Department of State, 10/10/1950, MT/HU.
4. Dennis C. Dickerson, "African American Religious Intellectuals and the Theological Foundations of the Civil Rights Movement, 1930–1955," *Church History* 74 (June 2005): 217–235; Dickerson, "Gandhi's India and Beyond: Black Women's Religious and Secular Internationalism, 1935–1952," *Journal of African American History* (Winter 2019): 59–82; Dickerson, "William Stuart Nelson and the Interfaith Origins of the Civil Rights Movement, in *Churches, Blackness, and Contested Multiculturalism: Europe, Africa, and North America,* ed. R. Drew Smith, Williams Ackah, and Anthony G. Reddie (New York: Palgrave Macmillan, 2014); Sudarshan Kapur, *Raising Up a Prophet: The African American Encounter with Gandhi* (Boston: Beacon, 1992); Quinton Dixie and Peter Eisenstadt, *Visions of a Better World: Howard Thurman's Pilgrimage to India and the Origins of African American Nonviolence* (Boston: Beacon, 2011); Gerald Horne, *The End of Empires: African Americans and India* (Philadelphia: Temple University Press, 2008); Nico Slate, *Colored Cosmopolitanism: The Shared Struggle for Freedom in the United States and India* (Cambridge: Harvard University Press, 2012).
5. "The Lucius E. Young Pledge Class," *Torch and Trefoil,* a publication of Young's fraternity, Alpha Phi Omega, Fall 1976; "This Soldier Didn't Have Time to Hate," *Tampa Bay Times,* 1/27/2003; updated 8/31/2005.
6. Tate, Travel Diary, 1950–1951, MT/HU.
7. Tate, "Finds Army Dictator Rules Negro GIS in Germany with Brutal Fist," *Chicago Defender* (national edition), November 4, 1950; Tate, "Officer Thumbs Nose at Army," *Afro-American,* November 4, 1950; Tate, "Tells Plight of Negro Officers at Kitzingen," *Chicago Defender* (national edition), November 11, 1950.
8. "Army Closing Kitzingen: JC Training Center Earned Condemnation," *Afro-American,* February 10, 1951; the paper's editor blamed the founding of the base on Lieutenant General Clarence Huebner, "an ardent admirer of segregation while serving as commander at Ft. Benning, Ga," who was with the European Command when the segregated base was created. Tate, "Royal Welcome Given Visitor to Infantry Base in Germany," *Afro-American,* November 23, 1950.
9. Tate, Travel Diary, 1950–1951, MT/HU.

10. Tate, BWOHP.
11. Tate, "I Visit the Pope," December 16, 1950, *Baltimore Afro-American;* Tate, BWOHP.
12. Tate, BWOHP.
13. "6,000 Miles to Cairo Where East Meets West: Howard University Professor Tells of Her Intriguing Visit in Egypt, Oriental Crossroads 6,000 Miles Away," *Afro-American Magazine,* November 25, 1950, MT/HU.
14. "6,000 Miles to Cairo Where East Meets West"; Tate, BWOHP.
15. Tate, Travel Diary, 1950–1951, MT/HU.
16. Letter from Tate to Horace Poleman, USIEF, New Delhi, November 12, 1950; Letter from Tate to Lloyd Steere, American Embassy, New Delhi, November 17, 1950, "Merze Tate," USIEF Files, Delhi; "Conference Board of Associated Research Councils, Committee on International Exchange of Persons, Fulbright Awards for the Academic Years 1950–1951, American Citizens," University of Arkansas, University Library, Special Collections, Fulbright Scholar Grantee Directories, 1950–1951; Letter from Tate to Fred Jochem, South-East Asian Division, State Department, Washington, D.C., January 17, 1951, "Merze Tate," USIEF Files, Delhi; Travel Diary, 1950–1951, MT/HU.
17. Tate, Travel Diary, 1950–1951, MT/HU.
18. Tate, Travel Diary, 1950–1951, MT/HU.
19. Uma Das Gupta, "Santiniketan and Sríninketan" (Kolkata: Visva-Bharati, 2009 reprint), Visva-Bharati University Library, Santiniketan. On the history and education of women in India, Geraldine Forbes, *Women in Modern India* (Cambridge: Cambridge University Press, 1996).
20. Tate, Travel Diary, 1950–1951, MT/HU. For his childhood recollections of Santiniketan and Calcutta, Amartya Sen, *Home in the World: A Memoir* (New York: Norton, 2021).
21. Tate, Travel Diary, 1950–1951, MT/HU; Tate to Lloyd V. Steere, American Embassy, New Delhi, November 17, 1950, "Merze Tate," USIEF Files, Delhi.
22. Tate, Travel Diary, 1950–1951, MT/HU; Tate to Lloyd V. Steere, American Embassy, New Delhi, November 17, 1950, "Merze Tate," USIEF Files, Delhi.
23. Tate to Lloyd V. Steere, American Embassy, New Delhi, November 17, 1950, USIEF Files, Delhi.
24. *Visva-Bharati News* 14, nos. 5–6 (November–December 1950): 32, Archives, Visva-Bharati University.
25. Tate Travel Diary, 1950–1951, MT/HU; *Visva-Bharati News* 14, nos. 5–6 (November–December 1950): 32–33, archives, Visva-Bharati University; Tate to Lloyd V. Steere, American Embassy, New Delhi, November 17, 1950, and January 17, 1951, "Merze Tate," USIEF Files, Delhi; Tate, "No. 1. Report to the United States Educational Foundation in India," received February 5, 1951, p. 2, "Merze Tate," USIEF Files, Delhi.
26. Tate, "No. 1. Report to the United States Educational Foundation in India," received February 5, 1951, "Merze Tate," USIEF Files, Delhi; Annual Report, 1950 Visva-Bharati.
27. Letter from Tate to Fred Jochem, South-East Asian Division, State Department, Washington, D.C., January 17, 1951, "Merze Tate," USIEF Files, Delhi; Travel Diary, 1950–1951, MT/HU.
28. Travel Diary, 1950–1951, MT/HU.

29. Travel Diary, 1950–1951, MT/HU.
30. "Overview: The Fisk Jubilee Singers' Travels in the Antipodes and South Asia, 1886–1890," John Hope and Aurelia E. Franklin Library: Special Collections and Archives, https://fiskmusicmusiceverywhere.omeka.net/exhibits/show/the_fisk_jubilee_singers_trave/overview--the-fisk-jubilee-sin.
31. Letter from Tate to Fred Jochem, South-East Asian Division, State Department, Washington, D.C., January 17, 1951, "Merze Tate," USIEF Files, Delhi; Tate Travel Diary, 1950–1951, MT/HU.
32. Letter from Tate to Jochem, January 17, 1951.
33. Letter from Tate to Jochem, January 17, 1951; Tate Travel Diary, 1950–1951, MT/HU.
34. Letter from Tate to Jochem, January 17, 1951; Tate Travel Diary, 1950–1951, MT/HU.
35. Letter from Tate to Jochem, January 17, 1951; "The Indian Institute of Culture, Public Lecture, 'Negro Life and Culture,' by Dr. Merze Tate (Professor of History, Howard University, U. S. A., Visiting Professor, Visva-Bharati, 4th January 1951," MT/HU.
36. Letter from Tate to Jochem, January 17, 1951.
37. Letter from Tate to Jochem, January 17, 1951; Tate Travel Diary, 1950–1951, MT/HU.
38. "Boys' Leader a Hit in India: Oklahoman's Fame Spreading in Orient," July 21, 1951. For more on Burr, see Gerald Horne, *The End of Empires: African Americans and India* (Philadelphia: Temple University Press, 2008), 189, 190–192.
39. Tate Travel Diary, 1950–1951, MT/HU.
40. Tate Travel Diary, 1950–1951, MT/HU.
41. "Dr. (Miss) Tate, an American Negro," *The Times of Ceylon,* March 7, 1951, MT/HU.
42. Newspaper clippings, "Geopolitics and Foreign Policies—Dr. Tate's Interesting Talk," *New Times of Burma,* March 24, 1951, and "Negro Professor's Lecture on Geopolitics," *The Sunday Nation,* March 25, 1951; "American Negro Educator to Lecture on Geopolitics," n.d., unknown newspaper. Tate left Rangoon for Mandalay where she was welcomed by two other Fulbright scholars and by faculty at the University College of Mandalay; Wilson and Elizabeth Hume to Tate, 6/30/1952, MT/HU.
43. *Visva-Bharati News* 19, nos. 11, 12 (May–June 1951): 104, 107, Archives, Visva-Bharati Library.
44. Tate, BWOHP.
45. Tate, BWOHP; "Scholar Pandit Nehru Impresses U. S. Visitor," *Afro-American,* July 21, 1951.
46. Tate, "Report of the Homeward Journey Through Southeast Asia and the Far East," "Departure from India, July 23, 1951," MT/HU. Tate prepared a nearly 100-page detailed report on her travels after India. Excerpts from much of the draft report are scattered in her archives. She may also have prepared a report on her time in India, Ceylon, and Burma, but it does not appear to be in her archives.
47. Tate, "Report of the Homeward Journey Through Southeast Asia."
48. Tate, BWOHP.

49. Tate, "Report of the Homeward Journey Through Southeast Asia."
50. Tate, "Report of the Homeward Journey Through Southeast Asia."
51. Tate, "A Journey to Angkor—City of Mystery," MT/HU. The trip began on August 4, 1951.
52. Tate, "A Journey to Angkor"; Aime Cesaire, *Discourse on Colonialism* (New York: Monthly Review Press, 2000), 52. The book was originally published in 1955 as *Discours sue lecolonialisme,* by Presence Africaine.
53. Tate, "A Journey to Angkor."
54. Tate, "Singapore, August 9–12, 1951," MT/HU.
55. Tate, "Singapore, August 9–12, 1951," MT/HU.
56. Tate, "Singapore, August 9–12, 1951," MT/HU.
57. Tate, "Manila—August 13–17, 1951," MT/HU.
58. Tate, "Manila—August 13–17, 1951," MT/HU.
59. Tate, "Manila—August 13–17, 1951," MT/HU.
60. Tate, "Manila—August 13–17, 1951," MT/HU.
61. Tate, "Hong Kong to Tokyo," MT/HU.
62. Tate, BWOHP; "Capital Spotlight," Louis Lautier, September 9, 1951; Tate, " 'Incomparable' Col. Harry F. Lofton: Slated Belatedly to Head Army School He Founded," *Afro-American,* September 15, 1951.
63. Letter from Tate to Allan F. Saunders, University of Honolulu, March 8, 1950; Letter to Tate from Willowdean C. Handy, Program Chairman, Pan-Pacific Women's Association, Honolulu, August 6, 1951; "Pan-Pacific Club to Hear Dr. Tate Speak on India," *Honolulu Advertiser,* September 4, 1951, MT/HU.
64. Tate, BWOHP; telephone interview, James Allen Thompson, 12/17/2014; obituary, "James Allen Thompson," *Capital Gazette,* 4/25/2020.
65. Telephone interview, Frances Thompson, 9/2021.
66. "Magellan Had Nothing on Howard's Merze Tate After 44,000-Mile Trip," *Pittsburgh Courier,* October 6, 1951; Tate, Chair's Report, Department of History, 1951–1952, MT/HU.
67. Tate, Chair's Report, Department of History, 1951–1952, MT/HU.

CHAPTER 7. "CHALLENGES OF OUR AGE"

1. Howard University Digital Archives, "University Officially Opened," *Hilltop,* 10/15/1951.
2. Tate to William Stuart Nelson, Dean, Howard University, 10/4/1955; Tate, BWOHP.
3. Tate to J. St. Clair Price, Dean, Howard, 10/29/1951, MT/HU.
4. Tate to J. St. Clair Price, Dean, Howard, 10/29/1951, MT/HU.
5. Tate to J. St. Clair Price, Dean, Howard, 10/29/1951, MT/HU.
6. Interview, Joseph Stevenson, 10/21/2020; interview, Joseph E. Harris, 11/17/2020.
7. Nancy E. Scott, WMU to Tate, 11/4/1951, MT/HU.
8. Tate, "General Conclusions," draft, n.d., MT/HU.
9. Letter from Cronkhite to Tate, 4/10/1952, 5/26/1952; Rupert Emerson to Cronkhite, 5/21/1952; Nancy E. Scott to Tate, 5/24/1952, MT/HU.

10. Tate, Syllabus, "The United States and Asia, 1945–1953," MT/HU. Thanks to Ichiiro Azuma for assistance in analyzing this document.
11. Tate, Interview, BWOHP.
12. Tate, Interview, BWOHP; Della Vance, National Achievement Club, to Tate, 3/17/1952, 4/7/1952; Tate to Vance, 3/26/1952, 10/29/1952; Alma Illery to Tate, 11/19/1952; Tate to Illery, 11/22/1952, MT/HU; "Dr. Merze Tate to Speak to Carver Day Luncheon," *Pittsburgh Courier,* 12/27/1952; Tate to Mrs. Emmanuel Friedberg, 11/24/1952, MT/HU; "Nehru No 'Stooge' Dr. Tate Says in Trenton," *Afro-American,* 12/15/1951; "India in Transition," *Philadelphia Tribune,* 12/8/1951; radio recording, "A.K.A. Story," 1/5/1952, MT/WMU.
13. "University Professor to Address Women's Forum," *Mount Zionite* (Knoxville), September–October 1951; Tate, BWOHP.
14. Tate interview, BWOHP.
15. American Friends Service Committee, Community Relations Program, Washington, D.C., no. 1, March 1952, and Tate to American Friends Service Committee, March 25, 1952, MT/HU.
16. Victor Daly, "Early History of the American Bridge Association," Victor Daly Papers, Schomburg Center for Research in Black Culture, New York Public Library; Janice Arenofsky, "Bridge Over Troubled Waters: The Story of the American Bridge Association," unpublished paper, p. 7; in author's possession, courtesy of Janice Arenofsky.
17. Albert H. Morehead, "Bridge: The A.C.B.L. Sets a Precedent," *New York Times,* July 22, 1956.
18. Daly, "President's Editorial: Right or Privilege," n.d.; Jim Wood, "25th Anniversary of Integrated Bridge in Washington," Daly Papers.
19. Daly, "President's Editorial: Sit Down for Bridge So That They May Sit Down to Eat," "President's Editorial: Bridge During the Crisis," "President's Editorial: A.B.A. Benefit Funds," n.d., Daly Papers.
20. "Fashions & Dancing presented by Xi Omega, Alpha Kappa Alpha Sorority, November 11, 1954, Willard Hotel, Program," MT/HU.
21. Radcliffe Award Citation, January 15, 1955, MT/HU.
22. Thelma Hayes to Tate (1953), MT/WMU.
23. Myrtle Tate to Merze Tate, 4/12/1953, MT/WMU.
24. Sonja Hollins interview, 8/12/2020; Tate, BWOHP.
25. "Academic Freedom in the United States," Fifteenth Annual Spring Conference of the Division of the Social Science, March 11–14, 1953, Howard University Press, 1953, MT/HU.
26. Federal Bureau of Investigation Documents, "Vernie Merze Tate," to author, June 30, 2014, under Freedom of Information/Privacy Acts request.
27. Federal Bureau of Investigation Documents, "Vernie Merze Tate." Tate requested and received a copy of the file and placed it in her archive.
28. Federal Bureau of Investigation Documents, "Vernie Merze Tate."
29. "Objective of the College Program," March 16, 1954, MT/HU.
30. "Objective of the College Program," 3/16/1954; Tate to Dean Carroll Miller, 3/19/1954, MT/HU.

31. "Objective of the College Program," 3/16/1954; Tate to Dean Carroll Miller, 3/19/1954, MT/HU.
32. Tate to William Stuart Nelson, 1/21/1956. Unsuccessful inquiries for summer jobs: Alonzo Moron, President, Hampton Institute, to Tate, 11/23/1954; Tate to Prof. Vander Velde, History Department, University of Michigan, 10/14/1955; Tate to University of Rochester, 12/4/1952; Tate to Thomas Cochran, History Department, University of Pennsylvania, 10/19/1955; MT/HU.
33. Tate to Vincent Browne, Howard, 1/21/1956, MT/HU.
34. Tate Interview, BWOHP.
35. "GENTLER SEX PLAY INTEGRAL ROLE: At Howard Women Make Up 25 Percent of the Faculty," *Howard Bulletin* (March 15, 1957): 19–21, MT/HU.
36. "GENTLER SEX PLAY INTEGRAL ROLE."
37. Tate, "*Out of Confusion* by Manmatha Nath Chatterjee," *Journal of Negro History* 39, no. 3 (July 1954): 220–221; Chatterjee, *Out of Confusion* (Yellow Springs, Ohio: Antioch Press, 1954).
38. Tate, "*The Bombay Meeting* by Ira Morris," *Journal of Negro Education* 25, no. 1 (Winter 1956): 47–49; Ira Morris, *The Bombay Meeting* (Garden City, N.Y.: Doubleday, 1955).
39. Tate, "The Punjab Massacres of 1947: Mano Majra by Khushwant Singh," *Journal of Negro Education* 4, no. 25 (Autumn 1956): 410–411; Khushwant Singh, *Mano Majra* (New York: Grove, 1956).
40. W. E. B. Du Bois, *Dark Princess* (New York: Harcourt Brace, 1928); Barbara Dianne Savage, *Your Spirits Walk Beside Us: The Politics of Black Religion* (Cambridge: Harvard University Press, 2008), 63.
41. Tate, "A Report on India," *Journal of Negro Education* 25, no. 4 (Autumn 1956): 412–413; Robert Trumbull, *As I See India* (New York: William Sloane Associates, 1956).
42. Tate, "The Awakening East," *Journal of Negro Education* 23, no. 1 (Winter 1954): 61–63; Eleanor Roosevelt, *India and the Awakening East* (New York: Harper & Brothers, 1953).
43. Tate, "The Awakening East"; Roosevelt, *India and the Awakening East.*
44. Tate, "A Personal Report on an American Negro in India," *Journal of Negro Education* 24, no. 2 (Spring 1955): 130–132; J. Saunders Redding, *An American in India: A Personal Report on the Indian Dilemma and the Nature of Her Conflicts* (New York: Bobbs-Merrill, 1954). Tate reviewed the book twice, although much of the content of the reviews overlapped. Tate, "An American in India," *Journal of Negro History* 40, no. 2 (April 1955): 186–191. Tate was not alone in harshly criticizing Redding's book: Wilbert Snow, "Ambassador to India," *Phylon* 16, no. 1 (1st quarter, 1955), 108–109; Stanley Maron, "An American in India," *Far Eastern Survey* 24, no. 7 (July 1955): 111; O. P., "AN AMERICAN IN INDIA," *The American Scholar* 24, no. 1 (Winter 1954–1955), 120.
45. Tate, "*The Pitiful and the Proud,*" *Journal of Negro History* 42, no. 1 (January 1957): 65–67; Carl T. Rowan, *The Pitiful and the Proud* (New York: Random House, 1956).
46. Tate, "*The Color Curtain,*" *Journal of Negro History* 41, no. 3 (July 1956): 263–265; Richard Wright, *The Color Curtain: A Report on the Bandung Conference* (New York: World, 1956); "Krishnalal Shridharani, Warning to the West," *Journal of Negro Education* 12, no. 4 (Autumn 1943): 654–655.

47. Tate, "*The Color Curtain,*"; Wright, *The Color Curtain.*
48. "Hunter Prof. Set for Trip Around World," *Atlanta Daily World,* 4/7/1955; Gladys P. Graham, "It Happened in New York," *Philadelphia Tribune,* 4/26/1955; "Feature educator," *Philadelphia Tribune,* 10/14/1955; James Hicks, "Feminine Front: Dr. Cartwright Confutes Press Try to Abase Bandung Conf.," *Baltimore Afro-American,* 5/21/1955; "Communism Was No Issue at Bandung—Dr. Cartwright Says Primary Purpose Was to Give Asians and Africans a Chance to Know One Another," *Pittsburgh Courier,* 5/28/1955; "Powell's Asia Reports Are Criticized," *New York Amsterdam News,* 5/21/1955.
49. "Payne Sends Exclusive Pictures of Asian-African Parley—African Nations Play Minor Role at Bandung," *Chicago Defender,* 4/14/1955; "Payne to Cover Afro-Asia Meet for Defender," *Chicago Defender,* 4/16/1955. Wright's mention of Payne featured a long anecdote about her hair in the Indonesian heat and humidity, a story later passed on by her biographer; Wright, *The Color Curtain*; James McGrath Morris, *Eye on the Struggle: Ethel Payne, the First Lady of the Black Press* (Amistad, 2015), 165–166.
50. Tate to Mordecai Johnson, 1/8/1957, MT/HU.

CHAPTER 8. "A WEARY RESEARCHER"

1. "3 Sacks Are in Educator's Bags as She Begins Pacific Safari," *Chicago Defender,* 4/19/1958.
2. Tate Travel Diary, 1958 and 1959; "Dr. Tate Does Research Here; To Write Paper on US, Hawaii," 1958, unknown newspaper; Marion Saunders to Tate, 4/29/1960, MT/HU; Tate, BWOHP.
3. Tate to Ernestine Cross, 5/10/1958; Tate Travel Diary, 1958 and 1959; Tate, BWOHP; Tate to "Mother & Herschel," 5/18/1958, MT/HU.
4. Tate to "Sister, and all the others," Nandi, Fiji, 5/29/1958, MT/HU; Tate, BWOHP.
5. Tate Travel Diary, 1958 and 1959, MT/HU; Tate, BWOHP; Tate to Spaulding, 4/17/1959; Tate to Ernestine, Wellington, 6/1958; Tate to "Ernestine, Theo, Thelma, Jim, Luella, all the others," Sidney, 7/6/1958; Tate to "Ernestine, Theo, Thelma, Mother, all the family," Sydney, n.d.; Tate to "Ernestine," Sydney, 7/11/1958; Tate to "Thelma," 7/21/1958, Canberra; Tate to Ernestine, Wellington, 6/1958; Tate to "Ernestine, Theo, Thelma, Jim, Luella, all the others," Sidney, 7/6/1958; Tate to "Ernestine, Theo, Thelma, Mother, all the family," Sydney, n.d.; Tate to "Ernestine," Sydney, 7/11/1958; Tate to "Thelma," 7/21/1958, Canberra; Tate to Myrtle Tate, New Delhi, 8/7/1958; Tate Travel Diary, 1958 and 1959, MT/HU.
6. Tate to "Sister and all the Family," Jakarta, 8/10/1958; Tate to "Ernestine," Djakarta, 8/14/1958; Tate to "Mother & Herschel's Family," 9/15/1958; Tate to Spaulding, 4/17/1959, MT/HU; Tate, BWOHP.
7. Tate, BWOHP.
8. Tate, BWOHP.
9. "Baptismorum Registrum, Mary Merze Tate, 6/10/1959," St. Anthony of Padua Catholic Church, Washington, D.C., copy provided by mail courtesy of Sister Janina, St. Anthony's Church, 10/21/2014; telephone interview with Frances Thompson.

10. "Baptismorum Registrum, Mary Merze Tate," confirmed 12/17/1961; thank you notes for special financial contributions from Rev. Joseph E. Norton, St. Anthony's Rectory, to Tate, 9/1982, and Fr. Bailey, St. Anthony's Rectory, n.d., MT/HU.
11. Letter from Lewis Giles to Tate, 10/21/1960, MT/HU.
12. Tate, BWOHP.
13. Tate, BWOHP.
14. "Maupin Tours, 1959 Russia by Motorcoach, Itinerary," MT/HU.
15. Tate, BWOHP.
16. Tate, "Expenses Incurred in Travel and Research in Connection with an American Council of Learned Societies Grant, Awarded March, 1959," and Tate, "First Progress Report, American Council of Learned Societies," MT/HU.
17. Tate, "Summer Research Project of Merze Tate, 9/30/1960"; James C. Evans to Lt. Commander Wesley Brown, USN, Honolulu, 7/26/1960, MT/HU.
18. Kenneth W. Thompson, President, The Rockefeller Foundation, to Tate, 11/15/1960; Tate to Thompson, n.d., but refers to prior letter; Thompson to Tate, 12/19/1960; Gerald Freud, Rockefeller Foundation to Tate, 4/25/1961, MT/HU; "Minutes of Rockefeller Board of Trustees Meeting, 12/6–7/1960"; Tate to Thompson, 9/23/1960, 10/17/1960, 11/9/1960, 11/30/1960, 1/9/1961; Thompson to Tate, 11/2/1960; Tate, Application, 2/27/1961. Letters of recommendation attesting to her brilliance and productivity came from Margaret B. Macmillan, a history professor at Western Michigan University, Cronkhite from Radcliffe, and her former Harvard professors Payton Wilde and Frederick Shuman; all in Rockefeller Foundation Files, folder "Howard University—Tate, Merze—Australian Expansion." Thanks to Katherina Rietzler for retrieving this information.
19. Kenneth W. Thompson, President, The Rockefeller Foundation to Tate, 11/15/1960; Tate to Thompson, n.d., but refers to prior letter; Thompson to Tate, 12/19/1960; Gerald Freud, Rockefeller Foundation to Tate, 4/25/1961, MT/HU "Minutes of Rockefeller Board of Trustees Meeting, 12/6–7/1960"; Tate to Thompson, 9/23/1960, 10/17/1960, 11/9/1960, 11/30/1960, 1/9/1961; Thompson to Tate, 11/2/1960; Tate, Application, 2/27 /1961; all in Rockefeller Foundation Files, folder "Howard University—Tate, Merze—Australian Expansion."
20. Letter from Thompson Webb, Jr., U of Wisconsin Press, to Tate, 12/18/1961, MT/HU.
21. Thomas J. Wilson, Harvard University Press, to Tate, 2/10/1960 and 7/10/1962; Lela R. Brewer, The Hawaiian Historical Society to Tate, 8/24/1962; J. G. Bell, Stanford University Press to Tate, 10/5/1962; Tate to Editor, University of Hawaii Press, 4/6/1960; Thomas Nickerson, University of Hawaii Press to Tate, 4/14/1960; Barnard P. Perry, Indiana University Press, to Tate, 6/22/1960 and 1/4/1962, MT/HU.
22. Tate received rejection letters from the following journals: *The American Historical Review*, 4/18/1960; *The Mississippi Valley Historical Review*, 5/5/1960 and 3/15/1961; *The New England Quarterly*, 8/11/1960; *New York Historical Association*, 2/16/1961; *Pacific Business Review*, 2/23/1962; *Pacific Northwest Quarterly*, 5/22/1963; *Oregon Historical Society*, 4/12/1960; *Political Science Quarterly*, 8/5/1960, MT/HU.
23. Tate, "The Sandwich Island Missionaries Lay the Foundation for a System for Public Instruction in Hawaii," *Journal of Negro Education* 30, no. 4 (Autumn 1961): 396–405;

Tate, "U.S. Diplomacy: Influence of Sandwich Island Missionaries and the ABCFM," *Oregon Historical Quarterly* 68 (1967): 53–74.

24. Tate, "U.S. Diplomacy."
25. Tate, "Sandwich Island Missionaries Lay the Foundation," 403.
26. Tate, "Sandwich Island Missionaries: The First American Point Four Agents," *Annual Report of the Hawaiian Historical Society* (1961): 3–19, 20. She elaborates this point in Tate, *The United States and the Hawaiian Kingdom,* 317–318, 12–13.
27. Tate and Fidele Foy, "Slavery and Racism as Deterrents to the Annexation of Hawaii, 1854–1855," *Journal of Negro History* 47, no. 1 (January 1962): 1–18, 18, 12; Tate, "Sandwich Islands Missionaries and Annexation," *Journal of Religious Thought* 20 (1963–1964).
28. Tate, "Slavery and Racism as Deterrents"; Tate, "Decadence of the Hawaiian Nation and Proposals to Import a Negro Labor Force," *Journal of Negro History* 47, no. 4 (October 1962): 248–263, 263, 261, 251. Tate had submitted both articles initially to the *Mississippi Valley Historical Review* but was told her work did not make a "sufficiently important new contribution to justify acceptance for publication." (This journal became the *Journal of American History* in 1964.) Letters from William C. Binkley, Managing Editor, The *Mississippi Valley Historical Review,* to Tate, May 5, 1960 and March 15, 1961. The work was welcomed by the *Journal of Negro History;* letters from W. M. Brewer, Editor, to Tate, 6/18/1962 and 10/26/1964.
29. Tate, "Decadence of the Hawaiian Nation."
30. Tate and Fidele Foy, "Slavery and Racism in South Pacific Annexations," *Journal of Negro History* 50, no. 1 (January 1965): 1–21, 8. Foy was a Howard graduate student.
31. Tate and Foy, "Slavery and Racism in South Pacific Annexations," 8.
32. Tate and Foy, "Slavery and Racism in South Pacific Annexations," 14, 18.
33. Tate and Foy, "Slavery and Racism in South Pacific Annexations," 21.
34. William C. Binkley, *Mississippi Valley Historical Review,* to Tate, 3/15/1961, MT/HU.
35. Tate, "Great Britain and the Sovereignty of Hawaii," *Pacific Historical Review* 31, no. 4 (November 1962): 327–348, 348; Tate, "Australasian Interest in the Commerce and the Sovereignty of Hawaii," *Historical Studies: Australia and New Zealand* 11, no. 44 (April 1965); Tate, "Hawaii: A Symbol of Anglo-American Rapprochement," *Political Science Quarterly* 79, no. 4 (December 1964): 555–575, 575; Tate, "Twisting the Lion's Tale Over Hawaii," *Pacific Historical Review* 36, no. 1 (February 1967): 27–46, 45, 46; Tate, "The Australasian Monroe Doctrine," *Political Science Quarterly* 76, no. 2 (June 1961): 264–284.
36. Tate, "Great Britain and the Sovereignty of Hawaii," 348; Tate, "Australasian Interest in the Commerce"; Tate, "Hawaii: A Symbol," 575; Tate, "Twisting the Lion's Tale," 45, 46; Tate, "Australasian Monroe Doctrine."
37. "Program of the Seventy-Seventh Annual Meeting of the American Historical Association," 12/28–30/1962, Chicago; Tate, "Comments on American Scientists and International Control of Atomic Energy, 1945–1946," read before AHA, 12/28/1962, MT/HU; "Program of the Seventy-Eighth Annual Meeting of the American Historical Association," 12/28–30/1963, Philadelphia.
38. "Valena Williams Joins Women's Peace Conference," *Cleveland Call and Post,* 3/31 /1962; Tate, BWOHP.
39. "Valena Williams Joins Women's Peace Conference."

CHAPTER 9. "A MODERN SCHOLAR"

1. Tate, "Application for a President's Grant-in-Aid of Research," June 15–September 15, 1963, MT/HU; Tate, BWOHP.
2. "Family Papers, Correspondence Allen and Fran, brother and sister-in-law, 1960–1970," MT/HU.
3. Telephone interview with Allene Thompson Martin, 10/13/2020.
4. Telephone interview with Allene Thompson Martin, 10/13/2020; telephone interview with Jay Thompson, 12/22/2020.
5. Tate, review of *W.E.B. Du Bois: A Study in Minority Group Leadership*, by Elliott M. Rudwick, *Journal of Negro History* 47, no. 3 (July 1962): 206–207; Washington Urban League to Tate, 1963, MT/HU.
6. Marian Neal Ash, Yale University Press, to Tate, 1/11/1963, 7/3/1963; David Horne, Executive Editor, Yale University Press, 8/5/1963; June Guicharnaud to Tate, 10/2/1963, 10/11/1963, MT/HU.
7. Tate to Guicharnaud, 10/9/1963, 10/11/1963, 11/13/1963; Horne to Tate, 10/14/1963. Duke's interest in her work was aided by Theodore Ropp, a prominent military historian; Theodore Ropp, Naval War College, to Tate, 1/5/1962, 5/27/1963, MT/HU.
8. Tate, BWOHP. Fall's most well known and influential works include *Street Without Joy: The French Debacle in Indochina* (Harrisburg, Pa.: Stackpole, 1961) and *Hell in a Very Small Place: The Siege of Dien Bien Phu* (Philadelphia: Lippincott, 1966).
9. Telephone interview with Mary Frances Berry, 5/12/2015.
10. Michael R. Winston, "The Howard University Department of History, 1913–1973," Howard University, 1973.
11. Telephone interview with Winston Langley, 6/29/2020. Thanks to Craig N. Murphy for alerting me that Langley had been a Tate student; email from Murphy to author, 1/2/2020.
12. Telephone interview with Winston Langley, 6/29/2020.
13. Telephone interview with Winston Langley, 6/29/2020.
14. Telephone interview with Winston Langley, 6/29/2020.
15. Tate, "Application for a President's Grant-in-Aid of Research, June 15–September 15, 1963," MT/HU; Tate, BWOHP.
16. Logan placed his diaries at the Library of Congress after keeping them in a safe deposit box, fearful that Howard would censor them. His papers at Howard include drafts on an unfinished autobiography drawn from the diaries, including these portions on Tate and others. Rayford Whittingham Logan Papers, Manuscript Division, Library of Congress. He refers to Tate repeatedly as a "bitch," an "ornery bitch," "The Bitch," "insufferable bitch," a "damned bitch," and "goddamned bitch." He attributed her behavior at times to menopause, accused her of trying to make him hit her, and called her incongruously both an "eel" and a "porcupine." Some among many examples are entries for 12/11/1954, 10/16/1955, 11/9/1955, 1/15/1956, 4/4/1956. In Rayford W. Logan Papers, Howard University, his draft "Autobiography," boxes 31–36, especially chapters titled "My Trials and Tribulations with President Mordecai W. Johnson and Professor Merze Tate," boxes 33 and 34. Logan diary entries on Catholicism: 6/17/1951, 8/31/1952, 4/29/1953. Others have written about Logan's treatment of Tate: Kenneth Robert

Janken, *Rayford W. Logan and the Dilemma of the African American Intellectual* (Amherst: University of Massachusetts Press, 1993); Linda M. Perkins, "Merze Tate and the Quest for Gender Equity at Howard University: 1942–1977," *History of Education Quarterly* 54, no. 4 (November 2014): 516–551. On Tate's silence on Logan: email from Janken to author, 12/1/2010.

17. Tate to Mary Bunting, President, Radcliffe, 2/25/1964, MT/HU.
18. "Intruder Stabs Howard U. Woman Professor," *Washington Post,* 1/25/1964; "Mystery surrounds knifing of Dr. Tate," n.d.; Mordecai Johnson to Tate, 1/28/1964; Mary Bunting, President, Radcliffe College, to Tate, 2/20/1964; Tate to Mary Bunting, President, Radcliffe, 2/25/1964; Allen Thompson to Tate, 3/22/1964, then stationed in Vietnam, MT/HU.
19. Tate to Frank Snowden, Jr., Dean, 3/16/1964, MT/HU.
20. "Dr. Tate say thanks at luncheon for friends," 11/21/1964, *Baltimore Afro-American;* letter to Tate from Sister Margaret Eileen, Providence Hospital, 3/13/1964, MT/HU.
21. "Report: An Investigation of Appropriate School Sites for Mentally Retarded Children in the District of Columbia," 1/25/1965, MT/HU.
22. Tate to Thelma Bando, Dean of Women, Morgan State College, 1/28/1965; Bando to Tate, 2/4/1965; Tate to Comptroller, Radcliffe College, 3/3/1969, MT/HU; Tate, BWOHP.
23. Tate to Rayford Logan, 11/13/1963; Frank Snowden to Tate, 3/12/1964. MT/HU.
24. "Effects of Nuclear Explosions on Pacific Islanders," *The Pacific Historical Review* 33, no. 4 (November 1964): 379–393 (with Doris Hull).
25. Horne to Tate, 4/27/1964; Tate to Horne, 3/26/1964; Bunting to Tate, 5/18/1964. It was a $900 subvention; MT/HU.
26. Tate, BWOHP.
27. Tate to Gudmundsen, 10/19/1966; Tate to Horne, 6/18/1965; Tate to Pamela Cocks, 5/23/1965, MT/HU.
28. Tate, *The United States and the Hawaiian Kingdom: A Political History* (New Haven: Yale University Press, 1965). Tate's second book on Hawaii appears to include material that had been edited out of the original and some additional research on the annexation debates; Tate, *Hawaii: Reciprocity or Annexation* (Lansing: Michigan State University Press, 1968).
29. Tate, *The United States and the Hawaiian Kingdom,* 308.
30. Tate, *The United States and the Hawaiian Kingdom,* 315.
31. Tate, *The United States and the Hawaiian Kingdom,* 312; Tate, *Hawaii: Reciprocity or Annexation,* 241.
32. Tate, *Hawaii: Reciprocity or Annexation,* 242.
33. Tate, *Hawaii: Reciprocity or Annexation,* 247.
34. Tate, *Hawaii: Reciprocity or Annexation,* 257–258.
35. Reviews of *The United States and the Hawaiian Kingdom:* Harold Whitman Bradley, *American Historical Review* 71, no. 4 (July 1966): 1459–1460; Donald D. Johnson, *Pacific Northwest Quarterly* 57, no. 2 (April 1966): 92; Richard W. Leopold, *Political Science Quarterly* 82, no. 1 (March 1967): 112–114; J. W. Davidson *Journal of Pacific History* 3 (1968): 231–233; Arthur Nagasawa, *Catholic Historical Review* 54, no. 4

(January 1969): 694–695. Reviews of *Hawaii: Reciprocity or Annexation:* Walter LeFeber, *Journal of American History* 56, no. 4 (March 1970): 933–934; Bradley, *American Historical Review* 75, no. 4 (April 1970): 1182–1183; H. Wayne Morgan, *Pacific Historical Review* 38, no. 2 (May 1969): 240–241; Jacob Adler, *Political Science Quarterly* 86, no. 2 (June 1971): 286–287. Harsh reviews of both of Tate's books were written by Charles H. Hunter, of the University of Hawaii, who after Kuykendall's death helped complete his colleague's unfinished third volume, which ended in 1893. Hunter disagreed with her unsympathetic portrayal of sugar plantation interests and her concerns for the fate of native Hawaiians after annexation. In his review of Tate's second book, he charged that she had benefited from materials shared with her by Kuykendall, citing one page out of her book. This incensed Tate, who was very respectful in print of Kuykendall and his work, and scrupulous in her note taking and attribution. She prepared a two-page rebuttal to the review saying that although Kuykendall had offered her suggestions, she never borrowed any notes or material from him. However, Hunter himself died suddenly, and her reply was not printed. Hunter, *Journal of Asian Studies* 25, no. 3 (May 1966): 508–509; Hunter, *Pacific Northwest Quarterly* 60, no. 2 (April 1969): 117; Tate, "MERZE TATE'S REPLY TO CHARLES H. HUNTER'S REVIEW OF HAWAII: RECIPROCITY OR ANNEXATION," MT/HU.

36. "Slavery Issue and Hawaiian History," *Honolulu Star-Bulletin,* 7/29/1965; "Negro, Indian Laborers Once Proposed for Isles," *Honolulu Advertiser,* 7/29/1965, MT/HU.
37. Charles E. Frankel, *Honolulu Star Bulletin,* to Tate, 12/4/1968; Tate to Frankel, 12/8/1968; Frankel, "Books: Of Piracy and Reciprocity," *Honolulu Star-Bulletin,* 12/3/1968, MT/HU.
38. "Entries for 1966 Francis Parkman Prize," 11/18/1965; "Memorandum," 11/12/1985; Records of Yale University Press, RU 554, Box 10, Folder 683, via email from Michael Brenes, Yale University Library Archives; "To the Members of the Jury," Columbia University, Office of the Secretary, 11/30/1965, from Office of the President, Central Files, Box 583, via email attachment from Jocelyn K. Wilk, University Archives, Columbia University; Tate, BWOHP; John Gudmundsen, History Editor, Yale University Press, to Tate, 12/13/1966, 12/22/1966, MT/HU. The Bancroft Award for 1966 went to Theodore W. Friend III for *Between Two Empires: The Ordeal of the Philippines* (New Haven: Yale University Press, 1965). The Parkman Prize was won by Daniel Boorstin for *The Americans: The National Experience* (New York: Random House, 1965); https://library.columbia.edu/about/awards/bancroft/previous_awards.html; https://sah.columbia.edu/content/prizes/francis-parkman-prize.
39. Reviews by Tate on Asia or the Pacific: Jacob Adler, "*Claus Spreckels: The Sugar King in Hawaii,*" *Pacific Historical Review* 36, no. 2 (May 1967): 231–232; R. Gerard Ward, "*American Activities in the Central Pacific, 1790–1870,*" *Journal of American History* 54, no. 3 (December 1967): 646–647; Gaven Daws, "*Shoal of Time: A History of the Hawaiian Islands,*" *The Annals of the American Academy of Political and Social Science* 384 (July 1969): 143–144; Louise H. Hunter, "*Buddhism in Hawaii: Its Impact on a Yankee Community,*" *American Historical Review* 77, no. 5 (December 1972): 1413–1414; Theon Wright, "*The Disenchanted Isles: The Story of the Second Revolution in Hawaii,*" *American Historical Review* 78, no. 3 (June 1973): 745; Jacob Adler and

Gwynn Barrett, "*The Diaries of Walter Murray Gibson, 1886, 1887,*" *American Historical Review* 79, no. 2 (April 1974): 597; Richard Tregaskis, "*The Warrior King: Hawaii's Kamehameha the Great,*" *American Historical Review* 5 (December 1974): 1627; Paul M. Kennedy, "*The Samoan Tangle: A Study in Anglo-German-American Relations,*" *Pacific Historical Review* 45, no. 1 (February 1976): 144–145. She also reviewed the third volume of Kuykendall's book as completed by two of his colleagues, one of whom was the late Charles H. Hunter, who had posted the negative review of Tate's book. Her review was gracious, and praised the authors for not disparaging Liliuokalani, although Tate's final paragraph was a long factual nitpick; Kuykendall, *The Hawaiian Kingdom, 1874–1893: The Kalakaua Dynasty,* Vol. III," *Pacific Historical Review* 37, no. 3 (August 1968): 359–360.

40. Ash to Tate, 4/21/1967; Gudmundsen to Tate, 5/12/1967, MT/HU; Tate, BWOHP.
41. Max Hall, Harvard University Press, to Angus Ross, University of Otago, 9/29/1967, 11/10/1967; Ross to Hall, "Report on Australia and New Zealand from the Tropics to the Pole," n.d.; "Correspondence relation to publication of Merze Tate's 'Australia and New Zealand form the Tropics to the Pole,' " Angus Ross Papers, Archives, University of Otago. Thanks to Dr. Miranda Johnson, University of Otago, New Zealand, for providing this to me; Tate, BWOHP.
42. Tate, "Report on Research Grant Awarded Merze Tate," summer, 1972, University Archives/HU. Tate explored the implications of the legal and political distinctions of territory and mandate as applied to Papua New Guinea in a series of articles in 1971; Tate, "Nauru, Phosphate, and the Nauruans," *The Australian Journal of Politics and History* 14 (1968): 177–192 (page numbers she cites are 186–192); Tate, "The Question of Development and Nationhood in New Guinea Since WW II," *Journal of Negro History* 56, no. 1 (January 1971): 43–53; Tate, "Australia and Self-Determination for New Guinea," *Australian Journal of Politics and History* 16 (1971): 246–259; Tate, "Recent Constitutional Developments in Papua and New Guinea," *Pacific Affairs* 44, no. 3 (Autumn 1971): 421–427; Tate to Edward Tripp, editor, Yale University Press, July 17, 1972; Tate to David Stewart Hall, Vice President, James Brown Associates, Inc., November 30, 1973, but signed "Lelia Kaliokalani"; Marie D. Brown, editor, Anchor Press/Doubleday, to Tate, January 12, 1978; Tate to Brown, February 21, 1978, in which she suggested Jacqueline Onassis as editor: "She is sufficiently sophisticated to understand the social background of Hawaii in the 19th century and has endured enough agony over the loss of loved ones to appreciate the anguish of Queen Emma"; MT/HU.
43. Tate, *Diplomacy in the Pacific: A Collection of Twenty-Seven Articles on Diplomacy in the Pacific and Influence of the Sandwich (Hawaiian) Islands Missionaries* (Washington, D.C.: History Department, Howard University, 1973); Jan Duncan, Review: *Diplomacy in the Pacific, Oregon Historical Quarterly* 74, no. 3 (September 1973): 279.
44. Herschel and Cynthia Cross to Tate, n.d.; Keith and Faye Tate to Merze Tate, n.d.; Ernestine and Theo Cross to Tate, n.d.; Keith and Faye to Herschel and Cynthia, 12/1/1964. Many letters in Tate's archive detail the struggle of family members in making decisions about their mother's care, MT/HU.
45. Mae Skinner to Tate, n.d., MT/HU.

46. "Church of Christ News—Obituary," March 1969, MT/HU.
47. "Dr. Tate Honored by County," 5/22/1969, clipping, unknown paper, MT/HU.
48. Letter to Gardiner, 12/15/1971, MT/HU.
49. "Merze Tate Fellowship Established at the Radcliffe Institute," Radcliffe: News from the College, spring 1971, MT/HU.
50. Tate to Matina Horner, Radcliffe College, 11/8/1974; Tate to Bunting, 10/6/1971; Bunting to Tate, 1/17/1972, MT/HU.
51. Tate to Horner, 11/8/1974; "Merze Tate Fellowship for women in research," *Washington Afro-American,* 6/26/1971; Carrie W. Elliott, Washington, D.C., to Tate, 7/1/1971, MT/HU.
52. Brooks is professor of history at Anne Arundel Community College, Maryland; Brooks, email to author, 3/23/22; Brooks to Tate, 5/20/1978, MT/HU.
53. Lydia Lindsey, "The Role of Immigration Policy, Race, Class, and Gender in Shaping the Status of Jamaican Immigrant Women Workers in Birmingham, England, 1948–1962," dissertation, University of North Carolina, 1992; Lydia Lindsey, interview, 12/9/2022. Lindsey is a professor of history at North Carolina Central University. Thanks to Kennetta Hammond Perry for alerting me to her connection to Tate.
54. Tate to Robert L. Owens, 5/8/1973, MT/HU. Logan returned to active teaching in January 1971 as Distinguished Professor of History.
55. Eaton to Tate, 11/18/1970; Winston to Tate, 1/12/1973, MT/HU.
56. Allison Blakey, interview, 5/31/2022. In 2001, Blakey left Howard for Boston University; he retired there as professor emeritus of modern European and comparative history.
57. Rayford Logan, *Howard University: The First Hundred Years, 1867–1967* (New York: New York University Press, 1969), 324, 600.
58. William Freehling to Tate, 1/14/1970; Tate to Freehling, 1/5/1969 [*sic;* 1970], MT/HU.
59. Tate to Gerald Wheeler, 10/4/1971; Wheeler to Tate, 5/31/1972; John Prados, U of Tennessee, to Tate, 6/8/1973, 6/12/1973; University of Oklahoma to Tate, asking if she wants to be dean; John Gerber, University of Iowa, to Tate, 6/25/1973; Tate to John Walter, Director, Afro-American Studies Program, Bowdoin College, 3/29/1977; Tate to John Garraty, Scribners, 9/10/1975. She applied for work on her new Africa project, but did not receive any funds and was told they had run out; Tate to Vincent Browne, 4/20/1976, MT/HU.
60. The Caucus of Women in History of the Southern Historical Association and the Berkshire Conference of Women Historians nominated her for a position on the AHA Council in 1972; Mollie Camp Davis to Tate, 11/29/1972; Kerber to Tate 6/28/1972, 12/20/1972, 1/26/1973, 3/1/1973; Tate to Dean Robert Owens, 1/3/1973 [*sic;* 1972]. Tate also later attracted notice from Barbara Solomon, who was researching her book on educated women, and William Banks, who was doing the same for one on Black intellectuals and scholars; William Banks to Tate, 3/10/1976; Tate to Banks, 4/1/1976; Barbara Miller Soloman to Tate, 12/2/1976, MT/HU. One of the earliest biographies of a woman historian was not published until 1996; Maxine Berg, *A Woman in History: Eileen Power, 1889–1940* (Cambridge: Cambridge University Press, 1996).
61. Nell Painter to Tate, 11/26/1975; Tate to Painter, 12/4/1975, MT/HU.

CHAPTER 10. "THE SINEWS AND ARTERIES OF EMPIRE"

1. Tate to Cronkhite, n.d., MT/HU. On the history of protests on black college campuses, see Martha Biondi, *The Black Revolution on Campus* (Berkeley: University of California Press, 2012); Jelani M. Favors, *Shelter in a Time of Storm: How Black Colleges Fostered Generations of Leadership and Activism* (Chapel Hill: University of North Carolina Press, 2019).
2. Honorary Degree Citation, "Merze Tate," 6/3/1968, Morgan State College; Tate, "Response to the Honorary D. Litt Degree," June 3, 1968, Morgan State College, MT/WMU.
3. Tate to Lorraine Williams, 9/28/1973; Tate Remarks, Dept of History, Howard University presents A Tribute to the Memory of Professor William Leo Hansberry, Howard University, 11/20/1972; Tate, "University Sponsored Research, Individual Application, 1942–1972," MT/HU.
4. Tate, "The White Man's Pan African Idea" (review of Lewis Snowden's *The Union of South Africa*), *Journal of Negro Education* 13, no. 1 (Winter 1944): 76–79; "Whites and Blacks on South Africa" (review of Selwyn James, *South of the Congo*), *Journal of Negro Education* 13, no. 1 (Winter 1944): 72–76; review, "Somaliland Under Italy's Heel," *Journal of Negro Education* 21, no. 4 (Autumn 1952): 497–499; review, "Africa, A Study in Tropical Development," *Journal of Negro Education* 38, no. 3 (July 1953): 335–339; review, "Who Are South Africans," *Journal of Negro Education* 23, no. 4 (Autumn 1954): 444–447; review, "A Fascist Land of Hate and Fear, 'Through Malan's Africa,' by Robert St. John," *The Journal of Negro Education* 24, no. 4 (Autumn 1956): 452–454; review, "Life of the Kikuyu," *Journal of Negro Education* 26, no. 4 (Autumn 1957): 484; review, "One Man's Africa, by John Seymour," *Journal of Negro Education* 26, no. 4 (Autumn 1957): 483–484; "The Cruelest of Accidents: review, 'The Revolution of Color,' by Thomas Patrick Melady," *African Forum: A Quarterly Journal of Contemporary Affairs* (1966): 134–136.
5. The university in 1963 had established the Hansberry College of African Studies, where he had served in 1963 as a distinguished visiting professor; Tate to Kalu Ezera, University of Nigeria, Nsukka, 1/10/1964; Hansberry to B. N. Chukwudebe, University of Nigeria, Usukka, 1/20/1964; Ezera to Tate, 3/13/1964; William Hawley, University of Nigeria, Usukka, to Tate, 6/26/1964; Tate to Hawley, 7/14/1964 and 8/11/1964; Tate to N. S. Alexander, Ahmadu Bello University, Zaria, Northern Nigeria, 8/19/1964; Tate to William Davis, Cultural Affairs Director, Addis Ababa, 7/20/1964; "MSU Gets Millions for Nigeria U," Michigan State University News, 10/29/1963; W. Patrick Strauss, Michigan State to Tate, 10/29/1963, MT/HU.
6. Tate, University Sponsored Research, 1942–1972; "Merze Tate's Report to Chairman," n.d., MT/HU.
7. Tate to Bernice Cronkhite, 10/24/1969; Tate to Mary Bunting, Radcliffe, 3/14/1970, MT/HU; Adom Getachew, *Worldmaking After Empire* (Princeton: Princeton University Press, 2019).
8. Tate, BWOHP; "Africa: New Railways for New Nations," *International Railway Journal* (September 1962): 24–32. On Trans-Gabon-Railway, Tate to M. D. Post, Bethlehem Steel Corporation, 5/17/1974; Post to Tate, 5/31/1974. On uranium mining and transport, Tate to Fred J. Stiglingh, Rio Tinto Group of Companies in South

Africa, 7/3/1974. On Guinea, Tate to Williams Whitney Halco Mining Inc., 2/23/1976; Whitney to Tate, 1/16/1976, MT/HU.

9. Tate, Travel Notes, "Church, Monrovia," 12/16/1973, MT/HU.
10. Tate, Travel Notes, "Church, Monrovia," 12/16/1973, MT/HU. Thanks to Wale Adebanwi for introducing me to the concept "enclave economy."
11. Tate to Miss W. Wilson, Department of Internal Affairs, Women's Division, Salisbury, Rhodesia, 1/29/1974; Tate, "Ethiopia Safari No. 1." MT/HU.
12. Tate to R. H. Behrens, U.S. Embassy, Morocco, 1/15/1974; Carter to Tate, 11/27/1973; W. Beverly Carter, Jr., to Frenise Logan, 12/18/1973; Tate to Carter, 1/22/1974; John and Daisy Withers to Tate, 12/7/1974, MT/HU.
13. Tate to Mr. Ross, Monrovia, 12/26/1973; Tate to Roger Baker, Department of Foreign Affairs, Rhodesia, 1/23/1974; Tate to Miss W. Wilson, Department of Internal Affairs, Women's Division, Salisbury, Rhodesia, 1/19/1974; "Buffet Dinner for Dr. Merze Tate," 12/21/1973, Salisbury, Rhodesia, MT/HU.
14. Tate to Mr. Ross, Monrovia, 12/26/1973; Tate to Roger Baker, Department of Foreign Affairs, Rhodesia, 1/23/1974; Tate to Miss W. Wilson, Department of Internal Affairs, Women's Division, Salisbury, Rhodesia, 1/19/1974; "Buffet Dinner for Dr. Merze Tate," 12/21/1973, Salisbury, Rhodesia. MT/HU.
15. Air Itinerary for Dr. M. Tate, West Indies—Latin America Travel Services, December 10, 1973–January 10, 1974; Tate to Roger Baker, Department of Foreign Affairs, Salisbury, 1/23/1974; Tate to Mr. Ross, 12/26/1973; Tate to Clay, 1/13/1974, MT/HU.
16. Tate to M. D. Post, Bethlehem Steel Corporation, Bethlehem, Pa., 5/17/1974; Tate to Job M. Lusinde, Minister of Transport and Communications, Tanzania, 1/15/1974; Tate to W. B. Whitney, HALCO Mining, Pittsburgh, 12/3/1974; H. C. Herling, South African Iron & Steel Industrial Corp., Ltd., to Tate, 4/22/1976, MT/HU.
17. Tate, BWOHP.
18. Tate to Mr. LePere, 4/30/1976, MT/HU; Tate, BWOHP.
19. Tate, "Travel Notes," South Africa; Tate, "Report On a University Sponsored Research Grant Under the Faculty Research Program in the Social Sciences, Humanities and Education," 6/30/1976; "Itinerary for Dr. Merze Tate," West Indies-Latin America Travel Service, Inc., Washington, D.C., MT/HU; Tate, BWOHP.
20. Tate, "Travel Notes," South Africa; Tate, "Report On a University Sponsored Research Grant Under the Faculty Research Program in the Social Sciences, Humanities and Education," 6/30/1976; "Itinerary for Dr. Merze Tate," West Indies-Latin America Travel Service, Inc., Washington, D.C. Tate, "Helen Joseph," MT/HU; Tate, BWOHP.
21. Tate, "Report On a University Sponsored Research Grant Under the Faculty Research Program in the Social Sciences, Humanities and Education," 6/30/1976; Tate, BWOHP.
22. Tate, "Report On a University Sponsored Research Grant Under the Faculty Research Program in the Social Sciences, Humanities and Education," 6/30/1976; Tate typing on letter from Eileen Fox, 2/16/1976, MT/HU; Tate, BWOHP.
23. Tate, "Report On a University Sponsored Research Grant Under the Faculty Research Program in the Social Sciences, Humanities and Education," 6/30/1976; Tate, BWOHP.
24. Tate, "Report On a University Sponsored Research Grant Under the Faculty Research Program in the Social Sciences, Humanities and Education," 6/30/1976, 13–14; Tate, BWOHP.

25. Tate to Mary Ida Gardner, YWCA, Dar Es Salaam, 7/16/1976, MT/HU; "Mary Ida Gardner," obituary, 2/15/2019, *Claremont Courier.*
26. Tate, "Report On a University Sponsored Research Grant Under the Faculty Research Program in the Social Sciences, Humanities and Education," 6/30/1976, 14–17.
27. Mary and Frenise Logan to Tate, 3/26/1976, 7/3/76; Tate to Frenise Logan, 5/5/1976; Tate to LePere, 7/19/1976, MT/HU.
28. Tate to Mr. and Mrs. LePere (South Africa), 7/19/1976; Tate to Mary Ida Gardner, Dar Es Salaam, 7/16/1976; Tate to Vernon Johnson, Director, USAID, Dar-Es-Salaam, 5/6/1976; Tate to Doris Hull, 4/1/1976, 4/26/1976; Tate to Dr. Khalil Mahmud, Ibadan University Library, 7/16/1976; Tate, "Report On a University Sponsored Research Grant Under the Faculty Research Program in the Social Sciences, Humanities and Education," 6/30/1976, 17–19; Tate to Michael Lacy, Woodrow Wilson International Center for Scholars, 9/23/1976, MT/HU.
29. Tate to Mary Ida Gardner, YWCA, Dar es Salaam, 7/16/1976, MT/HU.
30. Tate, "Comment on Dr. William Scott's Paper: Black American-Ethiopian Relations During the Italo-Ethiopian War—The Case of Dr. Malaku Bayen," ASALH, Cincinatti, 10/21/1972; Tate to Robert Owens, Dean, 7/1972; Tate, "The TanZam Railway: A Symbol of Nationalism Vs. Imperialism," ASALH, 10/1974, MT/HU.
31. James Spady to Tate, 10/28/1974, MT/HU; "James G. Spady, 75, Writer and Historian," *Philadelphia Tribune,* March 3, 2020.
32. Tate, "Iron-Ore and Liberia's Future—Africa and the World Panel," ASALH, 10/18/1975, Atlanta; Tate to H. C. Jerling, ISCOR, Pretoria, 7/29/1974; R. Pelletier, COMILOG, Gabon to Tate, 1/24/1975; Tate to Al-Tony Gilmore, 3/25/1976, MT/HU; Tate, BWOHP.
33. Tate, "American Pioneers in the Congo," ASALH, 10/1976, Chicago, MT/HU; Tate, BWOHP.
34. Tate, "Description of Subject," n.d., MT/HU.
35. Tate to Michael Lacy, Woodrow Wilson International Center for Scholars, 9/23/1976, MT/HU.
36. Tate to Charles Harris, Howard University Press, 4/13/1976, MT/HU.
37. Tate to Robert Owens, Dean, 4/5/1977; Tate to Michael Winston, 4/5/1977; Tate to Franklin, 4/26/1977, MT/HU; John Hope Franklin Papers, "Howard University—Correspondence"; Franklin to Tate, 4/29/1977. Thanks to Thavolia Glymph for retrieving.

CHAPTER 11. *"LIVING HISTORY"*

1. Tate to Matina Horner, 7/1/1976, MT/HU.
2. Schlesinger Library, Radcliffe, Papers of Black Women Oral History Project.
3. Tate to Ruth Hill, 11/28/1977, MT/HU.
4. "Suggested Topics to Be Included in Interviews for Black Women Oral History Project," MT/HU; telephone interview with Ruth Hill, 5/12/2015.
5. Ruth Edmonds Hill, ed., *The Black Women Oral History Project: From the Arthur and Elizabeth Schlesinger Library on the History of Women in America* (Westport, Conn.:

Meckler), 1991; Ruth Edmonds Hill and Patricia Miller King, eds., *Guide to the Transcripts of the Black Women Oral History Project* (Westport, Conn.: Meckler, 1990).

6. Susie Jones, BWOHP, July 11, 1977, 328.
7. Susie Jones, BWOHP, July 11, 1977, 355.
8. Susie Jones, BWOHP, July 11, 1977, 335, 345, 351; Frances H. Williams, BWOHP, October 31–November 1, 1977, 301, 306.
9. Dorothy Boulding Ferebee, BWOHP, December 28 and 31, 1979.
10. Ferebee, BWOHP, December 28 and 31, 1979, 472.
11. Flemmie Kittrell, BWOHP, August 29, 1977. This interview is not in printed collections but is now available via Schlesinger Library website.
12. Flemmie Kittrell, BWOHP, August 29, 1977.
13. Eva Dykes, BWOHP, November 30–December 1, 1977; May Edwards Hill, BWOHP, April 4 and August 9, 1978; Lena Edwards, M.D., BWOHP, November 13–14, 1977.
14. Eva Dykes, BWOHP, 219–220, 221.
15. Eva Dykes, BWOHP, 221.
16. Letter from Eileen Fox to Tate, July 1, 1974; Tate to Fox, July 25, 1974, MT/HU.
17. Eva Dykes, BWOHP, 221–222, 207.
18. Eva Dykes, BWOHP, 227.
19. Diane Kiesel, *She Can Bring Us Home: Dr. Dorothy Boulding Ferebee, Civil Rights Pioneer* (University of Nebraska Press, 2015), 239–240.
20. "Eulogy of Dr. Dorothy Boulding Ferebee," Patricia Roberts Harris, 9/20/1980; Harris to Tate, 2/29/1977, MT/HU.
21. "A Memorial Service for Dr. Flemmie P. Kittrell, 12/25/1903–10/1/1980," conducted by Rev. Kathryn L. Moore, Pastor, Douglas Memorial United Methodist Church, MT/HU; Kiesel, *She Can Bring Us Home,* 167.
22. Email from Ruth Edmonds Hill, Schlesinger Library, to author, 9/8/2010.
23. *Women of Courage: An Exhibition of Photographs by Judith Sedwick, Based on the Black Women Oral History Project, Sponsored by the Schlesinger Library, Radcliffe College* (1984), ed. Ruth Edmonds Hill.
24. Telephone interview with Joseph Harris, 11/17/2020.
25. "Merze Tate Fund for an Annual Seminar on Diplomatic History in the department of history, Howard University, 3/2/1977; List of Guests for Seminar Lecture, November 10, 1977; Tate, handwritten draft of names with explanatory notes, 10/25/1977; "News Bulletin, Merze Tate Seminar, Ambassador W. Beverly Carter, 11/13/1979"; "The Ninth Annual Merze Tate Seminar in Diplomatic History, 11/20/1985," MT/HU.
26. "Installation of the Archives and Memorial Dedication of the Prometheans, Inc."; Tate, "Prometheans Note Cards"; Earl L. Ginyard, National Vice President, Prometheans, to Tate, 7/7/1980, MT/HU; "Howard Univ. Prometheans Plan Reunion, 7/24/1993, *Pittsburgh Courier;* "Howard's Prometheans hold 50th reunion," *Philadelphia Tribune,* 8/13/1993; "History Department Continues a Tradition of Scholarship," The Graduate School of Arts and Sciences Newsletter, Howard University, June, 1978, MT/HU.

27. Joseph E. Harris, "Professor Merze Tate: A Profile," *Profiles* 2, no. 2 (December 1981): 1–24.
28. Harris, "Professor Merze Tate"; "Professor Merze Tate: A Profile by Joseph E. Harris and William M. Leak," draft copy, MT/HU.
29. "Acceptance Remarks, Merze Tate, Educator and Author, AASCU 1981 Distinguished Alumnus Recipient." Tate added handwritten changes to reuse the same speech for the 1984 dedication ceremony at WMU; "Dedication Proceedings, Education Library, Western Michigan University, Merze Tate Center for Research and Information Processing," MT/HU.
30. Conversation with Karen Stone, 12/9/2014; Tate to WMU, 9/25/1985, MT/HU.
31. Tate, "William Stuart Nelson: A Cosmopolitan and Universal Gentleman," 12/4/1977, MT/HU.
32. Tate, BWOHP; "Ethel Grubbs Dies," *Washington Post,* 6/26/1981; "Bernice Cronkhite Dies at 90; Radcliffe College Dean in 20's," *New York Times,* 8/5/1983; "Susie W. Jones, Greensboro civic leader, dies," n.d., included in letter from Lucille (no last name) to Tate, 1/6/1985, MT/HU.
33. Tate, BWOHP.
34. "Bridgebuilders Album, January, 1987," MT/HU.
35. "Gwendolyn Brooks," *Washington Post,* 9/25/1985; MT handwritten note on article: "I was there. Thanks to Claudia Tate," MT/HU; Brooks was among those profiled in Claudia Tate, ed., *Black Women Writers at Work* (New York: Continuum, 1983); Sharon Harley, email to author, with scans from guestbook for event, 5/12/2021; Sharon Harley and Rosalyn Terborg-Penn, eds., *The Afro-American Woman: Struggles and Images* (Port Washington, N.Y.: Kennikat, 1978).
36. "D.C. Native Among 32 New Rhodes Scholars," *Washington Post,* December 1985; *Radcliffe Quarterly,* March 1981, MT/HU. Perkins interviewed and corresponded with Tate as part of her work on Black women in higher education. On African women and female circumcision, *Washington Post,* 7/13/1985; "Bishop Tutu's Daughter Mpho Tutu," *Washington Post,* 10/27/1984; "UN's Decade of Women," *Washington Post,* 7/16/1985, MT/HU.
37. Tate to Lorraine Williams, 10/2/1983; Tate to Paul Knudstrop, WMU, 4/6/1983, MT/HU.
38. Tate to Paul Knudstrop, WMU, 4/6/1983; Tate to Helen Flaspohler, WMU, 7/12/1984, MT/HU.
39. Citation, Howard University, Honorary Degree, Merze Tate, 5/10/1986, MT/HU.
40. "1927 WMU Graduate Tells School: Thanks a Million," *Detroit Free Press,* 3/3/1990; "Ex-B.C. Resident Gives $1 Million to WMU Drive," *Battle Creek Enquirer,* 2/28/1990; letter from Agnes Cummings Haywood to Tate, April 25, 1990, MT/HU.
41. Tate to the Only Undertaker, Remus, Mich., 9/23/1985, MT/WMU.
42. "Diplomatic Historian Merze Tate Dies at 91," *Washington Post,* 7/8/1996; "Longtime Educator Dies," *Battle Creek Enquirer,* 11/20/1996.
43. Tate's Funeral Program and Funeral Home Guest Book, MT/WMU.
44. Telephone interview with Joseph Harris, 11/17/2020.
45. Funeral Home Book of Guests, Merze Tate, MT/WMU.

Acknowledgments

I am grateful to many people for helping me bring this book to print. My appreciation runs deeper than my written words can ever express, especially at this point when my vocabulary is exhausted.

Writing is a solitary endeavor, but the gathering of research materials always depends on the committed work of archivists and librarians who rarely receive the praise they deserve for collecting, preserving, and organizing the materials that make historical work possible. Their work at the institutions where Tate studied and worked contributed to the rich variety of archival records that undergird this project.

Howard University's Moorland-Spingarn Center has been essential to my career as a scholar of African American history. The dedicated staff there accelerated the processing of Tate's collection and patiently retrieved box after box so I could work my way through all of her papers and ephemera. Special thanks for that go to JoEllen El-Bashir, Ida Jones, and Richard Jenkins, longtime colleagues. More recently, Jaclynn K. Martin, Lela Sewell-Williams, Charice Thompson, and Sonja N. Woods helped me as I brought my research to a close.

The Schlesinger Library at Harvard's Radcliffe Institute holds the records and the interviews for the Black Women Oral History Project. Ruth Hill helped direct that work in the late 1970s, knew Tate, and granted me access to Tate's unpublished interview. I extend a special appreciation to Lauren Kientz Anderson as well.

The Zhang Legacy Collections Center at Western Michigan University has materials sent from Tate's home after her death in 1996 as well as records about her teachers and mentors and the history of the university. Sharon L. Carlson warmly received me there when I visited in 2015 and continued to help me after. Amy Bocko, WMU digital projects librarian, ably assisted me at the end of the project. It was during that first research trip to Kalamazoo in 2015 that I was able to meet with Sonja Bernard Hollins, a WMU alum who has worked to bring greater visibility to Tate.

At Oxford University, St. Anne's College is the successor to the Society for Home-Students where Tate studied. Imaobong Umoren first examined Tate's student file for me before I was able to travel there in 2014, beginning our connection as friends and colleagues. In the college archives, I was helped on site by David Smith and, after his retirement, Clare White.

Sandra Markum at Yale's Beinecke Library, Michael Brenes, Yale University Library Archives, and Jocelyn K. Wilk, University Archives, Columbia University, all provided needed information to me via email. Jennifer Higa assisted me at the Hawaiian Historical Society in 2019 on the beautiful grounds of the Hawaiian Mission Houses Historic site. Special thanks to Sister Janina at St. Anthony of Padua Parish, Washington, D.C., for providing copies of Tate's Baptismorum Registrum and information on her funeral mass.

At various times, colleagues elsewhere sent me information about Tate that they found while doing their own research: Dennis Dickerson, Vanderbilt; Laura Helton, University of Delaware; Katharina Rietzler, University of Sussex; and Miranda Johnson, University of Otago, New Zealand. Thavolia Glymph kindly reviewed correspondence between Tate and John Hope Franklin at Duke. Elizabeth Todd Breland helped me better understand the history of Black education in Michigan.

Conversations by phone, in person, and via email with those who knew Tate deepened my understanding of her. These include her former students and professional colleagues Mary Frances Berry, Allison Blakey, Lester Brooks, Joseph E. Harris, Sharon Harley, Thomas Holt, Winston Langley, Lydia Lindsey, Joseph Stevenson, the late Rosalyn Terborg-Penn, and Michael Winston. Allene Thompson-Martin, Jay Thompson, and their parents, Frances Thompson and the late Allen Thompson, were as close as family to Tate. Her fellow alum Karen Stone met Tate through their shared commitments to WMU; she helped ensure Tate's care as she aged as well as her last wishes.

As I mentioned at the outset, my work on Tate grew out of the Black Women's Intellectual History Collective, and I owe a special thanks to all of those involved with the project for their insistence that Tate needed a biographer. The Leverhulme Trust Research Project on Women and the History of International Thought in England was a similar cooperative effort, with special thanks to Patricia Owens and Katherina Rietzler, as well as David Armitage, Sarah Dunstan, Kimberly Hutchins, Glenda Sluga, and Joanna Wood.

My institutional home for my entire academic career has been the University of Pennsylvania. My work on this book would not have been possible without its generous financial support for research and travel. I also am grateful to the family of the late

Bernard and Geraldine R. Segal for funding my professorial chair. Colleagues in the Department of Africana Studies have watched me labor on this project while we worked together building a new department, especially Mary Frances Berry, Camille Charles, Carol Davis, Teya Campbell, Sean Fields, Gale Garrison, Grace Sanders Johnson, Eve Troutt-Powell, Dorothy Roberts, Tim Rommen, and Heather Williams.

Penn students served as research assistants in the early stages of my work. Natalie Shibley deployed her excellent digital and genealogical research skills in fact-checking and verifying information about Tate's family in Michigan. Cameron Brickhouse and Elise Mitchell both assisted me with other aspects of this project, as did Brittany Elliott, Alicia Lochard, and Eziaku Nwokocha.

Stephen Tuck at Oxford invited me to deliver the Faculty of History's Astor Lecture in 2016, where I spoke about Tate's time there in the 1930s. In 2018–2019, with his support, I was invited to return there as the Vyvyan Harmsworth Visiting Professor of American History at the Rothermere American Institute (RAI). I worked with colleagues there to host the 2019 symposium "Writing Black Women's Lives: Past and Present," which helped me with this project. Among those who presented were Judith Casselberry, Erica Armstrong Dunbar, Merve Fejzula, Farah Jasmine Griffin, Sinead Mceneaney, Tessa Roynan, and Imaobong Umoren.

At Queen's College, Alison and Paul Madden and Elaine Evers, as well as Jane Langdale, welcomed and supported me. My spiritual life was sustained by the superb music at Oxford, most especially that of the Queen's College Choir and the Christ Church Cathedral Choir.

Many other people helped make my time at Oxford working on Tate fruitful and interesting, including Jane Caplan, Patricia Clavin, Patricia Daley, Fiona de Londras, Marguerite Dupree, Peter Elborn, Oonah and the late Sir John Elliott, Kathryn Gleadle, Ruth Harris, Sarah Knott, Karma Nabulsi, Janet Howarth, Michael Joseph, Halbert Jones, Sinead Mceneaney, Lois McNay, Anu and Poorna Mysoor, J. C. Niala, Sarah Ogilvie, Lloyd Pratt, Pamela Roberts, Elizabeth Perez, Lyndal Roper, Amia Scrinivasan, Jane Shaw, Sophie Smith, Theresa Smith, Rick Trainer, Stephen Tuffnall, John Watts, William Whyte, Nick Witham, and Alexandra and Vyvyan Harmsworth.

While at Oxford, I benefited from presenting aspects of this project there and at other institutions, among them the North American History Seminar, Institute of Historical Research, London School of Economics; University of Kent, Canterbury; History Department, Warwick University; University of Sheffield; University of Nottingham; Baden-Wurttemberg Seminar, Heidelberg Center for American Studies, University of Heidelberg; Obama Institute for Transnational American Studies, University of Mainz; British American Studies Association Annual Meeting, Brighton. A special thanks to Gary Gerstle for a helpful session with the American History Seminar at Cambridge University.

Over the years, I also have shared my work on Tate elsewhere, including at Yale University's New Directions Symposium, African American Studies; Conference of the Collegium for African American Research, Université Paris Diderot; Clemson University; Radcliffe Exploratory Seminar, Harvard; University of Tennessee Humanities Center; Association for the Study of African American Life and History; American Studies Association; Society of Historians of American Foreign Relations; American Historical Association; American Political Science Association; and the African Episcopal Church of St. Thomas, Philadelphia.

Tate's time at Oxford in 1932–1935 and as a Fulbright scholar in Asia in 1950–1951 changed her life and her intellectual trajectory, and she always spoke of both in that way. During my time at Oxford, I approached my Penn colleague Lynn Lees, a scholar of British and East Asian history, about feeling the need to visit India, hoping she would talk me out of it. She not only encouraged me to go but made it possible by flying from Philadelphia to Doha to join me on a trip to Kolkata and Santiniketan. She also reached out to others in Kolkata who helped us: Geraldine Forbes, who paired us with Saptarshi Mallick for our trip to Visva-Bharati and its archives, and Debjani Bhattacharyya, who on a family visit in Kolkata spent time with us. Before the trip, I reached out to Adam J. Grotsky, executive director of the United States Indian Education Foundation in Delhi, who shared via email digital copies of Tate's many reports during her time in India. A trip to retrace Tate's time in Thailand was instigated by an invitation from Schuyler Alig, with generous assistance from Evelyn Cooke, Susanne Kerekes, Justin McDaniel, and Sally and David Michaels.

All writers need readers, and that was especially true in this case when I was stretched beyond my own fields and regions of study. I completed my first full draft during the pandemic, and despite that, many friends and colleagues made time during that exhausting period to read and offer suggestions that have made this a better book. Peter Agree brought all of his wisdom from years of publishing and editorial experience, along with his kindness and generosity. I am also deeply grateful to other friends and scholars who put aside their own work to read early drafts when I most needed it: Kathleen M. Brown, Bettye Collier-Thomas, Tiffany Gill, Farah Jasmine Griffin, Pamela Haag, Bruce Kuklick, Lynn Lees, Tiya Miles, Susan Pedersen, Brenda Gayle Plummer, Lyndal Roper, Stephen Tuck, and Judge Robert Williams, Jr. (a Howard student when Tate arrived there in 1942). For reading my book proposal or chapters, I thank Peter, Farah, and Lynn again, and Maxine Berg, Faith Childs, Thadious Davis, Erica Armstrong Dunbar, Drew Gilpin Faust, and Corrine Field. For sitting with the penultimate draft, I am appreciative to Kathy Peiss for that final push to completion. Adina Berk at Yale University Press embraced this project with enthusiasm and, along with Phillip King, helped make it a better book.

Along the way, I sought expertise from other scholars in the fields in which Tate worked, including Wale Adebanwi, Carol Anderson, Eiichiro Azuma, Carol A. MacLellan, Susan Pedersen, Ramnarayan S. Rawat, and Ramya Sreenivasan.

I write in this book of friendship networks with the first-hand knowledge that comes from being sustained by my own circles of friends and colleagues. You have already seen that in action from reading these acknowledgments.

Keeping me nourished and sane over these many years of work are many friends and neighbors, including Lynn J. Brown, Vicki and Robert Nix, Julia and Robert Williams, Darrell Tiller and James Davis, Ellen Harris, Debbie Harrison and Elaine Young, Julia T. Lowe, Joann Mitchell, Julia Sawabini, and Jeanne Stanley. Wilhelmena Griffin's continued care and conversations keep me in good cheer. Special kudos to Debra Williams for being both a longtime friend and my personal trainer. Peter Elborn has been a friend across the decades despite residing in London and Croatia. I am blessed as always by the presence of my godson Tyler Davenport, with thanks to his parents Amy Wilkins and the late Lane Davenport who also hosted me during the early stages of this project.

I recall with deep affection several other close friends who were there at the beginning, but did not live to see this book in print: Anne Campbell, Evelyn Lieberman, Sue Unsworth, Cheryl Wall, and Eve Wilkins, and Penn colleagues Deborah Broadnax, Robert Engs, Sheldon Hackney, Tim Powell, and Karen Wilkerson.

As in all things, I owe my greatest debt to my family, diminished now in numbers, but my roots remain in Virginia, close to the community of families that raised and guided me. Working on this book overlapped with the loss of my two remaining great aunts, Mrs. Corean Whitney and Mrs. Gracie Bell Williams, and of my beloved mother, Mrs. Mildred Savage Fields. Among her many gifts to her children were her faith, her intellect, her love of reading and music, and her quick sense of humor. The power of her loving spirit surrounds us as ever, and, often by surprise, can still make us laugh out loud.

To those of us who remain, as always, my deepest gratitude goes to my sister, Alice Annette Fields, and my sister-in-law and brother, Felita and Glenn Fields. Our next generation makes us proud every day: Erica and Jason Cartledge, Courtney and Chavis Smith, and Keauna Lyles and Sean Fields. It is their next generation that now brings us all such joy as we watch them come into their own with such verve and vitality: Khenan, Aubry, and Cole Cartledge, and Khloe and Ariana Smith. May they live in a world where there is peace and plenty for all.

Index